Models For Analysis of Social Policy:

AN INTRODUCTION

ADVANCES IN CHILD AND FAMILY POLICY

SERIES EDITORS

JAMES J. GALLAGHER AND RON HASKINS

VOLUME I

MODELS FOR ANALYSIS OF SOCIAL POLICY:
AN INTRODUCTION

Ron Haskins and James J. Gallagher

MODELS FOR ANALYSIS OF SOCIAL POLICY:

AN INTRODUCTION

RON HASKINS AND JAMES J. GALLAGHER
EDITORS

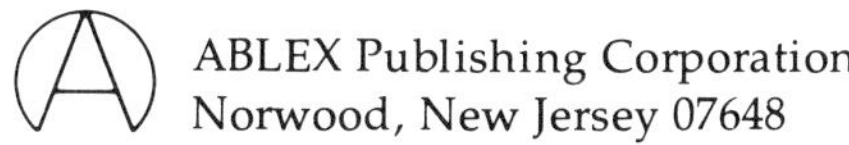
ABLEX Publishing Corporation
Norwood, New Jersey 07648

Second printing 1985.

Printed in the United States of America.

Library of Congress Cataloging in Publication Data
Main entry under title:

Models for analysis of social policy.

Includes indexes.
Contents: Models for policy analysis / Duncan MacRae,
Jr. and Ron Haskins—Models for policy analysis: child and family policy / James J. Gallagher—Policy analysis within a value theoretical framework / Robert M.
Moroney—[etc.]
1. United States—Social policy—Evaluation—Addresses, essays, lectures. 2. Evaluation research (Social action programs)—Addresses, essays, lectures.
I. Haskins, Ron. 1943- II. Gallagher, James John, 1926-
HN65.M56 361.6'1'0973 81-12856
ISBN 0-89391-084-8 AACR2

ABLEX Publishing Corporation
355 Chestnut Street
Norwood, New Jersey

CONTENTS

Preface to the Series

JAMES J. GALLAGHER

Emergence of the new field of social policy analysis, starting in the 1960s but accelerating in the late 1970s, is an intriguing phenomenon in the academic world that is worthy of study in its own right. This evolving discipline is clearly multidisciplinary in nature, drawing interest and contributions from such diverse bedfellows as the health sciences, economics, sociology, psychology, and education, among others.

Even more interesting than this multidisciplinary thrust from the academic community is that those in positions of power seem to be aware of this new movement and are generally attentive. The relationship between the keepers of knowledge and holders of power has always been a strained one. Truth, particularly when unpleasant, has rarely been welcomed by those at the seat of power. Those messengers who deliver such unpleasant truths run some very real risks, more psychological than physical these days. On the other hand, the academician rarely has a sense of the multitude of conflicting pressures and compromises that are the daily menu of the practicing politician, and often doesn't appreciate the many changes in directions that often must be taken to reach a political (policy) goal.

To appreciate this continued strain between knowledge and power, one need not invoke the memories of Galileo or Sir Thomas More. The current difficulties are well expressed in the agonies of the atomic scientists, aptly delineated in an extraordinary series of novels by C. P. Snow. Given this obvious and continued strain, why is there a current interest in pursuing what academia can bring to social policy formulation and implementation?

My own view is that the public policies of the 1960s are the stimuli for this review of relationships. Those policies were, by and large, designed to lead to a better life for all our citizens through improving the delivery of health, social, and educational services. The consensus held by both the political community and the lay public appears to be that after 15 years, the programs have largely come to grief, or have attained much less than was originally intended. Whether this outcome is the result of unrealistic expectations, poor policy formulation, or inadequate policy implementation is still a matter of personal interpretation.

Currently, there is a growing realization that attempts to improve American society can no longer be based on a "seat-of-the-pants," largely uncorrelated, and uncontrolled set of innovations. Such a strategy yields uncontrolled budgets and a corrosive cycle of over-expectation, disappointment, and despair. There appears to be a new willingness, tinged with some skepticism, to pursue what academia has to offer in improving policy design and implementation. What does academia have to offer? What it always has—the ability to organize systems of ideas into a pattern that allows us to bring order and new insights to the phenomenon under study.

This series on social policy analysis summarizes some of the latest ideas and methods that are being utilized by those social and health scientists most directly concerned with policy relating to children and families. Each volume in the series will be built around a particular theme so that contributors to a given volume will be focusing on a common topic. In this first volume, the theme is the development of models for analyzing social policy. Such model development is presented from a multidisciplinary perspective as we seek some usable procedures to bring clarity and comprehension to complex policy topics. In subsequent volumes, we will focus upon policy issues such as parent education, the needs of handicapped children and their families, maternal and child health, and children and families in poverty. In each of these volumes, there will be a mixture of general descriptions on the topic area plus the inclusion of specific policy analyses that attempt to bring insight into particular topics within the theme.

It would be inappropriate to conclude these introductory remarks without giving credit to the Bush Foundation of St. Paul, Minnesota, whose forward thinking has provided financial support for much of the analytic work that will be included in these volumes. The Bush Foundation has established training programs at four major universities—Michigan, Yale, UCLA, and North Carolina—and while the papers in this series will be based, to a large degree, on the work at North Carolina, the ideas and concepts in this series will undoubtedly reflect the interests of all four Bush centers.

Preface to Volume I

RON HASKINS AND JAMES J. GALLAGHER

Although the field of policy analysis is not new, it is currently experiencing great popularity. It is to be expected that like other fads, this one will also prove ephemeral. When the popularity has faded, however, the problems that serious analysts have been addressing for at least two decades will still remain. Indeed, given the Reagan Administration's current—and apparently successful—efforts to cut social programs, we might even argue that policy analysis is now more important than ever. As Aaron Wildavsky has so cogently argued, policy analysis is about program correction—it attempts to identify and document the weaknesses of programs and correct them.

I would like to suggest an analogy for the process social programs will go through in the next few years. The analogy is evolution. The engine of evolution is natural selection which, as Darwin and Wallace taught us, is the process whereby organisms best adapted to their environment—or in times of changing environmental pressures, the organisms most capable of adapting to new circumstances—proliferate, while those less flexible do not survive to produce offspring.

The role that policy analysis can play under such conditions of increased environmental pressure is to help identify those programs that produce the best outcomes, or show the greatest potential for producing good outcomes in the long run. An underlying assumption here is that policy analysis itself can face up to changing circumstances, and can identify bad programs that should not survive—and having found such programs, to say forthrightly that they are not having their intended effect. In this way, analysis might be expected to play a positive role in these rather austere times. It also helps insure that strong and vibrant social programs are perfected now, so that we will be ready for the next phase of expansion which lies ahead.

Two further points seem obvious. The first is that policy analysis is much better at comparing programs within a given social domain than across domains. Having established the analysis criteria, for example, one can determine what type of job training program seems most effective, or what changes in current training programs would likely produce the best outcomes. But how do we determine whether training programs are "better" on some set of criteria than food, income, or health programs? At present, the techniques to conduct this kind of analysis in a persuasive manner are almost completely lacking. However, if necessity is the mother of invention, perhaps one can expect fruitful efforts of this type over the next few years. In any case, it is now necessary to decide whether this health program is "better" than that education program, and whether this welfare program is better than that program for handicapped children. Analysts must attempt to develop means for making such comparisons.

Second, it is essential to remind ourselves that analysis is only one among a number of forces that will determine the fate of social programs in the years immediately ahead. Interest groups, decisions by powerful legislators and bureaucrats, and public opinion will also play their customary roles. Such, thankfully, is the way of democratic governments. Nonetheless, good analysis—persuasive in its methods, clear about the values on which it is based, and straightforward in its presentation—can influence each of these actors and constituents in the decision-making process.

This series of books is intended to play some small role in the use of systematic methods, grounded in reason, evidence, and valuative criteria for helping policymakers improve the decisions about social programs that must and will be made. In this volume, we set forth a number of methods by which social policy analysis can—and indeed has—been pursued. Further, the authors of individual chapters apply their method to various problems of social policy, in order to illustrate their procedures in a concrete way. Let us turn, then, to a brief comment on each of these chapters.

In the opening chapter, Duncan MacRae and Ron Haskins provide background information on the growth of policy analysis as a discipline. They also provide some general examples of analysis techniques that have or could be applied to social policy issues, consider some of the major problems that the discipline of social policy analysis must resolve, and summarize the analytic approach taken by the authors of the various papers in this volume.

In the next three chapters, we present three distinct approaches to social policy analysis. Somewhat grandiosely, we refer to these approaches as "models" of policy analysis. These approaches, developed respectively by James Gallagher, Robert Moroney, and Duncan MacRae, are similar in that all are concerned with defining the policy problem, selecting the analysis criteria, examining potential policies that could be used to attack the problem, and arriving at a policy choice. In addition, each author is concerned with the role of political feasibility in policy analysis.

On the other hand, the authors differ in the phases of analysis they emphasize, and in the particulars on their approach. Gallagher's model is governmental in perspective, and emphasizes program goals as a central concern of analysis. Gallagher also outlines two distinct types of policy analysis—one intended to select the best policy from among a set of alternative policies, and the other intended as a method of examining the effectiveness of policies already being implemented.

Moroney's approach is distinctive in at least two respects. First, he places values—or as he calls them, "first principles"—at the center of each analysis phase. As a result, Moroney emphasizes the importance of the analyst imposing his own values on his work, and of making these values explicit for all to see. Such an approach highlights the inevitable connection between personal values and policy choices, and forces us to make these connections explicit. Further, Moroney offers three first principles that may be applied to all social policies; namely, liberty, equality, and fraternity. After discussing the tradeoffs that necessarily occur when any one of these criteria is maximized, he builds an argument for the preeminence of fraternity in social policy analysis.

MacRae's approach is different from Gallagher's and Moroney's in two ways. First, MacRae is quite concerned with synthesizing analysis criteria. Analysts must always face the problems posed by multiple criteria. Thus, MacRae proposes various techniques—such as benefit-cost analysis—for expressing all criteria in comparable units of measurement which then permit synthesis. Second, MacRae adopts the perspective of what might be called "academic" analysis. In this role, the analyst is a "citizen-scholar" who bases her analysis on general ethical principles, and who publishes her results in academic journals, thereby initiating the process of scholarly criticism.

The chapter by Rud Turnbull, a lawyer, is unique in its focus on the law and the United States Constitution. This emphasis is extremely timely because judicial decisions by the United States Supreme Court have had and will continue to have a major influence on social policy. Turnbull uses one such decision—*J. L and J. R.* v. *Parham* (1979)—to illustrate legal analysis techniques that are comparable in many respects to the essentially nonlegal approach taken in the other chapters.

The chapter by Robert Strauss, an economist, was selected because it indicates the potential role of policy analysis in the actual formulation of public policy. Strauss was a member of Congressman Ullman's Ways and Means Committee staff when Ullman proposed an alternative welfare plan intended to improve upon deficiencies in President Carter's proposed welfare amendments. In telling what amounts to an historical story, Strauss demonstrates that elements of the policy analysis models discussed in this volume can, and have affected the positions of influential policymakers. More specifically, Strauss defines the criteria by which Ullman's staff developed their proposal, and then uses this framework of criteria to compare our current welfare system with the reforms proposed by Carter and Ullman.

In the final chapter, Haskins outlines some of the common ingredients of all the policy analysis approaches presented in this volume, and then discusses five current social policy issues to which policy analysis can be expected to be productively applied in the next several years.

Our work in bringing this volume to completion was aided by many individuals. We would like first to acknowledge the continuing support of the Bush Foundation of St. Paul, Minnesota for the grant that made much of this work possible. In particular, we thank Stan Shepard and Humphrey Doermann of the Bush Foundation who have provided our faculty and students the latitude to pursue their work.

Nor will we fail to acknowledge those people who, next to the authors, do the most and spend the most time in bringing a volume like this to publication. Florine Purdie, Sherree Payne, Ruth Kirkendall, Cathy Warren, and Denise Caldon typed and retyped the chapters more times than they care to remember or we care to admit. Kitty Jones and Amy Glass provided excellent assistance with library work. Of special importance is the superb editorial help we received from Susann Hutaff and Jennifer Mastrofski.

Finally, we recognize the probing criticism of our students who have repeatedly subjected our ideas to careful scrutiny, and have thereby forced us to sharpen our thinking.

About the Authors

H. Rutherford Turnbull, III, a former member of the Bush faculty and Professor of Public Law and Government at the Institute of Government, University of North Carolina at Chapel Hill, is now Professor and Chairman of the Department of Special Education at the University of Kansas. Mr. Turnbull, a lawyer by training, has been active at the county, state, and federal levels in legislation and litigation regarding handicapped children. He has been counsel for state and local educational and mental health agencies, and helped draft the federal regulations that implement P.L. 94-142 (Education for All Handicapped Children Act). He was the principal draftsman of North Carolina Statutes concerning special education, guardianship, and involuntary commitment. Mr. Turnbull is the author of more than 100 books and articles concerning mental retardation and special education, revenue sharing, and election laws. He has held three offices in the American Association on Mental Deficiency, and currently serves on the governmental affairs committee of the Association for Retarded Citizens of the U.S.A. Mr. Turnbull has frequently testified before Congress on education and mental health laws.

Robert P. Strauss, formerly a member of the Bush faculty and Professor of Economics at the University of North Carolina at Chapel Hill, is currently an Associate Dean and Professor of Economics and Public Policy at the School of Urban and Public Affairs, Carnegie-Mellon University. He was previously affiliated with the Institute for Research on Poverty at the University of Wisconsin, the Brookings Institution, the U.S. Department of Treasury, and the Joint Committee on Taxation of the U.S. Congress. In the latter position, he was one of the principal authors of Representative Ullman's welfare proposal that addressed many deficiencies in our current welfare system and in President Carter's proposed reforms of the welfare system. Professor Strauss's work as an economist has included, in addition to public welfare, an examination of occupational differences between men and women, analysis of under counts in the U.S. Census, the design of block grant programs, research index numbers for federal tax policy analysis, and the analysis of hospital costs. He is also the author of some 35 papers in professional journals.

Robert M. Moroney is a Professor of City and Regional Planning at the University of North Carolina at Chapel Hill where he is also a faculty member of the Bush Institute. He holds a Bachelor's degree and a Master's degree in Social Work from Boston College and a Master's degree in Public Health from Harvard. Moroney took his Ph.D. at the Florence Heller School for Advanced Studies in Social Welfare at Brandeis University. He has also held a number of policy-related jobs and consultantships, including work in the Office of Planning and Coordination of the Commonwealth of Massachusetts, the U.S. Public Health Service, and the Massachusetts Department of Public Health. More recently, Moroney has worked as an affiliated faculty member of the Center for the Study of Families and Children at Vanderbilt University, and is currently the editor of *The Urban and Social Change Review*. His recent books on analysis of family policy include *The Family and the State* (Longmans) and *Families, Social Services, and Social Policy: The Issue of Shared Responsibility* (U.S. Government Printing Office). He is also the author of some 35 books, chapters, and papers in professional journals.

Duncan MacRae, Jr. is William Rand Kenan, Jr. Professor of Political Science and Sociology at the University of North Carolina at Chapel Hill where he is also chairman of the undergraduate curriculum in Public Policy Analysis. He has previously held research or academic appointments at M.I.T., Princeton, Harvard, Berkeley, and the University of Chicago. He has published widely on legislative voting patterns, French politics, and values in policy analysis. Professor MacRae's recent books on policy analysis include *The Social Function of Social*

Science (Yale University Press) and *Policy Analysis for Public Decisions* (with James A. Wilde; Duxbury Press). He is currently preparing a book on social indicators.

Ron Haskins is Associate Director of the Bush Institute for Child and Family Policy and a Research Associate Professor with the Frank Porter Graham Child Development Center at the University of North Carolina at Chapel Hill. In addition to this book on policy analysis, Haskins has edited three other books on various topics in social policy (*Care and Education of Young Children in America*, *Parent Education and Public Policy*, and *Child Health Policy in an Era of Fiscal Austerity*), all published by the Ablex Publishing Corporation. Haskins has also participated in organizing various national conferences on topics in social policy analysis including parent education, federal and state health policy, and child development and social policy. With a background in research concerning the development of children from low-income and minority families, Haskins has published some 30 papers in professional journals and edited books.

James J. Gallagher, William Rand Kenan, Jr. Professor of Education, is Director of the Frank Porter Graham Child Development Center and the Bush Institute for Child and Family Policy at the University of North Carolina at Chapel Hill. He is the author of numerous books and articles on education, handicapped and gifted children, and policy analysis. These include widely used textbooks on special education (*Educating Exceptional Children*, with S. A. Kirk: Houghton Mifflin) and education of the gifted (*Teaching the Gifted Child*, Allyn & Bacon). A former Chief of the Bureau of Education for the Handicapped and Deputy Assistant Secretary for Planning, Research, and Evaluation in the U.S. Office of Education, Gallagher has considerable experience in developing and adopting models for program planning and evaluation. He is also the recipient of numerous Awards for distinguished service and scholarship including the Wallace Wallen award for contributions to exceptional children, the John Fogarty Award for Government Service, the Education Award from the American Association on Mental Deficiency, the Learning Disabilities Award from the Association for Children with Learning Disabilities, and the Certificate of Merit from the Association of the Gifted.

ONE

MODELS FOR POLICY ANALYSIS

DUNCAN MACRAE, JR. AND RON HASKINS

HISTORY AND DEFINITION OF POLICY ANALYSIS

Families and children are increasingly a focus for public concern. Although the family is a bulwark of privacy and freedom in a free society, it has nevertheless long been affected by public policy. Marriage, divorce, child support, property, education, public health, and taxation have been among the domains in which public policy has influenced family relations and the welfare of family members. More recently, societies aiming at greater cultural homogeneity or at fuller guarantees of equality of opportunity have also taken a greater interest in the education, health, and personality development of children. The recent increase in longevity has created additional problems in family care of the elderly. Moreover, growing concern with individual rights has also led to movements for the rights of women, children, the elderly, the handicapped, and the gifted, as well as to debates on public policies affecting their families.

Parallel with this growing concern is the development of a general approach to the analysis of public policies that can profitably be related to policies for families and children. This approach, known as *public policy analysis,* is a recent crystallization and synthesis of previous developments in applied research and decision science. We shall define this approach in general terms, trace some earlier developments, and then describe the present status of public policy analysis. Finally, we conclude with a brief statement of the distinctive features of the four models for policy analysis described in the chapters that follow.

Policy Analysis Defined

But what is policy analysis? To begin at the most general level, policy analysis is the application of reason, evidence, and a valuative framework to public decisions. There are almost as many specific approaches to policy analysis as there are analysts. Indeed, the purpose of this volume is to illustrate a number of these systematic models for analysis,[1] and there are many other approaches as well (e.g., Gil, 1976; MacRae & Wilde, 1979; Quade, 1975; Rein, 1976; Titmuss, 1974). However, most policy analysis models contain four essential components. A brief review of these components will provide a more substantive and concrete answer to the question posed at the beginning of this paragraph.

1. Definition of the problem. We need to learn how the various preexisting definitions of our problem may be transformed into the "analyst's problem," which is rephrased in terms precise enough to permit analysis.

2. Criteria for choice. Whether we use "objective functions" of operations research or systematic ethical criteria such as those of equity or benefit–cost analysis, we must formulate and use clear valuative criteria for the comparison of policy outcomes.

3. Alternatives, models, and decisions. Policy analysis involves comparison among possible alternative policies. The expected consequences of these policies are compared after being predicted by models of causation and are expressed in terms of the valuative criteria we have previously specified. On the basis of the values or disvalues of the alternatives, we then choose among them. One model of particular importance is the economic model of the free, competitive market, including possible departures from this model and means of coping with them. Numerous other relevant models exist which draw on knowledge from various natural and social sciences.

4. Political feasibility. Analysis of the prospects for enactment and implementation of a chosen policy is an essential feature of the larger analytic process. This topic draws on both political science and sociology, but also involves skills of nonacademic practitioners as well as much information that is specific to particular political situations.

Each of these components of policy analysis can be applied to formulation of nearly any public policy, whether it be a new program to support children, funds for a new road, or a decision about appropriate levels of hydrocarbons in the air. But the question now before policy analysis as a discipline is whether policy choice based on systematic approaches and a valuative framework (such as those proposed here) can lead to better policy decisions. After all, if analysis cannot improve decisions and thus benefit society, it should be abandoned as so much academic hocus pocus. The field, as it has developed, has claimed some successes but has also encountered criticism (e.g., Tribe, 1972); and the analysis of policies affecting families and children poses particular problems for the dominant approach that has developed so far.

Expert Communities and Public Policy Analysis

Careful and expert reflection on public choices is by no means a recent development; only the effort to organize it as a discipline is recent. Over the centuries, heads of state have sought the advice of counselors whom they have considered to possess expert knowledge (Goldhamer, 1978). As government became more democratic, citizens also sought such advice. These advisers have included priests, soothsayers, and diviners, as well as persons who by their knowledge or experience were acquainted with the ways in which policies are formulated and chosen. In our own society, for example, lawyers play a large part in policy advising. But in addition to lawyers, those seeking guidance have also turned to professionals and scientists with specialized, substantive knowledge of the technical feasibility and probable effects of policies. Engineers, physicians, planners, and natural and social scientists have been among those who have been asked for advice, or who sometimes have volunteered it.

These specialized fields have evolved since the late nineteenth century (Ben-David, 1971). Science has come to be cultivated as a career, focusing on published research shared by a community of peers in one's discipline. Scientific knowledge has thus come to be certified by the consensus of these communities rather simply by practical experience or by the authority of eminent individuals. The disciplines that correspond to these scientific communities have come to dominate the universities (Bledstein, 1976; Jencks & Riesman, 1968). When officials or citizens have sought advice or accorded credibility to advisers, the prestige systems of these disciplines have often been considered. The practicing professions, as well as the disciplines, have often given prestige to those of their members who have contributed to research communities.

Individual members of these scientific communities have made valuable contributions to the formation of public policy, but society has not yet discovered the best institutions for utilizing and sifting their advice while preserving the virtues of representative democracy. Sometimes the advisers have been simply confidants of governmental officials, such as Frederick Lindemann (later Lord Cherwell), who advised Sir Winston Churchill during World War II (Snow, 1961). At other times they have been distinguished scientists who have made use of their prestige to argue publicly for one policy or another, without necessarily receiving systematic criticism from their professional peers. Experts have been convened in royal or presidential commissions (Gallagher, Ch. 2; Komarovsky, 1975; Lazarsfeld & Reitz, 1975), have testified before legislative committees and courts and have been employed in staff positions in government or participated as consultants. New institutions such as the "science court" have also been proposed in which experts would present both sides of a technical question systematically (Kantrowitz, 1975).

In many of these institutional settings, the expert appears as an individual before laymen, received because of his prestige in some specialty. To a limited degree, his fellow specialists can engage in critical review of this testimony, but in reality the arguments of invited experts often go beyond the limited fields of competence in which their prestige has been earned. One example is the guru (Gallagher, Ch. 2) who becomes a leader on a wide variety of subjects, expanding his range of advice from matters on which expert colleagues might agree to values and speculations that are purely personal.

The value of this advice is often related to the promptness with which it is available as well as its broad coverage of relevant aspects of a problem; sometimes circumstances preclude the slow, public, partial assessments that the scrutiny of specialized colleagues might provide. Much of the power of modern science lies, however, in the collective process by which scientific research is guided and quality controlled (Ziman, 1968).

Especially in the controversial, value-laden, and imprecise domain of policy analysis, collective judgment of individual contributions is all the more necessary. We need to be sure that terms are defined precisely, that general principles are invoked logically rather than merely mustered for ad hoc justification, and that rigorous canons of empirical inference are followed. We need to show clearly which disagreements result from different value premises and which result from different views of the facts. We need also to separate these logical and empirical arguments from questions of the identity and motives of participants. These are difficult requirements that we ourselves may not meet in their entirety. But these standards of argument can be sustained and the quality of reasoning improved by processes of public criticism within communities of experts. We hope that this improvement in reasoning can contribute, in turn, to better public policies.

The narrow focus of specialized knowledge has led to a dilemma: experts must either limit their participation to a narrow area and thus deal with only a small part of a policy problem, or, venturing more widely, they must go beyond their area of competence—beyond the area in which their work can be reviewed by specialist peers. This dilemma has led some to seek another type of specialty in which the *range* of information bearing on a given problem may be drawn together by a single field of expertise (MacRae, 1976b). The professions have moved in this direction as professional schools have extended their concerns beyond the training of individual practitioners; medicine, public health, planning, engineering, and law have all drawn to some degree on the contributions of particular basic sciences and combined them in the service of practical recommendations. Those making these combinations may have had to depend on the more intensive expertise of narrower specialists; but they have seen the problems more nearly whole.

The foundations of public policy analysis may appear to have been laid in the work of the various professions concerned with public policies, but an important missing ingredient has been the systematic consideration of general questions relating to many different sorts of policy choice. The mathematical and computer aspects of general models relating policies to their effects have thus been developed in operations research and systems analysis. But equally important, public officials and citizens need to be able to compare the merits of devoting public resources to a wide variety of policies in terms of general value criteria—health versus education versus transportation, for example. What we need is a new and different type of expert community—if such a community is feasible—concerned with diverse policies and the overarching values in terms of which these policies may be compared.

To propose that such expert communities be cultivated—for example, in the form of a new discipline of policy analysis—confronts difficulties both in the academy and outside it (MacRae, 1976b). Within universities and colleges, such a proposal may appear to substitute a hybrid, mongrel base of knowledge for the more soundly based knowledge of the established disciplines. In the democratic political system, the proposal may also seem to risk interjecting a new priesthood into a political system that has already become distrustful of experts. Merely to suggest that there might be expertise in the ethical discourse of policy analysis is to invite accusations of either presumption or usurpation of judgments properly reserved for the citizen.

These questions and arguments lie at the foundation of policy analysis. We cannot do justice to all of them here, however, as we wish to concentrate on the question of quality control. Some of these academic and political questions have been discussed in other works (MacRae, 1976a; MacRae & Wilde, 1979).

Quality Control and Theory

In seeking an academic base for policy analysis, we wish to provide motivations for the quality control essential to insure rigorous reasoning, sound inferences from evidence, use of the best techniques available, and consideration of previous work. In any academic discipline these qualities are insured by the system of publication and research-reporting that submits findings and arguments to public expert scrutiny. The motive to publish involves a contribution to an expert community and the effort to gain the esteem of one's fellow experts through that contribution. Policy analyses, however, are often presented to lay clients rather than through publications. When this occurs, a major opportunity for independent, expert criticism unfortunately is closed off. An academic base for policy analysis, placing a premium on published reports, can help to define and enforce standards of reasoning and inference.

Such an academic base would resemble existing disciplines in its structure, but would not be identical with any of them. Existing disciplines provide motives for quality control; but their definitions of quality, related to their particular bodies of theory, are not always attuned to the needs of policy analysis. They reward a concern with general theoretical questions, often to the exclusion of the specific; yet, policy recommendations are ultimately highly specific in place and time. Furthermore, the disciplines encourage each researcher to work within the boundaries of a single discipline, whereas policy choice requires us to combine the contributions of various existing disciplines, as well as material that is the property of none. Finally, while most of the relevant academic disciplines discourage value judgments, policy choice is based on valuations. Policy analysis, therefore, requires another type of expert community, possessing somewhat different standards (but no less excellence), which may be called an *applied discipline* (MacRae, 1976a, Ch. 9). Policy analysis may benefit from becoming an applied discipline which would draw together, adapt, and synthesize contributions from various existing disciplines and professions in a field defined by its own internal logic. The theory of such a field would bear some resemblance to that part of welfare economics that considers the maximization of social welfare functions; it would extend, however, to include systematic ethical theory. This field would also require some familiarity with findings of all the sciences, insofar as they bear on choices relating to such general values. To specify the content of such a field is obviously an immense task. The field is actually in the process of development, however, and a sketch of its early development will suggest the ways in which its content is being defined.

The Development of the Field of Public Policy Analysis

The currently dominant model of policy analysis may be called the *economic-decisional model.* In terms of the general components of analysis listed above, this model uses as its criterion the maximization of a society's economic welfare, measured in terms of either the monetary value of production or the satisfaction of preferences. It stresses the model of a competitive market as a means of meeting this criterion. Major policy alternatives considered involve intervention in such markets to modify their operation if needed. The effects of such interventions are assessed, where possible, with the aid of formal models for decision. A number of methods characteristic of this approach are described in Stokey and Zeckhauser (1978). The "softer" components of this model for analysis, i.e., definition of the problem and assessment of political feasibility, are incorporated in the teaching of the major graduate policy schools with the aid of disciplines other than economics and decision science, and by practical experience in applied settings. Philosophical reasoning about the values to be sought does not occupy an important place in this model for analysis.

Applied welfare economics has been the chief foundation stone of the economic-decisional model for policy analysis. Its most important contribution has been a valuative criterion as to whether a public investment or expenditure is justified (i.e., whether its benefit to the economy exceeds its cost). By extension, this criterion can be applied to the comparison of one public policy with another. In principle, the relative merits of public expenditure on dams, schooling, health, police, and many other types of policy may thus be compared with one another. In these terms, public investment in any activity or program should be carried out only to the extent that its additional benefits exceed its additional costs.

Benefit-cost analysis is thus a procedure for estimating whether a proposed policy will make a net contribution to the welfare of society, and, therefore, whether it is worth undertaking. In this method, the welfare of society is measured by the net monetary benefit (benefit minus cost) which the policy will produce. Benefits include new goods produced and increases in earning capacity; costs include resources withdrawn from use in the private sector, as well as the monetary value of harm done by a project. Future benefits and costs are typically discounted, i.e., weighted at a lesser value than present benefits and costs. This practice requires close critical scrutiny when we consider long-term effects of policies for children. The numerical values of benefits and costs are usually estimated in terms of market prices, especially if these prices reflect true social value and do not involve government subsidies or taxes. Even for nonmarket effects such as pollution, crime, and the use of time, however, economists have produced estimates of their monetary value or cost.

The basic criterion of benefit-cost analysis is the *net benefit*, or excess of benefits (B) over costs (C), of a possible policy alternative relative to nonintervention or the status quo. Nevertheless, the benefit–cost ratio (B/C) is often used for comparing proposed policy alternatives. This is a derivative criterion (rather than the basic or defining one) but can be used to rank possible policies when costs are clearly identifiable as portions of a budget. If, in such situations, possible policies are ranked in decreasing order of the B/C ratio, choice of policies in this order will maximize net benefits.

We may not agree with the economic definitions of benefit and cost; but the intellectual self-discipline we can gain by thinking in these terms, whatever ethical system we may use for defining benefit and cost, is of great value. The economic notion of benefits and costs is, in fact, a highly systematic ethic that can be used for policy choice. For those of us who would use valuative criteria different from economic costs and benefits, the logical organization of benefit-cost analysis nonetheless constitutes a challenge to render our own value systems equally consistent (MacRae, 1976a, Chs. 4–8). Whether we wish to maximize human development, combine equity and efficiency, or limit a utilitarian ethic by human rights or by moral prohibitions against certain acts, a systematic ethic is necessary if we are to recommend a consistent set of policies.

The practical development of benefit-cost analysis received considerable impetus in the area of water resources. Following World War II, this branch of applied economics was taken up and became more respectable within the discipline of economics (Haveman & Margolis, 1977). Underlying the reasoning of benefit-cost analysis, and suggesting a general approach to predicting the effects of policy intervention on systems of action, has been the economic analysis of competitive markets. If government intervenes by a subsidy, tax, or price control on particular goods, economists are prepared to predict a set of ramified consequences for a market system. Changes will occur in the prices and quantities of factors of production required for the goods in question, as well as for complementary and substitute goods. The amounts by which these changes are likely to occur can sometimes be estimated from market data in the form of *elasticities*. All these sorts of predictions derive from microeconomics, which compares one static equilibrium state of the economy with another.

This economic approach has analogies in our intervention in political and social systems. A new policy typically intervenes in a system of activity; one of the most difficult aspects of modeling its effects is to anticipate the interactive effects between a new policy and existing policies. For example, a negative income tax policy extending "welfare" payments to the working poor may also automatically extend Medicaid payments to these recipients and thus cause an unintended increase in cost. Wildavsky (1979) characterizes an increasing interaction of this sort by saying that the "policy space . . . is densely rather than lightly packed" (p. 64).

Analysis of the competitive market has also given rise to a particular type of valuative criterion, that of *market failure*. An ideal competitive market has been shown to produce a special kind of efficiency. Government intervention can thus be justified only if conditions for such a market fail to obtain (e.g., monopoly, or external effects of production and consumption that escape market control), or if we wish to further values other than the efficient satisfaction of preferences, such as equity between rich and poor. Departures from the conditions for the perfect market create a *prima facie* case that government intervention might produce improvements, provided that this intervention is itself effective (Wolf, 1979). This line of reasoning leads analysts to ask first whether a competitive market could produce the effects desired, and if not, whether some policy correction might more nearly approximate such a market. It has led to proposals such as those for educational vouchers and effluent charges on polluters (Schultze, 1968, Ch. 6). If this perspective is applied to policies affecting children, we can ask whether there are deficiencies in the provision of services (e.g., day care) by the market.

The general approach of economics, which views behavior as guided by material incentives such as prices, has also been applied in other domains. In the case of crime control, it considers expected punishments as analogous to prices (Becker, 1976, Ch. 4); in education, it leads to the expectation that competency tests for students will induce teachers to teach more effectively. In either case, however, empirical research is needed to ascertain whether the model is correct and, if so, to what degree.

In addition to economics, a second major component of the economic-decisional model for analysis has been decision science, operations research, or the decisional component of management science. A basic text in this area is Raiffa's *Decision Analysis* (1968). This approach stresses that all choices, including the choice to obtain information, are to be judged in terms of the expected values which they promote in relation to their costs. More generally, decision science involves mathematical models such as those of difference equations and queuing (Stokey & Zeckhauser, 1978) which predict the temporal course of events as influenced by policies. The implications of such models can often be shown by computer simulation of the systems affected by policies.

Political science and the organizational aspects of management science have also been important parts of the graduate programs in public policy analysis. It has been recognized that we need not only to calculate the benefits and costs of policies but also to examine whether they are politically and administratively feasible. Experts in administration, organization, and legislation have thus participated in the training of policy analysts by working through case materials to illustrate their generalizations. Other disciplines and professions have been involved to a lesser degree; psychology, sociology, engineering, and public health, for example, have sometimes been part of instructional programs in public policy analysis or at least have cooperated with them. Ethics has also been a minor component of these programs.

One of the first policy-oriented graduate schools was the Woodrow Wilson School of Public and International Affairs established at Princeton University shortly after World War II. Much later, Harvard established the John F. Kennedy School of Government in 1966. The Rand Corporation, long a center for policy analysis, established a graduate school in 1970. Several universities, including Michigan, Minnesota, and California (Berkeley), modified or replaced schools of public administration by creating graduate schools of public policy. Duke University created an undergraduate and master's level program simultaneously in 1971. Moreover, a number of grants by the Ford Foundation in 1971 accelerated the process of establishing new training programs. Toward the end of the decade, the Alfred P. Sloan Foundation made grants in support of a number of undergraduate programs in public policy studies, some of which gave greater attention to philosophy and ethics as components of the field.

In October, 1979, the first annual meeting of the Association for

Public Policy Analysis and Management was held in Chicago. This meeting brought together representatives of the major graduate schools in the field and stressed the need for scholarly interchange and criticism of research in the field. Periodicals such as *Policy Sciences* and *Policy Analysis* had developed during the preceding decade, but further organization of the field seemed necessary. This meeting revealed not only the degree of consensus on the content of the field, but also some remaining controversies, including the question as to what values (other than those of applied economics) might properly be bases for policy analysis (MacRae, 1981).

SOME EXAMPLES

Economic Approaches to Day-Care Policy

So far we have explained the need for an expert community in policy analysis and traced the development of the dominant economic-decisional model for analysis. To be more concrete, we shall now illustrate the analysis of some policies affecting children and families as they could be carried out according to this model.

We first select as an example the policy choices relating to day care, and in particular possible government subsidies for the care of preschool children outside the home. This problem illustrates many features shared by other policy choices affecting families and children: (1) the choice between public and private action; (2) assessment of effects on children; (3) effects on the economy through freeing parents to enter the labor force; (4) equity between husbands and wives and between rich and poor; and (5) intergroup relations. Not all of these issues are salient in an economic analysis, but an economic analysis is nevertheless instructive.

In our assessment of day-care policies, estimating the costs of facilities and personnel is relatively straightforward (except for discounting, which we shall not discuss here). More difficult problems arise in estimation of the benefits. One study of a preschool project in Ypsilanti, Michigan (Weber, Foster, & Weikart, 1978), estimated benefits in the following way:

1. In comparison with a control group, pupils who had attended a preschool program were less likely to require special education, were retained in grade less often, and required less institutional care later; the reduction in cost of these services was considered a benefit.
2. Differences in number of years of school completed by experimental and control groups were converted into estimates of expected income in later life, counted as a benefit.

3. Parents' released time, i.e., the amount of time they could work or engage in other activities because their child was cared for by the program, was assigned a monetary value and counted as a benefit.

In addition, the pupils' foregone earnings, resulting from continuing their high school education rather than working for pay during that time, were counted as a cost. Another systematic account of the ingredients of such a benefit–cost analysis has been given by Halpern (1979).

A broader economic approach is taken by Nelson (1977, Ch. 6). He begins by estimating the value of the production of the child care "industry," including the extensive amount of child care done by parents. If this care were all provided by the market, it would cost $18 billion a year. He notes that demographic changes have led to a longer expectation of potential working life for women after the birth of their last child, and thus that investment in future earning power has become more rational for mothers. Therefore, Nelson suggests that a combination of increased productivity and possible benefits to children can justify public support of day care. Nelson's argument as we have summarized it does not fully justify government payment for day care instead of payment by the parents themselves, because the argument in favor of public support may rest, in part, on values related to equity.

A third economic analysis of day-care policies, paralleling Nelson's in several respects, is given by Rivlin (1977). She summarizes numerous arguments for and against public support of day care, many of which are qualitative and not expressed in monetary terms. For the particular question of whether New York City would benefit by encouraging welfare mothers to work, she does point out that the cost of a publicly supported day-care center for a mother of only one child would exceed the expected welfare savings. This is a calculation of benefits and costs from the city government's perspective, if not that of society as a whole.

In summary, the economic approach estimates monetary values for the benefits (or savings) from the provision of day care and compares them with estimated costs. When this approach is applied rigorously and to the exclusion of other criteria, it involves an effort to judge all benefits and costs in terms of their contribution to the satisfaction of preferences—with preferences taken as fixed and quantified in terms of prices.

Decision Analysis and the Evaluation of Screening Programs

Another major ingredient of contemporary public policy analysis is the systematic weighing of decisions. Where there are a small number of discrete alternatives, and where we can evaluate the possible outcomes that might result from each in terms of a quantitative criterion function, a convenient method for systematizing our reasoning is a decision tree (Raiffa, 1968; Stokey & Zeckhauser, 1978, Ch. 12; MacRae & Wilde, 1979, pp. 115–124). This approach is applicable, for example, to policies in which we consider giving a test to a population in order to find members who have some deficiency that is subject to treatment and improvement. Consider as an example a program for screening adults to see whether they have cancer of the colon (MacRae & Wilde, 1979, pp. 119–124). Figure 1 shows a simplified model by which we might consider the desirability of such a policy.

We start at the left-hand square box or "decision fork," faced with the choice between having no screening program (upper branch) and having a screening program (lower branch). Our task will be to decide which has the lesser expected monetary cost. If we choose the upper

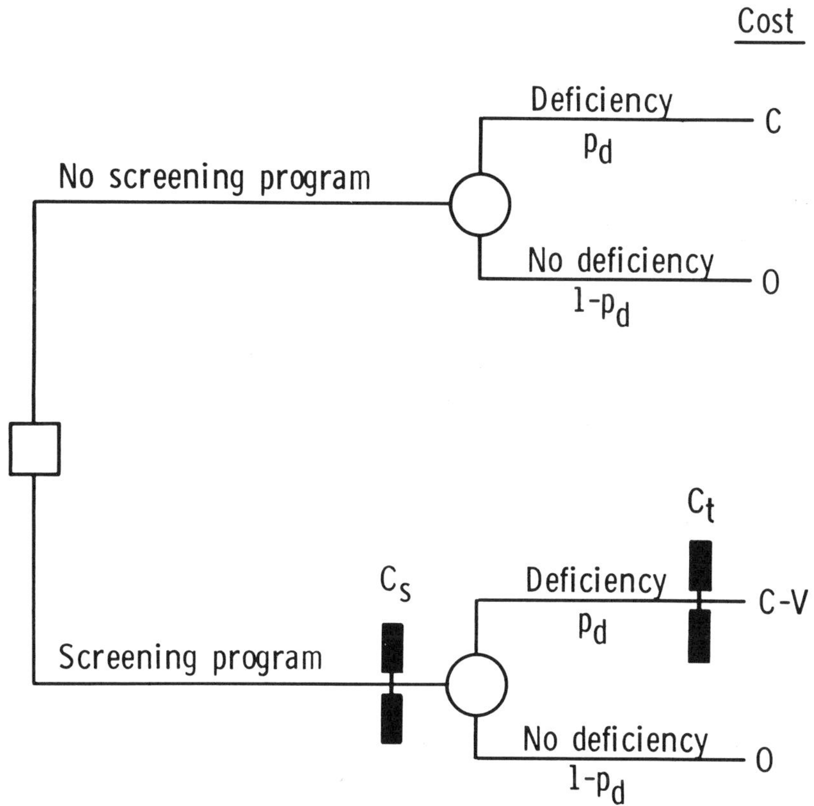

Figure 1.
A decision tree approach to analyzing cancer screening programs.

branch, we encounter a circle ("chance fork") at which one of two random events can occur. For the upper branch, the probability of the deficiency is p_d and its cost (relative to no deficiency) is C. For the lower, the probability of "no deficiency" is $(1-p_d)$ and its relative cost zero. Thus, the expected cost of the upper branch, per patient screened, is p_dC.

If we choose the screening program, we follow the lower branch from the decision fork and encounter a barrier or toll gate with price C_s, the cost of the screening test per patient. We assume that the screening test perfectly identifies patients with the deficiency, and thus encounter another chance fork with the same probabilities as before. Now, however, if a deficiency is found, we choose to treat it with additional cost C_t and reduced eventual cost $C-V$. The difference V is a measure of the benefit to a patient from treatment. Thus, the expected cost of the screening program per patient is:

$$C_s + p_d(C_t + C - V). \quad (1)$$

We then choose to undertake the screening program if its expected cost per patient is less than that of not having a screening program; i.e., if

$$C_s + p_d(C_t + C - V) < p_dC. \quad (2)$$

The terms p_dC on both sides of the inequality cancel, leaving

$$C_s + p_d(C_t - V) < O. \quad (3)$$

Expression (3) tells us that the net value of treatment per patient screened, $p_d\ (V - C_t)$, must exceed the cost per patient screened, but it also shows that the cost of screening C_s is expended on all patients who are subjected to the screening test, while the benefits come only to those who are treated. If we formulate (3) in terms of the net value of treatment, we can write

$$p_d(V - C_t) - C_s > O, \text{ or}$$
$$V > C_t + (C_s/p_d)$$

as the condition for choosing the screening policy. The value of treatment to an average patient treated must therefore exceed the cost of treatment C_t by (C_s/p_d), the cost of screening per patient *treated*, if the screening program is to be justified.

This line of reasoning shows us that in considering a policy such as an infant screening program, we must take into account not only the probability that a deficiency will be found in the population in question, but also the cost of screening in relation to this probability, the cost of treatment, and the value of treatment. Unfortunately, discussions of infant screening programs often fail to consider all these factors.

In this example we have dealt with expected values. It is the estimation of such values that leads us to choose the most useful statistical techniques for policy analysis, such as confidence intervals and regression. Techniques aimed merely at testing hypotheses (e.g., chi-square or analysis of variance) are of far less use for policy choice if they are used merely to show the probability that an observed value can occur by chance. Our very choice of probability levels at which to accept or reject a hypothesis depends on the benefit, cost, or other ethical values we attach to possible outcomes. Thus, conventional research statistics may be less useful than decision-oriented statistics—if policy choice is our main concern.

Models of Production and Exchange Within Families

Another promising extension of economic reasoning has taken place through the development of the "new home economics" and the analysis of household production; some illustrative theoretical papers are presented by Becker (1976; Chs. 5–7, 9–13). In this perspective we view the family as engaging collectively in production of "commodities" such as "the quality of meals, the quality and quantity of children, prestige, recreation, companionship, love, and health status" (Becker, 1976, p. 207). The time and effort of family members may be transferred between market production and unpaid family production; in return, other family members who receive benefits or who are altruistic toward one another may exchange their time and effort or share money or material resources. This theory has been developed in mathematical terms but can also benefit from research that measures some of its postulated but previously unmeasured variables (MacRae, 1978).

To indicate the potential importance of this approach to the analysis of family policy, we shall simply describe some of the types of family interaction to which it might apply.

Family interaction can reflect, or compensate for, the effects of the job market and other external influences on individual members. It involves transfers of resources—money, time, influence, information—from more fortunate family members to others. Family stability and instability may also reflect these external influences.

Whether family interaction effectively benefits those who need it depends on relations within the family—family structure, in sociological terms. Effects may depend not only on general family cohesion, but also on relations between particular pairs of members; such effects may extend to grandparents, cousins, and other relatives, or in some cases be limited to parent–child, husband–wife, or sibling relations. Finally, effects of interaction may extend beyond the family to informal living relationships similar to families and to friendship, neighborhood, and community relations.

Whether such transfers are socially desirable depends on their contribution to the general welfare as measured by some valuative criterion. Help to an unemployed family member may provide material well-being and self-respect. Aid by a wealthy family to a younger member (as, for example, by placing him in a major business position) may increase equality within the family but decrease equity between families. Marriage between two highly educated persons with high earning potential may have similar effects, accentuated by child-care arrangements that allow both to work.

Family interaction can also respond to members' new opportunities in the economy. When a second earner enters the labor force, salaries are shared but other demands arise. Career and job opportunities for mothers create a demand not only for day care but also for housework and child care by fathers and other family members. In some families this may lead to a reduction in working time by these other members. Upward mobility by junior executives can call for sacrifice and support by spouse and children who may have to relocate, substitute new friends for old, or see less of the "fortunate" family member. Some families adjust to such opportunities by living hundreds of miles apart; others respond by declining the opportunity.

Similar adjustments may be called forth by misfortunes as well—unemployment, illness, the birth of a handicapped child. Loss of a job may require a family member to seek employment in another place. Inadequate income may lead to moonlighting and thus to less contact with spouse and children.

All these examples suggest the desirability of further research on the family as an adaptive system, so that we can predict more successfully how families will react to a changing environment, including changes in public policies.

ANALYSIS OF CHILD AND FAMILY POLICY

The economic-decisional model for policy analysis faces special challenges when applied to policy choices concerning families and children. The rise in importance of child and family policy poses not only intellectual problems, but also problems in politics and in university organization in which various models for analysis will compete.

Of the many reasons for this increased importance, three in particular might be cited. First, the civil rights movement of the 1950s and 1960s, in addition to producing legislative gains for minority groups, served to heighten awareness of discrimination in American society. From an economic perspective, this discrimination was particularly evident in the marketplace, resulting in an unemployment rate among blacks nearly twice that for whites since the end of World War II and an average family income for blacks about half that for whites over the same period. Statistics such as these caused many policymakers and citizens to wonder how children reared in families suffering from these disadvantages could possibly compete in American social and economic life. It is hardly necessary to emphasize the fact that such concerns were based on the realization that our public and private policies affecting minority families appeared to represent a direct and powerful failure to promote the general welfare.

Largely as a result of the symbolic victories of the civil rights movement and the increased sensitivity to discrimination against minority families, the American government set about the task of devising policies to reduce discrimination and its effects. These policy initiatives, represented most clearly in President Johnson's War on Poverty, resulted in a second stimulus to the growth of interest in child and family policy. In particular, this stimulus was a growing realization that the many policy initiatives for children and families undertaken during and after the Johnson years did not seem to produce impressive results. Indeed, one now detects a widespread feeling among policymakers, social scientists, and the American public that programs such as Title I (of the Elementary and Secondary Education Act), Head Start, and the Comprehensive Employment and Training Act (CETA) simply do not work. As a result, a number of observers in the government and the academic community have turned their attention to examining why these and similar social programs failed (or achieved only minor success) and to seeing what new techniques could be developed to improve the programs. Thus, program evaluation and analysis of child and family policies have recently received increased attention as techniques that are expected in the long run to improve the success of intervention programs as well as generate new program ideas.

A third stimulus to interest in the analysis of child and family policy has been a growing feeling that the American family is in trouble. Commissions such as the National Advisory Committee on Child Development of the National Academy of Sciences (National Research Council, 1976) and the Carnegie Council on Children (Keniston, 1977) issued reports that played Chicken Little to the condition of American families. And a rash of books and articles by academicians (with titles like *The Family: Can it be Saved?*) both reflected and reinforced the feeling that American families were, as some would have it, falling apart. The basis of these gloomy calculations and projections was primarily the substantial increase in divorce rates, the widespread labor force participation of mothers—especially those with infants and young children—and the growing emphasis on child abuse statistics.

It should not escape our notice that each of these changes in the family immediately suggests a number of public policies. Indeed, if we take increased concern with child custody as an important part of policy addressed to the effects of increased divorce rates, availability of day care as a part of policy addressed both to divorce and to female labor force participation, and support of social services and improved data collection as part of policy addressed to child abuse, then we can argue persuasively that there have been substantial analysis and federal and state legislation prompted by each of these symptoms of trouble in the American family.

The point, then, is that each of these forces—the civil rights movement, the pervasive feeling that federal social initiatives undertaken during the 1960s achieved only minimal success, and increased concern with the state of American families and children—has contributed to growing dissatisfaction with social policy and the means by which it is created and implemented. This dissatisfaction has led in turn to a widespread interest in policy analysis among specialists in families and children.

These forces have brought to our attention a series of policy problems that are especially difficult to analyze, posing challenges not only to the individual academic disciplines but even to the new cross-cutting discipline of policy analysis. Indeed, there are a number of challenges more or less unique to the analysis of policies for children and families that must be considered; we shall consider only three of the most obvious ones. Some of these challenges are well known to practitioners of economic and decisional policy analysis; others go to the heart of its assumptions.

As suggested previously, various components of policy analysis, and especially the tendency to analyze alternative options systematically, estimate costs, and measure effects, have long been used by those interested in the mathematical and computer aspects of policy models, in program planning and evaluation, in systems research, etc. But the economic-decisional model for policy analysis has not actually been widely applied to policies as they affect children and families. Nor have specialists in child and family policy been greatly involved in the graduate schools of public policy. The valuative systems latent in their disciplines are, in fact, quite different from those of economics (MacRae,

1976a, Ch. 7); personality development and attitude change, for example, involve models of human behavior different from the economic notion that preferences are fixed. The models of possible policy consequences that arise from research in child development also differ considerably from economic models and are not easy to synthesize with them. In both theory and practice, therefore, the application of policy analysis techniques to problems of child and family policy has posed a number of challenges that bear emphasis.

Change of Preference

Preference satisfaction is an important criterion in economic models of policy analysis. Thus, in selecting between alternative policy options, the criterion of preference satisfaction leads the analyst to favor those policies consistent with people's preferences as revealed in their actual behavior or in opinion surveys. Occasionally, as in the case of educational vouchers, a primary justification for a policy is that it allows freedom of choice by those affected by the policy. Indeed, one argument for educational vouchers is that they will actually encourage diversity and thereby increase the range of available options. Such a policy outcome would presumably increase the likelihood that citizens could satisfy their preferences.

A special problem introduced by child and family policy concerning preference satisfaction is that, whereas economic models have usually assumed preferences to be fixed, there is abundant evidence that human preferences change, especially during the period of socialization. Moreover, as Skinner and many other psychologists would argue, preferences may be deliberately shaped by experience. This suggests that policies may not only satisfy or dissatisfy current preferences, but may also shape future preferences. A moment's reflection will provide numerous examples illustrating that this outcome of policy is more than just a logical possibility. To take just one historical example, mandatory public schooling was very controversial when Massachusetts first passed a compulsory attendance law in 1852. Yet within about 40 years, more than half the states had similar laws, and today we view free public schooling as a right that every child must enjoy (if not like).

There are two important ways in which people's preferences may be deliberately changed, namely, by education and by advertising (MacRae, 1976a, pp. 150–155). Education is often thought to change people's tastes in such a way that people who have more of it display a broader range of interests and spend more of their time on activities such as reading, participating in the political process, and watching educational TV instead of the "Dukes of Hazzard." Such changes in preferences have often been an explicit aim of educational activities and other publicly supported programs.

A second example of a change in preference through education is the attempt to train low-income parents, and especially mothers, to spend more time with their children in educational activities (Bronfenbrenner, 1975). Such programs attempt to shift parents' preferences from expending time in household tasks or leisure activities toward engaging in verbal activities with their young children. Since parent time investments in children are thought to induce intellectual development and, in the long run, school success, this example demonstrates that some government programs explicitly aim to shift preferences in order to increase the welfare of program participants.

Advertising is a second means by which preferences are thought to be systematically changed. Furthermore, a host of important child and family policy issues are raised by public attempts to regulate advertising. One clear example of government regulation aimed at changing people's preferences is the ban on TV cigarette commercials. Once the Surgeon General had determined that cigarette smoking was a major health hazard, the government initiated a series of programs designed to reduce the cigarette industry's ability to use advertising for the purpose of increasing the public's preference for cigarettes. Although the success of this campaign may be questioned, it does demonstrate that many policymakers believe people's preferences can be manipulated.

Priorities Among Social Programs

Especially in this time of tight money and concern with government spending, it seems wise to acknowledge that programs for children and families must compete for funding both against other social programs and against nonsocial programs such as defense, energy, and transportation. Since the number of dollars available for new programs is finite and, at least recently, rather small, those committed to the importance of such programs must be ready to set priorities and defend them.

But on what basis can such priorities be established? It is an axiom of political economy that government should attempt to invest its last dollar where it will do the most good. But how shall the good be defined?

One answer, suggested previously, is provided by benefit-cost analysis. Although some appear to use benefit-cost analysis to obfuscate their critics with the result that there is now considerable mistrust of benefit-cost approaches, the underlying idea of this valuative criterion is actually very simple. Thus, the primary question is whether a given expenditure, program, or policy will produce benefits that exceed costs—a positive net benefit. If so, the policy can be judged to constitute a wise use of public funds. The computation of net benefit assumes, of course, that both the benefits and costs of a policy can be accurately measured. If the policy in question concerns a new road, a dam, or a tariff on imported goods, there are problems in estimating costs and benefits, but they are often surmountable. But if the policy involves preschool education or a nutrition program for poor, pregnant women, the problems of assessing costs—and more importantly, benefits—are usually less tractable. Not the least of these problems is the fact that social scientists often do not know the actual effects of these programs, and that even where effects are known, the values of such benefits are difficult to determine.

Nonetheless, in principle at least, benefit-cost ratios provide a means of comparing social programs. Thus, for example, it may be possible to estimate the benefits of education programs by determining their effect on the probability of high school graduation and then using the dollar value of high school graduation over a lifetime of earnings to calculate the benefits of the educational program. Similarly, the effect of a given health program on work days missed because of sickness or premature death can be converted to dollar benefits. If the costs and benefits of two social policies can be estimated in commensurable units—such as dollars—the programs can be directly compared, thereby allowing policymakers to fund that program which produces the greatest benefits.

On the other hand, as suggested previously, it is not always possible to measure precisely either the costs or benefits of social programs. But of even greater concern is our choice of the benefit-cost standard itself. The value underlying benefit-cost analysis is increased contribution to production, and many have questioned whether this value should be the sole criterion of policy decisions. What about the intellectual satisfaction produced by educational programs, the value of feeling more robust and less worried that often results from medical care, or the well-being of an elderly person or a handicapped child? These values are not less important than increases in production, and the value of equity may be added to the list. But all these values suffer because they are very difficult to measure.

Thus, there are two aspects of the challenge to policy analysis offered by the problem of establishing priorities among child and family programs. The first is that few techniques are available to allow direct comparisons of the benefits produced by different social programs. Second, even in the case of the one technique that does allow such direct comparisons—benefit-cost analysis—the criterion of comparison leaves out important values which many citizens and policymakers would like to promote. Though one might wish to be more optimistic about solving these problems, it is difficult to foresee which techniques would allow comparisons among program effects on happiness, satisfaction, independence, and so on. Not the least of the barriers to knowing more about program effects on these variables is the problem of measurement.

Problems of Measurement

A third problem that must be faced by analysts of child and family policy is the difficulty of measuring the outcomes of social programs. One of the hallmarks of policy analysis is the attempt to bring data to bear on policy decisions. However, as the aphorism of computer science would have it, "Garbage in, garbage out." In other words, decisions based on data cannot be better than the data themselves.

And few would deny that the social scientists' ability to measure many of the hoped-for outcomes of child and family programs is primitive at best. Perhaps the clearest example of this problem is the evaluation of preschool programs in general and Head Start in particular. A number of the social scientists involved in the creation of Head Start have complained that most evaluations have focused on measures of intelligence (see Zigler & Valentine, 1979). Head Start was intended to influence, they argue, children's self-concept and motivation, as well as their intellect. Furthermore, Head Start was viewed as a Community Action Program that could serve as a focus of organization and self-help in low-income communities.

These, of course, are worthy objectives, and ones which may have a long-term impact on children, families, and even communities. But how are they to be measured? Social science has not produced a measure of self-concept or motivation that is as widely accepted and understood as the social science measures of intelligence. As a result, evaluations of Head Start and other education programs have tended, with few exceptions (e.g., Darlington et al., 1980), to focus on IQ and other standardized measures of intelligence.

Ironically, some of the most important outcomes of social programs can be easily measured, but—especially in the case of preschool and school-age programs—we must wait long periods of time before collecting such measures. Social scientists, policymakers, citizens, and program participants would all be very satisfied, for example, if Head Start, Title I, CETA, and other education and training programs could be shown to have an impact on employment and earnings. Both of these variables, of course, can be easily and precisely measured. But in the case of Head Start, for example, evaluation must wait 15 years or more to measure effects on employment.

Indeed, one of the reasons program evaluation of Head Start, Title I, and other education programs has relied on variables such as IQ, school achievement, and motivation is that these variables are thought to be associated with school success, and school success is thought to be associated with success in the job market. In this respect, IQ, school achievement, and similar measures are of interest because they are correlated with the variables of greatest interest, namely, employment and income. Direct measurement of these latter variables, however, would be preferable; yet we have very few careful studies of the relationship between education programs and job success. Nothing is known, for example, about the influence of Head Start on employment. It follows that two important objectives of policy analysis are to stimulate interest in such studies and insure that legislation for child and family programs includes funds for long-term evaluation.

Immediate Costs and Long-Term Benefits

We would argue, as would many social scientists, that longitudinal data may enable analysts to arrive at accurate conclusions about program effects. But the need for longitudinal data highlights the fact that many of the important effects of child and family programs occur only after a long time compared to the policymakers' terms of office. Roads can be built in a few years, buildings in even less, and military expenditures often result in many jobs being sustained or created very quickly. In each of these cases, politicians have a reasonable chance of still being in office when some of the results and benefits of their decisions become manifest. Policies of this sort have long-term effects as well, which need to be considered, but they also produce tangible results in the short run.

Unfortunately, we are now learning that the results of most social programs take decades or even longer to become apparent. In the meantime, policymakers may not have much to show for their investment. And, of course, the expenditures begin now. Thus, advocates for children's programs are often in the position of proposing expenditures intended to produce results that may not show up for a decade or two.

We have argued previously that feasibility is an essential element of most policy analysis models. This problem of immediate cost to produce long-term benefits is essentially a problem of feasibility. It follows that analysts must consider the extent to which policymakers may resist a program recommendation that will produce benefits only in the long term. Similarly, advocates must try to find ways to appeal to interests such as investment in future generations, as well as find short-term gains that provide temporary evidence that programs are working.

DIVERSE MODELS FOR POLICY ANALYSIS

Policy analysis is "the use of reason and evidence to choose the best policy among a number of alternatives" (MacRae & Wilde, 1979, p. 4). Probably all the authors in this book could agree on this broad definition, which can also be applied to the economic-decisional model. The various models for policy analysis that are described in the following chapters have much in common and may eventually be synthesized into a single approach. At present, however, they are still distinct—in part because of terminology, in part because of differing emphasis on various aspects of the analysis process, and in part because of differing values. What is a policy? How do we define "best"? What sequence should an analyst follow in carrying out a policy analysis? The five following chapters on policy analysis take somewhat different positions, explicitly or implicitly, on questions such as these.

Our approaches are distinguishable not only by our use of key terms, however, but also by our orientation to different audiences or reference groups. People in various disciplines, professions, and governmental roles stress different aspects of the evaluation and furthering of public policies, even when they all try to view the problem as a whole. They make use of the resources of disciplines and professions differently. They may also stress different basic value criteria, related to their professions and roles, just as economists tend to bring their own characteristic set of values to public problems.

Roles of the Analyst

One difficulty we face in describing policy analysis is that it may be practiced in various ways depending on one's social role (Meltsner, 1976, Ch. 1; Clark, 1976, pp. 72–74; Finsterbusch & Motz, 1980, pp. 7–9). Probably the most conspicuous role is that of the analyst trained in economics or in one of the interdisciplinary graduate schools of policy analysis who functions as a staff aide in Washington. A related role is that of the urban or social planner. In these roles, the criteria for policy choice often center about benefit-cost analysis, modified by the values and political constraints of the head of the employing agency.

The occupant of such a role may claim merely to be proposing means to ends given by others. He may base this claim either on the presentation of "facts" alone, or on the use of "consensual" value systems such as those of economics. In contrast to this adviser role is that of the informed citizen who takes a broader view of the values to be sought (MacRae & Wilde, 1979, Ch. 3) or who may work for one of the competing groups that seeks to influence government policy. Some policy analysts in this latter role consider themselves advocates for certain groups—children, for example—without seeking to balance the interests of such groups against other interests in society. Analysts often become advocates after they have concluded that a particular program or policy is desirable; but before making this commitment, if it is made in the name of the general welfare, they must use reason and evidence to show that their commitment furthers such a general value. One of the greatest pitfalls of analysis is to become committed, *in advance,* to a particular policy or group, thereby being blinded to evidence that runs counter to this predetermined commitment.

Analysts in either of the roles we have described may design policies as well as evaluate policies proposed by others. The role of planner probably connotes a greater responsibility for design than that of analyst. But even if we are given detailed policies or programs to compare, we cannot fail to notice that they might be improved by modification. Similarly, it can be only one step from the evaluation of an existing program to the realization that it might have been better designed or administered. The roles of designer and administrator (or implementer) are thus, in a sense, extensions of roles of the analyst.

Various other roles have also been proposed for the policy analyst. One such role is that of applied research on the fringe of an academic discipline. Members of an existing discipline may group together to study aspects of public policy that draw on their disciplinary expertise. Atomic scientists formed the Federation of American Scientists to discuss problems of nuclear warfare, international strategy, and other questions relating to their scientific expertise. Sociologists formed the Society for the Study of Social Problems; psychologists, the Society for the Psychological Study of Social Issues; and political scientists, the Policy Studies Organization. Such "fringe" associations (MacRae, 1976a, pp. 72–76) often meet together with the annual meetings of their parent disciplinary associations. They develop ethical systems closely related to central concepts of their disciplines. They tend to view practical problems from the standpoint of a single discipline, however, unless they can free themselves from this connection by bringing in expertise from other sources.

The very phrase "applied research" suggests a sequence that is taken for granted in the natural sciences: first one discovers the laws of nature, then one applies them to practical tasks. The widespread acceptance of this sequence has led to a downgrading of practical research on the grounds that it is merely derivative. Our unquestioning acceptance of the sequence from basic to applied may, however, have been harmful in some instances, especially in social science—and a similar suggestion has been made by Levins (1973) for agricultural research. In many instances, policy analysis can proceed directly from a practical problem to relevant research when information is required that cannot be supplied by basic science. At times, analysis can profitably make the detour of investing in basic disciplinary research on underlying principles which may connect policies to their consequences; but it need not always do so. Thus, the quest for a better world is a more general task than that of basic scientific research and need not be limited by the concepts and problem definitions of basic science. Policy analysis is thus an activity *sui generis* and not a mere application of principles discovered elsewhere.

An important feature of all public policy, particularly evident in family policy, is the central place occupied by the law. Family rights and responsibilities have been defined in Anglo-Saxon common law; changes in expected family relationships have led to challenges to some aspects of that law (Glendon, 1976). Most public policies are enunciated through legislation or through administrative decisions that are reviewed through legal procedures. One of the main approaches to the analysis of public policies that we present is therefore based on the law, and all policy analysis must take the law into account.

Practicing professions and the schools which educate professionals provide another role for policy analysis. A single profession can draw together contributions from various academic disciplines, and in this way circumvent some of the parochialism of the disciplinary fringe associations. If a profession is concerned with the delivery of a particular sort of service (e.g., health, education, social work), however, policy analysis within that profession may take the delivery of that service as the ultimate criterion for policy choice, rather than looking more broadly for other policies that will produce equivalent or better effects. Thus, health policy analysis, if conducted in medical schools, risks an excessive concern with the delivery of health services and a corresponding neglect of preventive measures operating through diet, exercise, work conditions, or the environment. Educational policy analysis conducted together with the training of educators may likewise focus on what schools and educational institutions can do, perhaps to the exclusion of the effects of parents, the media, and on-the-job learning. If members of given professions are considering policy choices, it is understandable to consider only what "we" can do; but for society's choices in allocating resources, a broader range of alternatives must be considered.

An additional developing role related to policy analysis is that of the evaluation researcher. This role usually takes the values for analysis from the goals of an organization or program. Most evaluation therefore begins by asking whether a program has fulfilled its goals. Evaluators less often ask whether the goals themselves are ultimately desirable, or whether the program has had unintended side effects that may be helpful or harmful. This field has been organized in a national association and has a growing literature. It provides quality control and covers a wide variety of policy areas. But insofar as it takes its valuative guidance from previously specified program goals, its practitioners limit their role to that of technician, providing means to given ends.

Perhaps the most desirable role—and the rarest—is for someone trained in policy analysis to *be* a political decision maker who is also concerned with the general welfare. Occasionally, federal cabinet officers have been trained in policy analysis; and perhaps Congressmen as well as their staff assistants can bring such training to the process of legislation. This combination of expertise and responsibility represents an ideal role that policy analysts should be prepared to take hypothetically. Even if their chances of attaining it are small, it provides a perspective combining design, analysis, enactment, and implementation.

The Models for Policy Analysis Presented in This Volume[2]

In Chapter 2 Gallagher presents a model for policy analysis that is governmental in perspective. It stresses the goals of policies or programs as a particularly important set of values, embodied in concrete targets, that must constantly guide the advocate or program manager. In the diagram in which he characterizes policy analysis, Gallagher separates goals from constraints. Moroney, in Chapter 3, makes a similar distinction; he defines "first principles" as centering on equity, and only at a later stage does he introduce costs as a criterion. Some advocates may even go so far as to favor a policy for day care or child health without calculating its costs. In this perspective, a policy may have one primary goal; if it is then put into effect, evaluators tend to concentrate their analysis on whether it has attained that goal.

A governmental perspective emphasizes one choice of objectives for a program. Examples of objectives for a day-care program might be a 10-point improvement in IQ by children from poverty by school age, a specified increase in the number of working mothers, or a reduction in the proportion of families below the poverty line by a given date. These objectives can be related to programs and models in at least three ways:

1. We can consider a specific program and predict its results, designating these results as objectives;
2. We can set forth objectives such as these and compare several programs as to whether each is likely to attain the objectives;
3. We can entertain the objectives as "ideal objectives," not simply predicted but held before the participants as targets at which to aim. Thus, the objectives may well exceed what a detached observer would predict as probably attainable. In this third case, the objectives do not correspond exactly to a predictive model.

In whichever way objectives were set forth, they could at the same time be part of a system of internal feedback for the program director and his superiors, whereby the relation between accomplishment and projections could be monitored. Objectives can thus be considered primarily as projected results in terms of which a proposed program is to be evaluated. If they are optimistic or inflated targets, they cannot, of course, be used for reasonable assessment of the expected benefits from the program.

Moroney's approach to policy analysis is distinctive in two respects. First, he emphasizes the role of values at each stage of the analysis. Second, he distinguishes between policy analysis, program planning, and evaluation, and offers a model to clarify the relations among these three activities.

The emphasis on values—or to use a term Moroney prefers, "first principles"—is implied in all the models discussed in this book. However, Moroney's chapter gives first principles a central place in virtually all phases of analysis. To a substantial degree, the importance of values is dictated by the fact that analysts do not simply find optimal solutions to problems that someone else defines; rather, analysts must define the problem in their own way. At one time in the development of policy analysis, policymakers assumed that the primary role of analysts was to use sophisticated techniques to find the optimal solution to problems presented to them. But it soon became apparent that analysts were often forced to redefine the problem before analysis could proceed. This, of course, gave analysts the opportunity to insert their own biases into the analysis process—under the cloak of objectivity (Nelson, 1977, pp. 27–28). Moroney's view is that the analyst *should* make these redefinitions. Moreover, the basis for selecting and defining problems should be an explicit set of first principles that is apparent to all concerned. These principles guide the analyst not only in selecting and defining problems for study, but in both choosing criteria to compare alternative policies and devising a plan of policy implementation.

Moroney also proposes a specific framework of first principles that represents the values most analysts attempt to maximize in analyzing social policy. These principles are liberty, equality, and fraternity. As Moroney points out, these principles are frequently in conflict—which is to say that policies maximizing one of the principles will usually undercut one or both of the others. Conservative Republicans, for example, will usually opt for liberty, particularly in economic matters. But as experience in all industrialized countries has shown, economics untempered by government interference produces huge differences in wealth between citizens. Indeed, some citizens and their families have no wealth or income. As a result, industrialized nations have tempered the free market with government transfer programs (welfare, unemployment insurance, social services, etc.). However, these transfer programs—enacted in the pursuit of equality—are financed by taxing corporations and relatively wealthy individuals. In short, such programs reduce the liberty of wealthy members of society to spend and invest in accord with their own preferences.

Thus, even among the first principles identified by Moroney, the analyst must have a well thought-out value position that will justify policies to maximize one first principle at the expense of the other two. For his part, Moroney supports fraternity (or community) as the primary value to guide analysis.

The second distinctive aspect of Moroney's approach is organizational. Unlike the other authors in this volume, Moroney provides a systematic distinction between policy analysis, planning, and evaluation. The first stage, policy analysis, is much like MacRae's approach in its emphasis on analysis of the problem situation, establishing criteria, generating alternative strategies, and making a choice between strategies. Having made a policy choice, then, the analyst next faces what MacRae calls problems of implementation. For Moroney, this phase involves setting specific objectives, establishing implementation criteria, and creating a program design for delivering services. In the third stage—evaluation—provisions are made for specifying program objectives, collecting data, and using these data to improve program performance.

MacRae's approach (see Ch. 4) is more characteristic of the academic analyst who seeks to optimize but who is less closely involved in the struggle for particular goals and objectives. He tries to put all the values involved in a policy choice—goals and constraints, benefits and costs—on the same footing.

Several of the other roles we have considered—staff analyst, planner, citizen-critic—fail to provide sufficient motivation to publish for an expert audience, which is needed for quality control. This motivation is more characteristic of a role that MacRae calls the "citizen-scholar"—a member of the applied discipline of policy analysis, who bases his or her analysis on general ethical principles rather than those of any particular organization and who seeks to publish the results for expert scrutiny. This role leads to a certain degree of generality in formulating the problem—for an audience such as the readers of this essay—in contrast, for example, with a detailed analysis of a particular piece of legislation at the state level. MacRae discusses day-care policies at the national level, with the hypothetical assumption that no public policies for day care presently exist. Such an approach is not realistic for consideration of an actual incremental addition to existing federal policies but can contribute to a scholarly discussion by bringing out many of the relevant issues.

Such a general citizen-scholar role may be useful for introductory teaching and may contribute to the academic respectability of policy analysis through concern with general principles. It must, however, be supplemented by more practical roles, more like those of the engineer or the professional with a particular specialty, that deal with highly specific details of policy recommendations. Only by communicating with decision makers about the specific choices they must make can policy analysts be effective. Thus, an emphasis on the role of the scholar, if not accompanied by these more practical roles, might risk establishing another interesting academic field with inadequate ties to practical choice.

In separating feasibility from desirability, MacRae classifies some elements of policy analysis differently from Gallagher. Gallagher (1976, p. 172; see also Ch. 2) presents a diagram including several valuative categories; for our present discussion the most relevant are constraints, resources, and criteria. Among the constraints is the availability of personnel, and resources include "public willingness to invest" and "sympathy for goals." Personnel are obviously essential to service programs, but MacRae's scheme of policy analysis separates the desirability of a program or policy from its feasibility. He proposes that we first estimate whether a program, properly functioning, would be worth public support, assuming the personnel would be available. He would then ask whether it could be enacted; here the public's willingness to invest and its sympathy for the program's goals enter. Finally, he would ask whether it could be implemented; at this point the availability of personnel is essential. If it is obvious at the start that personnel will not be available, however, he would not waste time on elaborate analysis of the program's desirability.

Turnbull's model for analysis in Chapter 5 centers on the provisions of the law and the Constitution. He first distinguishes genuine legal rights from mere claims, the latter not officially recognized by the law. Rights, once granted by law, are often unconditional in their expression. If, however, two such rights should conflict, it is the task of the courts to reconcile them. This is done by means of precedents, especially in Anglo-Saxon law, and occasionally by the enunciation of interpretive principles, and by the court's search for such principles in the intention of the legislature. The courts thus impose a certain consistency on the provisions of the laws, aided by whatever consistency prevails in the process of legislation. Legal philosophers have sometimes tried to aid and advise the courts by seeking deeper philosophical principles embodied in the laws.

The problem of interpretation and reconciliation becomes more serious, however, when we consider the principles of the Constitution itself. Turnbull points out that all legislation derives from powers granted by the Constitution, and that for the national government these powers are limited and enumerated. The acts of Congress are thus circumscribed in the Constitution. So, too, are the decisions of the courts in matters of constitutionality or constitutional rights. But here the problems are more difficult because of the brevity and vagueness of the Constitution itself; "interstate commerce," "freedom of speech," "due process of law," and "equal protection of the laws," for example, have been subjected to extensive and sometimes changing interpretation by the courts and by legal philosophers.

The result of this interpretation is a synthesis, but of a different sort from those discussed so far. The limits within which the law permits individuals, groups, and government to act are reasonably well established at any given time. Much controversy and some policy-making that affects children and families are conducted in the courts. Turnbull's chapter in this volume says much about the principles and procedures involved. But from another perspective, these judicial processes define the limits (at least in the short run) within which policies may be made by the legislative and executive branches *in terms of other criteria*. The Constitution, in this sense, is a prior constraint on principles such as those of benefit-cost analysis or other maximization criteria. It takes priority as a constraint just as certain moral principles do but is not itself the main source of criteria for policy analysis.[3]

In turning to the chapter by Strauss, we find a point-by-point analysis of a specific and concrete set of policy options aimed at improving America's welfare system. In Chapter 6 Strauss begins by proposing a framework for analyzing welfare policies that includes ten elements analysts should consider in evaluating and comparing welfare programs. These include a theory of poverty, a theory of intergovernmental regulations, cost, equity, feasibility, correctibility, incentives, certainty and risk, side effects on other programs, and coverage or participation. Strauss then conducts a systematic comparison of the current AFDC-Food Stamp welfare system, former President Carter's proposed reforms to the system, and the reforms proposed by House Ways and Means Committee Chairman Ullman.

The Strauss framework has much in common with the other models presented in this book. It differs from the other models, however, in that it is designed to apply only to welfare proposals, whereas the other models are general in the sense of being designed to apply to all problems of social policy. Furthermore, Strauss's framework does not provide for a restatement of the problem situation because the problem was defined for Strauss by his client, Chairman Ullman. But with the exception of restating the problem, Strauss's ten-element framework contains most of the analytical steps recommended by the Gallagher, MacRae, and Moroney models.

References

Becker, G. S. *The economic approach to human behavior.* Chicago: Univ. of Chicago Press, 1976.

Ben-David, J. *The scientist's role in society.* Englewood Cliffs, N.J.: Prentice–Hall, 1971.

Bledstein, B. J. *The culture of professionalism: The middle class and the development of higher education in America.* New York: Norton, 1976.

Bronfenbrenner, U. Is early intervention effective? In M. Guttentag & E. L. Struening (Eds.), *Handbook of evaluation research* (Vol. 2). Beverly Hills: Sage, 1975.

Clark, T. N. Policy research and urban public policy. *Policy Analysis,* 1976, *4,* 67–90.

Coleman, J. S., Campbell, E. Q., Hobson, C. J., McPartland, J., Mood, A. M., Weinfeld, F. D., & York, R. L. *Equality of educational opportunity.* Washington, D. C.: U.S. Govt. Printing Office, 1966.

Darlington, R. B., Royce, J. M., Snipper, A. S., Murray, H. W., & Lazar, I. Preschool programs and later school competence of children from low-income families. *Science,* 1980, *208,* 202–204.

Finsterbusch, K., & Motz, A. B. *Social research for policy decisions.* Belmont, Calif.: Wadsworth, 1980.

Gallagher, J. J. Planning for early childhood programs for exceptional children. *Journal of Special Education,* 1976, *10,* 171–177.

Gil, D. G. *Unravelling social policy: Theory, analysis, and political action towards social equality* (2nd ed.). Cambridge, Mass.: Schenkman, 1976.

Glendon, M. A. The American family in the 200th year of the Republic. *Family Law Quarterly*, 1976, *10*, 335–355.

Goldhamer, H. *The adviser*. New York: Elsevier, 1978.

Halpern, R. The economics of preschool education. In C. Silverman (Ed.), *High/Scope Report, 1979* (No. 4). Ypsilanti, Mich.: High/Scope Educational Research Foundation, 1979.

Haskins, R. A model for analyzing social policies. In R. Haskins & J. J. Gallagher (Eds.), *Care and education of young children in America: Policy, politics, and social science*. Norwood, N. J.: Ablex, 1980.

Haveman, R. H., & Margolis, J. (Eds.). *Public expenditure and policy analysis* (2nd ed.). Chicago: Rand McNally, 1977.

Jencks, C., & Riesman, D. *The academic revolution*. Garden City, N.Y.: Doubleday, 1968.

Kantrowitz, A. Controlling technology democratically. *American Scientist*, 1975, *63*, 501–509.

Keniston, K. *All our children*. New York: Harcourt Brace Jovanovich, 1977.

Komarovsky, M. (Ed.). *Sociology and public policy: The case of presidential commissions*. New York: Elsevier, 1975.

Lazarsfeld, P. F., & Reitz, J. G. *An introduction to applied sociology*. New York: Elsevier, 1975.

Levins, R. Fundamental and applied research in agriculture. *Science*, 1973, *181*, 523–524.

MacRae, D. *The social function of social science*. New Haven: Yale University Press, 1976. (a)

MacRae, D. Technical communities and political choice. *Minerva*, 1976, *14*, 169–190. (b)

MacRae, D. Review essay: The sociological economics of Gary S. Becker. *American Journal of Sociology*, 1978, *83*, 1244–1258.

MacRae, D. Valuative problems of public policy analysis. In J. P. Crecine (Ed.), *Research in public policy analysis and management* (Vol. 1). Greenwich, Conn.: JAI Press, 1981.

MacRae, D., & Wilde, J. *Policy analysis for public decisions*. North Scituate, Mass.: Duxbury Press, 1979.

Meltsner, A. J. *Policy analysts in the bureaucracy*. Berkeley: Univ. of California Press, 1976.

National Research Council. *Toward a national policy for children and families*. Washington, D.C.: National Academy of Sciences, 1976.

Nelson, R. R. *The moon and the ghetto: An essay on public policy analysis*. New York: Norton, 1977.

Quade, E. S. *Analysis for public decisions*. New York: Elsevier, 1975.

Raiffa, H. *Decision analysis*. Reading, Mass.: Addison-Wesley, 1968.

Rein, M. *Social science and public policy*. New York: Penguin, 1976.

Rivlin, A. M. Federal support for child care: An analysis of options. In R. H. Haveman & J. Margolis (Eds.), *Public expenditure and policy analysis* (2nd ed.). Chicago: Rand McNally, 1977.

Schultze, C. L. *The politics and economics of public spending*. Washington, D.C.: Brookings, 1968.

Snow, C. P. *Science and government*. London: Oxford Univ. Press, 1961.

Stokey, E., & Zeckhauser, R. *A primer for policy analysis*. New York: Norton, 1978.

Titmuss, R. M. *Social policy: An introduction*. New York: Pantheon Books, 1974.

Tribe, L. H. Policy science: Analysis or ideology? *Philosophy and Public Affairs*, 1972, *2*, 66–110.
Weber, C. V., Foster, P. W., & Weikart, D. P. *An economic analysis of the Perry Preschool Project*. Ypsilanti, Mich.: High/Scope, 1978.
Wildavsky, A. *Speaking truth to power: The art and craft of policy analysis*. Boston: Little, Brown, 1979.
Wolf, C. A theory of non-market failures. *Public Interest*, 1979, *55*, 114–133.
Zigler, E., & Valentine, J. (Eds.). *Project Head Start: A legacy of the War on Poverty*. New York: Free Press, 1979.
Ziman, J. *Public knowledge: The social dimension of science*. Cambridge, Mass.: Cambridge Univ. Press, 1968.

FOOTNOTES

[1] We deal here with several models *for* policy analysis, i.e., sets of steps or elements that may be followed in an analysis. These models should be distinguished from models that are causal statements or simulations that we use to predict the consequences of alternative policies (MacRae & Wilde, 1979, Ch. 4).

[2] Four of the models for policy analysis described in the following chapters have, in fact, been placed under a single set of categories—the "Bush model" used in our seminars (see Haskins, 1980); in order to stress their distinct features, we describe them separately here.

[3] Policy research may sometimes be directed at the choice of policies that best fulfills a constitutional provision; the Coleman Report's (1966) interpretation of equality of educational opportunity was indirectly related to "equal protection of the laws." The form in which legal argument is conducted, however, does not easily accommodate statistical reasoning about expected values.

TWO

MODELS FOR POLICY ANALYSIS: CHILD AND FAMILY POLICY

JAMES J. GALLAGHER

INTRODUCTION: THE AMERICAN FAMILY AND PUBLIC POLICY

During the past few decades, American society has revealed its continuing concern about the state of the family through a battery of policies designed to help the family cope with the stresses and problems of modern life. Support was made available through social work services, special educational provisions, more resources for better nutrition and health care, plus a variety of programs to insure that the consequences of poverty did not overwhelm the family and its individual members.

The need for models for evaluating the efficiency of these societal efforts and to determine what remains to be done has generated interest in policy analysis systems that can conceptualize these complex issues touching on all segments of the society. One such model as it applies to child and family policy is the focus of this chapter.

A number of attempts have been made to summarize trends in traditional family living arrangements. Bianchi and Farley (1979) summarized six major trends:

1. Age of first marriage has advanced, and a growing proportion of those who marry eventually divorce.

2. Women are much more likely now than in the past to head their own families.
3. A declining proportion of children live in families which include both their parents. At present, less than one-half of black children under 18 live with both their parents.
4. A much higher proportion of the nation's births occur to unmarried women.
5. Differences in family living arrangements are associated with substantial differences in economic well-being. Among both races, declining fractions of the population live within families where the per capita income level is high; increasing proportions live in families which have the lowest incomes.
6. The trend away from family stability can be seen in both black and white families. However, the shifts have been greater among blacks, and racial differences are now larger than when Moynihan wrote *The Negro Family* (1965), or at any other time since World War II. (p. 545)

None of these trends can be assumed to be totally favorable, to say the least, and a feeling has persisted that social policy can and should be used as a tool to improve family circumstances and to provide opportunities for better child development and family adaptation.

Schorr (1979) has argued that there are three major traditions in the United States which operate as a barrier to general family policy.

> First, our goals are individualistic. Though it may appear that the pursuit of individual development has reached new heights, liberation and egalitarianism (child in relation to parent, wife in relation to husband and vice versa) are ingrained in our national character reaching back to Colonial times. Second, as citizens we are profoundly suspicious of and opposed to government. . . . Finally, the nature of our political process does not lend itself to broad agreement on principles to which subsequent policies are subordinated. (p. 465)

Schorr feels that unless these traditions are eliminated or strongly reduced, then it is unlikely that major governmental policy related to families will be enacted.

For the reasons noted above, it seems likely that public policy around any broad dimension of American society such as the family will be done in piecemeal, issue-by-issue, decision making. Zimmerman, Mattessich, and Leik (1979) conducted a survey of Minnesota legislators on their attitudes toward family policies and goals. They concluded that the legislators reacted more favorably to those policies which helped families with special problems such as mental retardation, mental illness, child abuse, poverty, physical disability, old age, single parenthood, delinquency, minority group status, and unemployment. The legislators were much less approving of broad policy initiatives that helped *all* families with young children. It is clear that a broad and universal policy has less priority and less appeal than do specific policies in dealing with crisis problems.

The implication of this conclusion is that there will likely be a multiplicity of actions taken to deal with small parts of larger social problems. These actions will need careful analysis to see how they fit with other policies, and whether they add to (or even detract from) the well-being of all families.

The rapid growth of social policy analysis as a strategy has been documented in the MacRae and Haskins chapter. The recency of the movement is another phenomenon. The growing commitment of government at all levels to deal actively with social conditions within the society has stimulated a growing relationship between the academic community and the public policy arena.

PUBLIC POLICY AND THE ACADEMIC COMMUNITY: THE PAST

New methods usually emerge because of the failure of older procedures. Such is the case here. Two major strategies can be identified as having been employed by public policy leaders for gaining wisdom from academia in the last few decades.

The Commission Approach

The first of these could be labeled the "blue ribbon commission" approach. In this instance, a particular social issue such as delinquency, or the family, or welfare is identified. A commission composed of the most distinguished professionals available is then assembled and asked to give their best counsel and advice to the government on the true nature of the problem, together with their suggestions for ways to remediate the problem.

Some recent examples of the commission strategy are the Carnegie report on the family (Keniston, 1977) and the latest report of the President's Commission on Mental Health (1978). In the case of the Keniston report, the commission was assembled by a private foundation, but with a clear intent to affect public policy. The flaws in the blue ribbon commission approach lie in the difficulty of making a transition from what the experts know about the problem to some feasible or manageable government programs. Not infrequently, commissions make recommendations that are so impractical or so costly in their implementation that they are rejected out of hand by policymakers. Nor do commissions often give any serious consideration to the problem of inserting recommended new programs into an already existing service delivery network.

To take one example, a committee of the National Research Council (1976) recently published a book entitled *Toward a National Policy for Children and Families* in which a series of recommendations were presented by a panel of distinguished social scientists. Their first recommendation was a genuine blockbuster:

> A national policy for children and families should begin with a program to insure that families have the minimum income necessary to provide adequate food, shelter, and care for their children . . . No child should be deprived of access to a family living standard of at least half of the median family income level (after tax) for a substantial period of his or her childhood and this income should not fall below the government-defined poverty level even for shorter periods. This goal can be met by: increased levels of activity in the economy to reduce unemployment and draw more family members into the labor force, public employment and training programs for the low-skilled and the hard-to-employ, and direct redistribution of income. (p. 5)

Public policymakers viewing this recommendation realize very quickly that it calls for a major reform of our political and economic systems. No quantitative figures are provided which might suggest how much government investment would be required or what the expected output would be, to say nothing of possible unintended consequences of such a massive income redistribution policy.

Small wonder that most political figures classify such recommendations together with other pious goals, such as "no child with a health problem should be left untreated" or "all children should receive maximum educational opportunity." Policymakers know there is a gap, even a yawning chasm, between what is and what ought to be in society, but what they would like to know from academia are the dimensions, cost, and sequence of activities necessary to build a bridge between our current status and our goals. It is this information that academia has been unable to provide!

In general, study commissions have served admirably to summarize social problems but have rarely provided useful suggestions for new policies that were practical and capable of being implemented. Indeed, some cagey administrators or legislators have been accused of establishing study commissions in order to delay decision making on important, but painful, political issues.

An exception to the generally vacuous statements of commissions is the work on labeling of children by a commission established by Hobbs (1974). With the help of over 50 professionals who wrote on various aspects of the topic, Hobbs produced a scholarly state of the art on the effects of labeling upon children, together with a thoughtful consideration of alternative strategies and suggested pluses and minuses of each strategy. Even in this instance, however, the costs and consequences were not explicitly documented. Most commissions have neither the time nor the resources for such careful study and, consequently, their products often result only in restatements of the obvious, placing the difficult issues of cost and consequences back in the lap of the policymaker.

The Guru Approach

A second major strategy by which social science has influenced policy in the past is the *guru* approach. In this case, a particular agency or legislative committee identifies a distinguished academician whose judgment they trust to advise them on policy directions in a particular field. Thus, one may find the same individuals testifying repeatedly before congressional committees on major issues of health or education. Other professional gurus may be found on advisory councils of the various agencies or influential foundations. The limitations of this approach are that it depends on gurus adequately reflecting the more general consensus of their professional colleagues, and that it assumes gurus have the ability to make the required translation between what we know and the special problems of policy implementation.

What the public policymakers have often found, to their dismay, was that their particular guru did not reflect a professional consensus, nor did his expertise in pediatrics or psychology mean that he was able to make the important translation from academic knowledge to workable policy implementation. For example, an expert on the delivery of health services may not have a clear understanding of the organization of bureaucracy, the complex health delivery system, or the political issues that impinge on these organizations.

BARRIERS TO COOPERATION BETWEEN ACADEMIA AND DECISION MAKERS

There appear to be a number of forces that are operating to keep the academic community and the political community from capitalizing on their mutual interests.

Rivalry between Practitioners of Knowledge and Power

First, a natural rivalry exists between those who hold power and those who hold knowledge. Berle (1969), in his perceptive book on the uses of power, drew the analogy that every culture has its priests who collect and maintain knowledge and its kings who collect and use power. These two groups often find themselves in conflict with one another, and yet they are drawn together by their mutual dependence. Whereas the kings may be suspicious of the priests' knowledge, they need the priests' wisdom to make good decisions on complex professional and scientific issues. On the other hand, the priests may be concerned with the inappropriate uses of power, but they need the kings if they wish to translate their ideas into social action. In many respects, social policy analysis and its various offshoots provide a method of bringing together these two groups with their different values, objectives, and modes of performance.

Sense of Limited Resources

Our rapidly expanding social needs have forced us to focus attention on the almost unlimited demands that could be made on the public treasury by the perceived social needs of the citizenry (Wildavsky, 1964). Nevertheless, the first serious thrust of long-range planning and analysis seemed to emerge primarily as a result of the rapidly expanding budget of the Defense Department coincident with the Vietnam War (Rivlin, 1971). At that time, Secretary of Defense Robert MacNamara introduced a series of planning and decision models designed to bring under some degree of control the rapidly expanding budget from all four military services. These procedures required that agencies requesting resources make a clear statement of goals and objectives, an analysis of alternative strategies, and an attempt to evaluate performance from both a management and program standpoint in order to allow the key decision maker to reach some reasonable choices between competing programs and requests.

How Much Is Enough?

Figure 1 gives a breakdown of funds spent in North Carolina on a variety of programs for children. The figures are both impressive and puzzling. We can see a great diversity of resources being allocated, but how can we determine whether the right proportions are being spent to achieve important societal objectives? Should more money be spent on health or more on education? Does the comparison of child-care expenditures and education expenditures reveal an unmet need? We have limited tools to help us answer such questions and since each agency can be depended upon to ask for significant increases in their budgets each year, decision makers are faced with galloping budget growth while being relatively helpless in making informed judgments.

Planning as a "Foreign" Invention

It is sometimes difficult to remember that only a short two decades ago, key decision makers in the United States considered "ad hocism"

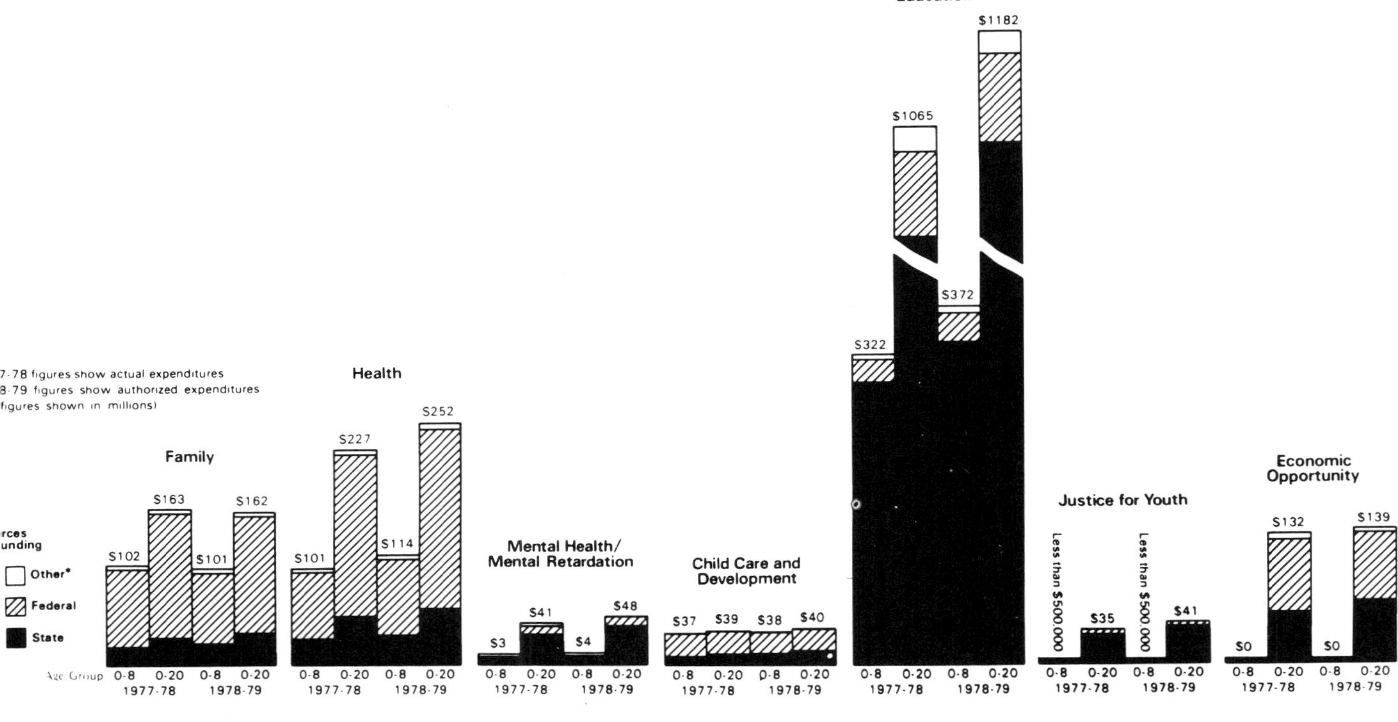

Figure 1.
Spending on children in North Carolina.

as a desirable way to meet our national problems. Our vast resources had allowed us to survive two world wars with little advance preparation and contributed to the feeling that anything was possible if we collectively put our energies and resources to the task. This feeling of naive optimism about our invulnerability against the ravages of time or unpleasant surprises has now diminished with our experiences in Vietnam and our energy shortages. We no longer believe we possess all the resources necessary to stand independent in the world (Heilbroner, 1974).

This new view that Americans must conserve and apply our limited resources efficiently has had a great deal to do with the growing development of, and interest in, planning and program analysis. Since we no longer appear to have the resources to do even the things we feel necessary, it becomes doubly important that we allocate existing resources effectively so as to gain maximum benefits from what we have.

Doubts about Program Effectiveness

One reason for the popularity of planning and program analysis comes from a concern about the effectiveness of various health, social, and educational programs. There can no longer be much doubt, for example, that the American public has grown increasingly skeptical about the values or quality of public education. The rapid development of minimum competency tests to insure basic skills in high school graduates is one clear indication of public suspicion that the public schools are not achieving their stated goals (Pipho, 1977).

The sharp increase in school bond rejections also suggests a lack of solid public support for education, and the cries for educational accountability heard throughout the land are symptoms of an important estrangement of the public from the educational establishment. The Coleman report (1966) presented the point of view that the quality of schools did not make much difference in school achievement, or at least was considerably less influential and important than family background. A follow-up volume by Jencks (1972) some years later continued the same message, i.e., the schools are less important than the home and social environment in influencing children.

Similar doubts have been raised about the effectiveness of programs such as Head Start (Cicirelli, 1969) and Title I of the Elementary and Secondary Education Act (Levin, 1977). An analysis which would differentiate effective from ineffective programs would obviously represent a major financial savings to the public. It would allow the establishment of other program elements of higher quality to replace those that do not seem to be working well (House, 1973).

The first generation of programs designed to attack such long-standing problems as poverty and mental illness has seemed to come up considerably short in terms of results, even though the costs of the programs are continually expanding. The situation has been summed up by Weiss (1975):

> There is apparently something wrong with many of our social policies and much social programming. We do not know *how* to solve some of the major problems facing the society. We do not apply the knowledge that we have. We mount limited focus programs to cope with broad gauge problems. We devote limited resources to long-standing and stubborn problems. Above all, we concentrate attention on changing the attitudes and behavior of target groups without concomitant attention to the institutional structures and social arrangements that tend to keep them "target groups." . . . The time has come to put more of our research talents into even earlier phases of the policy process, into work that contributes to the development of schemes and prototypes. We need more research on the social processes and institutional structures that sustain the problems of the society. (p. 25)

The strong trend to economy and program review now visible can probably be traced to ever-increasing budgets for social, health, and educational services combined with information on doubtful program success.

It is one thing to list the reasons why policy analyses are needed; another to suggest that they will be heeded, when drawn up. The extent to which social policy analysis now influences federal policy decisions can be judged by the presentation by an experienced legislative aide in the Congress (Andringa, 1976) of eleven factors that influence federal education legislation. Social policy analysis is ninth on the list, program evaluation studies are eleventh. The five most important influences are:

1. Personal judgment and values of usually no more than six to ten members of Congress and staff.
2. Strong views of respected and trusted friends.
3. Assumptions about the economy and the budget.
4. Public opinion and the popular media.
5. Strong views and efforts of major interest groups. (pp. 79–80)

Despite this currently pessimistic view, the disarray resulting from current modes of behavior makes it inevitable that decision makers will seek more predictable and defensible procedures.

MODELS OF SOCIAL POLICY ANALYSIS

Since policy analysis usually involves the collection or synthesis of data, it has often been compared to research and evaluation. Yet it has a distinctive character which differentiates it from both research and evaluation.

Policy analysis often uses secondary data analysis, rarely depends on an experimental design, makes explicit the value orientation of the analyst, and, above all, has a turnaround time of 3–6 months, which makes it potentially useful to policymakers. Many different formal definitions abound. Gil (1976) has defined social policy as principles or courses of action designed to influence:

1. Overall quality of life in society;
2. Circumstances of living of individuals and groups; and the
3. Nature of intra-societal relationships among individuals, groups, and society as a whole. (p. 25)

I am inclined to accept the definition of social policy analysis proposed by MacRae and Wilde (1979): "Policy analysis is the use of reason and evidence to choose the best policy among a number of alternatives" (p. 4). This defintion places the emphasis on *decision* rather than on mere *description*.

Zimmerman (1970) has identified policy analysis as having two essential characteristics; it is *decision-oriented* and *anticipatory*. Program evaluation or evaluation research, in its concern with program outcomes, is necessarily concerned with past performance which, in turn, may stimulate the search for new directions and approaches. Thus, on occasion program evaluation can be considered a part of policy analysis. Policy analysis also includes cost–benefit analyses of policy options in social, economic, and psychological terms with a view toward eliminating the unacceptable alternatives. By its very nature, policy analysis is value-conscious. In fact, Moroney, in Chapter 3, argues that value considerations form the heart of any analysis.

Beckman (1977) has tried to identify those techniques that form the essence of policy analysis. In his view these techniques include:

1. The identification of previous policies and their origins.
2. The identification of the historical and environmental context of decision alternatives.
3. The identification of values of groups coalescing for or against a particular problem solution and for the application of cost–benefit and equity efficiency criteria to policy options. (p. 20)

In Table 1, Nye and McDonald (1979) present three models of family policy research that distinguish it from advocacy efforts. Each procedure stresses secondary data analysis and nonprofessional audiences as the target group of the analysis activities. While values play an important part in analysis, there is a quantitative base for the analysis not required for advocacy. Still, there is a need for systematic and predictable methodology to be applied to the analysis.

TABLE 1: DISTINCTIONS BETWEEN FAMILY POLICY AND FAMILY POLICY ADVOCACY[a]

Family policy research activities	Goal or product	Method of analysis	Audience
Family evaluation research	An evaluation of the degree to which social programs have achieved their stated goals for individual family members and the family unit	Empirical: primary and secondary data analysis	Public policy decision makers and program administrators
Family impact analysis	An assessment of the intended and unintended consequences of specific policies and programs upon involved families	Empirical: primary and secondary data analysis, computer simulation	Public policy decision makers
Research for family policy	An assessment of the consequences of family structure and family types on family members and society	Research on secondary data analysis or interpretation	Practitioners, policymakers, lay public
Family policy advocacy	The endorsement and active campaigning for public policy and programs to improve family conditions and enhance the quality of family life	Nonempirical: positions taken based on commitment to basic family values and/or familiarization with existing family policy research	Public policy decision makers, legislators, and the voting public

[a] From Nye & McDonald, 1979, p. 474.

MODEL FOR POLICY GENERATION

Experience at the Bush Institute at the University of North Carolina at Chapel Hill has caused the author to distinguish two types of analysis. One type of policy analysis deals with the assembling of possible strategies to find the most viable approach to a given problem—a model for policy generation. The second approach involves analyzing the implementation of policies already in force to determine whether they are achieving their goals. Table 2 summarizes the major steps for each of the two models.

Each of these models bears close resemblance to an already existing decision model. This model, which has proved useful for program planning activities, owes its emergence to the interest of the federal government in controlling the cost of defense and social welfare programs (Rivlin, 1971). Figure 2 provides one schematic version of the

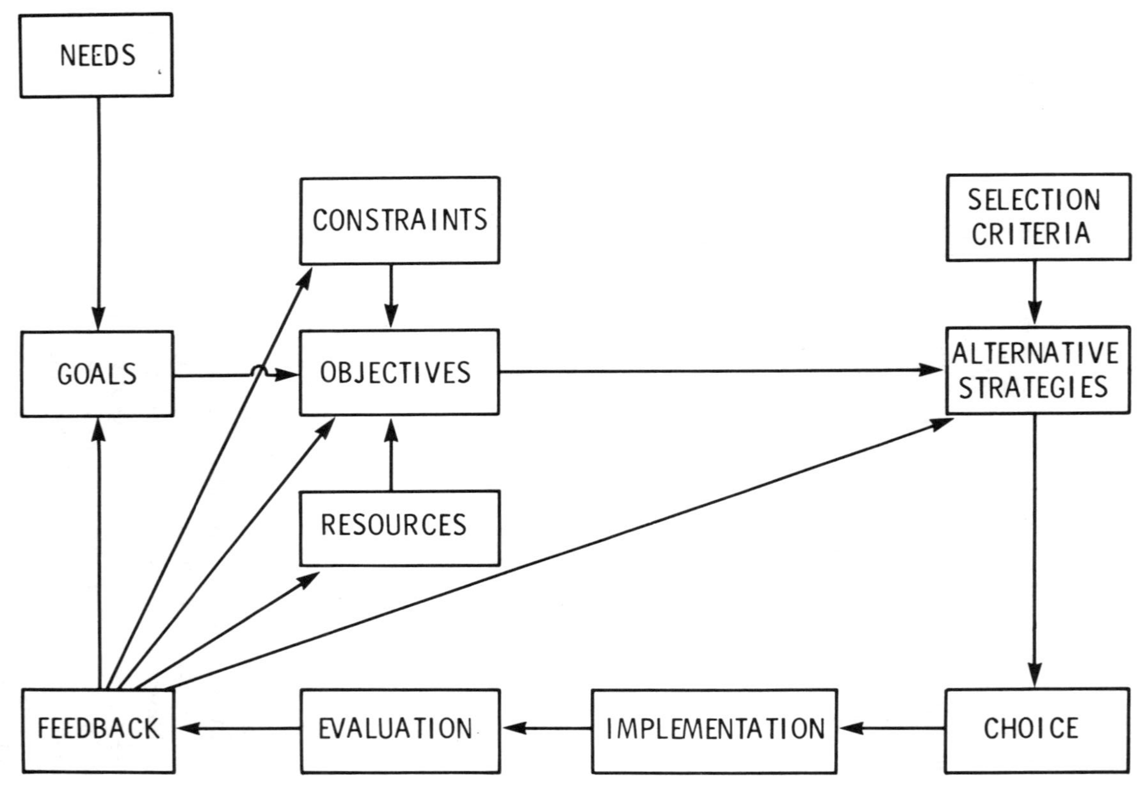

Figure 2.
A program planning and evaluation model.

TABLE 2: TWO MODELS OF POLICY ANALYSIS

Model of policy generation	Model of policy implementation
1. Restatement of the problem	1. Problem statement
2. Establishing analysis criteria	2. Current policy description
3. Synthesis of information	3. Value base for policy
4. Alternative strategies	4. Application of policy
5. Criteria for strategy choice	5. Program objectives attained
6. Implementation plan	6. Identifiable barriers to implementation
	a. Institutional
	b. Psychological
	c. Sociological
	d. Economic
	e. Political
	7. Recommendations for action

decision model (Gallagher, Surles, & Hayes, 1973). Although the decision model has many variations, all stress the importance of a clear statement of goals and objectives, analysis of alternative strategies, and identification of criteria for choice, as well as the inclusion of program evaluation and feedback in the planning and decision-making process. In remaining sections, I will elaborate on the actions required by each step of the two models outlined in Table 2 and show how these models link with the older decision model.

Restatement of the Problem

In policy analysis, the issues and problems are often chosen by the policymakers, which creates a situation quite unlike that in the research field in which the problem is generally chosen by the investigator. When the policy problem is presented to the analyst, is it often stated in limited or parochial terms and has to be restated before effective policy analysis can begin.

It is not uncommon for the analyst to face such questions as whether federal guidelines on day-care personnel should be endorsed, or whether PL 94-142 (the Education for All Handicapped Children Act) should be repealed. These are questions which must be reformulated to pose a larger issue if a meaningful analysis is to be carried out. The questions might be translated into "How does the kind and number of day-care personnel influence the developing child?" or "In what ways are we still not providing effective educational services to handicapped children and their families?"

The essence of a problem statement is that it have significant policy import, strategies available that are politically and professionally feasible, and data available, or easily accessible, which aid in the analysis. The redefinition of a problem also bears close resemblance to the more traditional statement of needs in the familiar decision model.

Needs. The first aspect of the decision model is a clear statement of *needs*. There must be an identifiable, definable, and quantifiable need before appropriate program elements can be designed. Needs statements can be very broad statements, such as "people are sick and not receiving appropriate health treatment," or "children are being poorly educated," or "there are no rehabilitation facilities for handicapped adults." However, for the needs analysis to be of maximum utility in the planning process, a much more precise, quantitative statement is required.

We want to know not only that "people are sick and not receiving treatment," but also their numbers and exact nature of their illnesses. This information would allow for some estimate of the type of treatment needed, as well as the number of additional professionals needed to provide treatment. If learning-disabled children need special education, for example, then a knowledge of how many such children exist will be essential in making budget estimates or personnel estimates of the resources required to meet their needs.

To illustrate the difficulties sometimes encountered in estimating needs, the number of learning-disabled children in the United States is estimated to be anywhere from 1–20% of the student population (Kirk & Gallagher, 1979). The wide disparity in these estimates means that from a half-million to 10 million children may have the presumed condition! Such diverse estimations of needs make it difficult, if not impossible, to provide a rational plan for dealing with the condition. This places a great responsibility on the analyst to sharpen the definition of the condition and reach some consensus from relevant professionals on the size of the needs.

In the past, so few services were available to youngsters and families with special problems that an overall estimate of the problem was not important because resources could be counted upon to fall far short of the minimum estimate anyway. However, as social programs have expanded in personnel and financial resources, it has become more important to be precise in estimating the number of children and families with unmet needs.

One example of a needs statement is provided by Mikow (1980) in connection with a policy analysis on displaced homemakers. Current estimates indicate that 50% of all first marriages will end in divorce

(Glick, 1979). Rising divorce rates, coupled with a relatively stable male mortality rate (which exceeds comparable female cohort rates), are reflected in the increasing incidence of women heading families. More specifically, in 1967, 11% of all U.S. households were headed by females; by 1977, the figure had risen to 14% (U.S. Bureau of the Census, 1978).

Female heads of households are significantly more likely to participate in the labor force. Seventy percent of all divorced women *must* work, and 85% *must* also care for children (Campbell, 1975). While a proportion of these households are composed of young women with minor children, a rapidly growing segment of this population, the displaced homemakers, are early middle-age and older upon entering the household-head status. The following list from the Department of Labor describes the characteristics of the displaced homemaker population:

(a) Has not worked in the labor force for a substantial number of years but has, during those years, worked in the home providing unpaid services for family members; and,
(b) (1) Has been dependent on public assistance or on the income of another family member but is no longer supported by that income; or (2) Is receiving public assistance on account of dependent children in the home, especially where such assistance will soon be terminated; and,
(c) Is unemployed or underemployed and is experiencing difficulty in obtaining or upgrading employment. (*Federal Register,* 1980, p. 33855)

It has been well-documented that families headed by women are more likely to experience poverty than male-headed families. As can be seen from Table 3, 57.4% of all female-headed households are clustered in the three lowest income categories, but only 18.2% of male-headed families are similarly grouped.

In 1960 there were 4.51 million families headed by women. By 1977, the number of families headed by women had grown to 8.24 million, a rate of growth four times faster than that associated with families headed by men (U.S. Bureau of the Census, 1978). As previously noted, female heads of household run a disproportionately high risk of being poor. In 1977, the median income for families headed by males was $17,517, whereas the median income for female-headed families was $7,765. While families headed by women comprise 14.4% of all families, they account for almost half (49.1%) of all families in poverty. Nearly one-third of all female-headed households (31.7%) lived below the federally established poverty line in 1977 (U.S. Bureau of the Census, 1979). The needs statement then is that over 8 million families are headed by women who are at risk for being poor, having dependent children to care for, and having few work skills.

TABLE 3: INCOME OF FAMILIES BY SEX OF HOUSEHOLD HEAD[a]

Income category	Male-headed Number (in thousands)	Male-headed %[b]	Female-headed Number (in thousands)	Female-headed %[b]
Under $4,000	1,490	3.0	1,725	20.4
4,000–6,999	3,274	6.6	1,724	20.4
7,000–9,999	4,262	8.6	1,398	16.6
10,000–12,999	4,824	10.0	1,080	12.8
13,000–15,999	5,130	10.4	766	9.1
16,000–19,999	6,907	14.0	717	8.5
20,000–24,999	7,855	15.9	537	6.4
25,000–49,999	13,556	27.5	477	5.6
50,000 and over	2,047	4.1	35	0.4

[a] Source: U.S. Bureau of the Census, 1979, Table 4, p. 40.
[b] Figures do not add to 100% due to rounding.

Goals. In the decision model there is usually a very close relationship between needs and goals. A goal is defined as a statement of general intent: if one identifies a need, such as "children are being poorly educated," then the goal becomes to "educate those children." A goal statement usually represents a direct statement of the intent to take care of an unmet need. As in the previous example, a goal for displaced homemakers would be to help women heads of households to acquire job-related skills.

An analyst may quickly discover that a single strategy such as "day care" may hide a variety of diverse goals or restatements of the problem. The particular strategy of increasing day-care services for preschool children receives support from many groups who may have quite different goals in mind. One group may argue that the goal of day-care programs is to allow more women to enter the work force by providing a satisfactory care setting for their young children. The goal of increasing women's participation in the work force may be a manifestation of women's rights, or of the more economic motive that the needs of the family unit require an income by the mother. A second and quite different goal for the establishment of day-care programs might be to enhance the early development of young children, particularly children who may be at risk for health, psychological, or developmental problems. Obviously, these two goals might generate different types of day-care programs.

The plan for an evaluation of program success would bring these different goals into play. In the first instance, "success" would likely be defined as an increase in the percentage of women in the work force who have youngsters in day-care programs. However, in the second case the definition of success would be improvement in the development or behavior of children in the day-care program. It is not unusual to find proponents of a given policy alternative approaching it from distinct, and sometimes contradictory, sets of goals.

Objectives. One of the major contributions to policy analysis from the MacNamara era was the demand that program objectives be stated in quantitative terms. A carefully stated objective requires a specific and quantitative set of program outcomes, together with some time limit for their attainment. A statement of objectives becomes an essential part of program evaluation; otherwise one would have a difficult time reaching a judgment regarding program effectiveness.

Thus, a generally stated goal such as "improvement of reading scores" must be translated to a specific objective, such as "third-grade children will gain 1.0 years in grade equivalent scores on the Metropolitan Achievement Test by June, 1981." This statement is precise in its quantification, in the instrument used to reach the quantification, and in the establishment of a time limit by which the gains are to be obtained. It is also clear that such a statement is more or less easily verifiable by standard evaluation techniques. The program director, and those wishing to review the program, can thereby have a clear and direct assessment of whether program objectives have been met.

However, the translation of broad, general goals to specific objectives in social programs is often not easy. For example, a general and vague educational goal of "improving self-concept through a special educational program" might well be translated into an objective statement of improvement by 20 percentile points on some self-concept scale. But if the particular scale does not accurately measure self-concept as originally conceptualized in the broader goal, then an illusion has been created. If the measurement of objectives is poor, it may appear that the general goal has been obtained when, in fact, all that has happened has been some change on a measurement instrument. Table 4 indicates the distinctions between goals and objectives.

There are two types of objectives used in decision models, administrative and program. *Administrative objectives* are statements related to the effective management or engineering aspects of the program. A common administrative objective in education could be "to hire three special education teachers necessary to carry out the program." One could then judge whether that objective had been obtained

TABLE 4: DISTINCTIONS BETWEEN GOALS AND OBJECTIVES

Goal (intent)	Objective (specific observable outcome)
We should improve the reading ability in the third-grade children.	Third-grade children in Jefferson Elementary School will gain 1.2 years in Grade Equivalent Scores on the Metropolitan Reading Test by June, 1981.
The number of socially aggressive outbursts in classrooms has to be reduced.	There will be a 20% reduction of behavioral attacks from baseline by Christmas as indicated by observer tally.
Parents of handicapped children will show less stress after parent programs are operational.	Parents will show a 25% reduction on scores on the Holroyd scale of stress after six sessions of our parent education program.

by merely identifying the appropriate persons on the personnel roster of the program. Successful attainment of administrative objectives does not imply that the program has achieved its program objectives.

A *Program Objective,* then, involves some change in the target group of the program, whether that change be childrens' behavior, parents' attitudes, or income level of the family. Some demonstrable change in a favorable direction is expected before one can pronounce a program effective, regardless of whether the administrative objectives have been successfully carried out.

The importance of measurable output in the decision model is apparent. Program input statements of "new teachers," or "more equipment," or "more pediatricians in rural areas" become important only when supported by demonstrable improvements in the targets of the program. Table 5 summarizes the essential relationship between needs, goals, and objectives through a specific example.

Establishing Analysis Criteria

In this second step of policy analysis, the variables forming the basis for analyzing the policy are established. In this stage the analyst's values come into full play, as well as the values of those who requested the analysis in the first place. In a society of diverse value systems, it is impossible to reach total consensus on the criteria to be used in analyzing issues (e.g., women in the work force or services to preschool

TABLE 5: RELATIONSHIP OF GOALS, OBJECTIVES, AND NEEDS

Needs (the problem)	A needs analysis has revealed that 20% of children in poverty areas do not receive minimum daily requirements of protein and iron in their regular diet.
Goals (statement of program intent)	Provide better nutrition for children who are in special need circumstances.
Administrative objective (necessary elements of the program in place)	Distribute supplies of nutritional supplements to centers or personnel charged with the responsibility of providing these supplies to children.
Program objective (expected changes in the target group)	Ninety percent of children previously identified as suffering from protein and iron deficiency would be found to have an adequate diet by September of this year.

children), but analysts should explicate clearly the values underlying the criteria selected.

In the decision model shown in Fig. 2, this stage of establishing analysis criteria is noted in the balancing of resources, constraints, and the selection criteria against which a strategy choice is made.

An example of such analytic criteria is provided by Samuels (1980) who established four criteria for evaluating a state screening program for young handicapped children. These criteria are:

1. *Vertical equity*. The unequal treatment of unequals so as to make them more equal. Since the rich pay more taxes for screening than the poor, universal screening would be consistent with a criterion of vertical equity.
2. *Efficiency*. Efficiency is defined as that use of resources that will produce the maximum benefit. If, for example, a state tracks 10% of 80,000 infants born in a given year, will this be an efficient use of resources? Will the infants identified and followed receive appropriate services, and if so, will the services be effective? More specifically, will the services produce effects that are of greater value than the combined cost of identification, tracking, and service delivery?
3. *Right to privacy*. Justice Brandeis once wrote that the individual's right to be left alone is the most valued right of civilized man. Collecting records of children at-risk and their families would seem to be in violation of such rights, unless careful protective devices are included in the program (such as parental consent required before data are transferred from one agency to another).
4. *Avoidance of stigma*. Stigmatization means that some individuals are labeled as different in a negative way from citizens not affected by the policy. The value underlying this criterion is that everyone has a right to benefit

> from governmental programs without having deficits, weaknesses, or pathology attributed to their character. (pp. 16–20)

These four criteria are not independent of one another, and the final policy selection will require some form of compromise. Also, different policy analysts might choose different sets of criteria by which to judge alternative strategies. The responsibility of analysts is to be forthright in stating their criteria and not try to search for some universal consensus, since differing values will always cause a choice of different criteria in the analysis. In this instance, for example, others might choose "treatment availability" or "diagnostic accuracy" as more important criteria for a screening program.

In the decision model, the final selection of objectives is shaped by *constraints* and *resources* (see Fig. 2). Each objective is proposed in spite of certain constraints and because of certain resources. If, for example, the objective is "to provide special education services for all handicapped children by 1981," the probability of achieving the objective is determined, in part, by constraints that limit its execution. Such an objective implies the need for massive new appropriations in the special education field. By leaving so little time to achieve the objective, time becomes a major constraint as well. If only 1 or 2 years remain to bring about important and significant organizational changes in large enterprises like the public schools, then time may be the crucial factor in determining whether the objective can be carried out. A third major constraint on this particular objective—in addition to money and time—is the availability of trained personnel who have the expertise necessary to provide special services for blind, deaf, mentally retarded, and other handicapped children.

On the other side of the coin, there are *resources* to be used in achieving the objective. In the case of educating handicapped children, for example, the past decade has seen a general public acceptance of the needs and rights of handicapped children which will allow special education programs to move forward. In addition, some major congressional appropriations have already been made to provide resources at the state and local level to achieve this objective. Therefore, two major resources are present, even though the constraints are also very severe and may eventually cause reconsideration of the objective to educate all handicapped children (Martin, 1976).

Synthesis of Information

In the third stage of policy analysis, the analyst draws together all available information from a variety of disciplines to determine the likely effect of each policy on each criterion. One potential reason for past failures of policy analysis had been the inability of analysis to encompass all professional areas that have a contribution to make. For example, a full consideration of a negative income tax policy option should include information from developmental psychology, sociology, cultural anthropology, economics, and psychiatry. Similarly, on an issue such as child care for poor families, an extraordinary amount of information on health care delivery and child development can be amassed in the consideration of possible alternative strategies.

This stage should be marked by a clear plan showing how the analyst achieved the synthesis of information, what reference areas were explored, and how the search was carried out. In this way the reader can assess how thoroughly the synthesis was conducted.

Generation of Alternative Strategies

In the fourth stage, the analyst must generate a range of alternative strategies for reaching the stated program objectives. The question is, how can reasonable strategies be generated, and on what basis can one choose between them?

The strategies chosen for consideration should have a reasonable rationale for meeting the stated goals and objectives. If more improved child care for poverty families is the goal, we would expect to see strategies that would provide some or all of the following:

1. Increased prenatal and postnatal health services for the mother.
2. Increased nutritional supplements to the newborn child.
3. Early child stimulation with special child development practices.
4. Greater work opportunities for the father that could provide more resources and more hope for a stable family.

It is understandable that different professional interest groups would lobby for their own favorite strategies in this set. One of the most important components of the decision model is the generation of a sufficient variety of strategies to accomplish the goals and objectives that have been established. A common flaw in public decision making appears to be a premature leap to a particular strategy without full and adequate discussion on the alternatives. Once the decision is made to publicly support a strategy such as "day-care centers" or "educational vouchers" or "medicare," then the decision maker is in a position only to defend the premature choice and is not likely to review alternatives that could accomplish the same objective with greater efficiency and effectiveness.

For example, with an increasing number of mothers of preschool children out of the home much of the day, there is a need for some kind of "surrogate parent" arrangement to meet the needs of the young child. Much of the discussion surrounding this issue has focused on one or two visible strategies that have been put forth as possible solutions, but there is a wider range of options that need study and analysis. A list of some options is presented below to illustrate the possible range:

1. The establishment of public day-care centers for all preschool children.
2. The establishment of public day-care centers and services for children with special needs (i.e., poor or handicapped children).
3. Child-care vouchers given directly to low-income parents that can be exchanged for child-care services of their choice.
4. A negative income tax which would provide more resources for low-income families to spend on child-care needs, as well as other needs.
5. Industry-supported child-care in which large industrial or commercial organizations would establish, for their employees, child-care services which allow the working mother to have her child near her during the day.

These strategies then can be arrayed against the set of criteria chosen for the analysis, as shown in Table 6.

Criteria for Strategy Choice

One stage in which the values of the analyst can play a significant role is in the establishment of the criteria against which to weigh the assembled strategies. A list of those in the present example can be noted in the matrix in Table 6. In an earlier stage, criteria were established that defined the analysis itself. In this stage, we are looking for dimensions of value that can separate the alternative strategies.

TABLE 6: CRITERIA FOR STRATEGY CHOICE (CHILD CARE)

Strategies	Cost	Available personnel	Political feasibility	Start-up time	Past experience
1. Public day-care centers for all Children					
2. Day-care programs for poor and handicapped					
3. Child care vouchers to low-income parents					
4. Negative income tax					
5. Industry-supported child care					

Many of these criteria can be counted upon to appear in almost any analysis while some will be specific to the given issue. *Cost* is an example of a universal criterion. Cost would appear to be a major negative factor regarding the strategy, "public day care for all." The costs for funding of such services would seem to exceed what the society is willing to invest at this time. The "day care for children with special needs" option would also be a substantial financial burden, but much less than services for all. The eventual cost of a program such as *educational vouchers* or *negative income tax* would be less certain and may need to be estimated by the analyst. Mutiplying the expected size of the voucher by the number of children estimated to need service will give an estimate of the total cost of that strategy.

Similarly, the projected cost of a negative income tax can be calculated, given certain assumptions of the level at which such a tax would begin and the number of persons participating. Needless to say, the validity of such projections relies heavily upon the validity of the assumptions used to make the calculations.

The resources needed to carry out a policy must be considered in choosing an appropriate strategy, as Sarason et. al. (1977) noted:

> We have never known a human service agency of any kind that asserted that it had the resources to accomplish its goals. (p. 19)

They go on to suggest that the seeds of policy failure often lie in the assumption of unlimited or increasing resources in both money and personnel:

> The problem [of providing adequate medical care] was defined in a way so that its solution *required* training many more physicians. Such a definition contains the "solution" but . . . it is a solution that renders the problem unsolvable. (p. 19)

Most of the strategies named above would seem to possess some serious problems of *political feasibility*. This is probably why major public decisions have not yet been taken on day care. The "public day care for all" strategy has encountered serious opposition, not only on the basis of its projected costs, but because of suspicions that day care may have a long-range negative impact on the child and family. Many persons maintain an image of an idealized American family unit with the father working and the mother staying at home to take care of the two or three children. They believe further that this family model is put "at risk" with the establishment of day-care programs. Those who are deeply concerned about the state of the American family are unwilling to do anything that might further erode the shaky bonds within the modern family unit. Such fervent opposition, even if presented by a minority of citizens, can have serious negative political consequences, and most prudent decision makers would rather avoid strategies with the potential for generating strong negative emotions.

In terms of the strategy of a *negative income tax* noted in Table 6, there are additional political concerns about providing "money without work" for anyone in this society, unless some special individual need or disability has been identified. Support for children who are obviously handicapped, or at risk for future handicaps, seems to have the greatest political viability. The support for programs for handicapped children has been large and manifest and has received, up to the present date, little visible public criticism. In terms of political feasibility, then, the strategy of providing day care for handicapped children would seem to be better than the others, though it would leave large numbers of nonhandicapped children without service.

The analyst should collect stated opinions of powerful political figures on these strategies, if available. Polls taken on the issue might be another source of data for the matrix, as would be the public position of groups such as the AFL–CIO, the Chamber of Commerce, or political parties.

Another dimension that might be included in the decision criteria is the start-up time for the initiation of a strategy, although start-up time would usually have to be estimated. Strategies 3, 4, and 5 in Table 6, for example, would require some form of legislation, which usually means that implementation would have to be considered in years rather than months. While state and federal legislation exists for Strategies 1 and 2, the essential problem in implementation would be the availability of trained personnel and the appropriation of considerably greater sums of money than is currently available. In the long run, such appropriation may take longer than passing new legislation. At any rate, the analyst probably needs to say something about the relative ease and quickness with which a strategy can be implemented.

The final criterion in Table 6 is common to almost all analyses. It represents an *estimate of the relative effectiveness* of the strategies by past experience. What does the accumulated literature say about the effectiveness of day-care centers to improve the development of young children? What has been the experience of the experiments on income maintenance? Are there lessons to be learned from those industry-supported day-care programs that have been tried? A thorough review of past experience would be expected as a means of completing the matrix.

It would be most unusual for one of the strategies to be superior to the others across all dimensions. If that were true, there probably would be no need for a policy analysis in the first place. It is up to the analyst and to those who wish to use the analysis to weigh the dimensions for relative importance. The analyst may be more impressed by past experience, while the decision maker may be more impressed by political feasibility and cost. No matter; the analyst should lay out the dimensions in the best possible fashion, while realizing that the decision maker may reach a different conclusion than the analyst would, given the power and authority of the decision maker.

Implementation Plan

This stage represents one of the most challenging aspects of policy analysis, for in this stage the analyst describes the possible design for putting the favored strategy into effect. It is not unusual to find policymakers struggling hard to establish a particular program or strategy, and then relax when the policy is established by executive order or legislative action. However, such programs often fail, not through inadequacy of concept, but through inadequate implementation.

Many new actors come into play when a large-scale social policy is implemented. Most of these actors have not had an opportunity, prior to implementation, to influence the policy design. Laws are passed by lawyers, but carried out by policemen. If the policemen are hostile or antagonistic to that particular law, implementation may have a difficult road. Similarly, in education, though a new policy can be established at a high administrative level, unless it receives the wholehearted support of those who have to carry out the policy—the teachers—then the policy is not likely to be effective.

The design of program evaluation can (and should) be a key part of any implementation plan. While specific program objectives sharpen our ability to make precise statements on expected program outcomes, there are also several reservations about the measurement of expected program outcomes as a sole indicator of program success. Such a procedure tends to overlook important *unintended consequences.* It is not unusual for an effect to occur in the program that was neither calculated nor anticipated. For example, one objective of a special education program for emotionally disturbed children might be a reduction of physical aggressiveness. We may well achieve our goal of reducing physical attacks on others but at the same time make the target children anxious or timid. Or the objective of a one-grade-level increase in reading in a Title I program may be obtained at the expense of having children hate school and become truant. It is clearly not sufficient in any program merely to rest the program evaluation on those objectives that have been stated by the program director.

One scholar in the evaluation field, Scriven (1973), proposed a system of "goal-free evaluation." Scriven recommended that evaluators ignore a project's stated goals and objectives and instead attempt to observe and measure everything that seems to be happening and make their assessment on that basis without any prior knowledge of specific goals and objectives that may bias their conclusions.

Most program evaluators will compromise between the two extreme positions of goal-directed and goal-free evaluation. They will pay specific attention to the stated program objectives, but will also examine other dimensions that can reasonably be assumed to be affected, either positively or negatively, by the program itself.

Unintended consequences are not necessarily negative. For example, an evaluation of an intervention program for preschool handicapped children might focus entirely upon the growth of the handicapped children. In doing so, the evaluator may overlook positive gains made by their families. Such gains might include more parental attention and affection to the siblings, better marital relations, and reduction of stress felt by parents. Unless the evaluator has some sense of other outcomes—in addition to those planned by the program—that might reasonably be expected, the implementation plan will not have been done well. This consideration speaks to the importance of having a program-knowledgeable person doing the program evaluation and implementation plan.

MODEL FOR SOCIAL POLICY IMPLEMENTATION

A second type of policy analysis focuses on the assessment of already-established policies which are in the process of being implemented. Instead of the analysis aiding the decision maker in choosing between policy alternatives, the analysis is now designed to help the decision maker determine how effectively the policy is being implemented. There is, in fact, a growing suspicion that when policy has proven to be ineffective, it is not so much because of an inappropriate choice of a policy alternative, but rather because of ineffective implementation. The stages that seem relevant in this type of analysis are listed in Table 2.

Statement of the Problem

In conducting a policy implementation analysis, the first step is a thorough review of the problem that generated the particular strategy in the first place. Unlike the policy generation analysis which gave the analyst considerable leeway in stating the problem, this implementation analysis is forced to take the problem as it was treated. For example, the policy of "education for all handicapped children" was stimulated in large measure by the continuing failure of local and state educational programs to provide comprehensive and adequate services to some handicapped children. School lunch programs were generated by the reality that many children seemed to be coming to school without adequate nutrition. The first step, then, in judging or evaluating a particular policy is to review the background of the problem that the policy was designed to solve.

The statement of the problem is necessary to remind the analyst of the forces that stimulated the current "solution." For example, one of the strongest movements in recent education has been the development and use of competency tests on a community or state-wide basis. The source of this movement has been rather clearly a public reaction to depressing news about public education. A sample of such news follows:

- Scores on the Scholastic Aptitude Test (SAT) have fallen from a mean of 473 on the verbal section in 1965 to a mean of 434 in 1975; and from a mean of 496 on the mathematics section in 1965 to a mean of 472 in 1975.
- In 1975, the National Assessment of Educational Progress reported a decline in science knowledge among American students between 1969 and 1973 equivalent to a half-year loss in learning.
- Twenty-three million Americans are functionally illiterate, according to a study sponsored by the U.S. Office of Education.
- Comparative surveys of writing skills show 19- and 17-year-old youth to be using a more limited vocabulary and writing in a shorter, more "primer-like" style in 1974 than in 1970.
- The American College Testing program has reported a decline in the average scores of students applying for college admission.
- The Association of American Publishers revised its textbook study guide for college freshmen in 1975, gearing the reading level down to the ninth grade.
- College officials, business firms, and public agencies are dismayed at the inability of younger persons to express themselves clearly in writing. (Clark & Thomson, 1976)

The rapid adoption of competency testing in states across the country reflected the view of educators that the general public wished to set some standards before awarding high school diplomas (Gallagher, 1979).

Policy Description

In this stage of the implementation analysis, a thorough description of the particular strategy to be analyzed is presented. This description should include the history of the policy, the sources of support for the particular strategy adopted, the goals and objectives of the policy, a description of who the major beneficiaries are supposed to be, and the means by which the policy was supposed to be executed.

In the case of the Education for All Handicapped Children Act

(PL 94–142), for example, there was a decade of legislation devoted to equalizing educational opportunities for handicapped children that preceded the legislation requiring states to provide an appropriate education for all identified handicapped children (Martin, 1976). In the body of legislation preceding PL 94–142, demonstration programs, incentive grants for states, support for training and research, and special help for groups with special problems such as the deaf–blind, were provided. All of this early legislation was designed to encourage states and local communities to give full service for all handicapped children. When, after a decade, it became obvious that many handicapped children still were not being served by local educational systems, court cases were introduced or threatened, and supporters of additional legislation at the federal level gathered sufficient momentum to pass PL 94–142.

It is not always clear, as in this case, what particular pieces of legislation were intended to accomplish. Supreme Court Justice Harlan commented on the Aid to Families with Dependent Children authorization as follows:

> We have before us a child born of the silent union of legislative compromise. Thus, Congress, as it frequently does, has voiced its wishes in muted strains . . . Congress sometimes legislates by innuendo.

It is not uncommon to see certain minor provisions in major pieces of legislation blossom forth into entirely new programs with little history or explicit rationale. The Early and Periodic Screening, Diagnosis, and Treatment Program (EPSDT) characterizes this backdoor approach to policy:

> The subsequent history of EPSDT must be read against this background: . . . an innovation of unknown complexity and cost, without a congressional sponsor, buried in a massive bill not principally concerned either with children or with health, and scheduled by one administration to be implemented by its unknown successor. (Steiner, 1976, p. 10)

Careful examination of the legislative history of a policy can provide insight on the origins of a particular policy and also give clues as to the implementation problems it created.

Value Base for Policy

In the policy generation analysis discussed above, I outlined the importance of conflicting value systems in determining the policy choice and the criteria for that choice. In implementation analysis, we attempt to tease out the values that appeared important in the decision to adopt the current policy. If the policy under study were aid to dependent children, what does such a policy indicate in terms of the social values that are implicitly or explicitly endorsed by such a policy? Are there conflicting values that lie hidden in opposition to the policy under study that were not strong enough to prevent its establishment, but may well be strong enough to hinder substantially its effective implementation? The value strongly held that the poor have caused their own problems and are undeserving of such aid surely is relevant here.

A program of amniocentesis and abortion upon demand may generate great opposition by local groups morally offended by such a policy, who will fight a type of political guerrilla warfare against it. The value base should provide us with an understanding of the major support and major opposition to such a policy.

In particular, the values become critical if services or resources are being allocated for some, but not all, of the citizenry. Much of the current social and health legislation focuses on target groups of persons with special needs. The poor, the handicapped, and the elderly have been the recipients of many policy initiatives with the obvious value of vertical equity being involved.

On the other hand, a different set of values must be searched for in special educational programs for the gifted and talented (Gallagher & Weiss, 1979). While a more sophisticated concept of "equal educational opportunities" can be invoked (each student should receive educational services according to his/her needs), another reason for supporting programs for the gifted is often revealed as the "societal good" or the "societal protection" that would be the expected output from such a program. In this view, special programs for the gifted students will help protect us from the Russians or Chinese or whoever is the current threat. The values revealed in the analysis often tend to uncover some of the causes for opposition that interfere with program implementation.

The development of the Individual Education Plan, a key provision in the Education for All Handicapped Children Act, and the requirement for parental participation in that planning, are indicative of some powerful values at work. The legislation requires the schools to include parents as participants in educational planning for their handicapped child, and that the written plan be on record and used to evaluate special education effectiveness. The values here are that parents should have some voice in their exceptional child's education and that the schools should be accountable to the public for its products.

Application of Policy

In this stage, the analyst examines how the policy was transformed into action. A law can be passed which addresses an issue in broad, general terms, but substantial legal interpretations have to be made for them to be understood by those charged with implementation. For example, a state policy mandating the teaching of citizenship by local schools might have to be interpreted differently in each local school district in the state, or a policy aimed at providing nutrition supplements to poor mothers may need to be interpreted by each county health officer.

Some degree of policy interpretation falls to the agency in charge of administering a program in order to specify how the law is to be applied at that level of government. In the case of legislation, this specification is usually accomplished by writing formal regulations or guidelines which govern implementation. Thus, one of the first actions in this stage of the implementation analysis is to make judgments on how faithfully such regulations interpret the original purposes of the legislation.

The second, and always critical, point in evaluation of policy implementation involves the extent of coverage of the policy. Are the number of clients who are supposed to be receiving services, or supposed to be affected by the policy, actually being touched by it? If the law suggests that *all* handicapped children and their families are to be served, then how close to that objective is the policy implementation? If a law is supposed to reduce or eliminate malnutrition, then what evidence exists to support the contention that the intended beneficiaries actually received coverage?

One example of translating policy to action is provided by the implementation of competency testing programs with exceptional children. In North Carolina, all eleventh-grade students are required, by law, to pass the competency test before receiving a high school diploma. The General Assembly which passed the law gave little or no guidance as to how exceptional children might be tested. As a result, following public hearings, the State Board of Education determined that all exceptional children (except the severely handicapped) would take the exam. The State Department of Public Instruction then designed special test adaptations for the handicapped, including Braille translations for the blind, scribes or special proctors for the orthopedically handicapped, special instructions for deaf students, and so on. The North Carolina Competency Test Commission held state-wide public hearings to survey interested groups as to how the test was being implemented for this special group. Most of the hearings and subsequent questionnaire findings seemed to indicate a general acceptance of the policy as implemented. In fact, most school systems now use these special adaptations of test procedures with exceptional children.

For many other policies, however, the regulations and other measures designed to implement the policy may bear little resemblance to the original intent of the policy, and may, in fact, serve as a barrier to full implementation.

Program Objectives Achieved?

The next step in the analysis is to judge whether or not the stated program objectives are being achieved. This stage comes closest to the existing field of program evaluation. The difference in this instance is that the policy analysts usually synthesize existing evaluation data; analysts rarely have the time or resources to conduct primary data collection themselves.

Thus, a new program might be established to help children with learning disabilities overcome their specific handicaps in order to become more efficient learners in the school, or a new program of mental health centers might assist individuals with mental health problems so that they behave more effectively and suffer less anxiety or depression. In each instance, the program leaders may have a general sense of their goals, but few quantifiable objectives. Evaluation of such programs depends, in some degree, upon a clear statement of what the policy intended.

Few programs have had as explicit a statement of purpose as Social Security:

1. To supplement social insurance as replacement of lost income to disabled and elderly workers.
2. To provide basic income support to the disabled and elderly who are unable to work and who have no social insurance benefits.
3. To correct the inequities and barriers to enrollment in the state programs.
4. To provide financial relief to state and local government.

However, many subparts of the familiar Social Security Act have less explicit statements of purpose and less successful outcomes and need to be considered separately from the parent legislation. One of the objectives of the Supplemental Security Income (SSI) program for handicapped children, a segment of the larger Social Security legislation, is to provide additional resources for the families of the handicapped. On that criterion alone, Breen (1980) raises serious questions regarding the success of implementation:

> Empirical findings confirm the hypotheses that participation rates of children in SSI are low and vary from state to state. Fewer than 25% of all SSI eligible children nationally are enrolled for benefits. State participation rates vary from 7.4% in Wyoming to 57.8% in Louisiana. (p. 2)

The evaluation of whether SSI funds received by the parents are used appropriately becomes a more difficult question, since no clear statement existed regarding the specific intention of the funds. Occasionally, analysts must establish their own criteria, making clear that the criteria were established by the analyst and not by the program designer or operator.

Barriers to Implementation

There are many barriers that may inhibit the full implementation of any policy. A number of the more important barriers can be classified under five headings: institutional, psychological, sociological, economic, and political. The proper identification of barriers to a particular policy implementation is especially important to the shaping of recommendations on what should be done next.

Institutional. A primary barrier to implementation may occur when a policy conflicts with established social or political institutions. In such cases, the policy may be actively opposed by representatives of those institutions. Health policy may flounder if the support of local public health departments is not apparent; education policy can be undermined by the covert resistance of the public schools; and successful social services are dependent on the support of the social work profession. A current example of such a barrier is the resistance by some unions to deinstitutionalization policy which now attempts to remove retarded or mentally ill persons from state institutions whenever possible. The unions oppose this policy on the grounds that the jobs of employees in these institutions, who are members of the union, will be endangered.

One of the most serious institutional barriers often interfering with the delivery of service is the procedure by which clients become eligible for benefits. One striking example is the bureaucratic maze that must be penetrated by parents applying for SSI benefits for their handicapped child. Breen (1980) has described the sequence necessary to receive these benefits:

1. The parent must become aware of the existence of the program itself—which is often no easy matter;
2. They then must go to the district Social Security office for a preapplication interview to see if they have a chance of qualifying;
3. The parent must then make a formal application and spend about 1 to 2 hours filling out the appropriate forms;
4. A claims interviewer must then pass on family eligibility for both income and handicap;
5. There is a state clearance that follows this step, often needing additional medical evidence to qualify the child as appropriately handicapped;

6. A federal clearance is then required to check the data provided by the state;
7. If one or the other of these clearances fails, the parent is informed by letter that they are denied SSI benefits;
8. If both state and federal clearances are positive, a message is sent to the U.S. Treasury;
9. The Treasury then sends a check to the parents of the handicapped child. (p. 79)

Given these hurdles, it is no surprise that only one out of every four eligible families collects SSI benefits or that the one factor associated with the proportion of eligible families participating in SSI from one state to another is the number of district Social Security offices in the state (Breen, 1980).

Psychological. Another barrier to policy implementation may come from a misreading of the reaction of individuals presumed to receive benefits from the policy. Even though services have been made available, the attitudes of potential recipients may prevent them from seeking benefits. Participating in some public programs, such as welfare, may be interpreted as demeaning or self-deprecating by eligible individuals who thereupon do not seek the services.

Another example of a psychological barrier to implementation is offered by the recent emphasis on parent programs. As an illustration of this barrier, consider the development of the Individual Education Plan (IEP) for handicapped children required by PL 94–142. The IEP is supposed to be a cooperative venture between a teacher and the child's parents, but substantial evidence indicates that the introduction of parents into educational planning for their children is considered threatening by some educators who may find ways to avoid parent involvement.

For example, the National Education Association (NEA) supported a study that visited selected school systems to investigate progress in the implementation of PL 94–142. The NEA reported no evidence of systematic programs to prepare parents for their role in the IEP development or conference. Another observational study of IEP conferences (Goldstein, Strickland, Turnbull, & Curry, 1980) concluded that they typically consisted of the resource teacher dominating the discussion while reviewing an already developed IEP with the parents. Thus, it would appear that neither teacher nor parents have been psychologically prepared for their role in developing an IEP. As a result, the IEP policy implementation seems to be floundering.

Similarly, in a survey of 1,500 planning team professionals in Connecticut, only two activities of a possible 24 were chosen as appropriate for parent involvement. These activities were "presenting information to the teacher" and "gathering information relevant to the child." Parents were primarily viewed as having a passive role as opposed to being active decision makers (Yoshida, Fenton, Kaufman, & Maxwell, 1978). We can conclude that a policy designed at the federal level to increase the involvement and authority of parents has been transformed at the local level into another information-exchange session in which the teachers maintain their dominant status and the parents become passive recipients or providers of information. The problem here is the reaction of teachers to a threat to their status.

Sociological. In some cases, policymakers may have seriously misread the cultural values of societal subgroups that were the target of particular policies. Policymakers might provide child-care services when, in fact, the cultural values of the subgroup may be for the mother to provide these services. Or special service provisions may run counter to long-term religious or cultural beliefs and as a result be rejected by recipient groups.

Many policy initiatives designed to deal with family problems can run directly counter to important values held by societal subgroups. At the present time, there is much concern among rural and politically conservative families about the possible negative effects of various child-care policies. There is substantial fear that day care is a means for taking the wife out of the home and breaking up the traditional family unit. This fear has aroused serious opposition to any state or federal program that would subsidize or otherwise provide help for child care, since such a policy is viewed as encouraging a family pattern that these groups find unacceptable.

Economic. The cost of any policy implementation has to be considered a potential barrier. The cost may be greater than the resources available, and thus the proposed service cannot be effectively delivered without a major increment in the allocation of resources. Thus, for example, a policy of comprehensive health services to all citizens, in order to be fully implemented, would imply a major reallocation of the society's resources. The failure to recognize the implications of such fiscal redistribution represents a primary reason for the problem of many policy implementations. The failure to anticipate the fiscal implications of well-meaning legislation is one reason why the government has garnered a reputation for breaking its promises (Gallagher, 1975).

At the present time, the implementation of the Education for All Handicapped Children Act is faced with such an economic barrier. A legislative promise was made when the bill first passed the Congress in 1976: by 1981 or 1982 the federal government would be paying 30–40% of the additional costs of educating handicapped children. At the present time, however, the federal government is paying about 12% of these costs, and there is little chance that the percentage will be significantly increased in the near future.

Political. Since many policies become associated with the political party that oversaw their initiation, such identification can cause some barriers as well. The opposition political party may wish to use a failure of policy implementation as a means of embarrassing their political opponents. To achieve this goal of harrassment, opposition political forces may delay, hinder, or reduce the resources available so as to guarantee a less than satisfactory implementation of the policy. These political forces can then point with scorn to the failed program as an illustration of the ineptitude of their political opponents who initiated the program.

Sometimes a specific policy is based on a political viewpoint or attitude that puts it in the middle between competing political groups. The concept of vouchers, for example, in which the individual citizen or family is provided with a voucher to purchase services from professionals, is popular with groups wishing to see a redistribution of societal power into the hands of individual citizens and away from professional groups or bureaucracies. Some see it as the social equivalent to the economic free-enterprise philosophy and support it on that basis. However, professional groups who see an erosion of their own capability to plan and organize services find these suggestions politically unacceptable and fight them.

Recommendations for Action

After the six steps outlined above have been completed, the final step of the implementation analysis requires that the analyst provide some recommendations for action. There are three major options the analyst has in making these recommendations. First, the analyst could present a hands-off recommendation. This would generally be the outcome if the analyst concludes that the policy is being implemented as well as can be expected at the present time. Although the policy implementation may be less than perfect, a judgment can be made that any attempt to substantially change the present situation might be counterproductive. Thus, an increase in the efficiency of implementation can be obtained only by major reform of the entire program that would require more effort, money, and risks than the small increase in program efficiency would warrant.

A second major option is to recommend substantial changes in the existing policy to make it more effective. The specific nature of the repair should emerge from an effective and accurate analysis. Such repair may merely mean more of one type of resource allocation, such as an increase in training programs, or a set of changes that improves delivery of services or communications between essential delivery systems. Such projected changes, of course, should emerge from delineation of the specific problems that have inhibited effective policy implementation in the first place.

The third major option involves replacing the current policy with some alternative. This is a more radical recommendation and is generally considered only when there is the most manifest failure of the policy. The "status quo" policy is sure to be defended vigorously by its original proponents, regardless of the results of any evaluation or analysis. Yet, sometimes an existing policy seems to be so destructive, or to produce such unusual, unanticipated consequences, that an analyst may wish to suggest a total reevaluation of the original policy decision.

Various alternative strategies considered and rejected when the original policy was enacted or some entirely new strategy could replace the defunct policy. The provision for sunset laws, where various programs automatically go out of existence unless some deliberate action is taken to save them by a legislative body, is a recognition of the fact that many policies tend to extend far beyond their useful time limit. The inertia of the policy itself, plus the commitment of adherents who are benefiting in some fashion from the policy, can cause even the most useless policy to have enough political support to carry it forward beyond its deserved time.

ROLES OF THE POLICY ANALYST

There remains a final question: what role should analysts play to see that their recommendations are adopted? Gallagher (1980) has pointed out that there are three rather distinct roles currently played by analysts. First, the analyst may function as a *technician.* In this role, the analyst primarily collects and organizes information to help the decision maker achieve better choices. The analyst tries to avoid showing personal policy preference on the grounds that this would extend beyond his mandate, and such advocacy might cast doubt on the objectivity of his reports.

This first role would generally be played by an aide or lower-echelon official to a policymaker. Information on child-care options or different modes of financing, for example, would be presented with no judgment offered by the analyst, clearly fixing the responsibility for the decision upon the policymaker. Many decision makers prefer this model and resent the analyst who attempts to present his own choice of the most desirable options.

The second role finds the analyst serving as a *counselor.* In this role, the analyst has an obligation to display the full range of options and alternatives to the decision maker and to point out the likely, unintended consequences or externalities of each alternative. In addition, the analyst is expected to make value judgments as to the best proposal or strategy. Such judgments seem to be well received when there is substantial agreement between the value system of the analyst and that of the decision maker.

In this role, for example, child-care options are presented with their advantages and disadvantages, but the analyst feels free to recommend the option that seems to have come off best in the analysis, always leaving room for the decision maker to weigh all options and reach a different choice.

In the third role, the policy analyst functions as an *advocate.* In this role, analysts are seen as having a responsibility for the achievement of desirable social goals. Their intimate knowledge of social problems and strategies for solving problems obligates them, in their view, to step into the policy field as vigorous supporters of the "best" way.

For such a role to be effective, the advocacy biases of the analyst should be apparent from the beginning so that no one will be surprised at the interpretations of the data. Sometimes, for example, the analyst has had a great deal of professional experience in advocating an increase in day-care funds or increased employment opportunities for women. Since everyone knows the bias, the analyst has a special responsibility to make sure the data and other information are not distorted by that personal bias; otherwise, the analysis is likely to convince only those who already support the position advocated.

All of these approaches can be observed in current use. The consumer of policy studies needs to know which of these three roles the analyst is playing. But, how can one guarantee the objectivity of these reports? Is it true that policy analysts are "hired guns" devoted to finding the answer most desired by their employers (Wildavsky, 1979)? We might look to the older sciences for an answer to this quandry. In doing so, we will find that the public impression of the objectivity of scientists is quite mistaken.

Indeed, there are few more passionate advocates than scientists for their own convictions. However, scientific objectivity comes from the process—the scientific method—and not from some superhuman effort on the part of scientists to ignore their own biases. We need a similar methodology in policy analysis to bring about the objectivity that cannot be provided by the policy analysts themselves.

The rapid emergence and continued development of the field of policy analysis make it certain that the analysis models presented in this chapter will be replaced with more efficient models. These "stages of analysis" have been presented with little confidence in their permanence, but with the confidence that steps in the direction of systematizing the analytic process are a fundamental necessity toward the stabilization of an often chaotic, impressionistic field.

We should not take comfort from the fact that policy analysis is currently more of an art than a science. That merely means that so little is known or standardized that individual practitioners are thrown back upon their own intuition and creative resources. It is in the best interests of both those doing the analyses and those who hope to use them that we take the necessary steps to move the field in the direction of the sciences as rapidly as possible.

References

Andringa, R. Eleven factors influencing federal education legislation. In S. Halperin & G. Kaplan (Eds.), *Federalism at the crossroads: Improving educational policymaking.* Washington, D.C.: Institute for Educational Leadership, George Washington University, 1976.

Beckman, N. Introduction: A symposium—policy analysis in government: Alternatives to muddling through. *Public Administrative Review,* 1977, *37,* 222–226.

Berle, A. *Power.* New York: Harcourt Brace Jovanovich, 1969.

Bianchi, S., & Farley, R. Racial differences in family living arrangements and economic well-being: An analysis of recent trends. *Journal of Marriage and the Family,* 1979, *41,* 537–551.

Breen, P. *Participation of disabled children in the Supplemental Security Income program.* Unpublished manuscript, Bush Institute for Child and Family Policy, University of North Carolina at Chapel Hill, 1980.

Campbell, A. The American way of dating. *Psychology Today,* 1975, *5,* 37–43.

Cicirelli, V. *The impact of Head Start: An evaluation of the effects of Head Start on children's cognitive and affective development.* Athens, Ohio: Westinghouse Learning Corp., 1969.

Clark, J., & Thomson, S. *Competency tests and graduation requirements.* Reston, Va.: National Assn. of Secondary School Principals, 1976.

Coleman, J. S., Campbell, E. Q., Hobson, C. J., McPartland, J., Mood, A. M., Weinfeld, F. D., & York, R. L. *Equality of educational opportunity.* Wash-

ington, D.C.: U.S. Govt. Printing Office, 1966.
Federal Register, May 20,1980, *45,* No. 99.
Gallagher, J. Minimum competency: The setting of educational standards. *Evaluation and Policy Analysis,* 1979, *1,* 62–67.
Gallagher, J. Some final thoughts: Social policy and the academic community. In R. Haskins & J. J. Gallagher (Eds.), *Care and education of young children in America: Policy, politics, and social science.* Norwood, N.J.: Ablex, 1980.
Gallagher, J. Why the government breaks its promises. *N.Y.U. Education Quarterly,* 1975, *6,* 22–27.
Gallagher, J., Surles, R., & Hayes, A. *Program planning and evaluation.* Chapel Hill, N.C.: Technical Assistance Development System, Frank Porter Graham Child Development Center, University of North Carolina at Chapel Hill, 1973.
Gallagher, J., & Weiss, P. *The education of gifted and talented students: A history and prospectus.* Washington, D.C.: Council for Basic Education, 1979.
Gil, D. *Unravelling social policy* (2nd ed.). Cambridge, Mass.: Schenkman, 1976.
Glick, P. Children of divorced parents in demographic perspective. *Journal of Social Issues,* 1979, *35,* 170–182.
Goldstein, S., Strickland, B., Turnbull, A. P., & Curry, L. An observational analysis of the IEP conference. *Exceptional Children,* 1980, *46,* 278–286.
Heilbroner, R. *An inquiry into the human prospect.* New York: Norton, 1974.
Hobbs, N. *The futures of children.* San Francisco: Jossey-Bass, 1974.
House, E. (Ed.). *School evaluation.* Berkeley, Calif.: McCutchan, 1973.
Jencks, C. *Inequality: A reassessment of the effect of family and schooling in America.* New York: Basic Books, 1972.
Keniston, K. *All our children.* New York: Harcourt Brace Jovanovich, 1977.
Kirk, S., & Gallagher, J. *Educating exceptional children* (3rd ed.). Boston: Houghton Mifflin, 1979.
Levin, H. A decade of policy developments in improving education and training for low-income populations. In R. Haveman (Ed.), *A decade of federal antipoverty programs.* New York: Academic Press, 1977.
MacRae, D., & Wilde, J. *Policy analysis for public decisions.* North Scituate, Mass.: Duxbury Press, 1979.
Martin, E. W. A national commitment to the rights of the individual—1776–1976. *Exceptional Children,* 1976, *43,* 132–134.
Mikow, V. A. *Displaced homemakers: Legislation, intervention, and policy implications.* Unpublished manuscript, Bush Institute for Child and Family Policy, University of North Carolina at Chapel Hill, 1980.
Moynihan, D. P. *The Negro family: The case for national action.* Washington, D.C.: U.S. Dept. of Labor, 1965.
National Research Council. *Toward a national policy for children and families.* Washington, D.C.: National Research Council, 1976.
Nye, F., & McDonald, G. Family policy research: Emergent models and theoretical issues. *Journal of Marriage and the Family,* 1979, *41,* 473–485.
Pipho, C. *Minimal competency testing.* Denver, Colorado: Education Commission of the States, June 1977.
President's Commission on Mental Health. *Report to the President from the President's Commission on Mental Health* (3 vols.). Washington, D.C.: U.S. Govt. Printing Office, 1978.
Rivlin, A. *Systematic thinking for social action.* Washington, D.C.: Brookings, 1971.

Samuels, H. R. *The North Carolina high priority infant identification and tracking program.* Unpublished manuscript, Bush Institute for Child and Family Policy, University of North Carolina at Chapel Hill, 1980.

Sarason, S., Carroll, C., Maton, K., Cohen, S., & Lorentz, E. *Human services and resource networks.* San Francisco: Jossey-Bass, 1977.

Schorr, A. Views of family policy. *Journal of Marriage and the Family,* 1979, *41,* 465–467.

Scriven, M. Goal-free evaluation. In E. House (Ed.), *School evaluation.* Berkeley, Calif.: McCutchan Pub., 1973.

Steiner, G. *The children's cause.* Washington, D.C.: Brookings, 1976.

U.S. Bureau of the Census. Marital status and living arrangements: March 1977. *Current Population Reports,* Series P-20, No. 323. Washington D.C.: U.S. Govt. Printing Office, 1978.

U.S. Bureau of the Census. Money income and poverty status of families and persons in the United States: 1978. *Current Population Reports,* Series P-60, No. 136. Washington, D.C.: U.S. Govt. Printing Office, 1979.

Weiss, C. Evaluation research in the political context. In E. Struening & M. Guttentag (Eds.), *Handbook of evaluation research.* Beverly Hills, Calif.: Sage, 1975.

Wildavsky, A. *The politics of the budgetary process.* Boston: Little Brown, 1964.

Wildavsky, A. *Speaking truth to power: The art and craft of policy analysis.* Boston: Little, Brown, 1979.

Yoshida, R. K., Fenton, K. S., Kaufman, M. J., & Maxwell, J. P. Parental involvement in the special education pupil planning process: The school's perspective. *Exceptional Children,* 1978, *44,* 531–534.

Zimmerman, S. Policy, social policy and family policy: Concepts, concerns, and analytic tools. *Journal of Marriage and the Family,* 1970, *41,* 487–495.

Zimmerman, S., Mattessich, P., & Leik, R. Legislators' attitudes toward family policy. *Journal of Marriage and the Family,* 1979, *41,* 507–517.

THREE

POLICY ANALYSIS WITHIN A VALUE THEORETICAL FRAMEWORK

ROBERT M. MORONEY

INTRODUCTION

Rein (1970) has suggested that social policy can be defined as the "study of the history, politics, philosophy, sociology, and economics of the social services" (p. 4). Within this context, he includes education, health, income maintenance, employment, and housing. His point is well taken in that no single academic or professional discipline can be expected to provide sufficient insight into, or the most appropriate framework for, analyzing social problems and then recommending effective policies and programs. He goes on to say that the analyst must "trespass on academic and professional domains in which he may have no special competence" (p. xii). The analyst's unique contribution, then, becomes one of identifying and understanding approaches used in the different disciplines and then synthesizing these into some meaningful whole.

More often than not, policy analysis relies on available data and existing research rather than on the collection of new data. What tends to distinguish policy analysis from traditional research is the way in which the questions are formulated as well as specific purposes of the analysis. Policy analysis sets out to produce something that legislators or administrators can easily translate into action, whereas traditional research attempts to provide a better understanding of social phenomena. Policy analysis relies heavily on research while research can stand by itself, although Bronfenbrenner (1974) has suggested that social science should rely on social policy for both vitality and validity. A further distinction is that policy analysis, to be useful, must be responsive to the needs of policymakers who often work under considerable time pressures. Researchers who inform a decision maker that the specific information requested will not be available for one, two, or more years soon lose their audience. Similarly, those researchers who inform the policymaker that although available research findings might suggest a course of action, these findings are tentative and in need of further replication, are called on less and less. When the best possible information may not exist, there is value in reexamining what is available and, through a synthesizing process, generating reasonable policy recommendations. The rationale for this approach is that available data are superior to intuition or one person's judgment.

This perceived nonresponsive attitude on the part of traditional social and behavioral scientists is probably a primary reason for an activity as ill-defined as policy analysis becoming a growth industry. It has literally filled a vacuum. Over the past 10 years, significant numbers of public policy curricula have come into existence and have attracted large numbers of undergraduate and graduate students. Today, policy centers draw considerable support from governmental agencies and private foundations and are found in most major universities. Much of this support has been developmental; i.e., concerned with finding appropriate methodologies and a framework for responding to policy issues.

Since there is little consensus as to a definition of social policy, its boundaries, or an agreed-upon methodology for analysis, each analyst must explicate his or her approach. This allows for a systematic dialogue among those who are engaged in analysis—a dialogue that might lead to useful clarification of the process. This chapter, like others in this book, attempts to begin such a dialogue. The approach taken by this author is shaped by a belief that social policy is concerned with a search for, and articulation of, social objectives and the means to achieve such objectives.

There are three ways to express public social policy. The first is through legislation which is the most accurate description of current social policy. Laws can be viewed as statements of social purpose in that they propose basic goals. Examples are the Federal Employment Act of 1946 which expressed the goal of full employment for everyone able to work, and the Housing Act of 1949 which stated that all Americans have "the right to decent housing, in decent surroundings of their own choosing." The second example falls under the general heading of "administrative decisions," more commonly referred to as "regulations." At the national level, the executive branch, responsible for implementing legislation, regulates through the development of operational statements (the translation of purpose into practice). Historically, every law passed might have dozens of administrative regulations which have the binding effect of law. For example, the 1962 Amendments to the Social Security Act state that applications for public assistance must be processed "promptly." In its regulations, the Department of Health, Education, and Welfare defined "promptly" as 30 days or less. The third way of expressing social policy is through judicial decisions. Although the courts are charged with upholding and interpreting law, over the past 25 years they have gone far beyond this function and have actually created policy. Examples include the Supreme Court's decision on school desegregation (see Wilkinson, 1979) and their ruling in a 1962 Connecticut test case striking down residency requirements for welfare assistance.

Defining social policy as a search for, and articulation of, social objectives as well as the means to achieve them presupposes a normative position expressing some sense of predetermined values. Nonetheless, this approach is built upon a number of nonideological activities (Moroney, 1976). Policy formulation requires analysis of the issue, including its dimensions and its implications. Policy formulation further necessitates a consensus of the body politic that the problem presents a current or future problem that should be addressed. Finally, policy formulation involves decision making, choosing among alternative strategies, and developing structures to carry out specific interventions, all of which are shaped by the current state of technology and the availability of resources.

Policy analysis clarifies and sharpens discussion but it cannot, nor should it, dictate what should be done. Ultimately, in a democratic society decision making is the responsibility of politicians who are held accountable by those they represent. Thus, social policy in this context is viewed as a blending of fact and preference that emerges from a continuous dialogue between the policy analyst, the policymaker, the policy implementer, and the American public. Although the process is neither orderly nor progressive (in point of fact, it is more likely to be an iterative process) and roles can become merged and the boundaries between the phases fuzzy, these are the primary actors in policy formulation.

In the remainder of this chapter, I will discuss policy analysis within the current policy literature, identify the tensions among basic approaches, and argue the benefits of a value analytic framework. Finally, the various components of a working model will be laid out and discussed.

POLICY ANALYSIS AND APPROACHES

Two distinct approaches to policy analysis can be identified in the literature. One approach—the dominant approach—emphasizes the process while the other approach emphasizes the purpose. The former begins with the notion that a policy can be defined as a "study plan," the product a rational exercise involving the determination of goals, the examination of alternatives, and the selection of a strategy (Kahn, 1967). Within this framework, policy formulation assumes rational decision making with the analyst functioning as a technocrat. Analysis is introduced only when the general policy has been worked out. Simply stated, the analyst accepts the "goodness" of the policy, saying to the decision maker, "Tell me *what* you want and I'll tell you *how* it can be achieved." The analyst does not determine goals nor does he or she have responsibility for selecting among alternatives. Rather, analytic activity is limited to the generation of alternatives and the application of various criteria to those alternatives. Traditionally, these criteria have tended to be grounded in economic analysis with specific emphasis on efficiency and cost effectiveness.

One example of this approach was the analyst's role in the welfare reform proposal introduced in the 92nd Congress (commonly known as the Family Assistance Plan). This proposal embodied the Administration's basic incentive mechanism for shifting recipient families from welfare to what became known as "workfare." To support the work programs, day care was to be expanded on a large scale with up to 90% federal reimbursement. The analyst, as technician, approached this issue with day care as a given (rather than one strategy among many) and identified alternative ways to deliver these services to the target population. Variables such as size of day-care programs, service packages, and staffing ratios were examined and eventually a modified benefit-cost analysis carried out. The results of the analysis were then given to a decision maker who would choose among the alternatives.

This approach, although somewhat narrow in scope, has strong support in the literature. Dror (1970, 1971), for example, describes the basic function of policy analysis as "identifying and documenting various alternatives within a range of decision possibilities." His seminal work on the emerging policy sciences over a decade ago is still one of the major influences on how analysts are trained and how they practice.

Dror (1970) suggests that the policy sciences "constitute a new and additional approach to the uses of systematic knowledge and structured rationality for the conscious shaping of society" (p. 137) and represent an integration of pure and applied research. Within the policy sciences, policy analysis provides "heuristic methods for the identification of preferable policy alternatives" (p. 139). Dror's analytical approach accepts three fundamental tenets: (1) a systems view, i.e., examining problems and alternatives in a broad way which tries to take into account all relevant variables and probable results; (2) a searching for an optimal solution within a "broad benefit-cost frame without being limited to environmental changes" (p. 141); and (3) "explicit and rational identification of the preferable alternative . . . with the help of a large set of techniques ranging from mathematical models to human gaming and from canvassing of expert's opinion to sensitivity testing" (p. 141).

In sum, Dror posits that policy analysis, based in the management sciences and a broad version of systems analysis, can provide the decision maker with the means to choose among proposed courses of action once a goal has been articulated. He suggests that such analysis can be viewed as heuristic for the identification and evaluation of alternatives and assumes that rationality and intellectualism are appropriate foundations of policy analysis. Even more important is his belief that knowledge provides authority to plan and act. Finally, the role of the analyst is that of technocrat.

Lasswell, who first proposed the concept of policy sciences, offers a similar perspective (1951). The purpose of the policy sciences is to augment, by scientific methods of decision making and data from the behavioral sciences, the process that humans use in making judgments and decisions. Whereas Dror argues for systems analysis, Lasswell (1970) sees the distinguishing characteristic of policy analysis as "tending toward contextuality in place of fragmentation and toward a problem-oriented, not problem-blind orientation (p. 6). Lasswell further suggests that this perspective forces the analyst to become less and less "method bound"; that the multimethod approach both reflects and contributes to contextuality and problem orientation; and that this is achieved through a synthesis of technique. Whereas Dror's approach is based on three fundamental tenets, Lasswell's approach emphasizes five components of analysis: (1) goal clarification; (2) trend analysis; (3) theory formation; (4) projection of future possibilities; and (5) invention, evaluation, and selection of alternative strategies. Unlike Dror, Lasswell does not see policy analysis as a linear process. Rather, he describes the activity more in terms of interaction, a moving "back and forth between images of the whole and particular details of time, place, and figure" (Lasswell, 1970, p. 13). Finally, though both Dror and Lasswell tend to view the analyst as a technocrat, Dror allows for something he calls "organized day dreaming" and Lasswell speaks of "creative flash", i.e., the examination of factual data in such a way that a creative rearrangement might occur and novel solutions be generated.

I have emphasized the views of Dror and Lasswell on policy analysis for a number of reasons. The first is somewhat obvious. Their approach is the dominant approach now found in both the policy sciences and the practice of policy analysis. Second, this approach, with its basis in the social and behavorial sciences as well as its belief in rationality, has important implications. Thus, the analyst as technocrat is viewed as a value-free or neutral scientist. By the time a problem is presented to the analyst it has already been defined, and tentative solutions have been identified. The analyst accepts the problem as given and begins a decomposing process, breaking the problem into manageable components for analysis.

Since the model presented in this chapter represents a significant departure from this dominant approach, it is important for the reader to understand the distinctions between the two approaches. First, I am reluctant to accept the notion that the analyst accepts the problem as given. In fact, I believe that the analyst needs to begin by analyzing the assumptions behind the problem statement. Consistent with this view, I reject the notion that analysts can be value-free, neutral technocrats. Rather, I argue that a normative approach is more useful for policy formulation. The analyst begins, not with the process, but with an examination of the purposes or objectives with which the policy purports to be concerned. Furthermore, a normative approach places emphasis on values as the basis for deriving criteria for analysis.

The process approach is not only limiting but also dysfunctional in that it emphasizes means while bypassing the issue of ends. By so doing, the process approach assumes that a fundamental consensus on societal goals or end states does in fact exist. Policy analysis within this framework is concerned primarily with issues of social engineering that are technical or administrative in nature. In reality, this fundamental consensus on goals does not exist, and the tendency to sidestep existing ideological conflict has resulted in policies that are both at cross-purposes with other policies and inconsistent or even contradictory. Policy has come to be viewed as a choice among neutral alternatives and analysis as an activity that assists decision makers in obtaining an optimal solution for some predetermined goal. Discussion tends to be concentrated on how services will be financed, organized, and administered. All too rarely does analysis focus on the nature, aims, and value of the services.

Recently, a number of committees, commissions, and individual scholars have stressed procedure and have not attempted to relate these procedures to a set of desired outcomes. Arguments are made in terms of who has what responsibility, e.g., responsibility in the public or private sector, and if the public sector, at what level of government? Should needs be met through the direct provision of services or indirectly through market mechanisms? If the latter, should the strategy be an income maintenance program such as the negative income tax, a family allowance program, a modified public assistance program, or a voucher system for certain categories of goods, e.g., housing, food, day care, or education? Whether this growing emphasis on procedures reflects a discouragement with the alleged failure of previous large scale programs, a distrust of government, or a lack of confidence in the government's ability to deal successfully with complex social problems, it does reflect a reluctance to sort out values and to define relationships between means and ends. This criticism is in no way meant to suggest that procedures are unimportant. The issues related to the financing, organization, and administration of services are critical, but they are dependent upon the purpose of the services. They address the issue of what can be accomplished given resources, knowledge, and technology. However, it should be underscored that these administrative and technical issues are, in fact, not neutral or value-free. In the absence of an identified purpose or outcome, means are inevitably chosen on efficiency criteria with primary consideration given to cost effectiveness in achieving narrowly defined objectives.

A VALUE-ANALYTIC APPROACH TO SOCIAL POLICY[1]

Titmuss (1968) defines social policy as the "study of the range of social needs and the functions, in conditions of social scarcity, of human organizations traditionally called social service or social welfare systems to meet those needs" (p. 20). He argues that the analyst must be concerned with the ends and not just the means of policy. When we direct our attention toward social policy objectives, we are usually concerned with their moral justification. To put this another way, how do (or may) supporters of a social policy aimed at a particular objective justify its pursuit? What alternative objectives can be morally justified? For Titmuss, values not only influence policy decisions, but the analyst should make these values clear, expose value choices that confront society, and probe and push the value assumptions underlying the development of policy. Rein's (1970) perspective is consistent with that of Titmuss. He discusses social policy as a concern for choosing among multiple, conflicting, and yet desirable goals, and suggests that no scientific rules exist to make these choices. Rein suggests that values provide the criteria by which we judge the desirability of a course of action (1976). Given the certainty of conflicting ideologies, there is never one "true" analysis. Rather, for any given social problem, there are potentially a number of different analyses, each one to be judged good or bad within the framework of its value assumptions.

Social policy, then, is concerned with social need and can be defined in terms of social purposes. It involves societal mechanisms to bring about social change, and values permeate the entire policy process. Values influence the selection of a specific policy issue and how it will be defined. Values are the basis for setting policy goals and objectives, for selecting criteria, for comparing policy options to achieve these goals and objectives, and for evaluating policies once they are implemented. Rein (1976) amplifies these points by suggesting that the study of social policy involves the interaction between values (found in statements of purpose or goals), operating principles (means to achieve these purposes), and outcomes. Thus, social policy is an articulation of the ideology between means and ends. Values concern both ends and means of public intervention involving normative propositions as well as assumptions about what public policy is and what it should be. Theory provides insight into factors that may be related to policy issues, interpreting how the world looks and how it might work in the future. Finally, research provides factual information relative to values, either repudiating or confirming existing beliefs about how people, institutions, and society function. Insofar as values are central to the policy domain and influence decision making, they must become central to policy analysis.

Since values have a subjective aspect and are inherently controversial, they cannot be addressed exclusively within a positivistic framework. Purists in the behavioral and social sciences, therefore, have been reluctant to explore the role of values in policy analysis since, they argue, values are outside the purview of the scientist. In some respects, their reluctance is warranted in that two extreme but complementary errors have been committed in the intellectural history of value studies (Dewey, 1939). One is the value-arbitrary error which holds that all values are equally good, a view which, says Dewey, if acted upon "would produce disordered behavior to the point of complete chaos" (p. 56). The other is the value-absolute error which asserts that the ultimate standards of valuation are a priori ends-in-themselves: "This theory, in its endeavor to escape from the frying pan of disordered valuations jumps into the fire of absolutism" (Dewey, 1939, p. 56).

Accepting Dewey's views implies that rational and scientific inquiry into the nature of values is a necessary activity. What is needed is an explication of values and the application of scientific method to the development of public policy as an articulation of favored values. Rein's (1976) comments are helpful in resolving the apparent scientific/prescriptive dilemma. He calls for:

> . . . an examination of goal concepts in their own terms but this task is difficult because there are no final solutions and no self-evident criteria against which to judge progress. Policy analysis is essentially involved with intractable problems. End values, societal goals, etc., are inherently controversial. They cannot be treated "scientifically" along positivist lines. Policy analysis involves the use of social science tools that produce inherently uncertain and incomplete findings, and these doubtful findings are then brought forward in an attempt to understand goals which are ambiguous and conflicting and where the elusive question of priorities is always dominant. It is nevertheless possible to cope with this intractability fairly sensibly. . . . The value-critical perspective does not make the assumption that there are discoverable causal relationships which are stable over time. . . . Research within the value-critical framework does try to discern patterns; it seeks general principles that take account of the context and co-mingle of facts and values. (p. 74)

Public policy, therefore, can be seen as the development of fact-value appreciation (Vickers, 1968) in order to make appropriate decisions. And policy analysis is, at least in part, an attempt to improve the quality of decision making by examining the fact-value implications of alternative courses of action. I am not suggesting, however, that policy analysts can develop a totally objective value calculus that fully rationalizes different value sets and multiple goals.

The position taken in this chapter is that policy analysis in general, and policy analysis concerned with families and children in particular, must deal directly and openly with values. Today's rallying cry that families should be strengthened will remain merely a slogan until the values implicit in this policy objective are identified and analyzed. It should be stated not only that families should be strengthened, but also why they should be strengthened. That families should be strengthened expresses a global value preference, but the slogan neither provides organizing principles for analysis nor brings to the surface important value differences among groups concerned with the state of families.

But, as argued earlier, there is not—nor can there be—a single calculus, just as there cannot be a single "true" or "correct" analysis. The values that inform policy analysis are the values that society espouses and there are conflicts inherent in the aspirations underlying the values. Take, for example, the expressed goals of liberty, equality, and fraternity. While all three may be desirable ends of social policy, they cannot all be maximized at once. In fact, more of one will inevitably result in less of the others. An emphasis on absolute liberty will lead to an individualistic, competitive, and productive society. An emphasis on equality leads to an equitable and egalitarian society, a society committed to reducing age-old inequities in the redistribution of resources and in access to opportunity. An emphasis on fraternity underscores the importance of community, the existence of common need and risk, and the necessity for shared responsibility but not necessarily a truly equalitarian society.

The real issue, then, is which value should be given primacy. If we begin with a communitarian first principle, absolute liberty is not possible in that social responsibilities are the sine qua non of fraternity. A similar conflict occurs, of course, if we emphasize liberty which results in a society of atomistic individuals.

Friedman (1962) is a major proponent of liberty as a first principle, while Titmuss (1968) argues for the primacy of equality and fraternity. In Friedman's view we must begin by extending freedom and choice because anything else is paternalistic and, in the long run, counterproductive to the economic and social well-being of society. This extension of freedom, Friedman argues, is best achieved through a competitive market which will not only be responsive to individual preferences but also achieve a proper balance between government, the private sector, and individuals. Competition will, in time, increase national wealth and provide society with the means to achieve social objectives. As Pruger (1973) has observed, Friedman builds his approach to social policy on an economic definition of man as one who interacts with others in bilateral, impersonal transactions:

> Under ordinary circumstances the exchange is impersonal . . . requiring no special effort or attention from either buyer or seller. Once the exchange has taken place, there is no residual or accumulation of unfulfilled obligations, and thus no inherent dynamic to extend the relationships beyond the time contractually specified. (p. 290)

Thus, individuals have the responsibility to act only in their own interests, and the idea of collective responsibility or welfare is nonexistent.

Titmuss, on the other hand, can be characterized as a communitarian who believes that we are by nature social beings with responsibility for others. In his view, industrialization and modernization with their emphasis on economic values have brought about community breakdown and alienation. Specifically, he argues that past and present approaches to social welfare are consistent with Friedman's view in that they emphasize a "we-they" relationship and have produced a divisive society. "We", the nonpoor, provide for a residual proportion of society because "they" are incapable of providing for themselves. This divisiveness is often reflected in our designing separate service delivery systems which are inevitably accompanied by stigmatization through means testing. Of importance is that both positions are value-laden and that, depending on which foundation one accepts, some options will be open and others will be closed. Both positions involve different views of society, the state, individuals, and families. Up to this point, the argument is simple enough, i.e., values shape both the policy process and policy analysis. The next section offers a perspective as to the purpose of social policy. It is influenced by what Boulding (1967) calls the search for common threads that unite all social policies and common denominators to evaluate heterogeneous policies. In his view, social policy analysis, unlike economic analysis with its clear structure and relatively simple body of principles, "looks like a sticky conglomeration of the ad hoc" (p. 6).

SOCIAL POLICY: PURPOSES AND FIRST PRINCIPLES

Titmuss (1968) views social policy as concerned with "different" types of moral transactions embodying notions of exchange, or reciprocal obligations, which have developed in modern industrial societies in institutional forms to bring about and maintain social and community relations. In this sense, the concerns of social policy are identified as essentially moral rather than technical. Titmuss is not alone in his definition of social policy as encompassing moral transactions and social relations. Schottland (cited by Gil, 1973) defines social policy as a "statement of social goals and strategy, a settled course of action dealing with the relations of people with each other, the mutual relations of people with their government" (p. 5). Boulding (1967) argues that the "objective of social policy is to build the identity of a person around some community with which he is associated . . ." (p. 8). Macbeath (1957) suggests that "social policies are concerned with the right ordering of the network of relationships between men and women who live together in societies, or with the principle which should govern the activities of individuals and groups so far as they affect the lives and interests of other people" (p. 2). Tawney (1964), in his work on equality, pays considerable attention to the issue of fraternity and fellowship as a prime concern for social policy . Others, such as Gil (1973) and Ponsioen (1962), view social policy in similar terms, i.e., as moral transactions and social relations.

These ideas also have a foundation in traditional sociology. Nisbet (1967) suggests that the "rise of sociology was a direct response to, or reflection of, new forms of associative life in Western Europe, forms that industrialism and social democracy brought with them" (p. 57). Within this tradition, community was viewed as:

> all forms of relationships which are characterized by a high degree of personal intimacy, emotional depth, moral commitment, social cohesion and continuity in time. Community is founded on man conceived in his wholeness rather than in one or another of the roles, taken separately, that he may hold in a social order. (p. 47)

As a social scientist, Nisbet then argues that most of the earlier sociologists were concerned with the idea and reality of a moral community. These social theorists include Comte, LePlay, Tonnies, de Coulanges, Weber, Durkheim, Simmel, and—from a radically different perspective—Marx. In their different ways, each of these writers indicts the excessive individualism, impersonality, acquisitiveness, and rational calculating of capitalistic society. It is not that they agree with each other. Marx, for example, suggests that the loss of community is a consequence of capitalism while Tonnies treats capitalism as the consequence of loss of community. Both Marx and Durkheim are critical of societies "in which economic activities and values have become separated from and commanding over all other spheres of collective life. The most intense social activity, was the least social" (Horton, 1964, p. 248). The outcome, all these thinkers agree, was anomie and alienation. Unfortunately, their prescriptions are not very useful. The enemies to be dealt with are the extension of bureaucratic forms of domination and its effect upon the quality of social life (Weber), capitalistic modes of production (Marx), and industrial society insofar as it eroded social solidarity and moral relationships (Durkheim). Still, the notion of a moral community is common to all.

Earlier, I pointed out that a number of social policy theorists viewed social relations as the primary object of social policy. Boulding (1967) develops this idea more fully when he suggests that social policy should be concerned with building an "integrative system," a system "that includes those aspects of social life that are characterized not so much by exchange in which a quid is got for a quo as by unilateral transfers that are justified by some kind of appeal to a status or legitimacy, identity or community. . . . By and large it is an objective of social policy to build the identity of a person around some community with which he is associated." Why? "Social policy has to concern itself with questions of identity and alienation for alienation destroys the grant system. By and large, it is the alienated who create social problems and the integrated who solve them" (p. 7). Boulding continues:

> One thing is clear: we must look upon the total dynamic process of society as essentially a process in human learning. . . . It is even clearer that the development of social integration is a learning process. We have to be taught to love just as we have to be taught to hate. Practically nothing in human life comes naturally. It is from vague and formless biological drives and the extraordinary learning potential of the human nervous

> system that the intricate structure of our personalities, our identities, our values and our communities are molded. (p.9)

And finally there is Titmuss (1971). In his brilliant analysis of the blood transfusion system, he argues that such a system:

> shows that detailed, concrete programs of political change—undramatic and untheatrical as they may often appear to be—can facilitate the expression of man's moral sense. Thus, it serves as an illustration of how social policy, in one of its potential roles, can help to actualize the social and moral potentialities of all citizens. . . . As individuals they [donors] were taking part in the creation of a greater good transcending the good of self-love. By contrast, one of the functions of atomistic private market systems is to free men from any sense of obligation to or for other men regardless of the consequences to others who cannot reciprocate and to release some men (who are eligible to give) from a sense of inclusion in society at the cost of excluding other men (who are not eligible to give). (p. 239)

Titmuss then goes on to argue that:

> The role of social policy has thus to be redefined in a broader perspective. In the past . . . social policy provisions were economically and politically justified as functional necessities. There was really little choice for society. The functional necessities of public health, factory and labor legislation, primary education and so forth made, in a sense, social policy inevitable. According to this interpretation of history, such limited or residual interventions by the state were needed to prevent the collapse of a particular kind of society and to operate as instruments of social control in relation to those elements in the population who threatened or were thought to threaten the established order. (p. 241)

Titmuss concludes that such a view of social policy gave rise to deterministic welfare theories and the belief that moral problems can be resolved by technical means and social engineering.

A PROPOSED MODEL FOR POLICY ANALYSIS

The model outlined in Table 1 emerges from the previous sections in that it is built upon the view that social policy involves the interaction between values, operating principles, and outcome or an ideology of ends and means. The model covers the broad arena of policy and has three components dealing with policy analysis, planning or program development, and evaluation.

Because this book focuses on policy analysis, the remainder of this chapter will deal primarily with the top panel of Table 1. I would, however, call the reader's attention to the fact that, unlike the other analysis models discussed in the other chapters, two types of criteria are defined by the model in Table 1. The first or policy criteria identify

TABLE 1: THE POLICY ARENA: A THREE-PART MODEL

Component	Description
	Policy Analysis
Problem analysis	Two components: Problem description and problem etiology. What is the problem? Who has the problem? What is the history of the problem? Why is it a problem? What are the causes of the problem?
Value criteria	Criteria are normative. They should flow from the problem analysis and reflect the ends the analyst wishes to achieve. A rationale for the selection of particular criteria should be provided.
Generation and review of alternative strategies	Alternative strategies are the various means that might be needed to address the policy problem. These means usually include provision of services, income transfers, or voucher proposals.
Strategy choice	Each of the criteria is applied to the alternative strategies and a strategy is recommended.
	Planning or Program Development
Setting specific objectives	Having selected a particular strategy, specific objectives—stated in terms of expected outcomes—must be stipulated.
Implementation criteria or policy variables	These are the criteria by which the selected program is operationalized. Included here are questions of population coverage, financing, quality of service, effectiveness, manpower requirement.
Program design	Included here are the issues of service delivery; e.g., by what means are the services to be delivered, how the services related to other programs, what organizations are responsible?
Implementation	How is the program actually delivered; e.g., timing, scale, etc.?
	Evaluation
Monitoring	Quantitative expectations of organizational performance for each area of program operations are specified here.
Evaluation	Data are collected on the outcome actually produced by the program.
Feedback	Outcome information both on program implementation and program effects is given to policymakers who can use the information to modify the program as necessary.

the goals a policy should achieve; the second or implementation criteria are used to specify how the policy goals are to be achieved.

Problem Analysis

The first step of analysis is to define—or in those instances when the problem is given to the analyst by a client, to redefine—the problem in the light of available knowledge. The analyst's function is to clarify the issue, synthesize and integrate what is known to provide a knowledge base, and define the issue with a major emphasis on identifying plausible etiological factors.

An example of this step might be helpful. Many efforts are initiated on the implicit assumption that the problem is fully understood and the solution known. In fact, problems are frequently stated in terms of solutions. Day care is an excellent example. As such, day care is neither a policy nor a problem. In fact, day care is but one of a number of possible policy options or solutions depending on the problem we are trying to address. Furthermore, as one possible solution, there are any number of day-care options, each of which is appropriate only within a specific definition of a problem. Dunlop (1978) argues that rationales for governmental involvement in child care generally fall into one of three categories. The first category includes reactive and maintenance-oriented interventions in which there is a concern for restoring a pre-established social order or meeting specific crises. Within this rationale, the purpose of interventions such as day care is not primarily to support children or families, but to meet other ends. Such was the intent of the Lanham Act of 1940. Centers for the care of children were created so that mothers could work in defense-related industries (Rothman, 1973). The opening of day-care centers has also been advocated as a means of attracting women to industries with an inadequate labor supply (Rossi, 1977), of creating jobs for trained persons who are in a declining industry (Steiner, 1976), and of making jobs for marginally employable women who have been given training aimed at reducing their dependency on public welfare (Woolsey, 1977).

The second general rationale is to create reform-oriented intervention focused on incremental social change. Unlike the maintenance-oriented intervention described above, the emphasis in this case is on supporting children and their parents. Dunlop (1978) identifies five types of reform-oriented intervention: (1) responses to changing social trends, especially demographic patterns and intrafamily relationships (Bronfenbrenner, 1978); (2) attempts to enhance child development (Angrist & Lave, 1973; Fein & Clarke-Stewart, 1973; Kahn & Kamerman, 1975; Rossi, 1977; Rothman, 1973); (3) attempts to increase parental competence (Brenner, 1970; Brim, 1959; Fein & Clarke-Stewart, 1973; Rothman, 1973); (4) concern for equal opportunity for women (Angrist & Lave, 1973; Kahn & Kamerman, 1975; Meers & Marans, 1968; Nye, 1974; Steiner, 1976; Woolsey, 1977); and (5) concern for community development (Amidon & Brim, 1972; Fein & Clarke-Stewart, 1973; Rothman, 1973).

The third category can be termed pro-active or radical reform (Kahn & Kamerman, 1975; Leiner, 1974; Rossi, 1977). Child care is viewed as a means, rather than an area of concern in its own right, to fundamental societal change. Two purposes of such reform have been suggested: (1) to facilitate comprehensive equality between the sexes (Bernard, 1971; Keller, 1974; Rossi, 1977); and (2) to create a collective consciousness and a "new people" (Leiner, 1974; Meers & Marans, 1968; Sidel, 1974; Talmon, 1974).

Building on Dunlop's analysis, we find day care proposed as a strategy to deal with a range of "problems," including employment and economic development, welfare reform, child development and parental competence, equal opportunity, community development, and reconstruction of society. In clarifying the policy issue—in defining or redefining the problem statement—the analyst is faced with two major tasks. The first task is to seek alternative strategies other than day care. For example, if the problem is restated as welfare reform, day care may not be the most desirable option. Rothman (1973), Angrist and Lave (1973), and Woolsey (1977) have all pointed out that the costs of providing day care are likely to exceed the costs of continued cash payments to poor mothers when there is more than one child. On the other hand, if the problem is defined in terms of equal opportunity for women, a day-care strategy is not likely to achieve its intended results if it is not accompanied by changes in the employment sector; e.g., job creation, job training, and effective antidiscrimination legislation. The second task in defining the problem concerns the form or content of day-care intervention once it is identified as a viable option. If the problem were to be cast in the maintenance-oriented category, day care issues would emphasize the physical safety of the child. Reform oriented intervention, on the other hand, would be concerned with child development. The specific form of day care, and especially the day-care curriculum, would be quite different in these two cases.

Criteria

Criteria, the next component of the policy analysis model, are concerned with the generation of appropriate objectives to be used in evaluating alternative strategies. Earlier, three fundamental values were discussed as constituting one framework by which to generate criteria, namely, liberty, equality, and fraternity. If we were to select liberty as the primary value, the analyst would probably generate criteria with an emphasis on choice, multiple modalities of services and benefits, a weighting toward the private sector, and a limited role for government. This is, of course, the position of Milton Friedman (1962). If, on the other hand, one were to begin with equality—as Rein (1976) and Gil (1973) would—there would be an emphasis on standards of fairness and opportunity as well as the need for redistribution. Rein (1970) states that "my profound conviction about the urgency of reducing inequities guides my policy analysis and offers a standard for judging policies" (p. xiv). Gil (1973) argues that "the distribution to individuals and groups, of specific rights to material and symbolic, life sustaining and life enhancing resources, goods and services . . . and the criteria underlying this distribution are, no doubt, the most significant issues of social policy development" (p. 22).

Whereas Friedman emphasizes the priority of liberty as a valuative criterion, and Rein and Gil emphasize the priority of equality, my own preference is to emphasize the importance of fraternity or community. The rationale for this emphasis was presented in the section entitled "A Value-analytic Approach to Social Policy." With community as a starting point, other criteria would tend to emerge, e.g., universal provision of services, funding of services that support rather than supplant parents, and emphasis on shared responsibility (Moroney, 1976, 1980). For the sake of explication, the remainder of this section will focus on universal services as a criterion essential to achieve community.

The universal provision of services is based on the recognition of common human needs, while the provision of exceptionalistic services emphasizes differences between people and usually implies a hierarchy among citizens. In arguing the case for universal services, Titmuss (1971) states:

> One of the principles of the National Blood Transfusion Service and the National Health Service is to provide services on the basis of common human needs; there must be no allocation of resources which could create a sense of separateness between people. It is the explicit or implicit institutionalization of separateness whether categorized in terms of income, class, race, colour, or religion, rather than the recognition of the similarities between people and their needs which causes much of the world's sufferings. (p. 238).

Exceptionalistic services, then, tend to stigmatize, to divide, and to create barriers to community, cooperation, mutual aid, and collective responsibility. Although universal services are no guarantee that these negative outcomes will be avoided, they do establish an environment in which individuals and families can be integrated into a network of supportive social relationships.

Universal and exceptionalistic services are best understood with reference to social welfare models. While these two approaches to providing services are ideal types (in the social science meaning of the term "ideal"), they do provide a way to understand divergent approaches to meeting social need. In the first or institutional model, there is a strong value commitment to universalist forms of welfare provision, supplemented where necessary by selectivist provision (Wilensky & Labeaux, 1965). Allocation for the selective services takes the form of positive discrimination rather than means tests. Social welfare services evolving from this model are viewed as the normal, first-line function of modern industrial society, necessary to deal with the risks and contingencies accompanying industrialization if individuals and families are to achieve and maintain satisfying standards of living. This model is based on the belief that, because of structural weaknesses, the market is not able to achieve a just allocation of goods and services, and that major institutions are needed to deal with such structural weaknesses.

The residual model, on the other hand, is based on the belief that social services should only come into play when the normal mechanisms of supply—the family and the market—break down (Wilensky & Labeaux, 1965). This model rests on moral assumptions about the self-evident virtues of competition and self help. Allocation takes the form of means tests which in practice stigmatize and by design provide disincentives. Services, when provided, deal with individual rather than structural weaknesses.

Proponents argue that universality of benefits and services is essentially egalitarian, that universality stresses social unity rather than divergence, and that universality is a major guarantee that potential recipients will avail themselves of the benefits and services so provided since such services are offered equally and without discrimination to all. Furthermore, the universalist position holds that the redistribution so achieved (because the high taxpayer contributes more and realizes less in relative terms) is more equitable than an exceptionalist system which may merely reshuffle resources among the poor. A universal approach has the further advantage of maintaining a high level of quality services since middle-class citizens are among the recipients and, as taxpayers, they are likely to be more influential than the poor in their demands. By contrast, the exceptionalist approach is based on the notion of two classes of citizens often resulting in two separate service delivery systems. Finally, the universal system is seen as relatively free from disincentives, both financial and psychological.

Still, to offer equal services or benefits to people in unequal situations is not to offer equality. This approach to providing services merely underwrites the existing inequalities between people. Examples of these types of benefits are tax credits for child care and various tax exemptions. To counter these types of services, selective services are proposed (i.e., services in which the poor benefit more than the rich, the handicapped more than the nonhandicapped, the underachiever more than the normal student, etc.).

A universal system, then, does not exclude the possibility of positive discrimination to rectify group injustices or meet the special needs of particular individuals and families. However, meaningful selective treatment of special needs is only possible (if we are concerned with community building, cooperation, and collective responsibility) given a generous universal system of benefits and services. Selective services, or positive discrimination, should be developed to meet the special needs of special individuals and families, and not to meet the needs of only the poor.

> The challenge that faces us is not the choice between universalist and exceptionalist social services. The real challenge resides in the question: what particular infrastructure of universalist services is needed in order to provide a framework of values and opportunity bases within and around which can be developed socially acceptable selective services aiming to discriminate positively, with the minimum risk of stigma, in favor of those whose needs are greater. (Titmuss, 1968, p. 135)

In explaining the various dimensions of universal provision, many authors refer to the family allowance benefit found in most Western countries. This program provides a cash benefit paid at a fixed rate regardless of the income of the recipient. However, since the family allowance is treated as taxable earned income, it is not of equal value to recipients but varies in relation to the level of tax they pay. There are, then, no cash benefits which are universal in value other than at the point of receipt.

Another dimension of universal provision that is important to understand is eligibility. Individuals or families qualify by virtue of being a member of a group—a group believed to need support because they are vulnerable. One must have children to claim family allowances; one must be over a certain age to claim retirement benefits. In some instances, the total population is determined to be in need (e.g., the National Health Service in the United Kingdom). In none of these programs is eligibility determined through means testing.

Another aspect of universal provision is that universal services are not free services. The critical issue is not the price paid but when it is paid. Under most universal services, services are financed through the tax system (usually through general revenue or special trust funds such as Social Security) and are not paid for by the consumer when the service is actually provided. Although proponents of the free market approach argue that the mechanism of financing universal services tends to curtail freedom to choose service providers, universalists suggest that this is not the case. For example, Britain's National Health Service, a universal system, allows patients to choose whichever doctor they prefer, not simply the one they can afford. Furthermore, the doctor can determine the appropriate course of treatment for the patient on medical grounds alone and not on ability to pay. Demand is relatively unrestricted and is determined by need. Decisions about the quantity of any human service needed are made between providers and consumers and are not determined by the government.

Two other aspects of universalism should be mentioned. Universal provision does not, by itself, address the issue of quality of services. Basically, it simply provides access to available services. Other mechanisms are necessary to deal with quality (regulations, certification, and the development of standards). Finally, it should be pointed out that a universal system may be universally generous or universally mean.

In summary, universal provision has been identified as a major criterion since it affirms the notion of common need and rejects a residual approach with its connotation of individual pathology or deficiency. A society that recognizes common social needs is less likely to be a divided society. Given a universal approach, individuals and families are more likely to use the service when needed and not be deterred because of psychological or financial barriers.

Implementation Criteria

As stated earlier, the approach offered here is, to some extent, a departure from more traditional models of policy analysis in that two distinct sets of criteria are introduced. The first set, discussed in the previous section, has been labeled "value criteria." These criteria are derived from first principles—such as liberty, equality, and fraternity—which in turn evolve from notions of society, social relationships, and social arrangements. In choosing among first principles, the analyst establishes a hierarchy since these principles cannot be simultaneously maximized. Choosing one will necessarily result in limiting others.

Implementation criteria are influenced by value criteria since some options will more adequately meet the requirements of the value criteria. For example, in providing day care, there are at least four options for government. Government could establish, administer, and deliver the day-care services (an option with both supply and demand dimensions). This public system could parallel our educational system. A second option would have the government intervene only on the supply side by providing funds for facility construction and the training of day-care providers. Precedents for this approach have been established in numerous manpower programs including the subsidization of professional training and the Hill-Burton Act. A third option can be characterized as demand-side intervention. Government pays for the service either directly or through vouchers, but does not directly increase the level of service provision. A fourth option would take the form of government intervention of both the supply and demand sides, but would also allow for private sector involvement.

Another implementation issue is the method of financing services. One option might be to expand current tax credits (which is consistent with the demand-side intervention); another would be to establish a special trust fund for payroll taxes (which would recognize the relationship between employment and child care); and still another option would be to establish financing from general revenues through the use of either categorical or block grants.

While all of the options under government's role and methods of financing are viable in the sense that each has precedents, not all are equally viable if value criteria have been introduced into the analysis. Earlier, I suggested that liberty, equality, and fraternity are meaningful organizing principles for the analysis and development of social policy. In choosing to maximize one of these, certain roles of government will be preferred over others, and some methods of financing will be more desirable than others. These issues can only be resolved, however, *after* the introduction of value criteria. The value criteria provide a framework to make such choices.

Finally, I would like to offer one comment about the issue of political feasibility. Within my approach to policy analysis, I tend to introduce this criteria only *after* decisions have been made on *what* is to be accomplished and *how* it might best be accomplished. The analyst can then decide whether the policy can be implemented completely or whether it needs to be phased in over time. The question of political feasibility is purposely placed at the end for good reason; if it were introduced at the beginning of the analysis and if it were given equal weight, we would quickly decide that nothing could be accomplished or would continue to make recommendations only for poor families thereby producing further divisiveness in our society.

SUMMARY

The ideas and approaches discussed in this chapter, while compatible in many ways with the models presented in other chapters, are somewhat unique. They are, furthermore, a significant departure from what most students of policy analysis today would consider appropriate within this field. Currently, policy analysis still relies on the management sciences, decision theory, systems analysis, and microeconomics. Policy analysis within this framework can be characterized as a decomposing process. The analyst, once given a problem, is expected to break the problem down into manageable components so that it can be understood and eventually manipulated or at least made susceptible to intervention. Following this, alternative strategies are identified and evaluated against a set of criteria. The results of the analysis are then given to the decision maker who will make the final choice. Over time, the accepted role of the analyst is one of a mere technician.

The position taken in this chapter is that such a formulation is incomplete and, more important, misleading. First, policy formulation is fundamentally concerned with making choices, and those choices are shaped by values. The role of the analyst is, then, one of clarification which in turn is accomplished by exposing the values implicit in any array of alternatives. Second, analysts are influenced by values which shape not only their view of society, social arrangements, and desirable outcomes but, just as importantly, their formulation of problems and their marshaling of evidence. Thus, it is not only useful but necessary to clearly specify the values that provide a framework for reaching a given policy recommendation. I call this approach a value-analytic approach.

Following this line of reasoning, I suggested that not only do values generate the criteria an analyst might use to evaluate existing policies or develop new policies, but also that three general values—liberty, equality, and fraternity—are the driving forces behind all policies, and that these three values cannot be maximized simultaneously. Whichever one is given primacy will result in limitations on the other two. I then offer a rationale as to why fraternity should be viewed as the more important of the three—a rationale that included both a discussion of how various social theorists and policy analysts have approached this issue and how it can be translated into first principles and policy relevant criteria.

The remainder of the chapter outlined a model for policy analysis. The model defined policy as covering three major areas, analysis, implementation, and evaluation. Since the focus of this book emphasizes policy analysis, the chapter concluded with a more detailed discussion of the components under that heading, namely, problem analysis and establishing criteria for formulating and evaluating alternative policies.

REFERENCES

Amidon, A., & Brim, O. *What do children have to gain from parent education?* Paper prepared for the Advisory Committee on Child Development, National Research Council, National Academy of Sciences, 1972.

Angrist, S., & Lave, J. Issues surrounding day care. *The Family Coordinator,* 1973, *22,* 457–464.

Bernard, J. *Women and the public interest.* Chicago: Aldine, 1971.

Boulding, K. The boundaries of social policy. *Social Work,* 1967, *12,* 3–11.

Brenner, R. (Ed.). *Children and youth in America: A documentary history* (Vol. 1: 1600–1865). Cambridge: Harvard Univ. Press, 1970.

Brim, O. *Education for child rearing.* New York: Russell Sage Foundation, 1959.

Bronfenbrenner, U. Developmental research, public policy and the ecology of childhood. *Child Development,* 1974, *45,* 1–5.

Bronfenbrenner, U. Who needs parent education? *Teachers College Record,* 1978, *79,* 767–787.

Dewey, J. *Theory of valuation.* Chicago: Univ. of Chicago Press, 1939.

Dror, Y. Prolegomenon to policy sciences. *Policy Sciences,* 1970, *1,* 135–150.

Dror, Y. *Design for policy sciences.* New York: American Elsevier, 1971.

Dunlop, K. *Rationale for governmental intervention into child care and parent education* (Center for the Study of Families and Children). Unpublished manuscript, Vanderbilt Univ., 1978.

Fein, G., & Clarke-Stewart, A. *Day care in context.* New York: Wiley, 1973.

Friedman, M. *Capitalism and freedom.* Chicago: Univ. of Chicago Press, 1962.

Gil, D. *Unravelling social policy.* Cambridge: Schenkman, 1973.

Horton, J. The dehumanization of anomie and alienation: A problem in the ideology of sociology. *British Journal of Sociology*, 1964, *15*, 280–291.

Kahn, A. *Theory and practice of social planning*. New York: Russell Sage Foundation, 1967.

Kahn, A., & Kamerman, S. *Not for the poor alone: European social services*. New York: Harper and Row, 1975.

Keller, S. Does the family have a future? In A. Skolnick & J. Skolnick (Eds.), *Intimacy, family and society*. Boston: Little, Brown, 1974.

Lasswell, H. The policy orientation. In D. Lerner & H. Lasswell (Eds.), *The policy sciences: Recent developments in scope and methods*. Stanford: Stanford Univ. Press, 1951.

Lasswell, H. The emerging conception of the policy sciences. *Policy Sciences*, 1970,*1*, 3–14.

Leiner, M. *Children are the revolution: Day care in Cuba*. New York: Viking Press, 1974.

Macbeath, A. *Can social policies be rationally tested?* London: Oxford Press, 1957.

Meers, D., & Marans, A. Group care of infants in other countries. In C. Chandler, R. Lourie, & A. Peters (Eds.), *Early child care: The new perspectives*. New York: Atherton Press, 1968.

Moroney, R. *The family and the state: Considerations for social policy*. New York: Longmans, 1976.

Moroney, R. *Families, social services and social policy: The issue of shared responsibility*. Washington, D.C.: U.S. Govt. Printing Office, 1980.

Nisbet, R. *The sociological tradition*. New York: Basic Books, 1967.

Nye, F. Sociocultural context. In L. Hoffman & F. Nye (Eds.), *Working mothers*. San Francisco: Jossey-Bass, 1974.

Ponsioen, J. *The analysis of social change reconsidered: A sociological study*. The Hague: s'Gravenhage, Mouton, 1962.

Pruger, R. Social policy: Unilateral transfer or reciprocal exchange. *Journal of Social Policy*, 1973, *2*, 283–301.

Rein, M. *Social policy: Issues of choice and change*. New York: Random House, 1970

Rein, M. *Social science and public policy*. New York: Penguin, 1976.

Rossi, A. A biosocial perspective on parenting. *Daedalus*, 1977, *106*, 1–32.

Rothman, S. M. Other people's children: The day care experience in America. *The Public Interest*, 1973, *30*, 11–27.

Sidel, R. *Women and child care in China*. Baltimore: Penguin, 1974.

Steiner, G. *The children's cause*. Washington, D.C.: Brookings, 1976.

Talmon, Y. The family in a revolutionary movement: The case for the Kibbutz in Israel. In R. Coser (Ed.), *The family: Its structures and functions*. New York: St. Martin's Press, 1974.

Tawney, R. *Equality*. London: Allen & Unwin, 1964.

Titmuss, R. *Commitment to welfare*. London: Allen & Unwin, 1968.

Titmuss, R. *The gift relationship*. London: Allen & Unwin, 1971.

Vickers, G. *Value systems and social process*. New York: Basic Books, 1968.

Wilensky, H., & Labeaux, C. *Industrial society and social welfare*. New York: Free Press, 1965.

Wilkinson, J. H. *From Brown to Bakke: The Supreme Court and school integration: 1954–1978*. New York: Oxford Univ. Press, 1979.

Woolsey, S. Pied Piper politics and the child care debate. *Daedalus*, 1977, *106*, 127–145.

FOOTNOTES

[1] This section is based in part on work that Paul Dokecki and I have carried out on a study concerned with strengthening families through public policy at Vanderbilt Institute of Public Policy Studies.

FOUR

COMBINING THE ROLES OF SCHOLAR AND CITIZEN[1]

DUNCAN MacRAE, JR.

The approach to be presented in this chapter is particularly concerned with the role of the scholar—in order to insure academic quality control—and that of the citizen—to stress the basic ethical criteria for choice of policies. Many other social roles are involved in public policy decisions, including those of the public official, the planner, and the lawyer; each role is likely to lead those who occupy it to emphasize somewhat different aspects of policy choice.

The scholar's role is important because it emphasizes the production of published work that can be reviewed and built upon by a community of scholars (Ben-David, 1971). This self-corrective critical process has served well in the development of scientific disciplines and has the promise of being extended to policy analysis. At present, however, this field does not yet have an organized literature or community of scholars. Rather, it overlaps with various disciplines, especially in their applied aspects, and even more with the professions. In the subfield of family and child policy, the relevant disciplines include psychology, sociology, anthropology, economics, and political science; related professions include education, pediatrics, psychiatry, other medical specialties, public health, nursing, social work, and law. Contributions from these disciplines and professions can fruitfully be combined in the subfield of family and child policy, as well as in policy analysis generally.

The quality control provided by a scholarly community is especially desirable for policy analysis because much analysis has to be done outside such communities. The results of these analyses are often embodied in private reports to clients rather than in publications—sometimes because they provide advantages to the client, but also often because they are done under time pressure or deal with specific and local details. A substantial body of analysis should nevertheless be subjected to a scholarly criticism of its methods and reasoning. To the extent that analysis cannot be judged simply in terms of its results, scholarly criticism may encourage the development of well-reasoned analysis rather than analysis based merely on successful salesmanship to the client (MacRae, 1976b).

Because scholarly publication stresses general rather than specific topics and encourages theoretical relevance, the approach I propose may pay insufficient attention to specific existing programs and particular proposals which effective analysis must consider. For this reason my approach, intended to relate to a scholarly community, will be somewhat incomplete in relation to practical policy recommendations.

I am also concerned with the citizen's role—one that scholarly communities often exclude because they fear it might introduce subjective and controversial values which would impair the objectivity of scholarly research. The citizen's role, however, can be a vital source of general value systems for policy analysis. Citizens concerned with the public interest must compare diverse policy alternatives in terms of general ethical principles and cannot delegate these value judgments to others.[2] Policy analysis, in this perspective, is a form of applied systematic ethics. It seeks to choose among alternatives in terms of general ethical principles applicable not only to families and children, but to persons in all roles and age groups. The policy domains to which it applies include the regulation of the economy, employment, health, education, taxation, the arts, foreign policy, and everything else that governments may do. In this sense the analyst, like the citizen, must be prepared to choose among all these possible government activities and compare them with activities in the private sector. Analyses cannot be based on valuative principles limited to the concerns of a single client group, profession, or discipline. This chapter will therefore emphasize the formulation of general ethical criteria for choice.

Because of this general concern, this type of policy analyst should always follow the general approach of benefit-cost analysis and ask, "How much?" How much should the government do for children as contrasted with other groups? How much should it spend on education, for example, rather than on health or crime control? This approach, seen from the perspective of a child advocate, may seem at times to be "against children"; but this is the role that citizens concerned with the general welfare must take—favoring each group or interest in society only up to a certain point.

THE ELEMENTS OF POLICY ANALYSIS

In the Introduction we have set forth a general model for policy analysis, which has provided a broad framework within which our four more detailed models may be placed. In the approach of this chapter, public policy analysis may be organized about the set of elements that we presented there (see also MacRae & Wilde, 1979):

1. Definition of the problem. We need to learn how the various preexisting definitions of our problem may be transformed into our "analyst's problem" which is rephrased in sufficiently precise terms to permit analysis, related to a system of values that provides criteria for choice, and which leads to recommendations that can be introduced into the decision processes of a particular political community. Analysis is not the same as scholarly research, however, and the analyst's problem may not require the gathering of new data.

2. Criteria for choice. Whether we begin with quantitative criterion of benefit-cost analysis (applied welfare economics) or with less systematized values such as rights, needs, equity, or human development, we must try to formulate and use clear valuative criteria for comparison of policy outcomes. Precise valuative discourse such as that of philosophy and economics can reshape the ambiguous values of citizens' discourse, but eventually the results of this technical discussion of values must be reintroduced into that discourse and understood by citizens.

3. Alternatives, models, and decisions. Policy analysis involves comparison among possible alternative policies. The expected consequences of these policies are compared after being predicted by models of causation, and are expressed in terms of the valuative criteria we have previously specified. On the basis of the values or disvalues of the consequences, we then choose among the competing policy alternatives. One model of particular importance is the economic model of the free, competitive market, including possible departures from the optimal properties of this model in terms of the economic value system. Numerous other relevant models also exist, drawing on knowledge from various natural and social sciences.

4. Political feasibility of enactment and implementation. Analysis of the prospects for enactment and implementation of a chosen policy is an essential feature of the larger analytic process. This topic draws on both political science and sociology, but also involves much information that is specific to particular political situations as well as skills of nonacademic practitioners.

In actual analysis these elements must be considered together rather than in sequence; but the sequence is useful for presenting an analysis or describing the field. In addition, the real process of analysis involves repeated cycles in which programs, once introduced, are evaluated retrospectively as part of the analysis of new policies.

DEFINITION OF THE PROBLEM

Policy analysis must center about comparison of some limited set of policy alternatives. A major task of the analyst is to choose the realm from which these alternatives are drawn—to specify the problem that calls forth the alternatives. This realm may be provided by the concerns of the analyst's clients or potential threats to their clients' values as these persons experience them—the "problem situation." It may also center on a new opportunity or discovery that provides possible policies of which most people are unaware, so that they must be informed about these possibilities. As the analyst moves toward systematic comparison of alternatives, he must formulate that version of the problem that will guide his analysis—the "analyst's problem."

Very often each group involved in a problem situation, concerned with its own interest rather than the public interest, will stress one particular value; the analyst's task (in the citizen role I am proposing) is then to try to reconcile or synthesize these values in some notion of the public interest or general welfare. Such a synthesis is not always possible, but sometimes the goals of various groups can be combined by means of an ethical system that provides for tradeoffs among them. This combination may not satisfy any of the groups completely. Moreover, there may be persons affected (such as children) who are not organized in vocal groups. The analyst should not assume that the major competing interest groups' views of relevant values include all the values that should be considered.

It is also possible to consider researchers' definitions of problems; researchers from an academic discipline will tend to seek questions amenable to their accustomed methods, concepts, and theories. Wildavsky (1979) argues that the policy analyst defines the problem so that it is "(1) worth solving from a social perspective and (2) capable of being solved with the resources at hand" (p.388). Researchers similarly seek to use the resources of their disciplines, but those of the policy analyst are more appropriate than those of the disciplines for reaching a policy choice.

Day care, which I shall use as a source of examples, is not a problem in the sense of a threatened value or a disparity between people's expectations and reality. Rather, it is a set of alternative policies aimed at dealing with values such as child development, equality for women, the desire of single parents to work (or of others to see them work), economic production, or rights. These values have come to the fore in public discussion because of changes in occupational and family roles (Kamerman & Kahn, 1979). Day care involves the care of preschool children during the day by persons other than their parents. In a general sense, the term includes babysitting, nursery school, and Head Start. But merely to try to formulate the issue in this way suggests broader questions.

One such question concerns the domain to which our analysis applies. Why should we use different principles for judging preschool policies from those for children, only slightly older, who have entered school? It is a rewarding intellectual exercise to try to apply the same principles to both. Even though public schools already exist and do not seem to present the same problems as day care, it is worthwhile in the long run to ask whether the schools should be as they are.

A second broader set of questions concerns the time during which children are separated from their parents. Will our judgments be different if it is part of the day, all day, or several days? Are we considering massive "ecological" intervention such as Bronfenbrenner (1975) has discussed, or a single, temporary separation? Our immediate concern may be the stress placed on a conventional set of family roles by the employment of women, but in a broader sense occupational as well as family roles may be considered as varying, including flextime and shared jobs. We may also ask what the separation from parents means to the child. What alternative persons or facilities are available? What are the goals of this separation—to provide parents with an opportunity for work or a vacation, to remedy deficiencies in parental care, or to furnish special learning or therapeutic opportunites for the child?

I raise questions of this sort to suggest the nature of academic policy analysis. Facing a particular immediate problem in our state or community, we would quickly reject or ignore most such questions as beyond the concern of the authorities in the time available. But such general questions, together with the valuative questions I shall discuss, provide some of the genuinely academic (quasitheoretical) concerns that make this aspect of policy analysis more than the highly specific and thus uninteresting activity that applied research is often thought to be by academics. Our task, in other words, is not merely to create a research literature but to build bridges between policy analysis and existing disciplines.

The analyst's problem may also be defined implicitly by the name used to designate a policy: Is it day care, nursery school, or Head Start? We sometimes find it difficult to draw back from the notion of a program with a single name and an associated dominant goal, and to view it in terms of a larger ethical system; but this initial detachment is often essential. Various political groups may label a program "liberal" or "conservative," but the analyst must be stubbornly independent of such labels.[3] One interesting example of the transformation of an issue concerns abortion: as recently as the 1960s it gained the support of conservative whites in southern legislatures as a means for birth control, but now that the issue involves the expenditure of public funds, conservatives oppose it.

Even though day care is one particular type of policy, the debates about it have nevertheless engaged a variety of general values, corresponding to definitions of the problem. Some of the main definitions given by participant groups are described by Woolsey (1977). They include concern with values of "workfare" conservatives, women, professionals, and persons concerned with vertical equity for the poor.

Two types of redefinition of the problem are especially noteworthy:

1. Efforts to synthesize some or all of the various values brought to bear on day care, such as those of the groups above;
2. Reconsideration of the means to these values, and thus bringing in policy alternatives other than day care. This approach will eventually lead me to consider income-maintenance policies.

These types of redefinition lead us to the next major element of policy analysis—the establishment of criteria by which the analyst will compare possible alternatives.

SYSTEMATIC CRITERIA FOR POLICY CHOICE

Careful reasoning is involved in public policy analysis, not only in our assessment of evidence and causal relations but also in the systematic formulation of our values. Consistent statement of our values is important both for consistency among our recommended policies and for discussion of valuative questions among scholars. The intellectual merits of analysis will be much clearer if we can demonstrate logical inferences from valuative principles to policy choices. Analysis should not mean starting with policy preferences and merely embellishing them with facts and values chosen after the policy itself is selected. Even though analysts will not necessarily agree on a single value system, a desirable condition for scholarly valuative discourse and for reasoning from values *to* policies is that each such system be clear, consistent, and general (MacRae, 1976a, Ch. 4).

The diverse criteria used in the assessment of policies for families and children provide numerous illustrations of the problems involved in rendering a value system consistent. Such problems typically arise when two or more criteria bear on a single choice and lead to contradictory results. Ultimately, in order to recommend a choice, we need to synthesize the criteria so as to tell whether a policy favored over others by criterion X, but not by criterion Y, is desirable on the whole. If we are advisers or technicians we can leave some of this task of synthesis to decision makers, but in the citizen role we have to choose between criteria when they conflict in this way.

Several methods are available to us for systematizing criteria (MacRae & Wilde, 1979, Ch. 3):

1. Separating political feasibility from other criteria and considering it in detail as a logically distinct aspect of the analysis.
2. Reducing disparate values to a common denominator, such as monetary value in benefit-cost analysis. Another type of common denominator may be provided eventually by measurements of the quality of life.
3. Characterizing some criteria as means to others. We might thus classify some criteria as "intermediate outcomes," and others to which they are means as "ultimate outcomes," restricting our analysis to the latter if possible.
4. Considering criteria in a strict sequence such that one is completely taken into account as a constraint before another enters (Rawls, 1971, pp. 42–44). This can be done only if the first criterion excludes certain policy alternatives but leaves a range of other permitted alternatives within which analysis can proceed. Examples are a ceiling on the cost of a project, or a legal or moral prohibition that excludes certain types of alternatives but permits a number of others that are judged acceptable.
5. When other methods of synthesis fail, using multiple criteria and presenting a comparison of alternatives with respect to each, the synthesis being made by intuitive judgment for the case at hand (see Keeney & Raiffa, 1976).

We shall now consider these methods of systematizing our criteria in greater detail.

Political Feasibility as a Separate Element

I have listed feasibility of enactment and implementation as a distinct element of policy analysis. One reason is that feasibility does not make a policy desirable; a policy no better than the existing situation would not be worth adopting, no matter how feasible it was. Feasibility is analogous to probability in that if it were measured by a number between zero and unity, the overall expected value of a policy could be characterized by the product of its value if it were certain (its desirability) and its feasibility. But it is not as clearly specifiable as a probability, because the feasibility of carrying out a policy may relate to the effort that we put into it, or to our success in persuading others to support it (MacRae & Wilde, 1979, pp. 49–51).

A second reason for separating feasibility from desirability in our analysis is that the feasibility of a policy alternative depends on the role one occupies. A government official or an interest group leader can accomplish more than an ordinary citizen; the resources of one profession may differ from those of another. Thus, an account of the feasibility of a policy, if linked to the specific situation and persons involved, is more personal and less universal than some other aspects of analysis. Conceivably a particular analyst might specify the roles and resources he assumes (much as he specifies his value system), but scholarly criticism of analyses of feasibility still seems difficult. Analysts nevertheless tacitly introduce considerations of feasibility into analysis of desirability when they prescreen the alternatives and remove obviously infeasible ones.

One ingredient of political feasibility in a democracy is the opinions or attitudes of our fellow citizens about policy alternatives. It is tempting, if we value democracy, to consider these attitudes as contributing to the desirability of policies. Nevertheless, if a program is desirable and can be implemented, we should not consider the public's attitudes toward the program, regardless of their foundations, as affecting its desirability. The public may not initially give the program sufficient support but may be open to reasoned persuasion. In other instances the public may be exceedingly enthusiastic about a program (such as research to find a cure for cancer), even when the prospects of the program's success are not good. It is our responsibility as citizen-analysts to try to inform and persuade our fellow citizens as to the merits of a proposed policy choice. Other citizens' initial views are therefore a condition of feasibility of a policy, but not necessarily a criterion of its desirability. Even if we consider consumer preference a major criterion for policy choice, we must face the possibility that consumers will prefer a means (e.g., health care) that does not effectively promote an end they desire (health). Citizen and consumer preferences need not simply be taken as given but can be informed and rendered more consistent through education and reasoned public discussion.

Quality of Life

The economic approach to policy analysis seeks to maximize the value of economic output or national income (Haveman & Weisbrod,

1975).[4] This definition of welfare is often supplemented by less systematic observations as to the effects of policies on equity. In combination, these criteria—welfare and equity—allow the analyst to take the perspective of a representative citizen who is not committed in advance to the exclusive welfare of any single group or to any particular policy, but seeks to compare various policy proposals evenhandedly.

My approach to policy analysis stresses this citizen perspective but seeks to introduce alternative noneconomic value systems. "Well-being," like "the good," "the general welfare," and "the public interest," is a valuative term that may be defined in various ways. Each such definition might constitute the basis of an ethical system for policy choice; various definitions might correspond, for example, to human development and perfection, to attainment of identity or reduction in alienation, to the satisfaction of preferences (akin to the economic definition), or to sentiments of well-being or happiness. It is the last of these meanings, based on asking people directly about their well-being, that has been the basis of a growing number of sample-survey studies that measure "subjective social indicators" (Bradburn, 1969; Campbell, Converse, & Rodgers, 1976). Though these measurements are less precisely adapted to policy choice than is benefit-cost analysis, they constitute an important philosophical contrast to the value of economic efficiency.

One presumed advantage of this sort of measure, if it could be made reliable, would be a greater emphasis on equity between rich and poor than is provided by monetary benefits and costs; rich and poor persons' descriptions of their well-being would count equally. Economists have, in fact, conjectured about a concept of "utility," which might vary nonlinearly with income. But they have seldom attempted to measure utility; cardinal measurement of utility has, in fact, been deemed to lack scientific justification (Arrow, 1962, pp. 9–10). Measures of happiness and satisfaction obtained from surveys have shown a modest (but far from perfect) association with income. Such measures, then, suggest an operational definition of "welfare" which, if it could be applied practically, might lead to the choice of different policies from those recommended by benefit-cost analysis.

A related development in the field of health policy has been the effort to measure "quality-adjusted life-years" as a valuative criterion. Weinstein and Stason (1977) have described ways in which a patient might judge a year under medication, or a year with the symptoms of a disease, to be equivalent in value to a certain fraction of a year in good health. This fraction would then furnish a measure of "quality" that could be combined with duration to provide a criterion for policy choice.

In considering policies affecting families and children, we may find that indices of quality and duration of life give results in greater agreement with our moral feelings than does benefit-cost analysis. Not only persons with low wage rates, but persons whose production is not sold in the market (such as housewives) might be treated more equitably if we judged the value of their lives in terms of time. Moreover, persons who do not produce appreciably in the ordinary sense might receive more consideration: the well-being of young children independent of their futures, of the handicapped, and of the elderly might also be taken into account in this way. This approach would come nearer to measuring consumption than production, and would do so in nonmonetary terms.

Goals

In much discussion of policies, the goals or purposes of a program are treated separately from its costs. I prefer, however, not to define goals separately from general ethical criteria that seek to include all of a policy's benefits and costs to society. Any policy should aim at increasing the general welfare, according to some system of values. To single out one value as its purpose and to neglect others seems at best a necessary evil, perhaps related to the choice of one profession or organization as the vehicle of a policy. We should try to consider as wide as possible a range of policy consequences and the values on which they impinge.

The goal of a child care policy might thus concentrate our attention on its effects on children, to the neglect of effects on other groups in society such as taxpayers. Conversely, if we focused attention on the goals of policies that are aimed mainly at other groups, but also affect children and families, we might neglect effects on children. Policies affecting taxation, employment, and equality for women all affect children as well; but because of the emphasis of the major groups supporting such policies, the effects on children may be neglected. Day care was supported during World War II, for example, primarily to increase production and not because of its effects on children.

Needs and Needs Assessment

A starting point in the analysis of social policy is often taken to be the needs of a potential recipient population. This approach is valuable because, in contrast to an economic assessment of demand, it provides for greater equity between rich and poor and allows professionals to assess the needs of potential recipient groups for goods or services they do not demand sufficiently in economic terms (e.g., infant nutrition or health services.) Thus, a frequent procedure when a policy for support of new services is contemplated is a *needs assessment.* This assessment usually takes the form of an enumeration of persons who suffer from particular problems or are deemed to be in need of particular services (Carter, 1966).

In connection with day-care policy, various observers have pointed out that children have needs not adequately expressed by parents' economic demand for care. Rivlin (1977, p. 444), for example, points out the problems of "latchkey" children; and Nelson (1977) notes the "appalling conditions under which poor working mothers leave their children" (p. 89). Here, as in the case of child abuse, we must consider policies that alter the family's internal distribution of resources to insure that children receive adequate care and protection.

The analysis of needs, however, risks a serious conflict among our recommendations for social policies if it is not connected with resources and costs. Gallagher (1976; see also Fig. 1 in Ch. 3) cites the example of proposals for special education, based on the needs of a population, that require an impossibly high number of specialized personnel. Some strategies, he points out, are "incapable of rational completion." Moreover, it is not simply the time required for training these personnel that makes these policies impossible; the cost of this training may well be so great that society could better expend these resources in other ways.

Conceivably the competing need-related claims of various professions and their politically active clients can be reconciled through political processes (Gates, 1975). This reconciliation may resemble that between "interests" in the courts, discussed by Turnbull in Ch. 5. With a limited budget, the political efforts of professionals, clients, taxpayers, and others will result in a division of public resources among various programs. Such a result may be more equitable than allocation by the market, and by involving professionals it may take into account those needs that are not represented by active public demand. We cannot be assured, however, that the resulting allocation of resources is the right one, according to any particular ethical system.

A difficulty with the categorization of needs of various types (as in a needs assessment) is that it fails to provide a quantitative basis to decide how much of each type of need should be served with our limited resources. The economic notion of demand is expressed as a *function* of the monetary price of a good or service; certain demands are more important to the individual than others and are distinguished according to the person's willingness to pay. The intersection of a demand function and a supply function, then, determines a market equilibrium which is efficient, if the necessary market conditions obtain.

This notion of intersection has been extended, at least in principle to public or collective goods (Musgrave & Musgrave, 1976, p. 53); and survey data might conceivably be used to ascertain the public's valuation of collective goods (Gramlich, 1977), corresponding somewhat to intensity of need.

Here again I suggest that economic reasoning provides a valuable intellectual model for any ethical system intended to guide public policy. Even if we should wish to avoid the inequities of an economic mode of analysis aimed only at serving dollar demand and wish instead to meet needs not adequately known to the client population, we should not immediately reject this formal type of reasoning. In place of an all-or-none notion of need we might well substitute a *need function* which requires us to estimate the importance of various alleged needs. Returning to Gallagher's example of special education, we must try to assess how much special education should be provided by society in the long run, taking into account the cost of training personnel and other necessary expenses. In the case of the handicapped, for example, society may be doing too little in some circumstances and too much in others. Society or its members should make some judgment, other than a purely political one,[5] regarding the proper allocation of its resources.

A step in this direction might be to characterize each need by the expected value of treating or serving it. For remediable conditions, the value of a cure might be estimated. For chronic conditions which cannot be completely cured, the increased well-being, life expectancy, or productivity resulting from treatments or other policies might be considered; in addition, reduced expenditures for later treatment might be considered as benefits. Values or benefits of this sort, if expressible in monetary terms, could then be compared with costs.

In economic terms, the primary indicator of need is low income. An indicator such as the poverty line is commonly modified by family size, and is increased in relation to the number of dependents. Further refinements, however, would consider the degree of dependency of each member (infants vs. teenagers), his or her possible contribution to family production (through chores or jobs), and other resources available to the family (property, savings, possibly even the availability of others for help). We return to these questions below in connection with equity.

Means and Ends

Our analyses can also be directed to a smaller number of more consistent values, if we focus our attention on ends rather than means.

Consider, for example, the value placed on the quality of day care or on quality of professional services generally. Much attention is devoted to measuring and monitoring quality (e.g., regarding the training of caregivers, amount of space available per child, and auxiliary services available). Yet what is of ultimate concern is the consequences, primarily for children, that result from care of better or worse quality. We need to know, for example, how children's personality development is affected by variations in quality, and how much these variations cost. The analyst's first questions about quality of day care should be, "How much good does it do? Is it worth the cost?"

We need not ignore quality of service delivery, but we should recognize this as a second-best measure or intermediate outcome of policies. We must give high priority in analysis, research, and data collection to seeing how much good is accomplished by "quality" service delivery—by examining its ultimate outcomes. The shortage of systematic research on this topic in the fields of health care and education is a serious obstacle to the reasoned comparison of policies. Newhouse, Phelps, and Schwartz (1974), for example, have argued that "even a substantial investment in delivery of more health services is not likely to produce any clearly measurable change in any dimensions of health, whether length of life or physical well-being" (p. 1352). In the field of child care, there is also a shortage of research on the effects of variations in quality of care and in monitoring of that quality, as I shall note later.

A second and even more important variable in assessing policies for families and children, which may be a means rather than an end, is the cohesion of the family itself. To some observers, family cohesion seems a value in itself; but from the perspective of an ethic that sees the good as located in human experience, the family is only one possible means to valued experience for its members and others. Its maintenance may contribute to that valued experience indirectly through developing the personalities of its members, increasing their productivity, or providing satisfying experiences in family interaction. Whether family stability is likely to produce these effects under particular conditions, however, is an empirical question that the analyst must study.[6]

Thus we might argue that sometimes family members are better off when the family is dissolved or when a member leaves it. The apparently high rates of marital dissolution revealed by the Seattle and Denver Income Maintenance Experiments (Hannan, Tuma, & Groeneveld, 1978) may have reflected opportunities to escape from unsatisfactory marriages. We need at least to ask which families should be kept together by policy incentives and which should not.

Moroney (1976) has argued that social policy should give more attention to providing incentives for families to care for their own dependent members, rather than transferring these functions into the hands of the state. But this is not to say that the preservation of an intact family is an end in itself. When an extremely dependent or disruptive member is removed from the family and cared for in an institution, there may well be a net benefit—if we can define this phrase clearly. We need to ask under what conditions, and to what ends, these caring functions of families deserve to be supported.

In advocating the preservation of the customary functions of the family, Moroney may simply be giving the benefit of the doubt to existing norms. Conceivably, a caring function can be performed with equal (or greater) net benefit in an outside institution. We may also find, however, that decentralized decisions provide fine tuning, or "coproduction" of services (Whitaker, 1980), conducive to greater efficiency or net benefit from family care. Without imposing intolerable burdens on the family, an elderly parent may receive more individualized care in the family, but with some external aid. The provision of home care for the elderly by public agencies may allow other family members to work or pursue other activities during the day, and thus provide benefits analogous to those of day care for young children. This home care permits an elderly parent to remain near his or her child, in familiar surroundings, rather than in a nursing home. It may even be cheaper than a nursing home. Similar considerations arise in the care of handicapped children. I have suggested, therefore, that more nearly ultimate criteria such as personal satisfaction, productivity, and cost can underlie our decisions as to whether to support the intact family. In these terms the maintenance of an intact family counts for nothing in itself, although it may well be a means to other human values.

Moroney argues, in effect, for the freedom of the family (a third variable that may be only a means) to decide whether to care for its dependent member, rather than for policies forcing that member out of the family in order to receive support. Freedom of choice is often mentioned as a desirable feature of public policies. In mentioning "fine tuning," however, I have suggested that only the *consequences* of that freedom for human welfare need be considered. This is analogous to the argument that an ideal free market provides efficiency of preference satisfaction and is desirable only for this reason—not for freedom itself. The reader may, of course, disagree with this value judgment, which relates to my utilitarian perspective, and consider freedom an ultimate end.

A fourth variable, in addition to quality of care, family cohesion, and freedom, which may well be considered a means rather than an end, is alteration of the structure of power in society. Latting (1980), for example, has examined the power relations on health planning boards between providers and consumers from poor minority communities. The question was raised as to whether an increase in power for these consumers actually led to an improvement in community health. The analysis seemed to presume that providers were insufficiently concerned with the community's welfare and that giving more power to community members would increase their welfare.

If we assume that those who command power or the means of production are necessarily exploitative, then power exercised by these persons is undesirable. On the other hand, it may be argued that some elites exercise their power or influence so as to serve the general welfare; most professionals would contend that their authority is used in this way. A judgment as to whether power is being exercised in a beneficial or harmful way can be complex, and may well depend on the value system or notion of the general welfare which we bring to the task; but I ask only that we bear in mind this relation between power structure, which may be only a means, and more direct measures of human welfare.

So far I have dealt with value criteria that apply to possible *consequences* of policies that we may choose. Principles of this sort are known in philosophy as *teleological* (from the Greek *telos,* or end) or *consequential* in that they aim at ends or consequences beyond the policy or the act itself. In contrast, we may consider *nonteleological* ethical principles or criteria, which consider an act right or wrong in itself, regardless of its consequences (MacRae & Wilde, 1979, Ch. 3). Some principles of this latter sort are absolute rights, constitutional rights, and moral prohibitions such as that against murder. Policy analysts must consider principles of the latter sort; but a greater part of their analysis is devoted to teleological principles of valuation, which require the prediction of consequences of policies.

Political and Cultural Autonomy

Analogous to the value of individual freedom, but more difficult to subsume in a general ethical system, is the question as to when one cultural group is entitled to exercise influence over another. This issue arises in consideration of differential effects of day care on different groups. Some studies have suggested that day care produces more positive results for low-income children than for middle-income children (Haskins, Finkelstein, & Stedman, 1978). Taken at face value, these findings would lead us to recommend policies that would induce more low-income families to place their children in suitable day care. Perhaps Head Start (seen as education rather than day care) has this advantage.

But the issue then arises as to whether one cultural, ethnic, or income group is making policies to alter the culture or modal personality of another. This issue arose for the Moynihan report (1965) on *The Negro Family* (Rainwater & Yancey, 1967) and for the "culture of poverty" hypothesis. It raises the nonteleological question: Should one group manipulate another group for what it judges to be the latter group's own good? Associated questions concern who should participate in the policy analysis and whether the proposed change really is beneficial.

The question whether government should intervene to change families and children involves the norms defining the boundaries and prerogatives of the family. In communist and socialist societies (the USSR, China, Cuba) and in Israel, there is greater intervention in family affairs by the state and community for goals of production, sexual equality, or socialization of the young. In Western Europe and the United States, a greater burden of proof has long rested on the government for such intervention; proof has required demonstration of improper care or cruelty on the part of parents (Marshall, 1970, pp. 136–137).

In the contemporary United States, an issue arises which is sometimes labeled "internal colonialism" by radical critics. Insofar as professionals are viewed as representing an exploitative outside group rather than part of the same population that may undergo change through socialization, policies for such change may be resisted. On the other hand, when policies for education (e.g., Head Start) are proposed and supported by the targeted population, the policies are accepted. Education and opportunity may be sought by minority groups for their children (Joffe, 1977, Ch. 5); socialization, culture change, and possibly even reduction of aggressive tendencies (Crain & Weisman, 1972) may seem an invasion of group rights. The issue is partly symbolic (Edelman, 1964, 1971), but it is true that education and day-care programs may affect personality development, culture, and other noncognitive variables.

The question of alleged exploitation can perhaps be dealt with not only by participation of those affected, but also (like the question of stigma, which we consider later) through furnishing universal rather than "selective" services. The Danish nationwide network of day-care centers is available to all at a fixed price, partially subsidized, and in addition includes "free places" for those who cannot afford the standard fee (Wagner & Wagner, 1976). Proposals for such an arrangement in the United States would raise the question, however, of whether the advantages of universal services are worth the additional cost.

Equity

So far, I have stressed ethical criteria that relate to individuals separately regarding either their welfare—such as preference satisfaction, personality development, or happiness—or their production, affecting others' welfare. But another extensive set of criteria is that designated as *equity,* which relates to the comparison of individuals or groups with one another. Related terms are fairness and justice.

Economists typically distinguish efficiency from equity (Okun, 1975), the former being incorporated in the logic of applied welfare economics and the latter not. Equity, in economic discussion, is ordinarily classified into two types: (1) horizontal equity, the equal treatment of equals; and (2) vertical equity, the unequal treatment of unequals so as to render them more equal. We may add to this the concept of "transitional equity" (Hochman, 1974), relating to the position of women and blacks in the United States. The handicapped, too, are claiming increasingly to be treated equally in certain ways (mainstreaming in schools), as are the elderly. Advocates of universal services are likely to stress human similarities, whereas advocates of selective services stress differences.

Vertical equity is most often invoked in the comparison of rich and poor. The very definition of poverty raises the question: Should the poverty of a family be defined only in terms of income (Moon & Smolensky, 1977)? The notion of vertical equity might be related to sex differences as well; indeed, some of the arguments in favor of day care seem to be claims for public compensation for inequality that a traditional family structure has imposed on married women.

Transitional equity, broadly considered, merges into the question of public compensation for past injuries. Even though long past, the wrongs done to slaves in America are sometimes considered a justification for special, present, compensatory policies toward blacks. Other historic claims by nations and ethnic groups for retribution or compensation can be traced for still longer periods.

A special situation involving questions of both equity and compensation concerns the role of the married woman in relation to day-care policy. From an economic perspective it is often suggested that monetary aid should be given to poor *families,* to spend on food, housing, day care, or other things as they judge best. Yet experiments with income maintenance (e.g., Rees & Watts, 1975, pp. 82–83) have shown that in families given such aid, there is a net movement of women out of the labor force rather than into it. It would appear from these findings that although day care is a means to mothers' employment and to increased family income, if income rather than day care were provided directly, many families would choose less employment rather than more.

A proponent of equity for women might argue, however, that the distribution of influence in existing families was inequitable—that the use of money given to the family is disproportionately controlled by men. An economist might argue that women wishing equality should make marriage contracts that permitted it—assuming that the marriage market could provide them with spouses willing to make such a contract. But in return, an advocate of women's rights might claim that the recently expanded consciousness of women has led to a realization that traditional family roles, within which many marriage contracts were made, were improperly defined. Such a conclusion would lead, then, to a historically temporary advocacy of government aid to women in those families where the marriage contracts were unjust.

In the longer run, if greater occupational equality were obtained in marriage for those couples who wished it, economic aid could again be given to the family as a whole rather than in such a way as to aid mothers specifically. As family structure changed, more fathers might wish day care to free *them* from home responsibilities. But then the question might arise: Is the bearing of children a burden (like illness, poverty, or handicaps) for which the state should assume responsibility? To accept this principle would indeed be a radical departure from traditional American norms in which families are largely responsible for the support and care of their own children. The needs of poor families have indeed been calculated in relation to numbers of children, and the poverty income level is adjusted accordingly. However, claims of nonpoor families for publicly aided day care could be less easily supported on this basis.

The claims of women to increased job opportunities, associated with the issue of day care, are also open to generalization when other groups make similar claims. The elderly, teenagers, and the handicapped are other groups who may wish to enter the labor force to a greater degree than prevailing norms have allowed. For a person who is considering working, we may ask whether the additional amount he or she produces will lead to a net social gain relative to the value of previous activities outside the labor market (e.g., child care). This last argument is based on the value of efficiency rather than equity; and even though it neglects equity, it has the advantage of allowing us to compare the merits of various groups' claims. It may also be a basis for distinguishing among employment claims of various elderly persons, for example, or among those of the handicapped.

The net social gain from employment does not correspond in general, however, to the results of one person's work and production alone. In an economy at less than full employment, new persons can be accepted into the work force without reducing the job opportunities for others. But as the economy approaches full employment, then, at least in the short run, job seekers compete with one another throughout the economy. The net increase in production resulting from the employment of a person may well be less than that person's own production if someone else's probability of employment is thereby decreased. Thus, there are not only various claims for equity in the job market; but a claim to employment based on one sort of inequity (women vs. men) may have indirect effects relating to another possible type of inequity (e.g., blacks vs. whites, young vs. old).

An important concept closely associated with the value of equity is that of stigma. A longstanding debate in Britain and America has focused on whether social services should be rendered on a *universal* basis (given to all citizens as a matter of right) or *selectively* (given only to the needy). One drawback of the latter approach, is the stigma attached to defining oneself as needy, as having to undergo a "means test." Because such a distinction among income groups seems to stigmatize those receiving state aid, advocates of universal services insist that certain basic services be available to all as a right (see Moroney, Ch. 3).

The stigma associated with means tests seems to result in part from the judgment of observers that the poor are responsible for their own situation. To declare oneself ill, blind, or over 65 and thus receive public aid is less stigmatizing because illness, handicaps, and age, unlike poverty, are viewed as ascribed rather than achieved statuses. But this difference raises the question whether under some circumstances poverty might not carry so much stigma.

A social label somewhat the opposite of stigma is the "deservingness" associated with a prior contribution to society, such as veteran status. This status has entitled veterans to a variety of social services and benefits. These benefits are given unconditionally, without further public inquiry into other aspects of the recipient's life.

Some public policies toward the poor ask not only about means, but also about personal behavior. Personal morality becomes a consideration, at least in the public's mind. Inquiries into personal and family behavior take place. One way of avoiding or reducing such inquiries is by the recipient's contribution to the values of the society; in the United States this can be done by working.

The advocate of selective social services would argue that there is a social cost in providing universal services to the nonpoor. Universal services require additional public funds; and even if taxes on the nonpoor are increased to pay for them, they still create inequities (childless couples pay for the education of others' children) and may force the nonpoor to spend their money for amounts or types of services different from what they might prefer. We are led, from this perspective, to ask first whether the degree of stigma resulting from a selective policy might be reduced, and second, just how much the social cost of stigma should be. If selective services save money for society, perhaps the recipients could be compensated for the stigma by getting more services.[7]

The negative income tax approach has been advocated not only on the grounds that it provides a work incentive for recipients, but also because it lessens stigma. Payments do require reporting of income; but since this program would be administered by the Treasury without the aid of professionals, it would presumably involve no detailed scrutiny of recipients' life styles. Moreover, by including the working poor, it would draw a gradual, rather than a sharp, boundary between recipients and nonrecipients.

It seems, therefore, that we need to direct more research and ingenuity toward devising selective policies that minimize the effective cost of stigma. (This, incidentally, seems another significant omission from disciplinary research.) Changes in bureaucratic procedures possibly could make the granting of aid less offensive and involve less invasion of privacy. We should try to incorporate stigma into a larger system of social values and disvalues in which there are possible trade-offs between one particular value and another.

Population Effects: A Noneconomic Criterion

It is difficult to study policies affecting the well-being of children without finding potential consequences of these policies for population size and distribution. If, for example, the well-being of children depends on their family's available resources, then we might advocate smaller families. Policies aimed at reducing family size do not affect children alone, however; they may also affect the autonomy of parents, the power of nations and ethnic groups, the amount produced and consumed in the economy, the relative benefits and burdens of age groups in the longer run, and the quality of life for those who share the earth's (as well as the family's) limited resources.

Any policy that lessens the burdens of caring for children can be expected—at least in an economic perspective—to increase the number of births. Thus, Rivlin (1977) points out:

> Another argument against a universal subsidy for day care, especially for the very young, is that it might encourage people to have more children

> at a time when there is a fairly general belief that a lower rate of population growth would be in the national interest. (p. 469)

The extent to which such incentives would exist is a difficult empirical question. But in our discussion of value criteria, we must note that the valued or disvalued effects of population change are not easily incorporated in the economic value synthesis. In economic comparisons, the desirability of alternative states of affairs is judged according to a fixed population's preferences among them. New arrivals may aid or harm those who are already here; but the welfare of the new arrivals themselves involves (in the economic perspective) the creation of new sets of preferences. The new arrivals' preferences are not even defined (i.e., have no meaning) for the state of affairs in which the new arrivals do not exist. Thus, policy alternatives that involve the choice of whether or not to increase the population cannot be compared (with each other) according to the preferences of any fixed set of choosers. It is true, however, that if we consider the national income or per capita income, we may compare one period of time with another even though the population changes.

Policies involving population change also raise the important value question as to the importance of quantity versus quality of life in our judgments of whether society is better off. It seems widely acknowledged today that population growth should be reduced; but there is less consensus (and little discussion) as to what our ultimate target should be. For some, the ideal may be a small population with a maximum quality of life; others argue for population expansion only to the point of maximum aggregate welfare. This issue seems not to be presently crucial because projected world population may well exceed even the second optimum; but it may eventually become more important.

Rights and the Law

Our effort to systematize the value criteria relevant to families and children has drawn together particular values by seeking common measuring units (such as money) or common ends to which particular values are means. We have also seen, however, that certain types of values resist this synthesis. Foremost among the types of values that resist synthesis are *rights*. The claim of a right, in the sense of ordinary discourse, is unconditional. Like a claim of need, it does not have an associated price tag that would allow it only if it is not too expensive relative to other social values. For this reason, some conservative observers of contemporary American politics believe that an escalation of claims and counterclaims of rights makes collective decisions increasingly difficult. Claims of rights to minimum standards of health and income, freedom of speech, equality for groups and their indemnification for past wrongs, liberation from past social bondage, and alternative life styles all seem difficult to reconcile except through a continued intensification of political struggle.

At the same time there are claims, based in part in the law, for rights of protection against the effects of new policies—especially those that would invade the autonomy of the family (Ramsey, 1978). If we are concerned with the abuse and neglect of children, we recognize immediately that the law does not permit spying within homes to detect actions of this sort. Nor does it allow the state, unless a strong case can be made, to remove a child from parental care and forcibly give him to substitute parents. This protection of the family seems to go even further than John Stuart Mill (1859) advocated: "[T]he only purpose for which power can be rightfully exercised over any member of a civilized community, against his will is to prevent harm to others" (p. 73).

To resolve conflicts among such unconditional principles is an almost impossible task for the rational ethical discourse described so far. There is, however, another mechanism for resolving some of them—the judicial system (as dealt with in Turnbull's contribution, Ch. 5).

Multiple Criteria

Even if we make serious efforts to synthesize our various valuative criteria into a single logical system, we may still fail to do so completely. Especially in a policy domain so complex as the one concerning families and children, such synthesis is difficult. This difficulty is illustrated in the tradeoffs we have to make in evaluating policies for day care. Day-care facilities have costs; they also have consequences for mothers' participation in the labor force relative to both equity and production as well as for children's personality development. Costs can be related to productivity in monetary terms. But even apart from the assessment of effects, the value of personality development is extremely difficult to express in monetary terms.

We may then simply express our values in terms of a minimum number of distinct dimensions of policy choice such as cost, equity, and personality development. Once we have done this, as citizen-analysts we must make specific or implicit comparisons among these dimensions to choose among policies. If, on the other hand, our role is that of an adviser rather than a chooser, we may present separate estimates of the effects of policies on these different dimensions and allow others to compare the dimensions.

Criteria may have to enter separately into our analysis, for several reasons. First, they may be conceptually distinct. Increased freedom and increase in the gross national product may be distinct in this way; so, too, may be the desire for health services and the desire for health. Second, we may be driven to use independent measures of criteria because of a lack of knowledge of causal relations; thus, although we may believe that education ultimately contributes to the well-being of members of society, we may have to use increases in test scores as a criterion because we cannot now estimate their relation to well-being. Finally, we may be unable to measure the value or disvalue of a particular policy consequence; we may believe that we should calculate the harm of polluted air or the unpleasantness of roadside litter as an economic cost, but we may not have adequate information to make this estimate in quantitative terms.

If, for these intrinsic or practical reasons, we must deal with distinct criteria for policy choice, we may still try to balance them against one another in various ways.

1. Cost-effectiveness analysis. If we wish to choose among alternative policies that produce an output measurable only in noneconomic terms, we may express the relation between output and cost as a quotient—a *cost-effectiveness ratio.* Thus, if the output is "increase in test-score points," aggregated over children, we may consider the number of test-score points added per dollar spent. In these terms we may compare programs having the same output, such as various education programs, even though we cannot compare programs of different types (such as educational and health programs) (Quade, 1975, p. 94).

2. Problem-specific numerical tradeoffs. Our inability to synthesize two value criteria *in general* does not prevent us from trying to do so in the particular case at hand. Thus, in the evaluation of environmental impacts of several possible highway routes in Georgia, a group of experts met and agreed on weights to be assigned to effects on trees, water supplies, soil, etc., and used these weights in comparing policies (Odum, Zieman, Shugart, Bramlett, Ike, & Champlin, 1976). Similar judgments may also be made by consulting members of an affected community, if they are able to translate their judgments into numerical terms. Problems of dealing quantitatively with multiple criteria have been discussed by Keeney and Raiffa (1976) and Stokey and Zeckhauser (1978, pp. 117–130).

3. Presentation of multiple judgments in matrix form. An analyst in the role of adviser may leave the combination of criteria to the policymaker or to the citizen by presenting a table showing how he judges each alternative policy under consideration as it affects each of the distinct value criteria. Quade (1975, pp. 59–60) presents the results of an analysis of alternatives for air transportation in this way, attributing this "scorecard" presentation to Goeller. An example of such a presentation in qualitative terms, for various day-care strategies discussed below, is given in Table 1: another table of this type is presented by Gallagher in Chapter 2.

4. Direct consensual procedures. On the basis of such a table—or bypassing analysis, without it—members of an expert group, decision-making groups, or affected communities may discuss alternative policies and seek to attain consensus. At the extreme, this discussion represents the political process without analysis. As more information is introduced into the process, an aspect of analysis enters. As the judgment is broken down into parts ("analyzed" in the literal sense), presumably a more systematic and consistent judgment can be made.

Day Care as an Example

By the preceding treatment of valuative criteria, I have tried to illustrate further the sense in which policy analysis is a form of applied

TABLE 1: MULTIPLE-CRITERIA ASSESSMENT OF STRATEGIES RELATED TO DAY CARE

	Alternative strategies		
Criteria	**Federal subsidy of day care centers**	**Federal vouchers for day care for the poor**	**Income maintenance such as negative income tax**
Probable cost	Intermediate; raised by quality requirements, but limited in function	Least, because it is limited to one function, one group	Greatest, because it extends beyond child care
Employment of women (and productivity)	More	More	Less
Child development	Greatest	Intermediate	Least
Freedom of family choice for recipients	Moderate	Greater	Greatest
Incentive to work	Increased	Possible "notch" (disincentive)	Greatest for main earner; possibly negative for second earner
Stigma	Depends on conditions for eligibility	Possible	Small

ethics. There may well be a limited number of valuative criteria common to many problems of policy analysis concerning families and children, even though different analysts may weight these criteria differently.

One of the advantages of studying day-care policies as an example is that they seem to bring out a great many of the values on this common list (for an alternative list of criteria, see Greenblatt, 1977, pp. 143–145). Let me simply recapitulate them.

1. *Cost.* Further consideration of cost might also involve the type of tax from which funds were derived, whether progressive or regressive and including its effects on incentives, and the extent to which recipient families share in paying for programs.
2. *Equity.* We assume that proposed policies will satisfy the condition of horizontal equity, e.g., by treating similarly situated persons in various political units equally. Vertical equity is involved in:
   a. Transfer of resources from rich to poor;
   b. Imposition of disadvantages, such as stigma, on the recipient population.

   An additional aspect of horizontal equity is involved if we consider equity among *all* families, rich and poor, such as might be involved in advocacy of universal provision of day care to all who wished it.
3. *Effects on children.* These include effects on:
   a. Intelligence;
   b. Social and personality development;
   c. Health;
   d. Satisfaction and well-being.
4. *Effects on parents.* These include:
   a. Reduced burden of family responsibility (Is this burden a duty, or, conversely, do all families have a right to be relieved of it? We are here led to nonteleological criteria.);
   b. Learning through involvement with the providing institution;
   c. Self-realization and development through work and other activities;
   d. Equity in distribution of responsibilities between parents (e.g., to what extent is this the parents' responsibility?).
5. *Effects on the economy.* Here I include both production and competition with others for jobs.
6. *Effects on providers.* We do not usually weigh providers' welfare heavily because they are less numerous and usually less needy than other affected groups.

The above list combines value criteria (equity, economic efficiency, human development, well-being, duty) classified according to the persons receiving the effects. The aim of our systematic treatment has been to limit the list of criteria. I have omitted the criterion of "freedom of choice," since its meaning is difficult to specify clearly and it seems a *means* to the other criteria listed. I have omitted "number covered" because it is not merely coverage but the *effects* of coverage that we should consider, and presumably all the criteria listed call for quantitative judgments as to how great the overall effect of one policy or another may be. We may also sometimes consider effects per capita in comparison with costs per capita. I have omitted "need" because the relevant consequences of a policy have to do with how much it will alleviate need, i.e., how much change in some criterion variable other than "need" it is expected to bring about. I omit "effect on the family," considering this a means rather than an ultimate end.

ALTERNATIVES, MODELS, AND DECISIONS

Having chosen our ends, we may now proceed to the more conventional aspect of policy analysis—finding policies that are most conducive to these ends.

Alternatives

Analysis in a narrow sense is concerned with determining whether one alternative policy is likely to have better consequences than another. In a larger sense, however, it may involve the design of policies themselves. A possible limitation of my contribution here is that I shall neither design policies in our illustrative area—day care—nor describe them in full detail.[8]

A major ingredient of analysis is our knowledge of the causal relations between policies and their results. The simplified schemes that we use to represent these causal relations are models, which may be mathematical, verbal, or expressed in diagrams or physical representations (e.g., of a bridge that is to be built).

Yet, preliminary models or initial judgments as to the consequences of policies are essential in the design of policies or programs. The proposal of alternatives is based on the supposition (often derived from experience with previous programs) that they will accomplish our goals or produce valued consequences. To propose them thus requires a preliminary model of the causal relationships between policies and values; but these relations may then be analyzed further and more explicitly.

We must look widely for possible alternatives. An approach that can sometimes deceive us is the quest for the origins or etiology of problems. We often presume that only by getting at root causes can we genuinely solve problems; but those causes may be difficult or expensive to alter. Conceivably, we can act more effectively and expeditiously on the "symptoms." Thus, methadone maintenance does not completely "cure" heroin addicition, but it may be a viable and preferable alternative. As another example, sickle cell anemia is considered genetic in origin, but it can be treated with the aid of the chemical urea. Some inadequacies in child development may result from the income distribution produced by the labor market, but reform of the labor market is not the sole remedy for income inequality. The policy analyst must seek alternative policies wherever they can be found.

In the realm of day care, I shall first list a few general alternatives or strategies and then indicate the great detail in which particular programs may vary.[9]

1. Do nothing or allow the status quo to continue. This is always a baseline for comparison with other policies (MacRae & Wilde, 1979, Ch. 4) and includes the projection of anticipated trends as they would develop in the absence of new policies;
2. Regulate certain modes of day care without subsidizing them;
3. Subsidize day care and impose standards as a condition of subsidy;
4. Provide for vertical equity more generally and directly through child-care vouchers or a negative income tax;
5. Gather more relevant information through experiments, either with policy interventions or instead of such interventions (MacRae & Wilde, 1979, Chs. 4 & 7).

A list of alternatives relating to existing national policies has also been given by the Congressional Budget Office (1978).

I stated above that "day care" is a set of policy alternatives. It is not the only alternative because it can vary along numerous dimensions, and some activities not called "day care" may nevertheless perform the same functions. A number of such dimensions are shown in Table 2, based on an outline presented by Haskins and Gallagher to the Bush Seminar, University of North Carolina at Chapel Hill. The number of dimensions of variation in Table 2 is so great that analysis of all of them—even neglecting their possible interactions—seems impossible if high standards of scientific inference are to be maintained. We should, of course, be able to combine various analyses and rely on previous studies; and if we assumed a specific role in connection with particular policy choices, some dimensions would be eliminated as politically infeasible. But in building the analytical literature we should try to contribute to a general perspective that will be useful to analysts confronted with a variety of specific problems—assuming that the problems and the models are sufficiently permanent to make such a general effort worthwhile. In this sample analysis I shall emphasize the five general alternatives listed in the preceding paragraph.

Models of Day Care: General Structure and Four Submodels

Our models of the effects of day care must take into account not only policy variables and their valued outcomes, but also uncontrollable

TABLE 2: DIMENSIONS OF VARIATION AMONG POSSIBLE CHILD CARE PROGRAMS

Characteristics of day-care program itself		
1. Minimum age of entry; age distribution 2. Characteristics of physical setting 3. Content of curriculum 4. Stability of caregivers	5. Adult-child ratios 6. Group size 7. Safety requirements 8. Staff characteristics 9. Staff training	10. Parent involvement (see below) 11. Supplemental services 12. Criteria for admission: family income, need for special treatment or care
Parent participation		
1. Curriculum decisions 2. Set regulations governing center operation 3. Control expenditures	4. Hire and fire staff 5. Visit the center 6. Participate in program	
Types of child care		
1. Center based 2. Family day-care home 3. Out-of-home individual arrangement with relative 4. Out-of-home individual arrangement with nonrelative 5. In-home individual arrangement with relative 6. In-home individual arrangement with nonrelative		
Supplemental services that might be offered		
1. Health care: immunizations, checkups, family care 2. Speech, hearing, vision testing	3. Dental care 4. Psychological assessment 5. Family counseling	
Role of government if it intervenes		
1. Provide subsidies to child care providers 2. Direct provision of care by established government run centers 3. Regulate and monitor all or some out-of-home child care arrangements 4. Provide combinations of the above		

or nonpolicy variables that interact with the policy variables. The state of the labor market, for example, may affect the employment opportunities for parents and their potential contribution to the national product. Haskins, Farran, and Sanders (1978), for example, have argued that: "Day care in the United States has tended to peak during times when women were needed in the work force—usually during major wars" (p.76). Thus, the policies we recommend might also depend on such nonpolicy variables. In the shorter run (years or decades), the need for day care may vary with the state of the economy; in the longer run (generations), it may vary with the nature of the society for which children are to be prepared (Fein & Clarke-Stewart, 1973, p. 147). Effects may also vary with the child's age or social class.

To organize and simplify model construction in relation to policy variables, I suggest four distinct types of submodels—three relating to the effects of day care on children and one relating to effects on parents:

1. Submodels of the "social and economic markets for child care." At any time there is a distribution of child care among various modes of care, from families to informal arrangements to centers and schools. We need to predict the response of this distribution to government policies and other influences. A subsidy, for example, that increases the supply of one mode relative to others, can change this distribution. When a new policy favoring a particular mode of care is instituted, however, we cannot simply assume that children will move from home care into the favored mode. Rather, some will move from care by relatives or neighbors into the new mode, and possibly as a result other children will move from home care to care by neighbors. This approach flows from economic reasoning and seems necessary to take into account some of the indirect effects of proposed policies. Note that the use of a marketlike submodel is not a matter of taste here. Noneconomists cannot avoid it by saying that they are seeking noneconomic values. No matter what values are sought, we need to know how many children (or adults) will be receiving them, and we must thus try to predict how many families will make use of one or another mode of care.
2. Cross-mode comparisons for effects on children and others. Such comparisons would predict the effects on children of their transfer from one mode of care to another; e.g., from home to center. Ideally, we need to make such comparisons for all the modes that are induced by models of type (1), but we do not appear to have nearly the requisite amount of information. For the comparisons attempted, it is helpful if we can assume that each mode has a single standard or average form. For example, as an approximation a "center" of a given type can be regarded as having a standard amount of state regulation; similar assumptions may be made for each mode compared, if the studies available provide us with this information.
3. We must also, however, examine the effects on children of variation in characteristics *within* any single mode of care, such as "centers." Similarly, a mode designated as "family care in a single-parent family" may encompass considerable variation.
4. Another market submodel concerns the employment and other activities of family members and others who are freed from child care. Their employment depends on the job market. A policy such as a subsidy to day-care centers will have effects on parental employment that are contingent on the state of the economy or on the relationship between parental job skills and local demand for them.

These four submodels, combined, constitute a framework for organizing relevant information. In considering each in greater detail, I would like to emphasize that the following sections are written from the perspective of a generalist in policy analysis rather than of an expert in child-care policy and related research. For practical utility, this perspective must be supplemented by expertise in both the relevant disciplines and the existing programs and politics.

Social and Economic Markets for Child Care

If we wish to assess the effects of a public policy that supports one particular mode of child care, we must estimate how many children are moved into that mode from other modes. In addition, we must try to estimate the effects of the "chains" of transfer of activities that occur: if a center is established in one neighborhood, not only may children move to the center from care by homes, relatives, and neighbors, but other children may then be able to receive care from the caretakers whose services become available. These former caretakers may also shift to other activities; we consider this possibility in the final submodel of "effects on parents and other caretakers."

I refer to "social" markets here, because nonpriced transfers of responsibility and activity are important for day care. Rearrangements of activities within the family and with relatives and neighbors need to be studied, if we are to predict some of the indirect effects of policies. The most useful information for this purpose consists of panel surveys conducted with the same respondents over time. In addition, theoretical reasoning may be helpful. A baseline for development of these models, however, is knowledge of the distribution of child care among modes at a given time. Haskins (1979) summarizes several surveys by pointing out that "a large majority of Americans who need child care use informal and non-market forms of care" (p.3).

In comparing day-care subsidies with general income transfers to the poor, for example, we need to know the possible reactions of families of various types. Presumably, if day care is subsidized, more families will take advantage of it than if they were to receive an equivalent amount of money. When monetary subsidies were provided in the New Jersey Negative Income Tax Experiment, however, the earnings and employment of women in two-parent families *declined* as a result of the income supplement; on balance, they moved *out* of the labor force rather than into it. This finding strongly suggests that for families of this sort, when new resources were made available in 1967–70, most families preferred to use these resources in such a way as to *decrease* the demand for child care outside the home (Pechman & Timpane, 1975, p.82). It is possible, however, that those families in which mothers remained in the labor force used some of the increased resources for day care.

Robins and Spiegelman (1978) have analyzed data from the Seattle and Denver Income Maintenance Experiments to provide an econometric model of the demand for child care. Studying two-parent families in which the mother was working (and thus not including those mothers who had left the labor force), they show the effects of family earnings, numbers and ages of children, and the presence of other adults in the family on demand for formal and informal market care. The demand for informal market care, for example, is increased by mother's earnings and decreased by the presence of alternate caretakers in the family. Studies of this kind can be extremely valuable in assessing the expected effects of policies, especially if they are extended to include single-parent families.

A market-oriented study dealing with parents' choices among modes of day care was carried out by Hill (1978). Reviewing models of the demand for child care in relation to price and other variables, Hill concludes that: "Households with working mothers reveal their preferences by purchasing at-home or informal market care for reasons that are economically rational" (p. 540). He finds little evidence that the market for day care operates in a fashion warranting government intervention: "The general consensus in terms of cognitive development or socialization is . . . that the benefits to society of publicly provided day care services are, at best, quite small" (p. 543). He does acknowledge that public policies may further equity—a criterion outside the economic framework of market efficiency—and that federal standardization of child care may be justified. But on the basis of current evidence, he proposes that "federal policy should be essentially neutral with regard to the promotion of one mode of care over another" (p. 544). Hill favors child-care vouchers, which permit a more restricted type of consumer choice than direct income supplements do and suggests that the government also provide information to consumers.

Cross-Mode Comparisons: Effects on Children

This aspect of the model—comparative effects of types of care on children—has been of particular interest to specialists in child development. From sampling this literature, I shall conjecture that we do not know enough to make clear distinctions among the effects of various modes of child care. This inference results from (1) a belief that for policy choice we need to demonstrate effects in experiments that resemble the proposed policy as closely as possible; and (2) a preference given to the free-market model by many policy analysts.

Care by fathers, grandmothers, other relatives, and nonrelatives outside licensed centers is widespread. As Fein and Clarke-Stewart (1973) observe: "There seems to be little evidence that these existing patterns [modes] are in and of themselves harmful and no evidence that they promote or retard the child's development. There are simply no comparative data on quality of care in noncenter, private arrangements vs. day care centers" (p. 44). Concerning the effects of day care on the mother-child relationship, Fein and Clarke-Stewart state: "Children who experience separation from the mother for some part of the day have not been studied extensively. Two . . . studies . . . suggest that arrangements of this kind do not necessarily lead to disturbances in the child's social attachments" (p. 64). Observations of this kind lead me to consider these noncenter modes of care as largely equivalent to parental care in their effects on children.[10]

One extensive study by Golden and his colleagues (1978) compares modes of child care in situations of actual practice. This study examined children in group, family, and home care over their first 3 years of life and considered a variety of outcome or criterion variables. Assignment of children to modes was not random, but the study made use of control groups stratified on variables such as income. Some representative findings were superior nutrition for children in group day care relative to family day care; superior Stanford-Binet IQ scores at the age of 3 years for children in group day care over family day care; nonsignificant differences between children in family day care and home-reared children on standard intelligence tests; and nonsignificant differences among groups in the three modes (group, family, and home care) in "everyday use of language or cognitive functioning outside of a test situation" (Golden et al., 1978, p. 130). This is the sort of study that seems most directly relevant to policy choice among modes of day care. But because such studies seem rare, I shall stress the lack of evidence rather than its presence in my recommendations.

An important variable affecting child development seems to be the continuity of caregiving persons (Fein & Clarke-Stewart, 1973, pp. 143–145). One means to assure greater continuity, and at the same time to give parents greater information as to what they are receiving, is to encourage care by relatives or neighbors. Here, the monitoring function is assumed by the parents rather than by a profession or the state. Perhaps this is a proper location of that function, except for those few parents who can be judged incompetent to choose.

There seem to be numerous inconclusive findings as to the magnitude and duration of the effects of day care on children's personalities. This lack of positive differences seems particularly acute when we limit our view to studies of actual public programs rather than academic or optimal conditions. As Ramey (1978) points out, "Just because . . . desirable consequences *can* occur for children in group day care does not mean that they *will* occur" (p. 12). I shall thus base my recommendations on the assumption that some of the major cross-mode differences are small.

From this assumption we are led to define some modes of day care as essentially equivalent to parental care. What are those modes? I find it hard to say precisely, but I suspect they are the modes chosen by competent parents, with adequate resources and information about their options, who cannot or do not wish to provide full-time child care themselves. Most of these modes require monetary payment by the parents. The type of policies I recommend center on making resources and information available to facilitate parental choice.

I do not wish to rule out the use of innovative modes of day care, but would stress that they should have the full support of the involved parents and that, if possible, these innovations should generate useful data for their subsequent evaluation (MacRae & Wilde, 1979, Ch. 6).

In advocating a marketlike model for the support of various modes of day care, I follow an economic approach. A contrasting view, put forward by Titmuss (1971) in his analysis of blood donations, resembles that of many child-care professionals who consider facilities paid for by parents as inferior. Careful study is needed to show the conditions under which they are inferior; economists consider the economizing motive a virtue rather than a vice.

An economic analysis by Weber, Foster, and Weikart (1978) of a preschool project in Ypsilanti, Michigan, for economically disadvantaged black children, does suggest that a 1-year project can be justified in these terms. These findings (discussed in Chap. 1) appear to resemble those of other studies, in that the effects of day care on intellectual development are more pronounced for children from low-income families than from middle-income families (Haskins, Farran, & Sanders, 1978). If this turns out to be a general finding, then this additional effectiveness would support vertical equity as a reason for making organized day-care programs especially available to the poor.

Intramode Comparisons: Structure and Regulation

We have simplified the problem of analysis by first comparing modes of care such as parental care, care by relatives, neighborhood care, and center care. But one of the major dimensions of policy variation concerns the possible differences *within* these modes, especially for centers. When public funds are expended directly on child care, public authorities can claim the right to regulate them—including specification of the numerous parameters listed in Table 2. Even within privately marketed modes of care, regulation is possible to prevent fraud or to place minimum limits on space, safety, or staff-child ratios. Conceivably, we might also be interested in differences among types of care within the mode "care by relatives"; though not subject to public regulations in general, they might be affected indirectly by public policies.

The enactment of Title XX of the Social Security Act speeded the codification of standards for day care (Cooper, 1977). Numerous academic experts and government administrators had participated in proposing a 1972 revision of the Federal Interagency Day Care Requirements (Cohen & Zigler, 1977). Yet, in an extensive reference dealing with such requirements (Dept. of Health, Education, and Welfare, 1977), there was little evidence of systematic research up to that time concerning the effects of particular regulations, or of their enforcement, on children. As Bronfenbrenner and his colleagues (1977) pointed out, "restriction of research to high-quality center-based care prevents generalization of findings to the kind and quality of day care available to most families" (p. 62). Nevertheless, Meyer (1977) has argued that "lower child-staff ratios tend to produce children who are quieter and less aggressive and who perform well on standardized tests" (p. 85). He added that the ratio alone may not be determinative of the effect, but that the overall size of the group of children and staff may also be relevant.

In response to this shortage of academic research on intramode comparisons, and to debate about federal day-care regulations, an extensive national study of the effects of center characteristics was initiated in 1974 by the Office of Child Development. A summary of the results (Abt Associates, 1979) showed advantages for smaller groups, higher staff/child ratios, and more child-related training for caregivers.

The fact that this study was carried out by contract to a nonacademic, policy analysis organization suggests that we are dealing with an important gap between academic and policy research. It is a good initial strategy, and one preferred in academic research, to see whether a new program works under highly favorable and controlled circumstances; but to recommend policies we must make the program work under *actual* circumstances, including systematic variations in administration and implementation. Engineers know this; basic scientists usually do not.

Research on the effects of inspection and enforcement also seems difficult to find; it may not fit the theoretical concerns of basic social science disciplines. It is, however, part of a broad methodological aspect of policy analysis, related to law enforcement generally (MacRae, 1980).

Effects on Parents and Other Caretakers

For some proponents of day care, its major goal is the freeing of women to work for pay. But as Woolsey (1977) asks: "(1) Is the public interest served in macroeconomic terms, by inducing more women to join the labor force? (2) Is the provision of day care by the government an important prerequisite to mothers, and especially welfare recipients, becoming employed?" (p. 137). She concludes that "the answer to the first question is far from obvious," and that "what matters most (for women's employment) is the existence of a job—when that is available, most mothers find some way to cope with the child care problems" (pp. 137–138).

The question of the availability of jobs may not, however, have the same answer in the long as in the short run. Conceivably, the economy can ultimately make use of productive persons, as it does in absorbing immigrants or the population growth from generation to generation. Women have indeed moved into the American labor force during the twentieth century, but this change may not correspond entirely to a net gain in production. Eventually, there may be a compensating move of men out of the labor market and into household production. To predict whether productive women can enter the work force without undesirably causing others to move out requires further economic analysis.

Policies aimed at creating job opportunities for women obviously have as goals greater equity between the sexes in the workplace, within the family, and in other social relationships. They may, however, increase inequity between families, if the capacity for greater, combined family earnings is enhanced in upper social strata more than in lower and leads to greater disparities in individual well-being between families in different strata. Payments from one family to another for child care can compensate only partially for this inequity. We must then seek to correct the added inequity by taxation. We often think of day care as making the difference between a mother's (or father's) working and not working. If a job is not available, of course, the mother may not work even if day care is available. But conversely, some mothers work in the absence of publicly aided day care; let us consider these cases separately in order to see the effects of day care on economic production.

If day care permits the mother's employment, we can simplify the analysis by making the approximation that only the mother's activities are changed by the availability of day care; the father does not adjust his activities. This assumption is exactly true for single-parent families. We then ask whether the net "production" of the mother is greater with or without the availability of day care. Without day care, the mother produces "quality of children" that may be compared with the same variable under day care. With day care, the mother works at a paid job, produces, earns, and buys services; the social cost is similar if day-care services are paid for from public funds. We then ask whether more valuable things are produced in the latter situation. Our judgment may vary, for example, with the number of children. A mother with special occupational skills may well make a greater social contribution by working for pay than by staying home with her children; but this comparison should include the less tangible, long-run value of child development.

An alternate viewpoint is that of the family that does not change its job arrangements but still avails itself of day care. In a wealthy family the wife might take advantage of the availability of a governess or a nursery school to devote more time to charitable and social activities. Of more concern to us for policy purposes, however, is the two-job family with flexible hours or part-time work in which day care relieves the stress, usually incident on the wife, of increased effort and reduced leisure when a job is combined with a traditional household role. Publicly supported day care may provide somewhat more time for the wife by reducing the need for earnings than full family payment for day care would permit. Weber and his colleagues (1978) synthesize the two viewpoints by placing a monetary value on parents' released time, regardless of its use.

The policy question is whether the additional equity and well-being within a two-job family justify the use of public funds for day care. As I have suggested, the question of need arises more clearly when the family is forced to hold two jobs because of poverty and when the stress falls on children who cannot be cared for adequately.

Not only parents but also other caretakers may be influenced by day-care policies. If children are moved away from one mode of care, other activities will be substituted by the people who formerly cared for those children. Some of these substitutions will occur through entry into the job market, others through the substitution of a new job for paid child care, and others through a shift to unpaid household production or leisure. The converse is true when a new mode of care is encouraged by public policy; some advocates of subsidies for child care have seen them as a means to employ community members who need jobs.

RECOMMENDATIONS

When recommendations must be made, one's policy analysis often seems incomplete; such an attitude is common among social scientists who must make practical decisions (Braybrooke & Lindblom, 1970, p. 3). But since the materials needed for a complete analysis ramify indefinitely into various fields and include information yet to be gathered, and since this situation is characteristic of the process of policy analysis, I shall proceed. Another option might be to present information and allow someone else to make the decision; but in the citizen role we are responsible for decision, not simply information. To present only the information of which we were certain might well bias our recommendation to the neglect of considerations that are intangible but equally important.

The most difficult question to answer here concerns the type of information needed for policy recommendations. Fein and Clarke-Stewart (1973) summarize scholarly research and point out the gaps between it and what is needed for policy judgments. Steinfels (1973) bases recommendations on a "liberal" sense of what children need, bolstered by examples drawn from personal observation. The latter case is persuasive; but I choose not to be persuaded, because of the apparent absence of both systematic experiments and demonstrations that particular detailed policies will work. Thus, on the Mondale-Brademas bill vetoed by former President Nixon in 1971, my skepticism leads me to side with the veto, and against the liberal majority in Congress and groups concerned with child care. But policy analysis calls for hard evidence rather than merely a sympathetic heart. In the period when we do not have new policies for day care, or even if an income-support policy should be enacted, research on the effects of day-care policies can continue.

I start, as indicated earlier, from the apparent shortage of conclusive findings regarding the effects of actual day-care arrangements on child development. A cautious approach would therefore be to allow families to choose modes of day care among their other options for spending; to try to regulate extreme instances in which parents leave their children without sufficient concern for the children's welfare; to encourage the provision of accurate information to parents about available opportunities for day care; and to stress income inequality among families as a major concern. Such an approach leads toward a general strategy of income maintenance; but if we should judge that day care has special benefits for low-income groups, it might also lead to limited initial subsidies, supplemented by child-care vouchers, for those types of child care found to be especially beneficial for poor children.[11]

I am not inclined to favor publicly supported day care as a right for all families, since families that are better off can pay for it themselves as well as choose whether they wish to spend their income in this way (Bane, 1976, pp. 84–85). I hope that the element of stigma that might result from singling out the poor for aid can be kept to a minimum by administrative procedures such as have been used in the various income-maintenance experiments.

An apparently undesirable feature of many proposals for day-care legislation (as well as for policies for the elderly) has been an insistence on unnecessarily high standards. In North Carolina, for example, the quality of care in public day-care centers is far superior to that in private centers (Abt Associates, 1978). Legislators and members of the public who are distrustful of unregulated spending choices by the poor seem to have sided with professionals and commercial providers who advocate "quality" or seek profits. The result is to deemphasize care by neighbors, relatives, and other nonprofessional, noninstitutional providers. The interests of large numbers of parents, contrasted with the smaller number who can take advantage of high-quality centers, seem to have been neglected in this political process. One exception to this tendency has been the recent enactment of a tax credit for parents who pay grandparents for child care.

Because of my reservations about existing and proposed day-care programs, I am led to recommend policies that will aid poor families to make their own decisions about day care in relation to their other perceived needs. My main recommendation is thus for a form of income maintenance, probably a negative income tax. This is a recommendation for a general strategy rather than for a highly specific program; but at least examples of this strategy have been tried experimentally. Some opponents of President Carter's income-maintenance legislation argued that a more incremental approach to income maintenance, making use of existing programs such as Food Stamps, may be more workable (see Strauss, Ch. 6). If resources can be supplied to poor families in this way so that they have the option but not the requirement to make use of day care, this would seem a step in the right direction.

In the meantime, experiments connecting child development with policy-manipulable variables should be encouraged. Findings on cognitive development (education) seem more encouraging than those on personality and social development. In spite of the controversy over the evaluation of Head Start, experimental programs of this sort seem desirable. The remaking of new generations in a pattern not chosen by parents, however, seems both difficult to predict and politically infeasible in the short run. As Fein and Clarke-Stewart (1973) put it: "There is no evidence that the solution to the problems of the family lies in group care of children per se" (p. 155).

I stress parental choice while noting that parents will not always choose what is best for their children. They may retain a child in a limited and parochial culture, perpetuating cultural pluralism but restricting the child's capacity for growth and mobility. They may also contribute to the development of children who are loyal to dissident groups at odds with other groups in society. They may also deal with gifted children only as "problems" rather than in terms of their potentialities.

My recommendation is thus for a negative income tax in which the level of support increases with the number of children. However, this is only one of several broad alternatives for income support in connection with child care, a more extensive set of alternatives has been examined in a cross-national study by Kamerman (1978). Dealing with aid for mothers of children under age 3, she distinguishes four major policy options:

1. Income-maintenance policies (direct cash transfers), to replace income foregone if a parent withdraws from the labor force and remains at home to care for a child;
2. Subsidized provision of out-of-home child care services for the children of working parents;
3. Income-maintenance policies (direct cash transfers) to permit parents to (a) purchase child care while they continue to work, or (b) substitute for earned income while remaining at home;
4. A combination of both income-maintenance policies and subsidized child-care services, provided sequentially.

My recommendation is for the third type of policy, which Kamerman analyzes for France, but with a negative income tax aspect rather than simple family allowances. A possible extension toward the fourth, characteristic of Sweden, might be considered.

Parents' opportunity to enter the work force seems again to be best left to family choices. The variety of market situations over time, and of family choices across families, seems too great for policymakers not to allow choice and readjustment of the system over time. Institutions must be able to expand and contract if possible.

The issues into which I have been led here—in effect, a redefinition of the problem—are largely issues of equity. The main type of equity that seems to me to call for public policy intervention is vertical equity between groups differing in income or resources. This is why I have stressed a policy of income transfers, such as a negative income tax.

A second type of equity concerns special burdens that individuals or families bear because of no fault of their own, such as the absence of a spouse or the presence of handicapped children. The ADC policy at its inception was viewed in this light, and only later did it appear that the absence of a "man in the house" could result from voluntary concealment or that the policy could contribute to family dissolution. Conceivably, a similar problem could arise in the concealment of income under a negative income tax policy.

By further extension, the mere presence of children seems now to be considered an inequitable burden that deserves compensation by government. Maternity leaves are increasingly provided for this reason—presumably because they tend to equalize the opportunities of women and men at work.

When we extend this reasoning to the care of children, however, we may meet the counter argument that families should allocate child-care responsibilities among family members themselves. If a woman has agreed to marry with the understanding that she will care for the children, it may not be government's responsibility to alter the marriage contract. If couples agree to divide child care in whatever manner suits them, then the question of equity relates to comparison among families, not between the sexes. Day care is then a provision for aid to families with young children relative to other families. It is an effort to equalize the burden of child care between families with more and those with fewer young children, and perhaps also to equalize burdens over the life cycle. For parents who enter the labor market, the temporary occupation of child-rearing may then be partly exchanged for longer-term accumulation and for the use of human capital in paid work.

We then encounter the paradox that families with more children must be given more support and that conceivably families may be thereby encouraged to have more children. France adopted the policy of *allocations familiales* partly in order to increase her population, but if it is possible to take a world perspective, such policies do not seem proper in the world today. Perhaps the pronatalist implications of such policies can be counteracted by other policies to reduce fertility, but I cannot propose a solution to that problem here. The question of support for children is important not only for human welfare but also for symbolic politics because illegitimacy and teenage pregnancies are seen as related to "welfare" policies.

The introduction of the analyst into the policy process seems to place a burden of proof on the proponents of social service programs—a burden that has not always existed in the past. It creates a counterweight to the informed judgment of the professional provider of services. In higher education, faculty members who are providers strongly resist such a burden of proof. Yet any profession claiming to produce an effect through service delivery should *invite* measurement of this effect as well as accept public questioning as to whether the effect can be produced in ways other than by professional services.

My recommendation of a negative income tax is encouraged by the fact that this policy has been partially enacted and evaluated extensively. The various income-maintenance experiments provide us with information rarely provided by policy-relevant academic research. They seem to show that low-income recipients use their supplementary income constructively. Neither the fears of conservatives (that recipients will stop working) nor those of professional providers (that recipient families will not know how to provide for their own needs) seem justified. The increased rates of family dissolution shown by the Seattle and Denver Experiments need to be considered, but I hope their undesirable effects can be kept to a minimum.

In the longer run, government may be able to enlarge the options of families who receive negative income tax support. Local day-care centers of various kinds in low-income areas, for example, may receive partial subsidies. But they are more likely to be monitored by families who use them—for efficiency as well as quality—if the families partially pay for them with their own money; experiments on this question are needed. Programs of this sort should be evaluated once they are in place; and comparative randomized designs will still be needed. Randomization is unfortunately inconsistent with free parental choice among modes (except for the choice to volunteer); but both sorts of comparison, based on families' choice of modes and on experimentation, are desirable. A significant program of randomized experimentation has been carried out at the Frank Porter Graham Child Development Center at UNC-Chapel Hill (Ramey & Haskins, in press).

I have stressed *informed* parental choice in recommending a negative income tax. Information may come from various sources; knowledge about care provided by relatives, neighbors, and existing day-care centers is developed from experience. Governments may supply additional information to parents, starting at a child's birth. But we need also to be able to move beyond what is customary and to innovate. How are parents to know whether to send their children to a new type of day-care center? Can we leave this to economic enterpreneurship? Such entrepreneurship often appeals first to the wealthy. But if social innovations, unlike material technology, are differentially suited to different social classes, we cannot expect them to "trickle down" the economic scale much like the automobile or television. Some ways of suggesting new possibilities to low-income parents are still needed. Perhaps the history of innovations such as Head Start will be instructive in this respect.

It is also possible, however, for professionals to argue against parental choice—especially when parents must pay.[12] Steinfels (1973) contends that day-care centers funded largely by parent-paid fees would "almost certainly [result] in custodial centers with minimum standards for staff ratio and programming" (p. 18). She also criticizes a "nursery school center" whose "educational program is geared toward producing good behavior rather than cognitive development," even though from a parent's point of view such a center "could appear quite attractive" for this and other reasons (pp. 122–124). She also expresses skepticism (p. 130) that for-profit day care has maintained quality and parent influence.

While favoring freedom of parental choice, I believe this choice may also be channeled in directions that promote vertical equity. Not only a negative income tax, but also the location and character of partially subsidized centers may have this effect. Researchers have given special attention to programs affording stimulation to deprived infants (Haskins, Finkelstein, & Stedman, 1978). If some encouragement can be given to programs of this sort, equity may be promoted (but see Herzog, cited in Bronfenbrenner, 1975).

The voluntary participation of families in publicly supported day-care programs may depend on the major purpose claimed for them. Even though I have tried to avoid the selection of a single, dominant goal and have advocated the guidance of policy choice by broad ethical systems, in considering feasibility I must return to the question of goals. In this respect, an "educational" goal has some advantages. If we are concerned with aid to low-income groups, we may be able to encourage their participation by stressing formal education, which is sought in day care more by lower-class than upper-class mothers (Fein & Clarke-Stewart, 1973, p. 173). Stress on education rather than "cultural therapy" may also be more acceptable to minority political organizations. Ultimately, however, the precise content of the education cannot be neglected; an important goal must be the capacity to function as a producer and citizen in the larger society.

Voluntary participation may also depend, however, on parents' resources, skills, and time. Klaus and Gray (1968) have perceptively discussed the difficulty of involving overburdened lower-class parents in intervention programs. The same difficulties may prevent them from actively controlling, in a participatory or a market sense, the centers in which they leave their children. For such parents, professionals may hope to substitute their own judgment; but this judgment must still be subjected to public scrutiny.

POLITICAL FEASIBILITY

The political feasibility of a policy proposal must always be assessed in specific terms, relating to that proposal and the contending forces at a particular time. Nevertheless, there are common elements shared by various policy proposals in a given policy issue area (Meltsner, 1972). For the national arena of policy for children over the last several decades, Steiner (1976) provides a survey of relevant organizations inside and outside government. Interested groups have ranged over the years from middle-class matrons to advocates for inner-city youth. More recently, advocacy groups for children with special illnesses, as well as the handicapped and the gifted, have emerged. Professionals have played a part, as have representatives of institutions providing services.

A contemporary perspective is provided by Munger (1979) who points out that "family policy has become increasingly a subject of attention at the same time that childlessness becomes more commonplace" (p. 5). Analyzing trends through the 1970s, he shows that the proportion of respondents to a national survey who were married males living in traditional households declined from 23% to 15%, while that of adults living alone increased from 10% to 19% (Munger, 1979, p. 3). Such trends define not only the conditions under which people may benefit from public policies (which we have considered so far), but also the support that policies may expect to receive. In the recent past a dominant factor seems to have been concern about the possible dissolution of the family, rather than a simple erosion of support for that institution.

The conditions for political feasibility of a negative income tax are illustrated by recent controversies over similar legislation. I shall not try to specify legislation in detail except to say that President Nixon's Family Assistance Plan (FAP), introduced in Congress first in 1969, is an example. The political experience of this bill, modified for current political circumstances, should provide us with a perspective on feasibility.[13]

A general survey of the politics of American welfare programs is given by Gilbert (1975) and by Strauss (Ch. 6). More specifically, the political history of FAP has been treated in detail by Moynihan (1973). He describes the origins of the bill in the advent of a new administration, in criticism of previous Democratic programs, and in an increasing skepticism of the contributions of professional deliverers of services to the poor. Success in the House of Representatives was obtained in part by skillful use of symbolism by Nixon, who portrayed an income-transfer policy as symbolically conservative. Wilbur Mills's conversion to support of the bill apparently assured its success. In the Senate, Moynihan and the bill's managers apparently let down their guard and were taken unawares by a devastating criticism launched in the Finance Committee by John J. Williams and Russell Long.

Could this scenario have improved in subsequent years? Several proposals for a negative income tax were aired under the Ford and Carter administrations with less success than Nixon's FAP. Moynihan felt that it had almost passed under Nixon, but as a Senator he subsequently swung to advocacy of New York interests more than of a negative income tax, which would have greatly aided the Southern poor. Possibly, the bill had advantages as well as disadvantages from Nixon's support: middle-of-the-road Republicans loyal to Nixon voted for a bill that they would not have supported if it had been proposed by a Democratic president. Mills's influence as Chairman of the Ways and Means Committee has no parallel now. Possibly the negative predictions of Cavala and Wildavsky (1970) were not so far off the mark as Moynihan had thought.

An important difficulty of the negative income tax was that it called for support by an ideologically central group in Congress against the two extremes. This difficulty was accentuated by the fact that the Southern poor, an important potential clientele, were not being represented by their Congressmen; there was no interest group for interregional equity. Efforts to gain support at one end of the political spectrum tended to lose it at the other. Such a voting pattern is relatively unusual in organized legislatures (MacRae, 1970). Thus, a dedicated coalition of supporters based on conventional liberal-conservative lines may be hard to construct. The passage of such a bill—even without any provisions for partial subsidy of local experiments in day care for the poor—may depend on the support of a politically skilled and dedicated president.

Since the Nixon proposal, we have seen additional efforts for federal support of day care itself and increasing support (under the Carter Administration) of federally regulated day care. It is interesting to speculate as to why such policies may have had a greater appeal to legislators than an income guarantee. One argument is that taxpayers, and therefore legislators, prefer to require the poor to be given specific goods and services rather than income. The reasoning supporting this preference may derive either from a distrust of the capacity of the poor to make prudent decisions, or from a broader distrust of governmental use of taxes for redistribution of income, related to the right of earners to dispose of their own income (Plattner, 1979). I have not included considerations of this sort in my criteria for analysis.

In combination with this concern on the part of taxpayers, however, there may be a related one on the part of professionals and providers, which would combine with that of taxpayers to lead to regulated center-based care as contrasted with the simple provision of money to families. While taxpayers may distrust poor families with respect to their morality and prudence, professionals and providers may distrust their capacity to choose quality care. The result may well be that the less organized advocates of free family choice are overcome by a combination of public moral feeling and professional concern for "quality." Alternatively, the professionals may ally themselves with liberals in favoring generous, but regulated, funds for day-care centers—even though the desirability of regulated day care has not been sufficiently demonstrated by research.

REFERENCES

Abt Associates. *A study of center-based day care in North Carolina.* Cambridge, Mass.: Author, 1978.

Abt Associates. *Children at the center: Summary findings and policy implications of the national day care study.* Cambridge, Mass.: Author, 1979.

Arrow, K. J. *Social choice and individual values* (2nd ed.). New Haven, Conn.: Yale Univ. Press, 1962.

Bane, M. J. *Here to stay: American families in the twentieth century.* New York: Basic Books, 1976.

Ben-David, J. *The scientist's role in society.* Englewood Cliffs, N.J.: Prentice-Hall, 1971.

Bradburn, N. *The structure of psychological well-being.* Chicago: Aldine, 1969.

Braybrooke, D., & Lindblom, C. E. *A strategy of decision.* New York: Free Press, 1970.

Bronfenbrenner, U. Is early intervention effective? In M. Guttentag & E. L. Struening (Eds.), *Handbook of evaluation research* (Vol. 2). Beverly Hills, Calif.: Sage, 1975.

Bronfenbrenner, U., Belsky, J., & Steinberg, L. Day care in context: An ecological perspective on research and public policy. In *Policy issues in day care: Summaries of 21 papers.* Washington, D.C.: Dept. of Health, Education, and Welfare, Center for Systems and Program Development, November, 1977.

Campbell, A., Converse, P. E.., & Rodgers, W. L. *The quality of American life.* New York: Russell Sage Foundation, 1976.

Carter, G. W. Measurement of need. In N. A. Polansky (Ed.), *Social work research*. Chicago: Univ. of Chicago Press, 1966.

Cavala, B., & Wildavsky, A. The political feasibility of income by right. *Public Policy*, 1970, *18*, 321–354.

Cohen, D. J., & Zigler, E. Federal day care standards: Rationale and recommendations. *American Journal of Orthopsychiatry*, 1977, *47*, 456–465.

Congressional Budget Office. *Children and preschool: Options for federal support.* Washington, D.C.: U.S. Govt. Printing Office, 1978.

Cooper, S. P. History of federal interagency day care requirements. In *Policy issues in day care: Summaries of 21 papers.* Washington, D.C.: Dept. of Health, Education, and Welfare, Center for Systems and Program Development, November, 1977.

Crain, R. L., & Weisman, C. S. *Discrimination, personality, and achievement: A survey of northern blacks.* New York: Seminar Press, 1972.

Department of Health, Education, and Welfare (Center for Systems and Program Development). *Policy issues in day care: Summaries of 21 papers.* Washington, D.C.: Author, November, 1977.

Edelman, M. *The symbolic uses of politics.* Urbana, Ill.: Univ. of Illinois Press, 1964.

Edelman, M. *Politics as symbolic action: Mass arousal and quiescence.* Chicago: Markham, 1971.

Fein, G. G., & Clarke-Stewart, A. *Day care in context.* New York: Wiley, 1973.

Gallagher, J. J. Planning for early childhood programs for exceptional children. *Journal of Special Education*, 1976, *10*, 171–177.

Gates, B. L. *Needs-based budgeting.* Paper presented at annual meeting of The American Political Science Association, San Francisco, 1975.

Gilbert, C. E. Welfare policy. In F. I. Greenstein & N. W. Polsby (Eds.), *Handbook of political science.* Reading, Mass.: Addison-Wesley, 1975.

Golden, M., Rosenbluth, L., Grossi, M. T., Policare, H. J., Freeman, H, & Brownlee, E. M. *The New York City infant day care study.* New York: Medical and Health Research Association of New York City, 1978.

Gramlich, E. W. The demand for clean water: The case of the Charles River. *National Tax Journal*, 1977, *30*, 183–194.

Greenblatt, B. *Responsibility for child care.* San Francisco: Jossey-Bass, 1977.

Hannan, M. T., Tuma, N. B., & Groeneveld, L. P. Income and independence effects on marital dissolution: Results from the Seattle and Denver Income-Maintenance Experiments. *American Journal of Sociology*, 1978, *84*, 611–633.

Haskins, R. Day care and public policy. *Urban & Social Change Review*, 1979, *12*, 3–10.

Haskins, R., Farran, D. C., & Sanders, J. Making the day care decision. *Parent's Magazine*, 1978, *53*, 58; 76–78.

Haskins, R., Finkelstein, N. W., & Stedman, D. J. Infant-stimulation programs and their effects. *Pediatric Annals*, 1978, *7*, 94–125.

Haveman, R. H., & Weisbrod, B. A. Defining benefits of public programs: Some guidance for policy analysts. *Policy Analysis*, 1975, *1*, 169–196.

Hill, C. R. Private demand for child care: Implications for public policy. *Evaluation Quarterly*, 1978, *4*, 523–545.

Hochman, H. M. Rule change and transitional equity. In H. M. Hochman & G. E. Peterson (Eds.), *Redistribution through public choice.* New York: Columbia Univ. Press, 1974.

Joffe, C. E. *Friendly intruders: Child care professionals and family life.* Berkeley: Univ. of California Press, 1977.

Kamerman, S. B. *Work and family in industrialized societies.* Paper prepared for Rockefeller Conference on Women, Family, and Work, September, 1978.

Kamerman, S. B., & Kahn, A. E. The day care debate: A wider view. *Public Interest,* 1979, *54,* 76–93.

Keeney, R. L., & Raiffa, H. *Decisions with multiple objectives: Preferences and value tradeoffs.* New York: Wiley, 1976.

Klaus, R. A., & Gray, S. W. The early training project for disadvantaged children: A report after five years. *Monographs of the Society for Research in Child Development,* 1968, *33* (4, Serial No. 120).

Latting, J. *Attaining consumer representation on Neighborhood Health Center boards.* Chapel Hill, N.C.: Bush Institute for Child and Family Policy, 1980.

Lynn, L. E. *Designing public policy: A casebook on the use of policy analysis.* Santa Monica, Calif.: Goodyear, 1980.

MacRae, D. *Issues and parties in legislative voting.* New York: Harper & Row, 1970.

MacRae, D. *The social function of social science.* New Haven, Conn.: Yale Univ. Press, 1976. (a)

MacRae, D. Technical communities and political choice. *Minerva,* 1976, *14,* 169–190. (b)

MacRae, D. Policy analysis methods and governmental functions. In S. Nagel (Ed.), *Improving policy analysis.* Beverly Hills, Calif.: Sage, 1980.

MacRae, D., & Wilde, J. A. *Policy analysis for public decisions.* North Scituate, Mass.: Duxbury, 1979.

Marshall, T. H. *Social policy in the twentieth century* (rev. ed.). London: Hutchinson Univ. Library, 1970.

Meltsner, A. J. Political feasibility and policy analysis. *Public Administration Review,* 1972, *32,* 859–867.

Meyer, W. J. Staffing characteristics and child outcomes. In *Policy issues in day care: Summaries of 21 papers.* Washington, D.C.: Dept. of Health, Education, and Welfare, Center for Systems and Program Development, November, 1977.

Mill, J. S. On liberty. In his *Utilitarianism, liberty, and representative government.* London: J. M. Dent, 1947. (originally pub., 1859.)

Moon, M., & Smolensky, E. (Eds.). *Improving measures of economic well-being.* New York: Academic Press, 1977.

Moroney, R. M. *The family and the state: Considerations for social policy.* New York: Longmans, 1976.

Moynihan, D. P. *The Negro family: The case for national action.* Washington, D.C.: U.S. Govt. Printing Office, 1965.

Moynihan, D. P. *The politics of a guaranteed income.* New York: Vintage Books, 1973.

Munger, F. J. The changing political context of American family policy: Some observations. *University of North Carolina News Letter,* April 1979, *44,* 1–5.

Musgrave, R. A., & Musgrave, P. G. *Public finance in theory and practice* (2nd ed.). New York: McGraw-Hill, 1976.

Nelson, R. R. *The moon and the ghetto: An essay on public policy analysis.* New York: McGraw-Hill, 1977.

Newhouse, J. P., Phelps, C. E., & Schwartz, W. B. Policy options and the impact of national health insurance. *New England Journal of Medicine,* 1974, *290,* 1345–1359.

Odum, E. P., Zieman, J. C., Shugart, H. T., Bramlett, G. A., Ike, A., & Cham-

plin, J. R. Totality indices for evaluating environment impact. In M. Blissett (Ed.), *Environmental impact assessment.* New York: Engineering Foundation, 1976.
Okun, A. M. *Equality and efficiency: The big tradeoff.* Washington, D.C.: Brookings, 1975.
Pechman, J. A., & Timpane, P. M. (Eds.). *Work incentives and income guarantees.* Washington, D.C.: Brookings, 1975.
Plattner, M. F. The welfare state vs. the redistributive state. *Public Interest,* 1979, *55,* 28–48.
Quade, E. S. *Analysis for public decisions.* New York: Elsevier, 1975.
Rainwater, L., & Yancey, W. L. *The Moynihan report and the politics of controversy.* Cambridge, Mass.: M.I.T. Press, 1967.
Ramey, C. T. *The group care of infants and young children.* Paper presented at the National Association for the Education of Young Children Conference, New York, August, 1978.
Ramey, C. T., & Haskins, R. The causes and treatment of school failure: Insights from the Carolina Abecedarian Project. In M. J. Begab, H. Garber, & H. C. Haywood (Eds.), *Prevention of retarded development in psychosocially disadvantaged children.* Baltimore: University Park Press, in press.
Ramsey, S. H. *Constitutional protection for the private realm of the family* (Working Paper No. 11781). Durham, N.C.: Duke Univ. Institute of Policy Sciences and Public Affairs, 1978.
Rawls, J. *A theory of justice.* Cambridge, Mass.: Harvard Univ. Press, 1971.
Rees, A., & Watts, H. W. An overview of the labor supply results. In J. A. Pechman & P. M. Timpane (Eds), *Work incentives and income guarantees.* Washington, D.C.: Brookings, 1975.
Rivlin, A. M. Federal support for child care: An analysis of options. In R.H. Haveman & J. Margolis (Eds.), *Public expenditure and policy analysis* (2nd ed.). Chicago: Rand McNally, 1977.
Robins, P. K., & Spiegelman, R. G. An econometric model of the demand for child care. *Economic Inquiry,* 1978, *16,* 83–94.
Steiner, G. Y. *The children's cause.* Washington, D.C.: Brookings, 1976.
Steinfels, M. O. *Who's minding the children?* New York: Simon & Schuster, 1973.
Stokey, E., & Zeckhauser, R. *A primer for policy analysis.* New York: Norton, 1978.
Titmuss, R. M. *The gift relationship.* New York: Pantheon Books, 1971.
Wagner, M., & Wagner, M. *The Danish national child-care system.* Boulder, Col.: Westview Press, 1976.
Weber, C. U., Foster, P. W., & Weikart, D. P. *An economic analysis of the Ypsilanti Perry preschool project.* Ypsilanti, Mich.: High/Scope Educational Research Foundation, 1978.
Weinstein, M. C., & Stason, W. B. Foundations of cost-effectiveness analysis for health and medical practice. *New England Journal of Medicine,* 1977, *296,* 716–721.
Whitaker, G. P. Coproduction: Citizen participation in service delivery. *Public Administration Review,* 1980, *40,* 240–246.
Wildavsky, A. *Speaking truth to power: The art and craft of policy analysis.* Boston: Little, Brown, 1979.
Woolsey, S. H. Pied-Piper politics and the child care debate. *Daedalus,* 1977, *106,* 127–145.

Footnotes

[1] I am indebted to members of the Bush Seminar, especially Ron Haskins, Robert P. Strauss, and James J. Gallagher, for comments on earlier versions of this chapter.

[2] A similar valuative stance is described by Wildavsky (1979) for "evaluative man": "He believes in clarifying goals . . . His wish is not that any specific objective be enthroned or that a particular clientele be served . . . To evaluative man the organization matters only if it meets social needs" (p. 213). Lynn (1980, p. 6) has also distinguished between an "academic" perspective on analysis and that of an analytic craftsman, favoring the latter for persons who wish to work in government. My approach is somewhat more like the former.

[3] The analyst, in assessing feasibility, must take into account the systems of values and factual beliefs (sometimes called ideologies) held by participants. The analyst's own system of values and beliefs should not necessarily be based on those of the participants; but an analyst may also choose to work with a particular group because of agreement with them or may be persuaded of the merits of their views.

[4] A characteristic of the state of the world, such as national income, which measures a desired condition and may be maximized with respect to a set of policy alternatives, is known as a social welfare function. Some ethical systems may be expressed in terms of such functions.

[5] I do not wish to disparage political decisions. They can create support for policies, educate people through participation, aggregate interests more sim-

ply than experts can, and provide a counterbalance to the interests and biases of experts; but they can also yield undesirable results when they are unreflective, shortsighted, or based on poorly chosen institutions.

[6] The family, as conventionally constituted, is only one of a variety of social groups that might produce such effects. Informal living arrangements, relations among neighbors, and congregate living for the elderly are other examples.

[7] The net welfare of the recipients could be adjusted in this way, but problems of equity and resentment might still arise relative to borderline groups who did not receive the services.

[8] Robert P. Strauss, commenting on an earlier version of this analysis, distinguished between a "blank piece of paper analysis" of day care and an "incremental analysis": "In the second case, one looks at existing institutions, sees if they are performing as expected, and makes suggestions for changes." I am admittedly slighting these aspects and in so doing, reflect the tension between an academic emphasis on general questions and the necessary specificity of useful policy analyses.

[9] I shall not consider major changes in the job market which allow parents more flexibility in their work hours. Such changes are often discussed, but do not seem feasible alternatives for public policy in the short run.

[10] There does appear to be some evidence that children who attend day care may be somewhat more aggressive than home-reared children (Haskins, Finkelstein, & Stedman, 1978). If subsequent studies show that this aggressiveness persists beyond the first few years of schooling, then increased aggressiveness may have to be considered a cost of day care.

[11] I have not dwelt on the problems of single-parent families resulting from desertion or divorce, but the absent parents' obligations may also be part of the problem of low-income in these families. Professor Irwin Garfinkel of the University of Wisconsin has proposed that enforcement of child-support payments through the tax system would alleviate this problem.

[12] It is not easy for an outsider to tell whether these professionals are the representatives of the future generation—or meddlers.

[13] Prospects for legislation of this sort under the Reagan Administration seem slight.

FIVE

TWO LEGAL ANALYSIS TECHNIQUES AND PUBLIC POLICY ANALYSIS

H. RUTHERFORD TURNBULL, III

INTRODUCTION

This book's purpose is to show how public policy, particularly as it affects children and families, can be analyzed. One important message is that there are different ways of analyzing public policy. Another is that the several methods, while sharing some common analytical tools, are essentially different in both their techniques and benefits in dissecting, explaining, evaluating, and giving direction to public policy.

No doubt, it is more helpful than not that more than one method exists. One technique (or a combination of techniques) may clarify public policy more sharply than others. But the risk is high that the different techniques' common components will be obscured and their relative usefulness, separately or in combination, hidden.

Lest that occur as a result of the ensuing discussion of the "legal" techniques, this chapter begins by restating the six components of the Bush model (see MacRae & Haskins, Ch. 1); it then sets forth in detail two techniques of legal analysis and applies them to a recent U.S. Supreme Court decision; and finally, it compares the legal model to the Bush model.

The basic components of policy analysis, as described by MacRae and Haskins, are: restatement of the problem; selection of analysis criteria; synthesis of information relevant to the problem; analysis of competing policy recommendations; communication of policy analysis and recommendation to policymakers; and development of strategies for enacting and implementing the policy recommendation.

As this chapter will show, the two legal analysis techniques involve some of these components more than others; significantly—since the legal analysis techniques are so different from the other techniques—they partake of all these components. The legal analysis techniques also share some of the components of the policy analysis methods described by Gallagher, MacRae, and Moroney. This, too, is important, because it suggests that, despite the sharp disparities between the legal and the other analysis techniques, there are commonalities. Accordingly, a policy analyst need not choose only one technique; indeed, public policy may be rendered more intelligible if more than one policy analyst were to work on the analysis and the analysts were to use more than one technique.

Before comparing and contrasting the legal analysis technique with the other methods, however, it is useful to describe it in the context of *J. L. and J. R. v. Parham* (1979), the Supreme Court's decision answering the question of how much procedural due process (judicial or other safeguards) is required by the Constitution before parents may admit their mentally ill, minor children to state hospitals. Parts one through seven will describe *Parham*, show why the case is important for policy analysis purposes, and demonstrate the usefulness of two legal analysis techniques (in the *Parham* context). Part eight relates the legal analysis techniques to the other policy analysis methods.

PART ONE: J. L. AND J. R. v. PARHAM

Under Georgia law, a parent of a mentally ill minor may apply in writing for the child's admission to a state psychiatric hospital. Upon application, the hospital's superintendent may admit the child for observation and diagnosis; if he finds that there is evidence that the child is mentally ill and "suitable for treatment" at the hospital, he may admit him for any period and under any conditions set by the hospital. Any child who has been hospitalized for more than 5 days may be discharged upon the parents' (or guardians') request; and the superintendent, even in the absence of a parental request for discharge, is under a duty to discharge any child who has recovered from his mental illness or who has sufficiently improved so that, according to the superintendent, hospitalization is no longer desirable.

In practice, parents normally do not seek to hospitalize their child until after outpatient treatment at local mental health clinics has proven ineffective. Also, the hospital admission team (consisting of a physician and at least one other mental health professional) interviews and examines the child, reviews his medical records provided by local clinics, interviews the parents, and then, based on the information it has obtained and other background information it can secure, diagnoses the child and decides whether he is mentally ill and likely to benefit from institutionalization. If admitted, the child is reviewed periodically by at least one independent medical review group regarding his condition and continuing need for hospitalization.

Counsel for minors admitted to Georgia hospitals challenged the state's statute and admission procedures and their clients' admission to those hospitals by filing a lawsuit seeking the following relief: (1), that the statute and practices be held unconstitutional on the basis that they deny the child his procedural due process rights under the Fourteenth Amendment to the Constitution (no person shall be deprived of life, liberty, or property without due process of law); (2), that the state be enjoined from enforcing the statute; and (3), that the plaintiffs be placed in "less drastic environment(s) suitable to (their) needs."

A federal trial court held the Georgia statute unconstitutional and granted the plaintiffs the relief they sought. The state then appealed to the U.S. Supreme Court, which reversed the lower court's decision and ruled that due process requires simply an independent medical decision-making process, which includes the thorough psychiatric investigation that the state presently uses, followed by additional periodic review of a child's condition; a more formal, judicial type of hearing is not required. Thus, the Court essentially affirmed Georgia's procedure and rejected the children's contention that they are entitled to a judicial hearing on the issue of whether they should be admitted to a hospital on their parents' initiative.

PART TWO: PARHAM AND THE ROLE OF LAW

For our purposes, it is useful to begin a description of the legal analysis techniques by considering the simplified statement of *Parham* given above, and asking, "What's going on?" Not unexpectedly, more than one thing.

First, "law" is functioning in its usual way. One role of law is to regulate the relationships between people and to resolve their controversies. The relationships in *Parham* are fairly typical of the type that surface in family-child public policy issues. There is the relationship of one citizen (parent) to another (child); the relationship of citizens (parents and child together or independently of each other) to the state;

and the relationship of one branch of government (the judicial) to others (the executive, in its capacity as enforcer of statutes regulating the placement of minors in mental hospitals). In addition, there is a resolution of the controversy between the parties (whether due process requires more than the Georgia statutes and practices provided).

But law is not the only social institution that accomplishes these purposes. Family members regulate their relationships with each other in nonlegal ways. In *Parham,* the relationship was parental authority over the child. Important family decisions are made without resort to a public forum (here, the hospital screening practices); private decision making is more often the rule than not in family matters. In *Parham,* the decision was about the place of treatment, and the decision had been made without third-party review. And families often resolve their disputes without resorting to lawsuits involving each other or public or private agencies.

Law, however, plays the role of regulating relationships and resolving controversies more prominently in public policy matters than nonlegal institutions (such as trade unions or professional associations, boards of trustees, and "family councils"). In a *Parham*-like situation, where one of the parties is a government and the other parties are family members, it is nearly inevitable that the law will be used to interpret and apply public policy decisions. Thus, in almost every case where a legislative decision has been made to regulate the relationships of private citizens among themselves or with respect to a public agency, or where a decision has been made by one of the parties to contest the regulation or another party's rights, the law will be used to interpret the decisions. In *Parham,* the decision was a public one—made by the Georgia legislature—which affected families by offering them publicly operated mental health care, but only after certain medical screening occurs to assure that the child is mentally ill and needs to be hospitalized. The function of the courts was to resolve the dispute raised by the children against the state. Thus, it behooves policy analysts to pay careful attention to the techniques by which "the law" (here, the Court) analyzes, interprets, and applies the policy.

The second thing that is happening in *Parham* (in addition to the law functioning in its usual way) is that each of the three real parties to the lawsuit—parents of mentally ill children, the children themselves, and the state's mental health system—has an interest in how "the law" operates. Stated another way, each has an interest in preserving or changing a public policy. It is by no means farfetched to say that each is a surrogate for unknown constituents—other parents, other children, and mental health systems in other states—that have similar interests. Hence, the Court in *Parham* not only will decide a policy issue that has profound effect on many people, but also will legitimatize or hold unconstitutional a policy made and applied by other branches of government. In doing so, the Court, as a branch of the federal government, will be deciding what policy must be followed by states and their three branches of government. Thus, it is important for policy analysts to recognize that the role of law is to affect policy as it relates not just to individuals but also as it relates to the functions of government.

PART THREE: RESTATING THE POLICY ISSUE IN PARHAM

It is now appropriate to return to *Parham* and, by introducing one of the legal analysis techniques, reexamine and restate the policies that are reflected in the state's statute and the relationships of family members to each other and the government. Stated alternatively, it is appropriate to develop Step One of the Bush model of policy analysis—restatement of the problem—by first asking what each party in *Parham* wanted, what the Court held each was entitled to have, and thus what the policy issues truly were.

The mentally ill minors (plaintiffs) wanted the courts to hold that the Georgia statute was unconstitutional, that any parental decisions to place them in hospitals must be reviewed by a court before placement, and that they were entitled to be placed in community-based treatment programs or similar less drastic environments suitable to their needs.

The state, on the other hand, argued its statute should be upheld for many reasons. First, it argued that its statute and the way community and hospital employees screen children before admission sufficiently protect them against errors in placement that thereby wrongfully deny them their liberty. Second, the state resisted the "less drastic" remedy that the plaintiffs sought on the grounds that the state had sought "substantively and at great cost to provide care for those who cannot afford to obtain private treatment." Further, granting the plaintiffs' request for "less drastic" placement, argued the state, would "divert public resources from the central objective of administering health care." Finally, the state resisted the plaintiffs' request for preplacement judicial hearings on the grounds that such hearings risk "aggravating the tensions inherent in families" and "erect barriers that may discourage parents from seeking medical aid for a mentally ill child." The state asserted thereby that its scheme for admissions would be less harmful to families than the plaintiffs' requested remedy.

It is not clear what parents of mentally ill children wanted in *Parham* since none was an actual party to the lawsuit. Some friend-of-the-court (*amicus*) briefs were filed by organizations made up of parents of mentally ill or mentally retarded children; the *amicus* briefs sought to overturn the statute. But the Court itself characterized parents' interests in almost benign terms ("the welfare and health of the child"), giving no further clue to parents' interests.

What is the public policy issue in *Parham*? Naturally, there is no single issue; examining what the plaintiffs and the state wanted reveals that much. The issues were, at the least, these:

1. The liberty rights of children (their rights under the liberty guarantee of the due process clause of the Fourteenth Amendment).
2. The amount of due process required by the Constitution in matters in which parents decide whether they will place their children in residential institutions for health, mental health, or other purposes. Essentially, this is a policy issue concerning the amount of protection children can obtain by using the Constitution to fortress them against decisions made about their interests by parents, the state, or both.
3. The degree to which parents may control their children and, inferentially, the degree to which any family member may control or be protected against decisions of other members.
4. The extent to which the law—as a regulator of relationships and resolver of disputes—should indulge in presumptions about the good or evil motives of parents and state mental health employees in child-hospitalization matters. Essentially, should any presumption be the basis for constitutional law that affects widely different families?
5. Whether public policy ought to address the process through which family decisions are made by assuring some kind of due process safeguards and reviews to children whose parents want to place them in mental institutions or whether instead public policy should simply prohibit families from making some decisions at all. This latter result would obtain if the plaintiffs asked for and received relief that had the intent or effect of creating community-based treatment, forestalling or completely drying up admissions to large mental hospitals, or both.
6. The rights of children to community-based or at least some other "less drastic" or "less restrictive" placement and treatment.
7. The rights of children to be free of institutional care because of the stigma attached to being an ex-mental patient and because of the uncertain benefit of, or the certain risks in, institutional placement.
8. The regulation of state mental health systems by legal—as distinguished from medical—criteria and means.

Parham, then, was a Pandora's box of public and private policy issues. But this did not become clear, at least for our purposes, until one of the major techniques of legal analysis was used—the technique of identifying the parties in a given case, their interests in the case, and their sought-for remedies. This technique—the interest analysis—now deserves close attention.

PART FOUR: INTEREST ANALYSIS

Interest analysis is a technique that carefully dissects everyone's stakes in a case and its possible outcomes. One performs an interest analysis by asking a series of questions in order to identify the true policy problem that the case presents: What is the public policy of the case and how will it affect various interested parties? These are policy analysts' proper concerns, and they will find the interest-analysis tool to be useful. This is so because the initial purpose of the interest analysis is to demonstrate how a policy might affect people by identifying who they are. It is not axiomatic that policymakers or analysts fully comprehend the potential range of a policy; they can, after all, overlook some of the people who may be affected. The interest analysis helps them identify that range, helps them take all affected interests into account.

I do not mean to suggest, however, that when an analyst or a court applies an interest analysis to a given policy or legal dispute, they are always seeking to satisfy or advance someone's interests and that the satisfaction of those interests is a criterion for the decision. On the other hand, using an interest analysis may help the analyst determine someone's interests, and, invariably, courts must advance one litigant's interests over another's.

Indeed, as is indicated below, the satisfaction of interests can be a first principle, but satisfying people's preferences or interests is not the first purpose of an interest analysis.

The first question in the interest analysis is always: who is directly affected by the case? Of course, the parties to the case are those who are affected directly; in *Parham,* J. L. and J. R. on the one hand, and the State of Georgia on the other. Quite obviously, however, J. L. and J. R. represent, or stand in for, people like them; they are surrogates for the other mentally ill or mentally retarded minors in Georgia who might be placed in state institutions by their parents under the state's laws and administrative procedures. By the same token, the state is a surrogate for the many states that have similar laws and procedures or those that have different laws and procedures but a common interest in preventing or keeping to a minimum the amount of judicial involvement in their admissions procedures. So the second question is: who is affected indirectly?

The third question is the obverse of the first two: who is not affected by the case? This is not so easy to answer as might appear at first blush. One might think that mentally ill or mentally retarded adults are not affected, simply because they are not minors. To assume this, however, would be wrong, for some mentally handicapped adults have been adjudicated incompetent and can be admitted to state hospitals on the application of their guardian. In many respects, they are like minors because they are legally powerless to object to their admission and accordingly want and need safeguards to assure that they, too, are not placed erroneously in a state facility or incur needlessly the stigma of having been institutionalized.

One might also assume that "normal" minors are not affected by *Parham* because they are not mentally ill or mentally retarded and therefore are unlikely to be placed in an institution by their parents. This, too, would be a false assumption. *Parham* was formulated as quintessential "children's rights" case: the fundamental issue raised by the plaintiffs was the degree to which minors should be entitled to have legal procedures to safeguard them against the damage they would suffer from mistakes their parents or the state might make.

Similarly, one might assume that parents of "normal" children are not affected by *Parham* because their children are not mentally handicapped. This is another false assumption, because their right to control and raise their children (for example, by securing institutionalization to treat mental conditions) was very much an issue.

Another assumption concerning whose interests are not at stake might be that *Parham* affects only the institutionalization procedures of state mental health systems, nothing more. But a review of what Georgia argued—that both its institutional and community-based mental health services would be affected by the Court's decision—shows that all public providers of mental health services had an interest in the Court's decision.

Still another assumption might be that *Parham* is only a children's rights case in which the issues were focused solely on children, families, and their relationships to governments. Yet *Parham,* although it undoubtedly started primarily as a children's rights case, also was the battleground between two groups of professionals—providers of mental health services, some of whom resisted the due-process safeguards that J. L. and J. R. sought, and reformers of mental health services, many of whom were also providers but who included many lawyers wanting to make an indirect attack on institutions and institutionalization. *Parham* might have been a beachhead for the law-based reformers; instead, it became the sanctuary of the status quo in mental health.

Thus, the third question in the interest analysis might seem the easiest to answer but probably is the most difficult as well as most illuminating once it is answered. "Who is not affected?" is an important question because it serves double duty. It helps identify many more people or groups who are indirectly affected than might appear to be as a result of answers to the first two questions. It also helps the analyst anticipate some of the subtle consequences that could flow from a policy decision. Once the analyst knows who is affected, he can better anticipate, or at least think about, the consequences of a policy.

The fourth question raised by the interest analysis is a logical extension of the first three; namely, how are people affected? In the children's rights view of *Parham*, the proper inquiries are: how will mentally handicapped children be affected, and how will nonhandicapped children be affected? In the parents' rights view, the questions are the obverse: How will parents of handicapped minors, nonhandicapped minors, and adjudicated adults be affected? In the law-reform view of *Parham*, the analysis will revolve around the likely results of one decision or another on the state's mental health system and the degree to which the law—in the form of procedural safeguards in advance of institutionalization—will shape the form and future of the system.

Finally, the interest analysis asks, what is each affected person or group likely to do, and how are they likely to react to one result or another? In a sense, this question is a rephrasing of the fourth question. But it explicitly requires an examination of the anticipated or unanticipated results of a policy decision. Furthermore, it impels the analyst to relate the affected groups' interests to other criteria for policy analysis because their response to the policy decision may be determined by such criteria.

Those criteria include the following: first principles, such as Moroney's inquiry into the relationship of a person to the state or of people to each other; optimization of individual preferences, such as MacRae's concern with distributing scarce resources in order to provide the greatest good; and political support and feasibility, similar to the constraints and resources of Gallagher's model.

Any decision on the merits in *Parham* inevitably implicates first principles: a parent's relationship with his or her child or to the state, or the parent's and child's joint relationship to the state. What effect will *Parham* have on parents, children, and the state? That question is a first-principles issue that the interest analysis helps answer.

Does *Parham* reach a "greatest good" result? Does it leave the community and institutional mental health system open or close it down? Does it foreclose parents and children as well as the state from making one kind of choice or another, from satisfying one type of preference or another? While the interest analysis alone will not provide all the answers to these questions, it will provide some.

Will the *Parham* decision cause law reformers to seek legislation that requires judicial review of placement decisions, the Court having made it clear that the states may interpose such review on placement decisions? If so, will law reformers have sufficient political support? What resources can they bring to bear on the *Parham* result in post-*Parham* action? These are issues that the interest analysis might help answer.

Thus, an interest analysis that explicitly requires the analyst to examine anticipated or unanticipated consequences of a policy also helps him understand how affected groups may respond and on what grounds; that is, the analyst will be better able to predict the basis for the reaction of affected groups. When those bases are related to such criteria as first principles, optimization of individual preferences, or political support and feasibility, the analyst will be able to apply those criteria to his policy analysis task. One criterion for policy analysis thus feeds into others.

PART FIVE: "INTERESTS" AND "RIGHTS"

It should be clear by now that *Parham* furnishes a complex example of family-child-state policy and policy analysis, and that the many interested people and systems affected by *Parham* cannot all be satisfied with any given decision. There are simply too many competing claims asserted by the interested parties.

How, then, is the Court to decide which interests it will recognize, which claims it will legitimize? This question confronts every policy analyst; it is almost never the case in family-child-state policymaking and policy analysis that all interested parties are unanimous in their choice of policy. Even widely supported notions about mandatory education and compulsory vaccination, for example, are opposed by some families on religious grounds. Choices between claims are inevitable. For purpose of the law (which is to say, for purposes of a social institution that makes policy by regulating relationships between people or their governments or both and resolving their disputes with each other), the choice depends in part on whether one party or another has well-established or emerging "rights."

It is important at this point to distinguish between rights on the one hand and claims or interests on the other. In *Parham,* the distinction is blurred but nonetheless discernible. The state argued that its procedural safeguards were constitutionally adequate because, among other reasons, they had the effect of underpinning parents' traditional *rights* to govern their children. There were no inconsistencies, said the state, between its preadmission procedures and parents' rights to seek and obtain mental health treatment for their children, i.e., parents' rights to govern and control their children. The fact of the matter, argued the state, is that parents always have had the right to control their children and the few judicially or legislatively created incursions on that right (e.g., in the case of child abuse) are distinguishable from the institutionalization decision because the parents' actions in these cases have greater adverse consequences for the child than institutionalization. Accordingly, children have no *right* to object to their parents' placement decisions and, by like token, parents have a general, but not unlimited, right to institutionalize their children. This much, said the state—and the Court agreed—is settled law.

J. L. and J. R. responded by arguing that they have a right not to be institutionalized without more elaborate procedural safeguards because they have their First and Fourteenth Amendment rights to be free of unnecessary bodily restraints.

Stripped bare, the state's argument is one that attempts to preserve or advance its interests and claims by investing them with constitutional rights. So, too, in the case of the minors. Each party sought to prevail by elevating their respective "claims" or "interests" into "rights."

Claims and interests are no more than assertions by a given party that the policymaker should tilt the scales in that party's favor. The strategy of any lawsuit is to align claims and interests with rights, to demonstrate that such claims and interests have been recognized by other courts in similar cases to be worthy of recognition and enforcement. The strategy repeats itself in other policymaking forums; the oft-heard "children's rights" cry resounds in legislative and executive arenas as well as the courts. I do not mean to suggest that the adversarial process necessarily leads to good policy. As I indicate in Parts 8 and 9 below, there are important reasons why the adversarial process does not assure good policy. Instead, I intend here only to describe how defenders of one policy or another use the law to advance their claims.

Rights, on the other hand, are claims or interests that are *enforceable* by legal processes. Parents' rights to religious liberty under the First Amendment normally shield them against governmental action which attempts to "protect" the child against parental religious beliefs. For example, the religious liberty of Amish parents to raise their children in the Amish faith and exempt them from compulsory school attendance laws is enforceable by the parents through the courts (*Wisconsin v. Yoder*, 1972).

Another example will help to demonstrate that claims or interests are simply assertions about how policy issues should be resolved but, unlike rights, are not enforceable against the policymaker. Indeed, rights are claims and interests that have been elevated to an enforceable status and must be taken into account by the policymaker. Minors have the right to secure an abortion during the first trimester of pregnancy and are not required to obtain their parents' consent for the operation; their privacy rights to an abortion are enforceable against not only their parents but also against those state legislatures attempting to circumscribe the rights by granting parents the opportunity to object to the abortion (see also *Planned Parenthood v. Danforth; Bellotti v. Baird*).

Parham is a classic example of the dispute-resolving role of law in family-child-state policies, precisely because it requires a balancing of the competing rights of the state, the parents, and the minors. The choice between claims or interests was made all the more difficult because the parties properly argued that their interests were based on rights—that they had claims and interests that they could legally enforce against each other.

PART SIX: RIGHTS AND FAMILY POLICY ANALYSIS

It is not terribly profitable to discuss rights without also discussing their origin and uses. After all, the policy analyst who attempts to explain, evaluate, or give direction to public policy affecting children, families, and governments should know more than simply that rights are weightier matters for him to handle than claims or interests.

To discuss the origin of rights, it will be helpful to inquire why *Parham* was ever brought to bar. The answer is not that parents and children have possibly competing interests. It is, instead, that the state acted by allowing a rather relaxed review of parental decisions to institutionalize a child and by providing state-operated institutions. Without state action, the family-child issues would have been purely private matters that could have been resolved by means other than resorting to litigation based on constitutional rights. It was only after the state acted that the parties could assert their constitutional rights because the Constitution is the linchpin for resolving public-law issues. Thus, the policy analyst must ask whether there is state action, whether that action may provoke a confrontation of rights, and whether those rights are grounded in constitutional or other law. If the answers are "yes," the analyst should be prepared to confront the limitations that the Constitution imposes on state action.

The Federal Constitution is a document of limitations. It begins by setting forth the powers of the three branches of the federal government and reserving to the people or the states any rights not explicitly granted to the federal government. It also contains a Bill of Rights further limiting the powers of the federal government. Likewise, state constitutions reflect the powers the state's citizens have granted to their government and the limitations they have imposed on it by their own bills of rights.

It is axiomatic that any governmental action must be grounded in an explicit or implied power contained in the Constitution. To challenge as unconstitutional a law enacted by a legislature is to assert that either the legislature had no authority to enact the law or that the law, although based on a constitutional power, offends a countervailing limitation on government as in a bill of rights. For example, the state's decision to operate mental hospitals must be based on some authority granted in the state constitution; hospital admissions procedures and policies must be grounded in turn on some power that the legislature has delegated to hospital administrators; and neither its laws nor its regulations may offend any article of the Bill of Rights. In *Parham,* there was no challenge to the state's power to establish and administer mental hospitals; such a power accompanies the power to enact laws for the general welfare.

This discussion of rights is intended to make two simple points. First, courts do not become involved in public policy analysis and public policy decision making concerning children and their families unless there is some type of state action. Second, when courts do become involved, they must examine the source of the state action, i.e., whether it is grounded in a grant of power and whether the action itself exceeds any of the limitations imposed by the Constitution.

It behooves policy analysts, therefore, to inquire not only into the source of power for a policy decision, but also into the limitations on that power. By the same token, analysts ought to ask whether there is existing law; if so, how does it affect the proposed policy, and, if not, is new law needed and will it be constitutional?

PART SEVEN: THE FUNCTIONAL ANALYSIS

Up to this point, I have concentrated on how to use the technique of interest analysis in analyzing public policy; explained the important differences between interests and claims on the one hand and rights on the other; and argued that policy analysts should be concerned about the origin of rights of both governments and individuals. I turn now to a second technique of legal analysis—the functional analysis.

As is the case with the interest-analysis technique, the functional-analysis technique begins when the analyst asks a series of questions about what governments and people are doing in a given circumstance; namely, who (or what government) is doing what to whom, how, and why? These questions can be cast in somewhat more sophisticated terms and applied to the *Parham* case. What functions is the state performing in maintaining mental hospitals and allowing parents to place their children in them with only medical review of the admissions decision? Or to put these questions in a still more sophisticated form, what functions do parents and the state together perform in providing for children's institutionalization? The policy analyst is making a fundamental inquiry, no matter how he asks the question: What is the policy's purpose and is it served? The simpler the question, however, the easier it is to get to the heart of the matter. Who does what to whom, how, and why?

Consider the children. One function of hospitalization is ostensibly to treat children who cannot under present circumstances be treated elsewhere. Hospitalization might provide them with acceptable diagnosis, treatment, and posthospitalization plans and services. It might provide them with a safe haven from the debilitating effects of living with parents who cannot or will not care for them. It might provide them with refuge from the demands of living in normal society or a nonaccepting community. On the other hand, confinement might jeopardize them physically, mentally, and socially by placing them in conditions that are themselves damaging and stigmatizing.

How does hospitalization affect parents? It might relieve them of the heavy burden of caring for their handicapped child. At the same time, hospitalization might also attenuate the already strained ties between parents and children. It need not have this effect; indeed, hospitalization or other placement of a child outside the parental home (whether for short-term diagnosis, short-term respite care, or longer-term treatment) can enable parents to carry out their responsibilities. But it can also have the unwanted effect of encouraging parents to surrender their child-rearing responsibilities to the state. The issues of parental responsibilities, parental capabilities, and parental "dumping" of their children surface under a functional analysis inquiry.

What does institutionalization do with respect to other functions of government? For one thing, it may remove the most seriously impaired children—and therefore the ones who are the most difficult and expensive to deal with—from the local schools. It might also exclude such difficult children from foster-home placement, thereby making foster care easier to obtain for less severely impaired children and, therefore, an easier program for governments to operate. Institutionalization may also feed children into existing state facilities, thereby enabling the state to collect federal or private funds for the treatment and maintenance of the children and use those revenues to liquidate bonded debt on the hospitals, or for operating expenses, or both. Institutionalization might direct children into a large service-provider system, turning them into patient fodder for professionals employed in hospitals or deriving their jobs from functions of government that relate directly or indirectly to the hospitals' operation. After all, the decision to admit a child to the state hospital was made by a state employee, relying on evaluations developed by state or other government employees. The locus of the decision-making authority is an excellent clue in applying the functional analysis. Institutionalization might also alleviate the pressure on community-based mental health systems and funding by providing a well-established and traditional alternative to community-based care. At the very least, hospitalization assures the continuation of institutional care and its availability for people whom the community-based system cannot or does not want to treat; hospitals and hospitalization remain the places and procedures of last resort, providing outlets to providers of mental-health care as well as to parents of mentally handicapped children. Finally, institutionalization enables the state to act in its *parens patriae* role; hospitals are places where the state can discharge its function of looking after those who cannot take care of themselves. More than that, hospitals are places of confinement for people who are dangerous to others (not just themselves) but who have not committed a crime or cannot be tried or convicted of a crime because of their mental disabilities.

What does institutionalization do to the relationships that might be established between nonhandicapped and handicapped children and adults? For one thing, it separates the able from the disabled and segregates the latter into their own facilities and communities. It also doubly labels the disabled by categorizing them as not only "handicapped" but also as "ex-mental patients," potentially driving them further apart from the nonhandicapped majority and thereby assuring that they will remain members of a minority. And it can forestall—if not altogether prevent—the possibility of their integration into and participation in mainstream society.

These questions—what does the policy do to whom, how, and why?—are indispensable in policy analysis. They help analysts flesh out their interest analysis by suggesting that some previously unaccounted-for people may have certain interests in a policy. Thus, mental health service providers and nonhandicapped citizens have important interests in institutionalization. Furthermore, these questions may help the analyst anticipate the effects of a proposed policy or evaluate the effects of extant policies. Thus, in the *Parham* case, was the purpose of the admissions law and procedures to help children, their parents, or others, did it have that effect, and will the *Parham*-established doctrine make any difference? These questions may also help the analyst determine which level or agency of government (federal, state, or local; public health, mental health, social services, or education) should or could perform the duties the policy will impose.

Like interest analysis, functional analysis is directed first at identifying and then at advancing the values and welfare of people affected by a given policy. Interest analysis requires examination of their values and welfare from their point of view, while functional analysis requires the same examination but from the perspective of those who are producing the effects. The results of using these two techniques, however, should not be different. Both seek to dissect the policy so that its true effects can be anticipated and studied. While both techniques can be useful in advancing someone's claims, neither expressly serves advocacy purposes in the hands of an impartial or disinterested policy analyst.

PART EIGHT: COMPARING AND CONTRASTING TECHNIQUES OF LEGAL ANALYSIS AND THE ROLE OF COURTS WITH THE BUSH MODEL OF POLICY ANALYSIS

As I pointed out in the introduction, the interest and functional analyses are simultaneously like and unlike the Bush analysis model. The time has come to compare this legal model with the various steps of the Bush model. The point of this exercise is to demonstrate that various techniques of policy analysis are useful and that policy analysts should use more than one model to adequately dissect, explain, evaluate, and give direction to public policy.

Step One of the Bush model calls on the analyst to restate the policy problem. The interest analysis helps in doing this by holding the policy up to the light of many views. It is as though the analyst were examining a diamond through each of its facets. Thus, the problem is studied through the eyes of everyone who is directly or indirectly affected, including those who, at first blush, appear not to be affected at all. The functional analysis helps in restating the problem because it directs the analyst's attention to how and why governments are acting. Functional analysis is tangentially concerned with interests and rights, but it addresses frontally the effects of a policy as well as how and by whom the policy will be carried out. In doing so, it tends to show that the problem is not what it may at first appear, but rather something entirely different or radically more complex, although of the same genre.

Step Two of the Bush model requires the analyst to select criteria by which to evaluate a policy. The legal analysis is particularly helpful to this end because it sets forth criteria that help the analyst dissect the problem and apply certain values to its solution. Thus, the legal analysis demands that the policy be examined to determine whether the government that will carry out the policy has the constitutional authority to do so, the necessary statutory power to complement its constitutional authority, or the necessary executive rule-making power to carry out the grant of power. The legal analysis also imposes a duty on the analyst to satisfy himself that there are no constitutional or statutory restraints on the government and thus on the government's ability to formulate and carry out a policy. Thus, the two major criteria for legal analysis are the constitutional grants of power to governments and the constitutional limitations on power (i.e., the rights of individuals).

In Step Three of the Bush model, the analyst synthesizes information about a policy and the criteria by which it is analyzed. Although the legal techniques seem to be particularly helpful in Steps One and Two, there can be no doubt about their shortcomings in this step.

The trial of a case is supposed to be the means by which the judge resolves a conflict between parties, according to law, by determining the facts of the case, deciding which are dispositive of the legal issues, identifying the legal issues, applying the dispositive facts to the applicable rules of law, deciding which litigant prevails and why, and entering a judgment granting relief to the victor. But these procedures of legal decision making are purely hypothetical, and reality does not often match the ideal.

There are several reasons for this unhappy but unavoidable result and thus for the relative inability of the court to synthesize information. First, the adversary process is as much designed to obscure as to illuminate the truth. Counsel for the parties do not play the role of dispassionate analysts; instead, they are zealous advocates.

Second, the process itself normally relies on evidence (on the facts) that is unfamiliar and often unacceptable to social scientists, whose evidence normally is carefully (and nonadversarily) derived data. Accordingly, social science evidence and legal evidence do not serve as identical information that can be synthesized.

Nor are courts required to use social science data. If the data are presented to the courts, however, the courts will find it difficult to avoid using them. But the facts that courts attempt to determine relate fundamentally to the effect of one person's actions on another. In *Parham,* for example, the effects of institutionalization on children, their parents, and the mental health system were not dispassionately examined in the way that good practice requires a social scientist to examine such effects. Thus, the facts that are relevant to legal analysis and courts as policymakers can differ markedly from those relevant to other policymakers; by the same token, the type of facts that undergird the legal-analysis model can differ from the data that are the foundation for other models of policy analysis.

Moreover, courts remain relatively free to rely on assumptions or presumptions concerning the proper relationship of the parties to each other. Courts are reluctant to abandon precedents and to reject or modify the assumptions or presumptions of earlier cases. By contrast, social scientists engage in activities that can confirm, modify, or reject previous work.

Finally, courts are under no obligation to use social science research as, for example, by examining the effects of their previous decisions on large numbers of people.

To have pointed out these differences in how courts and social scientists use facts is not to say, however, that courts never use social science data, never challenge the assumptions or presumptions of precedents, or never consider the effects of their decisions on large numbers of people. In its very feeble way, the *Parham* decision illustrates an unsuccessful effort of a less than intellectually honest court to use social science data.

Moreover, simply because courts do not use social science data in the same or similar ways as other policymakers does not mean that the tools of legal analysis are less valuable to policy analysts than other analysis techniques. Nor does it mean that lawmakers other than judges (such as legislatures, executive rule-writers, or attorneys presenting their clients' cases to courts or other decision makers) do not use such data. They do, as do courts, but their opportunities to do so are less constrained than those of the courts. To the extent that courts and other consumers of the tools of legal analysis use social science data honestly, law may evolve to reflect the knowledge that social science generates—law and the social sciences may become progressively integrated. But a courtroom is not the most suitable forum for such use and integration.

A third reason the court does not synthesize facts very well is that expert witnesses and their expert testimony often are not used. Even when they are used, they may or may not be persuasive, depending in part on their personal characteristics (essentially, initial credibility and sustained credibility under cross-examination), the prohibitive value of their evidence, and the extent to which the decision in a case hinges on their evidence.

Fourth, judges are not policy analysts; true, they must synthesize facts and apply them to legal issues, but they usually are constrained by what the litigants have presented in the trial.

Fifth, when a case is appealed, the Appeals Court can select which facts or information it thinks most relevant to support the decision it wishes—or is compelled by precedent—to reach. *Parham* perfectly illustrates this selective process because the Court paid careful attention to data concerning the amount of time that preadmission judicial hearings might require of staff psychiatrists and psychologists, but it did not point out the false assumptions in the data or that the data were incorrectly calculated.

Sixth, courts are bound by precedents, i.e., by decisions of higher courts in previous cases raising the same issues of law and based on the same or indistinguishably different facts. Unlike other policy analysts, courts do not have wide latitude to consider policy on a blank slate or to dramatically reverse policy directions. Indeed, counsel in any major constitutional litigation must persuade the court to use the precedents creatively and apply facts (particularly those presented by expert testimony) and precedent imaginatively. In short, synthesizing information is one step in the Bush model that the legal analysis does not accommodate or accomplish easily.

Steps Four and Five of the Bush model require policy analysts to select a particular policy from among the competing policy recommendations and to communicate their recommendations to policymakers. Courts—the forums where legal analysis techniques are applied to public policy matters during trials—do indeed examine competing policy recommendations and, in a sense, communicate recommendations to policymakers. They examine competing policies in the sense that they hear from both sides of a case concerning the facts (data in other forums of policy analysis and decision making) and applicable law (criteria for policy analysis); and they make recommendations by issuing decisions and entering orders in the case, thereby establishing precedents that may be followed by other courts in similar cases.

It is necessary at this point to make it clear that courts use techniques other than the interest or functional analysis to reach decisions. As noted, they pay (or are supposed to pay) careful attention to the facts and decide the case solely on the basis of the facts. But that does not prevent the courts from being selective about the facts or deciding that one cluster of facts is more important than another (the so-called "dispositive facts"). They are bound by precedent, which either restricts them in their decision or, when counsel and courts become creative about precedents' use, enables them to reinterpret the usual rule of law and apply it in new ways to establish new rules of law and thereby new policy. They follow, or reinterpret and apply imaginatively, the legal doctrines and principles of the precedents. "Equal protection," "substantive due process," and "procedural due process" are constitutional guarantees that courts give meaning through interpretation and application. Through this process, courts have created legal principles and doctrines that help them decide how to reach decisions and which decisions to reach in a given case; they serve the dual role of being analytical techniques and substantive rules of law. Courts often adhere to presumptions established by precedent or the legislature; the presumptions (e.g., that mothers are entitled to their child's possession in child-custody cases) help the court decide how to consider a case as well as what decision to make.

In addition to these strictly legal techniques for deciding cases and rules of substantive law (criteria that are applied by the policy analyst as part of his duty to examine competing policy recommendations), courts also analyze and decide cases (make policy recommendations) by using techniques and bases for decision that are not so purely legal. In Justice Holmes's words, courts respond to "the felt needs of the time." In Mark Twain's words, courts also "read the election returns." Judges and justices often bring to their jobs preconceived ideas about the court's role in the scheme of government; some believe the courts should exercise self-restraint and decide cases on narrow or strict constructionist grounds, while others believe that courts should be activist and prone to create new law or create new policies. And many judges and justices experience moral outrage and believe that a case presents facts that are "shocking to the conscience" and thus they grant remedies (make policy) that may be beyond the boundaries of precedent.

Whether they rely solely or partially on the interest or functional analysis, and whether they bring other criteria to bear on how they decide a case, courts do follow Steps Four and Five of the Bush model. As the Bush model implies, a primary method for analyzing competing policy recommendations is to investigate the impact of previous and current policies. Courts do this by considering precedents, relying on them or distinguishing them from the case at bar and making them thereby inapplicable, and by considering whether the precedents have worked and are therefore to be followed in the case at hand.

Finally, the Bush model calls upon analysts to develop strategies to enact and implement their policy recommendations. Again, the legal-analysis techniques and forums do not perform this role well. Courts can point out the deficiencies of policy that others have made or implemented, measuring those deficiencies against the applicable legal criteria. They can even suggest how policymakers might cure the deficiencies (how a properly drawn statute or acceptable practice will pass constitutional muster). And, occasionally, they can retain jurisdiction over a case or order a party to take certain action to implement their decision. But their role traditionally is to decide a case and enter an order of judgment in favor of one party or another. The court is not a legislating body with the power to decide what strategies should be enacted to carry out a given policy. Nor is it an executive body with the power to decide how to comply with a strategy or what strategies to adopt to implement a policy.

PART NINE: THE CONSTRAINING POWER OF LAW ON POLICY

In summary, courts are proper forums for policy analysis and decision making; the techniques they bring to bear in analyzing policy can be useful to other policy analysts; they follow more or less adequately the steps of the Bush model of policy analysis. But they are not, nor were they ever intended to be, more than marginally sufficient for the purposes of policy analysis, decision making, and evaluation. Their principal duty is to resolve disputes and enable the law to perform that important political and social function· only tangentially do they contribute to policy analysis, decision making, and evaluation.

And even in their tangential role, they serve largely as inhibitors or constraints, for they are bound, in the end, to apply the Constitution—the body of fundamental law—to public policy controversies that find their way into court. The Constitution and the techniques that are used to apply it (e.g., the criteria and the techniques of policy analysis) bring policies to the bar of "justice" by asking whether a family-child-state policy can prevail over some counter policy. MacRae correctly notes in his chapter that the Constitution is a prior restraint on other principles for policy analysis, decision making, and evaluation. But it is nonetheless an important one; it limits other policies, it has its own inherent limitations, and it is of increasing significance to policy analysis because of the rising number of family-child-state policy matters that courts are called upon to address.

SIX

INCREMENTAL VERSUS COMPREHENSIVE WELFARE REFORM[1]

ROBERT P. STRAUSS

INTRODUCTION

Since the late 1960s, our system of cash and in-kind transfers has been viewed critically by analysts and politicians of virtually every political and philosophic persuasion. Beginning with a Presidential Commission, HR1, and more recently the Better Jobs and Income Program (BJIP), Presidents Nixon and Carter have sought to evaluate and reform what has frequently been called the "welfare mess." Attending this interest in change has been the creation of a significant intellectual community devoted to studying the welfare system and alternative welfare programs.

Against this decade-long research and political effort, one must contrast the reality that comprehensive reform of the welfare system, as contemplated by Presidents Nixon and Carter, has not been achieved. Instead, the existing system of cash and in-kind programs has been changed, sometimes markedly, but without the elimination of any programs. This amendment and refinement process, sometimes called "incrementalism," may be more consistent with the Congressional legislative process, especially in the absence of a catastrophic crisis which might mobilize wide-scale institutional change.

The purpose of this essay is to provide a framework within which one can analyze alternative welfare reform proposals in the sense of categorizing and examining issues which implicitly or explicitly must be dealt with by welfare reformers. The framework is first developed in terms of issues which should be addressed, and then Carter and Ullman welfare plans are compared and contrasted. The Carter plan was widely viewed as comprehensive welfare reform while the Ullman plan was widely viewed as an "incremental" welfare reform proposal. The major objective here is to ascertain, through the use of the evaluation framework, if there are inherent difficulties with a comprehensive approach to welfare reform. Another objective is to identify logical interdependencies among issues which affect the entire structure of a proposal.

In order to put the analysis in subsequent sections in historical perspective, some background about the Carter proposal is in order. Recognizing that the problems of low-income families involved not only the manner in which they received cash and in-kind (Food Stamps, housing, child care, etc.) assistance, but also matters of access to private and public sector jobs, President Carter—with the approval of House Speaker Tip O'Neill—was able to have the House of Representatives create an ad hoc Welfare Reform Committee to consider the President's proposal. While the Committee was composed of Representatives from the three substantive House Committees having jurisdiction over various aspects of federal aid to the poor (Ways and Means, Labor, and Agriculture), the Committee was never formally a creature of the House Rules. Therefore, it did not have formal jurisdiction over the President's welfare reform proposal, nor did it have the authority to authorize or appropriate any public program. Also, the Committee was under no requirement to operate under the rules of the House with respect to procedure.

In terms of composition, the Welfare Reform Committee contained members from the Ways and Means Subcommittee on Public Assistance and Unemployment Compensation, from the Agriculture Subcommittee on Domestic Marketing, Consumer Relations, and Nutrition (chaired by Congressman Fred Richmond of New York), and from the Labor Subcommittee on Employment Opportunities (chaired by Congressman Hawkins of California). Most remarkable was the appointment by the Speaker of the House of James Corman as chairman of the Ad Hoc Committee along with the appointment to the Ad Hoc Committee of the standing Committee chairmen. Thus, one had the anomalous situation of a member of Ways and Means chairing a committee which inclued the chairman of Ways and Means.

Congressional staff work for the Ad Hoc Welfare Committee was done by Dr. Ken Bowler, Staff Director of the Ways and Means Subcommittee on Public Assistance and Unemployment Compensation, Susan Grayson, Staff Director of the Labor Subcommittee on Employment Opportunities, and John Kramer, Special Counsel to the Agriculture Committee. With regard to tax matters, staff work was performed by the author and Dr. Randall Weiss, both of the staff of the Joint Committee on Taxation. General staff support was also provided by Margaret Malone and Vee Burke of the Congressional Research Service of the Library of Congress, Bill Hoagland and John Korbel of the Congressional Budget Office, and staff from various executive departments.

Concerned about the nature of President Carter's proposal, Congressman Ullman sought early in the history of the Carter effort to dissuade the President from submitting a comprehensive bill to the Congress. He was concerned about the cost and the philosophical shift which a centralized and complete welfare system would represent. When it became apparent that President Carter would submit a comprehensive plan, Ullman sought to construct an alternative to the President's bill and brought together a small staff composed of Dr. Wendell Primus of the Ways and Means staff, the author, and Dr. Randall Weiss which advised him throughout the deliberations of the Welfare Reform Committee.

Below, I outline a comparison between the incremental and comprehensive approaches to welfare reform. Principal among my concerns will be matters involving the cost of various alternatives, the equity and fairness of the proposals, and also whether the proposals would admit of implementation.

An underlying purpose of this essay is to identify why proposals originating from the academic community have significant difficulty in being accepted in the practical world. Having served on both sides of the fence—as a staff aide to the Congress, and as an academic who has generated ideas which have been brought before the Congress—my interpretation may have some value both for analysis in the academic community and the government.

A FRAMEWORK FOR ANALYZING WELFARE REFORM POLICY

Rationale for the Framework

Any comparison of such a large-scale enterprise as reforming our welfare or tax systems must contain values and presumptions about what is important. Such a framework must permit the analyst to compare differences and similarities between proposals and to identify problems in the design of welfare proposals. The framework is sufficiently general to contemplate not only the welfare proposals which were immediately before the Congress, but also other proposals which seek to change laws affecting Aid to Families with Dependent Children (AFDC) or the Food Stamp program. It is hoped that this framework, while sufficiently general, also provides a fair benchmark against which we may compare various welfare reform proposals.

The Framework

There are, in my view, ten areas which any welfare reform proposal must explicitly or implicitly address. I discuss each of these briefly and indicate why a proposal to change the existing welfare system would attempt to address each of these issues.

Theory of poverty. Any welfare proposal, or for that matter even the existing system of assistance to the poor, is based on assumptions as to why people are poor and what society's obligation is to assist them. For example, if one believes that income redistribution is a basic obligation of modern government, and that every member of society should be assured some minimum standard of living—regardless of their ability to produce—then it follows that financial assistance is an entitlement; i.e., an inalienable right of each individual or family to control at least a minimum level of resources. Taking this a step further, if one believes that this right is inalienable, one may also conclude that it is independent of any requirement that an individual work. The absence or presence of a work requirement for those receiving public assistance may then be viewed, in part, as an implicit statement of the theory of poverty underlying the program. Similarly, if part of a proposal involves educational opportunities or educational requirements of the poor, then the underlying theory of poverty is that poor people lack marketable job skills which society ought to provide.

Theory of intergovernmental relations. Because we have a federal system of government, it follows that a program of assistance to individuals must address the question of federal versus state responsibilities.

These questions of relationship between the central and state governments are often overlooked, despite the fact that since the enactment of the Social Security Act during the Depression, virtually all of our social welfare programs have been financed, at least in part, by the federal government but administered entirely by the states on behalf of the federal government (pursuant to federal guidelines and strictures). Any proposed change to the existing system of income transfers to the poor must address this intergovernmental aspect of the current system and define what is the desirable or more appropriate relationship between the federal government and the states.

There are a number of alternative federal-state relationships. Under a centralized theory of federalism, not only would income redistribution be the primary responsibility of the federal government, but it would also be controlled and administered entirely by the federal government with the states acting as passive bystanders. Another possible relationship, which might be described as a decentralized form, would involve complete abrogation of the income-redistribution responsibility of the central government to be accomplished instead by state government. Under this form, the states not only would have primary responsibility for redistributing income throughout the nation, but would also exercise the financial and administrative functions. There are, of course, variations between these two polar caricatures of our current system; however, it is useful to provide them to highlight the importance of intergovernmental relations when addressing changes to our existing system of public welfare.

Cost. This issue—how much proposed changes to the existing system would cost—is addressed directly by virtually all welfare reform proposals. An important consideration when examining the cost of welfare reform is its cost by level of government, both in the near and long term. As will be seen in our discussion of the two proposals before the Ad Hoc Welfare Reform Committee, the matter of cost turned out to be quite important, and in retrospect was the major factor in the ultimate defeat of the comprehensive approach.

Equity. Financial assistance to the poor is, by definition, a redistributive public activity. Accordingly, issues of equity are implicitly or explicitly raised by those who seek to change the existing system of financial assistance. It is useful here to outline the concepts of equity which will be used below. These include vertical equity and horizontal equity. With respect to vertical equity, at issue is whether the benefits provided are sufficient to meet the basic needs of families, and whether the benefits are progressive or regressive when viewed on an after-tax and after-transfer basis. A further important question of vertical equity is whether individuals who are provided financial assistance receive more than they pay into the tax system. The concept of vertical equity becomes especially important when one examines the benefit levels and tax rates of individuals at the edge of poverty.

Horizontal equity concerns the treatment of individuals in the same pretax, pretransfer circumstances. At issue is whether these individuals are treated the same by the transfer system. For example, it is not clear whether a 28-year-old person earning $3,200 yearly and a person getting Social Security of equal value are in different economic circumstances; however, the tax and transfer systems view their situations differently. Similarly, whether or not a family of two adults with two children and a family of one adult with three children, both with the same earnings, are in the same circumstance may be viewed as problematical.

Finally, when examining the issues of vertical and horizontal equity, it is important to determine how the transfer system treats individuals and family units over time. To the extent that resources are scarce and limited to providing assistance to needy individuals at any given moment, we must question whether proposed expenditures will be accurate in assisting only those currently in need. Similarly, one should determine whether programs of assistance have a chance of helping individuals to the point that their dependency on the public transfer system is diminished.

Feasibility. Academics are usually not overly concerned with questions of feasibility. On the other hand, elected officials seem preoccupied with whether proposed changes in current practice can indeed be achieved. Three forms of feasibility may be distinguished for analytical purposes. First, is the change managerially feasible, i.e., can the new policy be managed efficiently to achieve its goals? Second, can existing institutions reasonably expect the policy to be implemented smoothly, given current and proposed resources as well as institutional constraints? The feasibility concerns of elected officials seem quite pragmatic, for such officials need to take into account the resistance and inertia which existing institutions have to change. It may well be that a given policy could be managed if a new organization were started from scratch, but there is usually an existing delivery system which employs thousands of well-intentioned individuals throughout the country who may or may not wish to change. Third, we must be concerned with political feasibility. Here the analysts' problem is straightforward: Are there enough votes in the House of Representatives and the Senate, given their disparate interests, to assure that the proposal will be adopted?

Correctibility. The issue of correctibility entails consideration of the reform's effect on existing practices and institutions, and in particular whether adoption of the change will preclude subsequent corrections in the system. A closely associated question is whether the proposal will generate information about its effects on practices and institutions so that the new system will be allowed to self-correct through time. A simple example will illustrate the issue of correctibility. Under President Carter's welfare reform proposal, Food Stamps would have been eliminated. Before eliminating such a major program, however, the analyst may want to determine how difficult it would be to reinstitute in-kind transfers were it found that the elimination of Food Stamps had a deleterious effect on the welfare of poor people. Radical reforms that sweep aside many existing practices and institutions may, in fact, not permit such correction.

Incentives. Academic researchers—and especially economists—who have looked at questions of income redistribution have been preoccupied with the issue of incentives. There have been numerous experiments, involving many millions of dollars, which have attempted to determine whether new forms of financial assistance to the poor would materially affect their willingness to work. But we should also be concerned with the degree to which a proposed change contains mechanisms designed to induce institutions and delivery systems to achieve desired goals. For example, where a proposal seeks to improve the accuracy of payments to the poor and thereby eliminate erroneous payments to the nonpoor, we should ask whether the proposal includes meaningful incentives for the reduction in such error rates. Similarly, we should determine whether the proposal includes incentives for the creation of new jobs for the poor and whether there is accountability in the new institutions administering the program.

Certainty and risk. Any proposal for changing existing institutions must involve some risk. At issue is the magnitude and the probability distribution of such risks. These risks in the context of welfare reform entail not only whether more poor people will be helped at a lower administrative cost, but also whether there are significant risks of cost overrun.

Side effects on other programs. It is convenient to view the welfare system as an independent slice of greater society and to consider only questions of whether the millions of individuals, currently poor and not receiving assistance, would begin to receive cash assistance under proposed reforms. In fact, however, there are numerous programs of cash and in-kind assistance to the poor. Thus, the question arises as to whether proposed changes in welfare would have any unexpected effects on service delivery demands on other parts of the welfare system. For example, both the President's and Congressman Ullman's proposals would have increased the number of individuals eligible to receive welfare benefits. Since Title XX of the Social Security Act provides a variety of social services to individuals who qualify for welfare, and since the Medicaid program pays for the medical care of the same individuals, there would have been significant increases in demand for both Title XX and Medicaid benefits. However, neither proposal addressed this indirect problem.

Participation. Until very recently, there has been little research examining the relationship between the number of individuals eligible for a public program and the number who actually enroll in the program. It has been estimated that, because of misrepresentation on the part of applicants and lax enforcement of eligibility requirements on the part of administrators, more than 100% of the individuals eligibile for AFDC in New York City actually participated (Boland, 1973). On the other hand, it has been estimated that the participation rate in the Food Stamp program has been under 50% (MacDonald, 1977); the participation rate in the children's portion of the Supplemental Security Income (SSI) program appears to be even lower, about 25% (Breen, 1980), and the participation rate of adults in SSI was found to be under 50% (Strauss, 1977). Any cost projections for a welfare reform proposal, of course, are dependent on accurate estimates of participation rates. Furthermore, the analyst should be concerned with how well or how poorly a given welfare reform proposal addresses the issue of under- or overparticipation.

ANALYSIS OF THE CARTER AND ULLMAN WELFARE REFORMS WITHIN THE EVALUATION FRAMEWORK

Theory of Poverty

An examination of welfare law—especially the AFDC and Food Stamp programs—suggests that the poor and their children have been accorded a right or entitlement to a minimum standard of living from the federal government. However, examining the evolution of these programs suggests that there has not been a consistent theory of why the poor are poor. Nevertheless, recent years have seen increased emphasis on encouraging adults with school-age children to work. Indeed, a part of these work requirements in the AFDC and Food Stamp laws has been the stricture that refusal to accept an available private sector job should entail a diminution of welfare benefits. This policy suggests that the theory of poverty implicit in our current welfare system is that the poor are poor because of inadequate job opportunities. Note also the implicit presumption that children of the poor are best cared for by their parents during their early years.

In addition to Food Stamps and AFDC, another important program of income support is the Supplemental Security Income program (SSI) which provides categorical assistance to the elderly and disabled who are poor. Unlike Food Stamps and AFDC, there is no presumption in SSI that the elderly and disabled should obtain private sector jobs.

In the case of SSI, lack of employment is not viewed as cause of poverty; in fact, there is no work requirement under the SSI program.

Under the Better Jobs and Income Program (BJIP) submitted to the Congress by President Carter on September 12, 1977, and under Congressman Ullman's incremental counter proposal, HR10711, the relationship between beneficiaries of cash and in-kind assistance and the job market was altered. Both proposals attempted to provide public jobs to the poor and, in effect, make the federal government the employer of last resort. Both programs have significant public sector employment programs, although the Carter jobs program was much larger than Ullman's program; the BJIP jobs program had no ceiling on the number of public sector jobs to be created.

Under BJIP, beneficiaries of cash assistance would be on the "lower tier" of cash assistance for a short time during which it was assumed they would look for work. If jobs were not available from the private sector, the federal government would provide public sector jobs. The waiting period prior to provision of public sector employment was quite nominal, only 4 weeks.

Under the Ullman proposal, the discrepancy between cash and in-kind benefits and public-sector wages was greater, and also there were more numerous incentives to take private sector jobs. For example, tax credits were provided to employers to encourage them in hiring low-income individuals. The waiting period for public-sector employment was much greater under the Ullman proposal vis-à-vis Carter's proposal, thus providing a greater incentive for individuals to take a private sector job.

Both proposals stressed the relationship between the job market and poverty of individuals. In effect, both proposals subscribed to the theory that employment opportunities are a significant determinant of low-income status; both proposals implicity rejected the "culture of poverty" theory which holds that poor individuals remain poor because their behavioral patterns and attitudes, which are passed from generation to generation, represent an adaptation to poverty and not to the world of work (Lewis, 1965).

Theory of Intergovernmental Relations

Under current law, a fragmented approach to fiscal federalism prevails. A consistent thread among the several welfare programs which have been candidates for reform in recent years has been the assumption that states should deliver services and thus act as the fiscal agent of the federal government. One also finds in current law the presumption that federal employees should not directly provide eligibility and benefit payment services. For example, Food Stamps is entirely federal in that the rules determining the level and rate of reduction of benefits, as well as overall eligibility, are entirely federal. Food Stamp benefits are also paid entirely from federal funds. However, the individuals actually deciding who will and will not receive Food Stamp benefits are state employees paid from federal and state funds. AFDC is partially federal and partially state financed. Most eligibility requirements are set forth in the Social Security Act. A few eligibility requirements are left to the states based on the submission of a state plan to the federal government. However, AFDC is entirely administered by the states.

Perhaps most indicative of the contradictory nature of the fiscal federalism theory implied by our current welfare system is the fact that under AFDC the basic guarantee level of cash assistance (the amount a family receives if they have no earnings) is set by the states, with the federal government setting the *rate* of benefit reduction (the rate at which benefits decrease as income increases). Thus, we now have 51 different benefit levels throughout the country. In addition, the costs of administering AFDC and the cost of the assistance itself are shared between federal and state government, and in some instances costs are even shared by the states and their localities. This is, if you will, a "federal partnership approach" to the provision of cash assistance to the poor.

A second form of intergovernmental relations may be observed with regard to the current SSI program. Under the SSI program, cash assistance is entirely financed by the federal government, and administration is entirely federally controlled by the Social Security Administration. This small program of 5.2 million beneficiaries in 1979 is the only example of federal service delivery directly to the poor. Note, however, that there is no work requirement and individuals are categorically eligible on the basis of income, assets, age, and health status. Under AFDC and Food Stamps, family composition is an additional consideration, and the AFDC and Food Stamp programs serve considerably larger number of individuals, about 12 million in the case of AFDC and nearly 20 million in the case of Food Stamps.

The Carter proposal consolidated several existing programs; namely, SSI, Food Stamps, and AFDC, all of which would have been consolidated into one program of cash assistance. On the other hand, the states would continue to set guarantee levels with federal matching of costs. The extent of the matching of federal funds to state funds would be federally determined, as would the income and wealth levels that determine eligibility. However, administration of these provisions would be left up to the states or the states and their localities. Thus, under the Carter proposal there would be a perpetuation of the state (or state and locally) administered system.

Under the Ullman proposal, there was very clear delineation of intergovernmental responsibilities. States were again viewed as fiscal agents of the federal government as is currently the case with Food Stamps. Local, optional administration of AFDC was eliminated from current law, leaving only state administration of eligibility determination. Eligibility and benefit reduction rate would be entirely federally defined. Federal and state costs would also be clearly defined, with no matching on the part of state governments. Finally, over time state payment for AFDC would be phased out, except to the extent that the state made errors in administering the program.

An interesting intergovernmental aspect of the Carter proposal was the relationship of federal and state governments in the attempt to create jobs. (See also the discussion below on incentives.) Under current law, the Work Incentives Now (WIN) program provides about 25,000 public-sector jobs for the able-bodied poor with school-age children. Under the WIN program, responsibility for job creation, job counseling, and referral of such individuals to private sector jobs is a shared responsibility among the Secretary of Labor, the governor of each state, his advisory counsel composed of labor and management, and the state and field offices of the state employment services. Thus, unlike AFDC and Food Stamps, which have a fairly clear delegation of final authority to the federal government and the state governments, respectively, WIN's job creation, job counseling, and job referral have no final delegation of adminstrative responsibility. This may explain why the WIN program has not been very successful over the years.

The Carter program would have relied on the Comprehensive Employment and Training Act (CETA), prime sponsors to create jobs, rather than the existing WIN program. Note that CETA would force localities to create the jobs. However, if localities failed to create jobs, the states would, in effect, be forced to continue matching their funds with federal funds to finance the cash benefits to which unemployed individuals would be entitled. Such a system, of course, would punish states for the failures of localities.

Under the Ullman proposal, in contrast, states would be responsible for creating jobs under a revised WIN employment program which clarified the administrative control of WIN. The restructuring of the relationship between the federal Department of Labor and the state so that the WIN program—and therefore the Public Sector Employment program—would be put on the same basis as AFDC was mandated by the Ullman proposal. Under the Ullman proposal, each state would provide to the Secretary of Labor, as they then provided to the Secretary of HEW, a plan of how they would administer the job creation program. Ullman's proposal matched the source of fiscal liability for potentially higher benefit costs with the source of control over the job creation program. Thus, under the Ullman program, if jobs were not created by the states, the states would have to pay for cash benefits entirely.

The Carter proposal's absence of clear responsibility for administration of the cash portion, and the absence of a matching of fiscal responsibilities and administrative responsibilities for the job program, would probably have created reverse incentives for the states not to create jobs for individuals. To the extent that individuals who initially take public-sector jobs can obtain marketable skills useful in the private sector, the Carter program would continue dependency rather than diminish it because the intergovernmental aspect of the program was not clearly defined. On the other hand, the Ullman program continued existing relationships, although clarifying these relationships by centralizing them at the state level. Thus, the Ullman proposal may be viewed as superior to the Carter proposal in that the level of benefits was entirely determinative within the framework of federal law. Under the Ullman proposal, both the guarantee level and the rate of reduction were federally determined, state by state, and could not be altered by the states unless they financed higher benefits entirely at their own expense. On the other hand, the Carter proposal was indeterminative because the federal government was forced to match—on an unlimited basis—state funds in meeting the state-determined guarantee level.

Cost

A complete history of welfare reform in the late 1970s will undoubtedly include details of the various cost estimation techniques used by the Administration and the Congressional Budget Office (CBO) to provide accurate price tags for the various welfare proposals. Existing welfare programs which were under discussion—AFDC, Food Stamps, and SSI—amounted to about $42 billion in 1982 dollars (CBO, 1978). HEW claimed that the Carter proposal would cost an additional $2.8 billion in 1982. On the other hand, when the Congressional Budget Office (1978) provided its cost estimates of the Carter proposal, it estimated that the incremental federal cost for BJIP would be $17.4 billion in 1982. By the time the Welfare Reform Committee completed its deliberations on the Carter proposal, the estimated 1982 cost had increased to almost $25 billion.

The very large disparity between the HEW and CBO estimates may be explained by several factors. First, the HEW figure was a net figure which included as offsets increased revenue to the federal government from proposed legislation. In particular, it was assumed that 7.9 billion additional dollars from the excise tax on crude oil could be directed to the program of welfare reform. Second, HEW made some very modest estimates of the number of individuals who would continue to receive cash assistance under the unemployed parent (AFDC-UP) segment of their program. Third, it was assumed that many private-sector and some public-sector jobs would be made available and thus relieve welfare costs. Fourth, HEW planners assumed that participation in the welfare system, under the consolidated program of cash assistance, would not change at all. CBO made rather different, and more reasonable, assumptions about the availability of private-sector jobs and behavioral responses to the Carter proposal. Congressional skepticism of the $2.8 billion cost figure was widespread and adversely affected the Department's effectiveness before the Committee.

Under the Ullman proposal, the additional cost estimated by Congressional staff was between $7.5 and $8 billion; HEW estimated the Ullman proposal cost to be $12 to $15 billion. Thus, the program which left Food Stamps intact, left the SSI program untouched, and had a ceiling on public sector jobs, was thought by HEW to be more expensive than the Carter proposal which would have consolidated and increased eligibility for all three programs.

It should be noted, of course, that neither incremental nor comprehensive welfare reform was enacted by the Congress. The enormous additional outlays entailed by either program at a time when the budget was in deficit and a recession quite likely, led the Congress to conclude that it could not afford the cost of either reform program. Subsequently, in late 1979, the House of Representatives did pass an incremental welfare bill modeled on the Ullman proposal. However, the Senate had not taken up the matter by late 1980.

The intellectual history of welfare reform that has yet to be written should, in my opinion, involve a rather careful discussion of the cost estimation techniques used by proponents and opponents of particular welfare proposals. HEW began its analysis with a complicated and undocumented computer program, known as the KGB model, which contained routines for estimating the behavioral responses of individuals to the provisions of specific welfare proposals. This program was used in calculating the final number of eligibles. The model was not made available to Congressional staff for a considerable time, and its accuracy could not therefore be independently checked.

Cost estimation for the Ullman proposal was done by the Ways and Means and Joint Tax Committee staffs who used data based on existing welfare programs. Thus, for example, estimates of the additional cost of the Food Stamp program caused by more generous eligibility requirements were done by using a sample of 1977 Food Stamp beneficiaries. Similarly, the cost of the enhanced AFDC program was estimated using data on a sample of AFDC recipients by state. Of particular importance is the fact that these two samples were drawn from the operating welfare system and represent a 1-month slice of history in 1977. By contrast, the KGB model was based on data from the Survey of Income and Education (SIE) which contained annual information about individuals' work histories and earnings. As such, the SIE required that individuals recall their earnings and hours worked over the prior calendar year—a technique guaranteed to introduce error. Ultimately, HEW began using these program data files to calculate the cost of alternative incremental welfare reform proposals. Without research beyond the scope of this essay, it cannot be said with great accuracy that the use of those program data files led to more inaccurate predictions of cost than the predicions made by the staffs of the Ways and Means and Joint Tax Committees.

Equity

In 1978, the poverty line for a family of four, as determined by the Social Security Adminstration, was approximately $6,770. Column 1 of Table 1 shows, state by state, the value of AFDC cash and Food Stamp benefits available to a mother with 3 children in 1979. Taking the $6,770 figure as a benchmark, anywhere from 50% to 120% of the poverty line was provided throughout the United States, depending on the state in question. Of course, the $6,770 is a national estimate and cost of living varies considerably, both within and between states, as well as between urban and rural areas. However, at the outset, despite the question of cost of living differences, one may ask whether the benefit variation among the states shown in Table 1 is horizontally equitable. Guarantees, and thus benefits, vary significantly depending upon the state in which a family of four might reside.

This comparison of benefits among the states for a similarly situated family has often been described as the "welfare problem." Welfare benefits are generally much lower in the South than in other parts of the country, and this discrepancy has been the source of much criticism. Another horizontal equity consideration reflected in Column 2 of Table 1 is the relationship of guarantee levels among contiguous states. It is often claimed by states adjacent to New York, for example, that if they raise their welfare levels to the level of New York—which is among the highest in the country—they could well experience a significant in-migration of poor individuals from New York. Of interest,

TABLE 1: COMPARISON OF GUARANTEE LEVELS BY STATE AND BETWEEN-STATE BENEFIT DIFFERENCES FOR THREE WELFARE PLANS IN 1979

	Current law				Carter proposal				Ullman proposal			
State	(1) Guarantee level	(2) Av. guarantee in contiguous state	(3) Contiguous state differential	(4) % Differential	(5) Guarantee level	(6) Av. guarantee in contiguous state	(7) Contiguous state differential	(8) % Differential	(9) Guarantee level	(10) Av. guarantee in contiguous state	(11) Contiguous state differential	(12) % Differential
Alabama	$3932.	$3899.	$ 33.	.0085	$4452.	$4452.	$ 0.	.0000	$4452.	$4452.	$ 0.	.0000
Alaska	7704.	—	—	—	7704.	—	—	—	7173.	—	—	—
Arizona	4469.	5392.	−923.	−.2064	4469.	5392.	−923.	−.2064	4452.	5491.	−1039.	−.2333
Arkansas	4268.	4241.	27.	.0062	4452.	4655.	−203.	−.0456	4452.	4640.	−188.	−.0423
California	6242.	5315.	927.	.1486	6242.	5315.	927.	.1486	6527.	5293.	1234.	.1891
Colorado	5267.	5284.	−17.	−.0032	5267.	5284.	−17.	−.0032	5442.	5245.	197.	.0362
Connecticut	6821.	6135.	686.	.1005	6821.	6135.	686.	.1005	6159.	6414.	−255.	−.0414
Delaware	5099.	5528.	−429.	−.0841	5099.	5528.	−429.	−.0841	5244.	5587.	−343.	−.0653
Washington, D.C.	5326.	5217.	110.	.0206	5326.	5217.	110.	.0206	5498.	4980.	519.	.0943
Florida	4335.	3932.	403.	.0930	4452.	4452.	0.	.0000	4452.	4452.	0.	.0000
Georgia	3932.	4048.	−116.	−.0295	4452.	4452.	0.	.0000	4452.	4452.	0.	.0000
Hawaii	8222.	—	—	—	8222.	—	—	—	7065.	—	—	—
Idaho	5771.	5733.	38.	.0065	5771.	5733.	38.	.0065	5640.	5674.	−34.	−.0060
Illinois	5486.	5408.	78.	.0142	5486.	5408.	78.	.0142	5527.	5627.	−100.	−.0181
Indiana	4998.	5481.	−483.	−.0967	4998.	5481.	−483.	−.0967	5885.	5482.	403.	.0685
Iowa	6006.	5742.	264.	.0440	6006.	5742.	264.	.0440	6018.	5794.	224.	.0372
Kansas	5746.	5297.	450.	.0782	5746.	5297.	450.	.0782	5423.	5376.	47.	.0087
Kentucky	4662.	4954.	−292.	−.0626	4662.	5028.	−366.	−.0786	4753.	5040.	−287.	−.0060
Louisiana	4133.	3843.	290.	.0702	4452.	4452.	0.	.0000	4452.	4452.	0.	.0000

Maine	5326.	5595.	−269.	−.0505	5326.	5595.	−269.	−.0505	5498.	5678.	−180.	−.0327
Maryland	4931.	5306.	−375.	−.0760	4932.	5306.	−375.	−.0760	4932.	5253.	−321.	−.0651
Massachusetts	6015.	6300.	−285.	−.0474	6015.	6300.	−285.	−.0474	6169.	6195.	−26.	−.0042
Michigan	6636.	5070.	1567.	.2361	6636.	5070.	1567.	.2361	6593.	5470.	1123.	.1703
Minnesota	6250.	5971.	280.	.0447	6250.	5971.	280.	.0447	6348.	6034.	314.	.0494
Mississippi	3396.	4066.	−670.	−.1974	4452.	4452.	0.	.0000	4452.	4452.	0.	.0000
Missouri	4839.	5148.	−309.	−.0638	4839.	5236.	−397.	−.0819	4772.	5239.	−467.	−.0979
Montana	5469.	5590.	−121.	−.0222	5469.	5590.	−121.	−.0222	5215.	5534.	−319.	−.0611
Nebraska	5796.	5442.	354.	.0611	5796.	5442.	354.	.0611	6027.	5354.	673.	.1117
Nevada	5007.	5756.	−749.	−.1496	5007.	5756.	−749.	−.1496	5017.	5777.	−760.	−.1515
New Hampshire	5595.	6012.	−417.	−.0745	5595.	6012.	−417.	−.0745	5678.	5911.	−233.	−.0410
New Jersey	5830.	5869.	−39.	−.0067	5830.	5869.	−39.	−.0067	5895.	5923.	−28.	−.0048
New Mexico	4612.	4943.	−331.	−.0717	4612.	5060.	−448.	−.0972	4611.	5093.	−482.	−.1045
New York	6687.	6237.	450.	.0674	6687.	6237.	450.	.0674	6593.	6044.	549.	.0832
North Carolina	4368.	4260.	109.	.0248	4452.	4715.	−263.	−.0590	4452.	4596.	−144.	.0323
North Dakota	5796.	5754.	42.	.0072	5796.	5754.	42.	.0072	6027.	5649.	378.	.0627
Ohio	5141.	5380.	−239.	−.0464	5141.	5380.	−239.	−.0464	5055.	5546.	−491.	−.0971
Oklahoma	5284.	4766.	518.	.0980	5284.	4895.	389.	.0737	5262.	4859.	403.	.0767
Oregon	6468.	5849.	619.	.0957	6468.	5849.	619.	.0957	6410.	5911.	499.	.0778
Pennsylvania	5822.	5411.	411.	.0705	5822.	5411.	411.	.0705	5933.	5408.	525.	.0931
Rhode Island	5704.	6418.	−714.	−.1252	5704.	6418.	−714.	−.1252	6480.	6164.	316.	.0488
South Carolina	3672.	4150.	−478.	−.1302	4452.	4452.	0.	.0000	4452.	4452.	0.	.0000
South Dakota	5544.	5761.	−217.	−.0392	5544.	5761.	−217.	−.0392	5385.	5786.	−401.	−.0745
Tennessee	3932.	4362.	−430.	−.1095	4452.	4658.	−206.	−.0462	4452.	4602.	−150.	−.0336
Texas	3864.	4574.	−710.	−.1838	4452.	4700.	−248.	−.0557	4452.	4694.	−242.	−.0544
Utah	5830.	5063.	767.	.1316	5830.	5063.	767.	.1316	5857.	5041.	816.	.1393
Vermont	6695.	6099.	596.	.0890	6695.	6099.	596.	.0890	6065.	6147.	−82.	−.0135
Virginia	5502.	4667.	836.	.1519	5502.	4767.	735.	.1336	5027.	4775.	252.	.0501
Washington	6376.	6120.	257.	.0402	6376.	6120.	257.	.0402	6461.	6025.	436.	.0675
West Virginia	4780.	5212.	−432.	−.0903	4780.	5212.	−432.	−.0903	4564.	5140.	−576.	−.1262
Wisconsin	6536.	5914.	622.	.0952	6536.	5914.	622.	.0952	6707.	5964.	743.	.1107
Wyoming	5250.	5613.	−363.	−.0691	5250.	5613.	−363.	−.0691	5083.	5594.	−511.	−.1006

Source: Congressional Research Service (1979).

therefore, is the average maximum AFDC and Food Stamp benefits available to individuals in states contiguous to any given state. Column 2 shows this average figure. Thus, for example, Massachusetts, which has a guarantee level of $6,015 for a family of four, has neighbors whose maximum benefit level averages $6,300. Column 3 shows the difference between the state in question and the average for contiguous states. Negative differences indicate that the state is relatively low in its provision of assistance and Food Stamps compared to neighboring states. Thus, Arizona, which has a guarantee level of $4,469, is $923 below its neighbors. These disparities among contiguous states may be viewed as undesirable because they cause undue pressure for migration.

If one takes the average of Column 1, the average guarantee among the states is $5,399 with a standard deviation of $1,004. Thus the coefficient of variation is 18.6%. One may view the national equity problem as the extent of the coefficient of variation in the column of guarantees.

One of the remarkable characteristics of the Carter proposal was that the complex matching requirements, which would appear to have changed current law dramatically, actually left the matching rate identical to current law. The level of benefits under the Carter proposal is represented in Column 5 of Table 1 and is the larger of the minimum guarantee, $4,452, and current law in 1979. The mean guarantee under Carter's proposal is $5,491 with a standard deviation of $875. The coefficient of variation in benefit levels is 15.9%.

The Ullman proposal, which as noted previously contained federally mandated guarantee levels and benefit reduction rates, did provide for interstate variation in benefit levels. It did so by tying the minimum guarantee to 30% of the median family income for a family of four in each state (based on pretax, pretransfer income). Column 9 of Table 1 displays the guarantee levels that would result under this fixed formula proposal. Overall, the average guarantee would be $5,470 with a standard deviation of $798 and a coefficient of variation of 14.6%. This constitutes about a 25% reduction in interstate benefit differentials and a 1% reduction in the amount of contiguous state disparities. Thus, if one compares the Carter and Ullman proposals to current law, one finds that interstate disparities are reduced by the Ullman proposal. Moreover, under the Ullman proposal there would be much greater certainty in benefit levels among states since guarantee levels would be entirely federally mandated. By contrast, under Carter's proposal, there was the possibility that states might continue to exacerbate the interstate differentials because the matching rates would effectively be the same as current law, i.e., between 50% and 80% depending on the state's inverse per-capita income.

Over time, both the Carter and Ullman proposals would increase the amount of assistance available in response to inflation. The impact of this increase under the Carter proposal would have been to freeze the relative distribution displayed in Column 5 of Table 1. Under the Ullman proposal, states which had relatively low benefit levels would have had their guarantee levels increased by more than the inflation rate until reaching a predetermined target level. This target level was set at a specified fraction of median family income. On the other hand, states whose guarantees were above 30% of the median family income for a family of four would have had their guarantee levels eroded by inflation until they reached the target. Thereafter, the guarantees would be indexed by the inflation rate. Table 1 assumes such erosion has occurred in the few states whose guarantees in 1979 exceeded 30% of the median family income.

An important source of cost differentials between the Carter and Ullman plans was the increment in guarantee level resulting from differential family size. Under the Ullman plan, the increment was not available, and the guarantee level was fixed based on a family size of four. Under the Carter proposal, on the other hand, there were mandated increments for family size. The Carter program should thus be viewed as being superior to the Ullman proposal as well as superior to current law which increments differentially depending on the program in question. Under Food Stamps, for example, the guarantee level is now incremented based on budget studies and on inflation rates in the cost of food. AFDC on the other hand does not change unless acted upon by the states.

Single individuals receive no cash assistance under any federal program and thus are eligible only for Food Stamps. Under the Carter proposal, single individuals would have been provided cash assistance. Similarly, intact families are not eligible for assistance in some states because these states have not adopted the optional AFDC-UP (Unemployed Parent) program to assist intact families. Again, under current law, the guarantee level for intact families in states which have adopted the AFDC-UP program is entirely under the control of the state.

Thus, with regard to equity considerations that depend on family size or family composition, the Carter program may be viewed as superior both to current law and to the Ullman proposal. Also, the Carter program was universal in coverage, whereas current law does not provide assistance to individuals or to childless couples. The Ullman proposal continued current gaps in coverage and did not provide assistance for single individuals and childless couples.

Another aspect of equity involves the responsiveness to changes in the economic circumstances of families. Under the Carter proposal, a long accounting period (6 months) was proposed. As a result, families that had sudden changes in employment or marital status that resulted in inadequate incomes could not become eligible for benefits until the 6-month waiting period had elapsed. Under the Ullman proposal, a 1-month retrospective accounting period was used, which made the proposal quite responsive to changes in income circumstances. To offset the increased cost which a very short accounting period might entail, the Ullman proposal contained an ingenious program of "recoupment" of excess welfare benefits which would be administered through the tax system. Under recoupment, beneficiaries who had significant earnings for part of the year were required to pay back excess transfer payments when filing their taxes on April 15. For such beneficiaries, the transfers of cash and Food Stamps were viewed in effect as loans which, due to the overall annual earnings of the beneficiaries, were to be repaid at the end of the year.

Both the Carter and Ullman proposals made the earned income-tax credit, which is available under current law, immediately refundable through the withholding system. Interestingly, this feature of the Carter and Ullman proposals was enacted as part of the tax reform act of 1978.

Feasibility

With regard to managerial feasibility, the Carter proposal might be viewed as bordering on a disaster. For example, the Administration recommended the creation of computer centers to be run by each of the states. These state computers would feed into a central computer system in Baltimore to be controlled by the Social Security Administration. Discussions with computer experts from the academic community and the Department of Defense indicated that such a computer system would be larger than anything currently known to exist. This would include the ARFA system, which took 10 years to become operational. Moreover, the General Accounting Office, which investigated the manner in which the Administration administered computer resources in the SSI program, reached the conclusion that the Social Security Administration should not be permitted to have any additional computers until it used those currently in storage. When reviewing the computer component of the Carter proposal, the Welfare Reform Committee voted down the Administration's proposal for a national computer network with the state control of the input information. An important consideration in making this decision was the Committee's belief that to have state control of input and federal liability for part of the cost would insure high levels of erroneous information and higher federal cost.

Both the Carter and Ullman proposals presumed that there would be large-scale, public-sector job creation. To date, the country has not had much experience with programs on the order of $8 to $13 billion—the price tag associated with the jobs portion of the Carter bill. Until very recently, the Comprehensive Employment and Training Act (CETA), has not been an income-conditioned, job-creation program. Rather, it has been a way to achieve employment stability through local governments. Several studies have demonstrated that CETA has simply resulted in keeping municipal employees from being laid off as a result of fiscal conditions at the local level. It would be reasonable to question, therefore, whether the jobs portion of either the Carter or Ullman proposal would be managerially feasible. The Carter proposal appeared to be analytically neat in that there would no longer be a Food Stamp or an SSI program. Instead, there would be one administrative unit to provide cash assistance to the needy. However, serious doubts about the computer capability essential to such a system lead one to question its feasibility. By the same token, the consolidation of the Food Stamp and AFDC programs entertained under the Ullman proposal, which would entail a single application form, a more common definition of income and assets, and a more consistent definition of the filing unit, still leads one to question whether even this more modest consolidation could be managed.

The Carter proposal maintained the current practice of state or state and local administration, and at the same time maintained state level computerization. By contrast, the Ullman proposal moved to state-only administration, which while logical, would take considerable time to implement. States such as Michigan, which have gone from a state-local system to a state-only system, have taken anywhere from 3 to 5 years to smooth out relations between state field offices and the state central office. While the Ullman proposal achieved a responsiveness in the provision of assistance by using a short accounting period, it relied on recoupment of excess welfare payments through the tax system in order to maintain overall cost control. But the Internal Revenue Service (IRS) and the Department of Treasury's review of recoupment raised serious questions about whether such a system could be managed. IRS claimed that forcing its agents to go into low-income areas of core cities could cause significant difficulties in raising even very modest sums of revenue. With regard to the refundability of the earned income-tax credit proposed by Carter and Ullman, it is likely that we will now have some real experience with the degree to which the tax system can provide such welfare benefits through the withholding system.

Whether existing institutions would be able to successfully implement the proposed changes is very much an open question. The

Carter proposal was relatively silent on how its new program of cash assistance would be administered. As noted, there was significant skepticism about the ability of computer technology to administer an on-line system of eligibility determination and benefit payout for 25 to 30 million individuals. The Ullman proposal required very clear changes in operating procedure and would have required substantial coordination between the Food Stamp and AFDC programs. The Departments of HEW and Agriculture were required to issue joint regulations and presumably something like this could be achieved. Also, the public service, job-creation portion of the Ullman proposal was to be administered through a revised WIN program. While clarity and symmetry were an important part of the Ullman proposal, it is still unclear whether existing agencies, especially the Employment Service and the federal Department of Labor, would accept these clarifications of responsibility. On the other hand, ambiguity can be an important source of authority and power, and may permit states to more naturally evolve efficient relationships between the local employment service office and the federal department itself.

The political feasibility of the Carter and Ullman proposals is quite easy to assess and in retrospect indicates why comprehensive welfare reform did not occur. In late 1977, the Food Stamp program was materially amended after considerable debate in the Congress. The 1977 amendments to the Food Stamp law resulted from urban, liberal interests and rural, conservative interests liberalizing Food Stamp benefits. The effective date of the amendment was not until 1979, so the Carter proposal could be viewed as trying to erase a series of changes which the Congress had made, but not yet put into effect. Also, the Carter proposal contained, as indicated earlier, a fair amount of deception as to its ultimate budgetary impact. Furthermore, the draft bill contained numerous technical errors. Both these factors antagonized the Congress. Coupled with the lack of agency support for the program by providing accurate analysis to the Congress, it was easy to predict that the Carter proposal would never be broadly accepted in the House or Senate.

The Ullman proposal benefited from being much less costly and more technically coherent than the Carter bill. As the Carter bill worked its way through the Welfare Reform Committee, it was clear that a vote on Carter versus Ullman would be quite close. History notes that on that up or down vote, the Ullman bill lost and the amended version of the Carter bill won. What history does not report, but which was factually the case, was that Ullman elected not to ask two of the Ways and Means Committee members of the Welfare Reform Committee, who would have responded if asked, to support his bill. The close vote by the Welfare Reform Committee for the Carter bill meant that welfare reform in the House was dead, for a close vote in a friendly, liberal committee meant that the Carter proposal could never be passed by the full House of Representatives.

Beyond the issue of aggregate costs, the political feasibility of the Ullman and Carter bills hinged in good measure on whether the states (especially representatives of the National Governors' Conference) supported either proposal. An important element in their support was the degree of fiscal relief provided to the states. Lobbyists for the Governors' Conference named a price tag of $1.5 billion as the minimum amount of fiscal relief they would accept in exchange for their support. For those who were ultimately involved in the negotiations between the Administration and the Governors' Conference, or between the Congress and the Governors' Conference, it is a sad commentary that fiscal relief became a far more important issue than providing financial assistance to the poor. In retrospect, the price tag of $1.5 billion may have been the stumbling block for any welfare reform proposal to the Congress.

Correctibility and Impact on Future Options

The Carter bill, because it was a comprehensive proposal, was properly viewed by the Congress as a high-risk proposition. If the "cashing out" of Food Stamps was not successful—and there was reason to believe that low benefit states might be unwilling to give the poor significant additional amounts of cash instead of Food Stamps—there would be no easy way to provide assistance to the poor. In short, once eliminated, the Food Stamp program might prove very difficult to bring back. In this respect at least, the Carter proposal must be given a low score on correctibility. The Ullman proposal, on the other hand, because it constituted a series of incremental changes in current AFDC and Food Stamp law, was probably more correctible than the Carter proposal. However, neither proposal systematically generated information which could be used to redirect the program if it departed from its intended course. Under the Ullman bill, penalties were imposed on states whose error rate was above certain thresholds; however, there has been little experience with the use of error rate penalties in encouraging states to improve their administration of the AFDC or Food Stamp program.

While the Ullman proposal constituted an incremental consolidation of AFDC and Food Stamps, it should be noted that it would permit later, complete federalization of the program by combining Food Stamps and AFDC into a cash program. Carter's proposal, on the other hand, was a national program from the outset, although as previously noted, it presented serious questions of feasibility. If one takes administrative and managerial feasibility into account, and especially if one takes political feasibility into account, in retrospect one can say Ullman's proposal rather than Carter's would be the long-run comprehensive approach to welfare reform because it permitted incremental changes in the welfare system which could be evaluated in stages. The Carter proposal, because it was not very feasible, might be viewed as futile rather than comprehensive.

Incentives

Significant research has gone into the work incentives implied by current AFDC and Food Stamp law. If one takes into account the benefit reduction rates under AFDC, Food Stamps, and the earned income-tax credit, there is a net tax on earnings of 75%. Put another way, individuals who earn a dollar get to keep only 25¢ as a result of the reduction rate inherent in AFDC, Food Stamps, and the earned income-tax credit. There is evidence that such implicit tax rates discourage work. Under the Carter proposal, the single-parent family would face an implicit tax rate of 60% on earnings of up to $333 per month, and 65% thereafter. While this implicit tax rate is below current law, it is still quite high. Under the Ullman proposal, single-parent families would face an implicit tax rate of 53% on earnings up to $416 a month, 73% on earnings of $416 to $595 per month, and 53% again on earnings above $595 per month. Ullman thus achieved a lower effective tax rate on earnings up to $416 a month than either Carter or current law, and then a much higher tax rate than Carter from $416 to almost $600 a month. Thus, incentives under the Ullman proposal, although more complicated than under the Carter proposal or current law, certainly would provide more incentive for low-income families to work and thereby avoid complete dependency on public largess.

With regard to incentives for improved administration, it is clear that current law provides only very modest incentives and penalties for maladministration of AFDC, and absolutely none under the Food Stamp program. Under the Carter proposal, there were no incentives for improved administration, and in fact by separating the states' responsibility for inputting data into the computer system from the federal government's control of payments, it probably created some perverse incentives for greater errors than we currently suffer. Ullman, by contrast, required states to pay half the value of errors on Food Stamps and AFDC in excess of 5%. Errors would be measured under the Ullman plan for both under- and overpayments.

With regard to incentives for job creation, it is fair to say that current law creates no positive incentive for local employment offices to create jobs for the poor. In fact, there has been widespread criticism of the current "balanced employment" formula which allocates employment service money. Local employment service offices have been accused of "creaming" their employment pools for those individuals who are most readily employed. As a result, the hard-core poor are often the last to be employed. Under the Carter proposal, there were few incentives for job creation. In fact, because job creation was to occur at the local level under CETA prime sponsors, while fiscal responsibility for new cash beneficiaries was placed at the state level, there was apt to be no incentive for creating new jobs. Under the Ullman proposal, by contrast, states were to pay two-parent benefits entirely without federal assistance. On the other hand, public sector wages were to be entirely federally funded. This created a strong incentive at the state level to create public sector jobs rather than to pay state-financed benefits.

Currently, there are very few private sector incentives to employ the poor. While there has been for some time a WIN tax credit to employers of certain qualified low-income individuals, the tax credit has been widely criticized as ineffective. The Carter program did not provide any new incentives to the private sector to hire individuals, while the Ullman program, through its targeted new jobs credit for poor individuals, did provide employers with significant tax advantages in excess of those available under the WIN credit for hiring the poor. Under the new jobs credit, tax relief to employers was available if they hired individuals who had not taken a private sector job after 4 weeks of waiting. Public sector jobs would only become available after 8 weeks of waiting time.

Accountability is not very apparent under current AFDC or Food Stamp laws. Indeed, no state has ever had its federal funds for AFDC cut off because of maladministration. Appeals which are state-controlled under AFDC are quite complicated and vary among states. Under the Carter proposal, recipients were accorded additional rights and the appeals procedure was clarified. Administration of the Carter proposal was thought to be enhanced by providing access to tax return information. These disclosure provisions could have become quite controversial and constituted a new invasion of privacy.

Under the Ullman proposal, as noted above, there were fiscal sanctions against nonperformance of AFDC and Food Stamp administration. The penalties for such errors could be construed to constitute accountability. However, because the effectiveness of such incentives has never been evaluated, it is not clear whether they would have been effective.

Side Effects on Other Programs

Under current law, eligibility for AFDC also provides eligibility for social services under Title XX and for medical assistance under the Medicaid program. Among welfare assistance programs that are federally financed, the Medicaid program has grown most rapidly and has also caused the greatest administrative problems for the states. Under the Carter proposal, Medicaid eligibility would have been materially increased because individuals currently getting Food Stamps would instead receive cash assistance and thereby become eligible for Medicaid. This would mean that somewhere between 8 and 12 million additional individuals would have been added to the Medicaid rolls. The Carter proposal contemplated this increased enrollment and had some recommendations to the states that they create two types of Medicaid programs—the old and the new—and, in effect, perform a dual eligibility determination under the new welfare system. However, during testimony before the Welfare Reform Committee, it became clear that states would feel inordinate pressure to make all new cash beneficiaries eligible for Medicaid. This would have greatly increased the cost of the administration's program.

Under the Ullman proposal, because Food Stamps was kept intact, there was not likely to be any massive increase in Medicaid eligibility. In states which would be raised to the $4,200 minimum for a family of four, there was likely to be some increase in Medicaid eligibility; however, the increase was not expected to be nearly as large as that under the Carter proposal.

SUMMARY AND CONCLUSIONS

This essay comparing the Carter and Ullman welfare reform proposals leads one to conclude that the Carter proposal, because it was far more costly, administratively complex, and poorly thought out in terms of incentives, was not likely to achieve the comprehensive reform it sought. Indeed, any thoughtful observer of Carter's welfare reform proposal might have concluded that it was doomed from the outset. Disingenuous cost estimates, coupled with politically unrealistic suggestions for change in the wake of recent Congressional action, were bound to elicit Congressional disfavor. The Ullman proposal reflected a much more coherent approach to welfare reform and a much greater sensitivity to current institutions and practice. Nonetheless, neither proposal was enacted by the Congress, perhaps because of the worsening fiscal situation, the Proposition-13 mentality, and the need to address other more pressing concerns—especially energy legislation.

Designing a system of laws that will, with a reasonable probability, actually achieve greater welfare equity is clearly a very difficult task. The issues of how the federal government should relate to the states, whether incentives will in fact be workable, whether the levels of certainty and risk associated with change are within reason, and whether the proposal will have some unexpected effects on existing programs and thereby increase the level of chaos in the welfare system, are all quite difficult to assess when designing a new system. Moreover, the kinds of detail and information required to coherently build a proposal which addresses the concerns laid out above, are certainly at the limit of our current technical knowledge. In many instances these requirements are well beyond the sort of information which the academic community may be reasonably expected to accumulate.

Welfare reform, when viewed in an academic context, has been almost entirely a matter of incentive effects on willingness of the poor to work. The matters of whether the state should administer the system or continue to share that responsibility with their localities and whether the structure of the WIN program makes administrative sense are not issues which the academic community has addressed very extensively. Nor are they matters about which agencies of the federal government—responsible for administering these programs—have reasonably complete information. Yet, within the context of contemplating change, these are natural questions which the legislative branch of government must address. Change of any sort involves risks—particularly, risks of making the system less workable and less equitable. But the role of analysis should be to demonstrate how such risks can be minimized.

This review of the Carter and Ullman proposals leads one to the conclusion that the Ullman proposal was the more likely and workable step in achieving welfare reform. There is an additional lesson to be learned if one accepts the evaluation provided here. This lesson concerns the manner in which such proposals should be authored. The Carter proposal had a long and complex period of gestation which involved participation by all the relevant executive branches of government—the Treasury, the Departments of Agriculture, Labor, and HEW—as well as participation by representatives of the poor and some participation by Congressional staff. Such a complex process was bound to cause many compromises which, when initiating a proposal, may decrease its overall coherence. By contrast, the Ullman proposal was written by three individuals in response to something that had already been proposed, namely, the Carter proposal. Smaller groups of individuals can, of course, always create a more coherent document. Of course, it is not clear, had both proposals been submitted to the normal Congressional process of consideration by the three standing Committees of the House and their respective subcommittees, how either proposal would have fared. Nonetheless, other things being equal, a coherent and internally consistent proposal based on careful analysis will stand a decent chance of enactment and implementation. The role of policy analysts is to produce such proposals—whatever their political fate might be.

References

Boland, B. Participation in the Aid to Families with Dependent Children Program (AFDC). In Joint Economic Committee, Subcommittee on Fiscal Policy (93rd Congress, 1st Session), *Studies in public welfare: The family, poverty, and welfare programs—Factors influencing family instability* (No. 12, Part 1). Washington, D.C.: U.S. Govt. Printing Office, 1973.

Breen, P. *Evolution of Supplemental Security Income benefits to disabled children: History, analysis, and public policy implications* (Bush Institute for Child and Family Policy). Unpublished manuscript, University of North Carolina, 1980.

Congressional Budget Office. *The Administration's welfare reform proposal: An analysis of the program for better jobs and income.* Washington, D.C.: U.S. Govt. Printing Office, May 1978.

Congressional Research Service. *Background material on selected income maintenance programs.* Washington, D.C.: Author, January 1979.

Lewis, O. *La Vida: A Puerto Rican family in the culture of poverty—San Juan and New York.* New York: Random House, 1965.

MacDonald, M. *Food stamps and income maintenance.* New York: Academic Press, 1977.

Strauss, R. P. Information and participation in a public transfer program. *Journal of Public Economics,* 1977, *8,* 385–396.

Footnotes

[1] The author wishes to thank Dr. Wendell Primus of the Ways and Means Committee, U.S. House of Representatives, for his comments on an earlier version of this manuscript.

SEVEN

SOCIAL POLICY ANALYSIS: A PARTIAL AGENDA

RON HASKINS

INTRODUCTION

The purpose of this book has been to describe the emerging enterprise of social policy analysis and to outline some of the methods by which this enterprise might be pursued. In the concluding chapter, I have two straightforward purposes, namely, to identify and summarize the common elements in the models described in the previous chapters and to outline some of the social problems to which these models can be applied. The latter section will serve as a brief introduction to topics that will be addressed in subsequent volumes of this series.

COMMON ELEMENTS OF MODELS FOR SOCIAL POLICY ANALYSIS

For all their differences, the authors of this volume—as well as other analysts such as Gil (1976), Stokey and Zeckhauser (1978), Wildavsky (1979), and Titmuss (1974)—would probably agree that analysis involves at least five distinct but related activities: (1) describing the problem situation; (2) specifying criteria; (3) generating alternative strategies; (4) selecting a "best" policy; and (5) assessing feasibility. In characterizing each of these activities, my intent is to be succinct rather than comprehensive. Readers can consult the various chapters for further details and differences of emphasis.

The Problem Situation

The objectives of defining the problem situation are to document the problem that makes people think a policy is needed, to describe current and previous policies that have attempted to deal with the problem, and to describe the social or political groups that have an interest in the policy. A good analysis of the problem situation will demonstrate how (if at all) the general welfare is threatened, will describe the nature and extent of the problem, and will demonstrate that some public action needs to be taken. After completing an analysis of the problem situation, we should feel that we have a good understanding of the dimensions and causes of the problem and that some—as yet unspecified—action should be taken to solve the problem.

An important aspect of defining the problem situation is to demonstrate not simply that society faces a problem but that society has an interest in how the problem is resolved. We want to know, as a *sine qua non* of the justification for a policy, that the general welfare is threatened by the problem's existence and will be advanced by its solution.

Criteria

Criteria specify the ends we design policies to achieve. For the sake of convenience, it is helpful to think of two types of criteria. Universal criteria[1] are outcomes that we hope to maximize or minimize by virtually any social policy. The universal criteria that one frequently encounters in political debate about social policy include efficiency, stigma, equity, and preference satisfaction. In brief, these criteria define good social policies as ones that: produce a maximum effect for a given investment of resources, avoid labeling program participants as inferior to other citizens, consider the redistribution of income such that people with less money benefit relatively more from the policy, and allow choices so that citizens can maximize their personal preferences.

In addition to these general or universal criteria, it is usually appropriate and useful to specify criteria that are applicable to a specific type of policy. Such criteria are often necessary because the hoped-for outcomes of various types of social policies are quite diverse. Thus, for example, we may want a day-care policy that produces intellectual gains among participating children, and we may want an adoption and foster-care policy that increases the stability of children's living arrangements. These two outcomes are very different, yet each is well suited to its particular policy area. Policy-specific criteria, in other words, supplement universal criteria by specifying the outcomes we seek in particular social domains.

If criteria embody the ends we seek, what is the source of these ends and how can they be justified? Some analysts duck the issue by allowing others—policymakers, administrators, funding agencies—to specify the objectives of policy and then define the analyst's role primarily as identifier or inventor of the means to achieve these ends. At the other extreme are those who hold that some values are absolute, certain, and beyond the need for justification—such as the Ten Commandments or the Bill of Rights.

A different approach to identifying criteria is frankly to acknowledge that the analysts' values underlie much of the analytic process and require that analysts present and defend the values from which their criteria emerge. The advantage of specifying values for all to see is that people then have no doubt about what precisely the analyst aims to achieve and why.

Unfortunately, justifying the values underlying the analysis criteria is often a difficult and lengthy undertaking. Rawls (1971), for example, penned a very thick book attempting to establish the preeminent place of equity in the goals of society. In direct contrast to Rawls's perspective, Milton Friedman (1962) has written a series of essays to establish the preeminence of freedom, particularly in economic matters, in the hierarchy of values that policy should aim to achieve. Friedman begins by establishing the philosophical and practical reasons for the importance of freedom and then applies his perspective to selected areas of social policy such as education, discrimination, jobs, income redistribution, and welfare programs.

For our purposes, the books by Rawls and Friedman are important, not simply as elaborate and refined justifications of particular value positions, but as illustrations of the relationship between fundamental value positions and specific policy criteria. These general valuative systems are important, not only because they provide the basic justification for particular criteria and make the analyst's values explicit, but also because they provide a guide in orchestrating the tradeoffs that are a necessary evil in policy analysis.

Tradeoffs are deliberate sacrifices of one criterion in favor of another criterion. Doing one thing reduces our ability to do another; investing in one program reduces the resources available to invest in another program; eating our cake prevents us from having it too. These are facts, and no analyst, policymaker, or citizen can avoid making these hard choices between desired ends. The immediate function of criteria is to help us make such choices; the underlying function of a general valuative system is to provide a systematic basis for selecting the criteria to be maximized when tradeoffs are necessary.

An example suggested by Friedman may clarify this issue. The first principle that follows from the attempt to maximize individual freedom is that the scope of government must be limited—the best government governs least (Friedman, 1962, p. 2). According to Friedman—not to mention the authors of the Bill of Rights and the Declaration of Independence—big government inevitably reduces individual freedom by imposing laws, regulations, taxes, and similar constraints on individual and corporate initiative. It does not follow, however, that government should never intervene in the economy or the decisions of individuals. Poverty, for example, is a problem to which government might properly address its efforts. However, in so doing policies should conform as nearly as possible to the principle of governing least in order to maximize individual freedom. Thus, in-kind programs such as Food Stamps and housing would not be favored since they restrict the freedom of individuals (in this case, welfare recipients) to fulfill self interest by making their own choices. By contrast, a negative income tax which provides individuals with cash is a better program because it allows individuals the freedom to enter the marketplace and make their own choices. Similarly, a negative income tax can be designed so that recipients always have an incentive to work.

One further word about criteria seems appropriate. As MacRae has argued in Chapter 4, multiple criteria are a problem because some of the criteria are almost always incompatible (i.e., in maximizing one criterion we minimize others). The argument I have just presented implies that a valuative framework is one solution to this dilemma because it tells us which criteria are most important to preserve when making tradeoffs. Another approach is to synthesize the criteria in such a way that each can be measured by a common yardstick. The most widely used technique for synthesizing values is to measure outcomes on all criteria in dollars and to maximize a combination of the criteria by selecting the policy that produces the greatest net dollar benefit.

Alternative Strategies

Having summarized the problem and specified the criteria to be maximized, the analyst now wants to identify all the policies that might be used to attack the problem. Usually, the strategies are well known. Some are currently in force, some have been tried on a limited basis by states or localities, some may have been tested on a small scale by social experiments, and some may have been implemented in other countries. In the main, new ideas for programs to solve social problems are not the outcome of policy analysis. Even in the case of "innovative" social programs such as Head Start, the negative income tax, or Health Maintenance Organizations, a little study reveals that the essential ideas behind the innovations have been known for many years—and, indeed, that similar programs had been previously attempted on a small scale.

Thus, inventing new programs to solve social problems is not as important a part of policy analysis as selecting the best program from among known alternatives. The primary end of social policy analysis is to compare the long-term effects of various programs in solving social problems and provide an explicit rationale for selecting policies that maximize the public good.

Information Synthesis and Policy Selection

The analyst now collects and analyzes information to estimate the outcomes of each alternative strategy in terms of each criterion. The gathering of information is an extremely catholic activity; the analyst has no choice except that of examining information produced by many disciplines. Moreover, analysis usually involves familiarity with federal and state budgets, as well as with statistics published by the Bureau of the Census or any of the various administrative departments of the federal and state governments.

Although survey data may enable the analyst to describe the dimensions of a problem, in most cases experimental data are required to make predictions about the effects or outcomes of various strategies. This is the part of analysis in which social science is able to make its greatest and most distinctive contribution. Unfortunately, the particular studies that may provide data about outcomes come from a variety of disciplines. In the case of day-care policy, for example, most of the information about effects of day care on child development comes from developmental psychology and education; data about the effects of policy on consumer choice come from economics; and data about effects of day care on health come from pediatrics and public health. Since each of these disciplines has its own professional organizations and journals, as well as its own unique network of informal contacts that facilitate the rapid distribution of research information, building a cadre of policy analysts who can move easily across disciplinary boundaries will be a formidable undertaking. But this undertaking is especially important, because insights from many disciplines provide analysts with the breadth of perspective that is essential to sensitive analysis.

A final point about information synthesis and policy selection is in order. In most cases, decisions about social policies must be based on best estimates. Even the very best information concerning policy outcomes, such as that yielded by the income maintenance experiments, is subject to substantial error. Thus, even under the best of circumstances (i.e., when good information is available), predicting the outcome of various policy alternatives is far from an exact science. For this reason, statistics of probability and confidence intervals are usually more valuable than statistics suitable for hypothesis testing. In any case, the advantages of policy analysis are that it makes the basis of decisions explicit and allows us to select policies based on the probability that they will produce a specified outcome—not that we can assure policymakers that specific policies will "solve" specific social problems.

Feasibility

A charge to which all policy recommendations are subject is that they are impractical. Gallagher (Ch. 2), for example, argues that commissions and committees of experts often produce a large list of recommendations that, if funded, would break the national treasury and if implemented would produce chaos.

Thus, the analyst must always be sensitive to at least two types of feasibility. First, an analysis must be conducted with awareness of *political feasibility*, i.e., the probability that the recommendations will actually be enacted by a legislative or administrative body. If, as Wildavsky (1979) has argued, policy analysis is as much art as science, among the least scientific aspects of analysis is the assessment of feasibility. What is involved here is the analyst's assessment that the temper of the times, the political composition of legislative and administrative bodies, the personalities and political commitments of key legislative personnel, and the strength of other proposals vying for funds would, taken together, hold some possibility that the recommendation will receive support. If the analyst judges that support would not be forthcoming for the recommendation most favored by other aspects of the analysis, two choices are possible. First, the feasibility of enactment may be improved by retaining the recommendation, but reducing its scope or attracting political support to increase its feasibility. Second, the analyst may recommend a less preferred strategy that has greater political feasibility.

Given the uncertainties of assessing political feasibility, the analyst must be alert to the possibility of making recommendations in ways that make them more appealing and therefore more feasible. Showing that a particular program can produce benefits that exceed costs, for example, increases a policy's appeal to people of all political persuasions. The analyst must not, in other words, overlook the fact that political feasibility is not a static concept; the feasibility of a recommendation can be greatly influenced by the arguments and data used to support the recommendation and by the individuals and groups that can be won over by these arguments and data.

Although feasibility is an important aspect of analysis, there is at least one circumstance in which the immediate feasibility of a policy might be deliberately ignored, namely, when the analyst wishes to increase the policy's long-term feasibility by calling attention to the proposal and making it a part of normal academic and political discourse. This approach is especially likely to be taken by commissions or by professional organizations. To cite an example mentioned by Gallagher (Chap. 2), both the National Academy of Sciences (National Research Council, 1976) and the Carnegie Council on Children (Keniston, 1977) have recently published extensive reports that supported a negative income tax for families. Although the political situation of the late 1970s (and, perhaps, even the political situation that seems almost certain to prevail during the first half of the 1980s) is not favorable for major new social programs, both reports did succeed in popularizing the notion of a negative income tax and in informing a large constituency of social scientists, professionals, and interested citizens of the characteristics and advantages of a negative income tax.

A second aspect of feasibility that requires attention might be called the *feasibility of implementation*. Many policies are enacted in Washington with great fanfare only to flounder on the constraints imposed at the state and local level. Some of these constraints may be political—as when local officials disagree with a particular program—but many are not. Other problems with local implementation include lack of clarity in guidelines, conflicting programs, lack of trained personnel, incompatibility with local attitudes, etc. The point is that even if a policy recommendation is feasible in the sense that it can be enacted and funded by a legislative body, it does not follow that the recommendation is feasible in the sense that it can be easily implemented at the point of service delivery. The analyst must be sensitive to both types of feasibility.

A PARTIAL AGENDA FOR SOCIAL POLICY ANALYSIS

My purpose in this section is to highlight some of the current social issues that would profit from policy analysis of the type described in this volume. The intent is to provide concrete examples of the social problems currently on the federal agenda and to indicate the general directions that policy analysis of these issues might pursue. The topics covered are by no means exhaustive, but each problem has received attention by Congress and the states in recent years and seems certain to remain on the agenda for the next decade and beyond. Moreover, these problems will receive more elaborate treatment in subsequent volumes of this series. In this respect, the following discussion constitutes a brief introduction to the types of social problems to which we will apply the analysis models described here.

Poverty and the Distribution of Income

An important question of social policy is the distribution of income that a society maintains. To a substantial degree, income determines the extent to which an individual or family can participate in the economic and social life of the community. Furthermore, in a market economy the distribution of goods and services is determined by what people demand. People enter the marketplace and "vote" for a distribution of goods and services by making decisions to purchase. A problem of equity is introduced, however, because each individual's influence is weighted by the amount of money she has to spend. Thus, relatively wealthy people have a greater influence in determining what goods and services are available than relatively poor people—many of whom may have virtually no vote at all.

It is not difficult to document the extent to which American society has permitted this type of inequality. First, blacks have always been behind, and in spite of efforts such as the War on Poverty, welfare programs, education and training programs, they still remain considerably behind whites. As one indication of the economic problems experienced by blacks, consider that the rate of black unemployment has been twice that of whites since the end of World War II. In 1977 the earnings of black males who worked full-time were only 69% as much as the earnings of white males, and blacks, who are about 12% of the U.S. population, held only 2% of the jobs in the top 5% of the salary distritution (Thurow, 1980, pp. 185–186). Similar numbers could be cited for women. The point is that income—even for those who work full time—is unevenly distributed in American society. The policy question is what degree of income inequality is acceptable to citizens in our society.

In addition to the problem of income inequality between groups, American society also continues to face the problem of poverty. Using 1978 figures, we find that about 25 million persons—nearly 20% of the population—had incomes that placed them below the government-defined poverty line (U.S. Bureau of the Census, 1980). Poverty was not, however, equally divided among subgroups in the population. About 15% of the elderly were poor, 41% of black children lived in poverty, and 37% of female-headed families were poor (Keniston, 1977, p. 27).

Governments at all levels are well aware of these figures and spend vast sums of money to assist the poor and to redistribute money from those with more to those with less. Indeed, in 1978 direct government transfer payments amounted to $224 billion (Office of Management and Budget, undated). Thus, about 10% of the GNP was accounted for by the various levels of government taking money from some people and giving it to others (Thurow, 1980). And these figures do not include in-kind programs, such as job training and Food Stamps.

What is the effect of these programs on poverty? Thurow (1980, pp. 156–157) suggests one answer. In 1977, the 40% of the population with the lowest wages received a little more than 9% of earned income. By contrast, the top 40% received 74.5% of all earnings. However, after the effects of government transfers have been taken into account, the lower 40% received 17% of all income, while the top 40% received 65.7%. Thus, the effect of government transfer programs was to reduce the excesses of a system that produces great differences in family income (see also Plotnick & Skidmore, 1975).

Though no one should belittle this achievement of government policy, critics can nonetheless point to important deficiencies in the current system. First, the gap between the lowest and highest income by any measure is very great. Indeed, as Wiles (1974) has shown, the distribution of income in the United States is less equal than that of any other industrialized country. Using a measure called the "semi-decile ratio" (obtained by dividing the income of families at the 95th percentile of the income distribution by the income of families at the 5th percentile), Wiles shows that the ratio for the U.S. is more than 13. For Sweden, by contrast, the ratio is 3.

Of course, few disagree with the premise that wage differentials are needed to maintain motivation. But is a semi-decile ratio of 13 really necessary to maintain work and achievement incentives? Although no precise answer to this question is possible, Thurow (1980, pp. 200–202) has suggested an interesting empirical approach. If we confine our attention to white, male, full-time workers, we find that the income of those in the top quintile is only five times that of workers in the lowest quintile. Since this distribution of earnings appears to be enough to maintain work incentive among white males, is there reason to suppose that any greater spread is necessary to sustain incentive among other workers?

A second problem with current income policy is that it grossly violates the criterion of horizontal equity which stipulates that equals should be treated equally. To select just one example from one federal program, a mother with two children on AFDC in Mississippi gets monthly benefits of $87.52. The same mother and child in New York would receive $366.33. No one has yet produced a cogent argument that would justify this characteristic of our welfare system.

Another major problem with our current system of income supports is that it does not adequately encourage initiative. Recipients of Aid to Families with Dependent Children (AFDC), for example, have very little incentive to earn money because earned income reduces their AFDC payments by a substantial amount. Indeed, in some cases the implicit tax rate in the AFDC program is greater than 100%. What we need, of course, is a system of income redistribution that allows poor people to keep part of what they earn so that there is always incentive to work.

These three problems with our system of income transfers are not exhaustive. Other closely related problems—such as the fiscal burden on states, inequities in our tax system, fluctuating rates of employment, and the lack of help for the working poor—might also have been discussed. The point is that the American economic system has not provided adequate and reliable income for all families. Since most of society's social problems are concentrated in families having inadequate incomes, it stands to reason that a long-term solution to many social problems is contingent on achieving a just distribution of family income. Means by which such a distribution could be achieved, and the moral and economic justification for such reforms, is a high priority for social policy analysis.

In recent years, two widely publicized commissions of social scientists have recommended that the federal government adopt some sort of negative income tax program (Keniston, 1977; National Research Council, 1976). Among other things, such a program would guarantee each family a certain minimum level of income. Thus, the federal government would guarantee every family that regardless of its fortunes in the marketplace, there would be an income level below which they could not fall.

A potential problem with this proposal, as suggested earlier, is that its political feasibility might be questioned. On the other hand, under President Nixon, a negative income tax bill (called the Family Assistance Plan; see Moynihan, 1973) was actually passed by the House of Representatives. Unfortunately, the bill died in the Senate. That Nixon initiated and strongly supported this bill suggests that Republicans and other conservatives may be able to support such legislation.

This type of proposal is, after all, administratively less complex than the current array of categorical programs; it does provide strong fiscal relief for the states; it does answer the problem of horizontal equity; and we can now cite data to show that it produces reductions in work effort that are moderate (Keeley, Robins, Spiegelman, & West, 1976) or minor (Pechman & Timpane, 1975). Each of these characteristics of the negative income tax is likely to have considerable appeal to conservatives. Thus, although there may be problems of political feasibility associated with a negative income tax, perhaps the possibility of creating such a system in a time of fiscal conservatism is greater than many would imagine.

In any case, as Strauss (see Chap. 6) argued so persuasively, some very important questions should be analyzed in order to improve the negative income tax proposals that many hope one day will be adopted. First, careful attention should be given to the nonlabor force effects of income maintenance programs. The four income maintenance experiments (in New Jersey, Iowa/North Carolina, Gary, and Seattle/Denver) have produced a great deal of information on the effects of income supports on fertility, health, education, and marital stability. If we are to project all potential costs and benefits of an income guarantee program, all of these outcomes must be considered and, if possible, synthesized. Second, the manner in which a new welfare system will replace the current system needs careful attention. Substantial bureaucracies already exist at both the state and federal levels. What role, if any, are these bureaucracies to play in a new system? Third, which current programs would be replaced by a universal program of income assistance? In 1979, for example, the Food Stamp program spent only about 20% less than AFDC. In addition, we have housing programs, health programs, and day-care programs, among others, that are directed in whole or in part to the poor. Should all these programs be "cashed out" and the money included in a new universal income program? If so, what is to be done with the bureaucracies that have grown up around these programs?

Care of Young Children

Certainly not a new issue, child care is likely to continue for some time as a policy question of major importance. Two reasons justify this conclusion. First, there are nearly 20 million children under the age of 5 in the U.S., and more than half of these have a mother who works full or part time. Furthermore, the frequency of employment among mothers continues to climb, thereby indicating that the demand for extrafamily child care (and after-school care) will continue to increase.

Second, many child development professionals believe that preschool programs are necessary to insure adequate development among poor children. Thus, groups such as the National Association for Education of Young Children, the Day Care and Child Development Council of America, and the Children's Defense Fund will attempt to keep day-care legislation on the public agenda.

Since President Nixon vetoed the Mondale-Brademas bill in 1972—a bill which would have quickly made up to $5 billion available for child-care programs—there has been only tepid Congressional support for new day care legislation. Nonetheless, given the increasing need for child care and the interest of professionals, it seems certain that day-care legislation will remain on the public agenda for the foreseeable future. In the meantime, there are important issues that require analysis.

First, what types of day care should receive support? The current day-care market includes, among others, centers with more than 12 children, family day-care homes with 6 to 12 children, neighborhood sitters with 2 or 3 children, and care by relatives. Not more than 10% of children are in centers (Coelen, Glantz, & Calore, 1979); by contrast, well over half are in more informal arrangements such as care by relatives and family day-care homes (Haskins, 1979). Yet most federal money now supports centers (Rivlin, 1978), a policy that does not seem well justified. Unless there is good reason to suspect that market transactions do not fully measure the social value of a commodity, government intervention to restructure the market is not justified. If a strong case can be built to support the notion that centers help children develop more fully and maintain these gains, then government emphasis on funding for centers may be justified. Currently, however, this case does not appear very strong (Haskins, 1979; Hill, 1978). Current and future government funding of day care, then, should be more neutral with regard to the types of care receiving support.

There is also need for consideration of the mechanisms by which government provides financial support for day care. Currently, four funding mechanisms are used by the federal government: (1) direct subsidy of food for lunches and snacks; (2) direct creation and funding of programs such as Head Start; (3) reimbursement by the federal government, in conjunction with state and local government administration, to day-care providers for services to children from low- and moderate-income families through Title XX of the Social Security Act; and (4) provision by the government of a child-care income tax credit for families who pay taxes. This system of funding, though cumbersome, does provide at least something for every type of family.

But a central question that requires analysis is how funding would be provided by any major new program. There are two general mechanisms by which such expansion might be achieved. First, the government could increase the supply of day care by direct funding of programs—as is currently done in Head Start. This mode of funding, which was the mode adopted by the Mondale-Brademas bill and the recent comprehensive day-care bill sponsored by Senator Cranston, seems to be favored by professionals both inside and outside the government. By funding programs directly, the government is able to control program characteristics (e.g., the provision of educational curricula, staff-child ratios, parent participation, etc.)

The second general type of funding is vouchers. In this case, government funding would not affect supply directly nor would it control program characteristics. Rather, this policy is based on the assumption that parents know what is best for their children and will choose what best meets their own—and their children's—needs. If current supply conditions are any indication, a voucher policy would likely favor a diverse market dominated by informal arrangements such as family day-care homes, care by relatives, and neighborhood care. Such a market would be very difficult—if not impossible—to regulate.

Analysis is also required to determine the need for and effects of other government activities such as regulation and providing information. Regulation has already received, and continues to receive, a great deal of attention. In 1968, the Department of Health, Education, and Welfare published a set of guidelines known as "Federal Interagency Day Care Requirements" (FIDCR), but these guidelines have never been fully implemented. After 3 or 4 years of study and administrative problems, the FIDCR guidelines have now been revised. However, the 96th Congress refused to pass the new guidelines, probably because the staff-child ratios specified in the document were judged to be high and because federal regulation is not currently in political favor.

Nonetheless, federal and state regulation of day care remains a central question. Imagine a continuum of regulation extending from mere fire and safety guidelines on one extreme to curriculum requirements and staff-child ratios on the other. The question for analysis is where the line should be drawn along this continuum. Virtually no one would disagree that government has a right to establish and enforce fire and other safety regulations, but many doubt that a case can be made to justify regulation of curriculum, group size, and staff-child ratios (see Hill, 1978).

To the extent that government regulations are moderated, parents should be expected to create and enforce their own "regulations." In order to assist parents in this responsibility, three things are necessary.

First, parents should have extensive information about the types of care available locally. As Nelson (1977), Nelson and Krashinsky (1974), and Hill (1978) have suggested, government policy may have a role to play here. For example, government could provide funds for local day-care coordination committees that could serve as information clearing centers for parents.

Second, parents must be able to have complete access to day-care programs at all times. Such access would enable parents to inspect the type of care being provided. In some cases, parents might organize to provide periodic checking on a regular basis. Although day-care management might object to this procedure, openness could be a part of the day-care regulations enforced by state and county agencies when complaints arise (see Nelson, 1977, pp. 98–102).

Third, consumer sovereignty can be further promoted if parents have the power of "exit", i.e., the ability to leave a care situation they find unsatisfactory (Hirschman, 1970). In order for the threat of exit to have an impact on providers, the market must be diverse and fluid in order to provide parents with real and immediate alternatives. In a market dominated by state-funded institutions, as is the case with public schools, the threat of exit is relatively ineffective. But in a diverse market of competitors, providers would need to be responsive to consumers or they would go out of business.

Day-care policy, then, poses many interesting challenges to the analyst. As is often the case with social policy, recommendations that have come from professionals heretofore have often not been well reasoned and dispassionate. What is needed now is careful attention to ways that policy can stimulate supply, maintain diversity, promote quality, and increase consumer sovereignty.

Family Dissolution[2]

No social problem has caused more alarm in recent years than the substantial increases in divorce rates. Beginning in the 1960s, the American divorce rate has climbed to the highest level ever recorded and the highest rate of any nation in the world (Glick & Norton, 1977). There are currently more than 5.9 yearly divorces per 1,000; in 1980, more than 1.1 million marriages will terminate in divorce (National Center for Health Statistics, 1980). Well over one-third of new marriages end in divorce, and for some states, such as California, the rate is above 50%. Perhaps of greatest importance, a large number of children are involved in these divorces. Glick and Norton (1977) have estimated that 45% of today's children will live for at least some time with only one parent; the figure for black children may be as high as 80%.

There are at least four issues associated with divorce that are in need of dispassionate analysis. The first of these, and the most difficult, is whether the government has a right to intervene in the marriage and divorce decisions of individual citizens. On the one hand, the analyst might argue that government, as the concrete embodiment of the general welfare, can intervene in any social problem which threatens the nation's well-being. On the other hand, some would see great danger in government intervention in marital decisions. The Bill of Rights reflects the traditional American concern for individual freedom, and the deep-seated fear that centralized power can cause mischief by attempts to regulate human relations. Among the most fundamental of these relations is the right to make and, under certain specified circumstances, break contracts, including marriage. Although Western governments have tended historically to exert some constraints on marriage through regulation—most notably in laws that stipulate the conditions of divorce—a number of legal scholars (e.g., Glendon, 1976) have concluded that the tendency in recent years has been for government to reduce its role in regulating marriage.

The analyst concerned with divorce must invest careful thought in the justification for government policy addressed to controlling mariage and divorce. Perhaps the best solution to this problem is for the government to withdraw from the regulation of marriage and divorce and to design policies aimed at ameliorating the effects of divorce.

Which raises the second issue of consequence in analyzing divorce policy. Among the more important contributions that social science research can make to policy analysis is the generation of data concerning the effects of social conditions. With regard to effects of divorce, one established body of research concerning the effects of father absence on children's behavior and development has, somewhat surprisingly, failed to show substantial negative effects (Herzog & Sudia, 1973). On the other hand, a more recent body of work on the effects of divorce, and especially the longitudinal work of Hetherington (1979; Hetherington, Cox, & Cox, 1978), has demonstrated rather serious negative effects on IQ, school adjustment, and family relations. These effects appear to be especially powerful for boys. The conclusion one would draw from this body of research is that divorce is indeed a threat to the normal development and behavior of children. It would appear, then, that policy addressed to ameliorating the effects of divorce—as distinguished from policy designed to regulate divorce—may be justified by virtue of the deleterious effects of divorce on children.

A third important issue in designing social policy addressed to the problem of divorce is the timing of intervention or support programs in the marriage-divorce cycle. Burnett (1980) has proposed that analysts divide the marriage-divorce cycle into three phases, each of which would require distinct types of support programs. The first phase is before marriage, at which time premarital counseling and contraceptive services would be most helpful. During marriage—the second phase—a number of support policies may be appropriate in helping couples increase their marital satisfaction and stability. These programs would include marital counseling, marriage enrichment, tax rate equalization, day-care vouchers, flexible employment, extending AFDC to two-parent families, and parent education.

The third phase in the marriage-divorce cycle is during and following divorce. Programs appropriate at this time would include mediation services to help couples achieve satisfactory custody and child support arrangements, support groups for single parents and adolescents, training of family heads (usually females) who have been out of the labor market for many years, day-care support, flexible employment, and enforcement of child support payments.

Although I cannot present the necessary arguments and data here, one view of the divorce problem would hold that the most serious consequence of marital dissolution in the United States today is the association between female-headed families and poverty. About half of all poor families are female headed, and 32% of female-headed families live in poverty—as compared with 5% of husband-wife families (U.S. Bureau of the Census, 1979). A primary reason for the drastic rates of poverty among female-headed families is that the level of child support payments is shockingly low. Indeed, Garfinkel (1980) has reviewed data showing that in 1975, only 20% of nonwidow female households received *any* child support payments.

It might be argued, then, that child support payment is the area in which government intervention is most justified and would do the most good. Divorce settlements are contracts; thus, failure to pay child support represents breach of contract. Parents who have agreed to a child support settlement and who subsequently fail to fulfill its terms are legally culpable and should be brought to justice. In addition to being legally culpable, such parents have violated moral obligations to their children. Government policy designed to force these parents to meet their obligations is clearly justified both because government has the power to enforce contracts and because such policy would represent a step toward making parents live up to a responsibility to which they have previously agreed—by participating in procreation and usually by agreeing to a child support settlement. That government policy of this type is feasible and practical has been amply demonstrated by recent experience with federal child support enforcement (Adamson & Dobelstein, 1981).

Teenage Parenthood

Like the other social policy issues discussed here, teenage parenthood is a complex and challenging problem. It is a problem of long-standing duration; it involves serious conflicts between individual rights and family rights; it intersects with other social policy issues such as abortion, foster care, adoption, and day care; and it concerns delicate value issues that are not necessarily the province of government.

Unfortunately, many people have based their beliefs about trends in teenage pregnancy on a widely circulated 1976 report by the Alan Guttmacher Institute. This report, *Eleven Million Teenagers,* referred to increased adolescent fertility as an "epidemic." But in fact, fertility rates among girls of ages 15–19 have fallen slightly since 1950. Fertility rates among adult females have fallen even more quickly, however, with the result that a greater proportion of births are to adolescents. Currently, about 1 of 5 births—or about 580,000 per year—are to girls 19 or younger (Oohms & Maciocha, 1979).

Of what consequence is early childbearing? To begin with the mother, we should first recognize that teenage childbearing is one among a nexus of variables that are all intercorrelated. These variables include low education, background of family poverty, low job skills, and low educational aspiration. Some investigators have held that teenage childbearing in and of itself may be overrated as a condition that keeps the mother and her child in poverty (Cutright, 1973). Recent research suggests, however, that early childbirth reduces years of schooling, increases family size, and for those pregnant adolescents who marry, increases the probability of marital dissolution. All these conditions are associated with low occupational status, low earnings, and welfare (Moore, Hofferth, Caldwell, & Waite, 1979; McCarthy & Menken, 1979; Waite & Moore, 1977). Recent research, then, shows that early childbearing, through its effect on intervening variables, does in fact increase the likelihood of long-term poverty.

Nor is the adolescent mother the only person affected by early childbearing. Her infant is also at risk for a number of negative outcomes. These begin even before birth with higher rates of miscarriage, continue through the birth and neonatal periods with elevated probabilities of birth complications such as prematurity and low birth weight, and continue into the years of early childhood and beyond as the adolescent mother attempts to rear the child under conditions of poverty and—frequently—unstable living conditions (Alan Guttmacher Institute, 1976; Keniston, 1977; Oohms & Maciocha, 1979).

In addition to the teenage mother and her child, the mother's family is also heavily affected by the early birth. Especially among black adolescents, the mother and her baby usually live with the mother's family and the maternal grandmother often plays a central role in child rearing. Indeed, innovative research by Furstenberg (1976) showed that among 400 pregnant adolescents in Baltimore, 90% continued to live with their families during the pregnancy, 61% were still with their families 1 year after delivery, and a surprising 45% were still there 5 years after birth. These results have significant policy implications to which I will return.

Finally, one must mention the adolescent father and his family. Although little is known about the role played by these parties in supporting the mother and child, it would appear from most studies that their role is relatively minor (Oohms & Maciocha, 1979). Nevertheless, it seems reasonable to expect that the father may be a potential source of psychological and financial support and should therefore be kept in mind when policy is formulated.

Based on this review of the problem situation, let me suggest four principles that should condition the analysis of policy for teenage parenthood. First, it has long been recognized that one of the leading causes of school dropout is pregnancy. Since years of schooling is associated with a number of important variables such as occupation, income, and marital stability, it seems clear that an important focus of policy should be to keep pregnant adolescents in school or help them return to school following delivery.

Second, Furstenberg's (1976) research produced the important finding that teenage mothers who remained with their families received more financial support and child care than mothers who left their family unit. Furthermore, this support was associated with a number of important outcomes, such as increased probability of completing high school and increased earnings for the adolescent mother. Thus, the apparent importance of the mother's family should be carefully noted by analysts of teenage parenthood. In many respects, both the current legal situation and the stance of some professional organizations seem to have the effect—unintended though it may be—of increasing the potential for conflict between teenage mothers and their families. A series of Supreme Court decisions—and especially *Planned Parenthood* v. *Danforth* (1979) and *Belotti* v. *Baird* (1979)—have affirmed the right of teenage girls to seek and receive birth control information and abortions without the knowledge of, or consent from, their families. The respective rights and responsibilities of adolescents and their families represent a classic confrontation of values of the type that seems to be the rule in family policy (Caldwell, 1980). Nonetheless, one might hope to devise policy that minimizes such confrontation and promotes reconciliation or continued harmony between the pregnant teenager and her family. Steinfels (1979) has suggested a number of policies that could promote such outcomes.

The third principle that should condition policy analysis in this area is that the teenage mother and her infant may have a special claim to public support. Because adolescent females have such poor job skills, low education, low income, and high levels of responsibility, policy should attempt to insure good—and early—prenatal care, high quality delivery services, and educational and financial support following birth. An ancillary question that deserves careful analysis is the extent to which this support should include publicly provided child care.

Fourth, analysis of policy for teenage parenthood should include careful attention to means by which teenagers can avoid rapid second pregnancies. There is currently an unfortunate tendency for teenage mothers to become pregnant a second time. This substantially reduces the mother's chances for returning to school, acquiring better job skills, and even remaining with her family.

Finally, because of the historical persistence of teenage pregnancy, especially among black youths (Gutman, 1976), analysts should consider the possibility that, from the teenage girl's point of view, pregnancy is less a mistake or problem than a desired achievement. How long can we continue to doubt that persistence of adolescent pregnancy must imply that sexual activity, pregnancy, and childbirth have a positive and adaptive function for adolescent girls in modern American society? Furstenberg's (1976) work has shown that pregnancy can elevate the teenage mother's status within her family, and that the new infant is a valued object of attention and affection within the family unit. Pursuing this line of reasoning, the analyst might also consider the implications of Ogbu's (1978) thesis that black adolescents are well aware of the odds against economic success for blacks in American society, and that this realization causes a turning away from mainstream educational and economic institutions and toward culturally sanctioned roles such as child rearing.

The importance of these considerations is that true prevention may involve less jawboning and birth control information in favor of greater emphasis on creating economic and social opportunities for modern youth. Of particular importance in creating such opportunities may be policies that would strengthen what Berger and Newhaus (1977) have called "mediating structures" such as youth groups, the church, and community organizations.

Foster Care[3]

Foster-care policy in the United States is a dramatic example of the problems which must be faced by social policy analysts. Current foster-care practice is the outgrowth of a long history of policy evolution (Cox, 1980); although the private and public sectors are deeply involved, disparate state laws currently dictate and regulate practice, there are nearly as many systems of foster care as there are local departments of social services, and data concerning prevalence and outcomes is very sketchy. Nonetheless, the last decade has seen a substantial increase in public attention to the problem of foster care (Fanshel & Shinn, 1978); in response to this concern the federal government has recently enacted new legislation, the Adoption Assistance and Child Welfare Act of 1980. In addition, cases currently pending before the Supreme Court (especially *Doe* v. *Delaware)* could have far-reaching effects on the practice of removing children from their natural parents. Thus, despite the difficulties of analyzing foster-care policy, the next few years would seem to be a propitious time for thorough study leading to specific policy recommendations.

The foster-care system, although it varies from state to state, might be described as follows. For a variety of reasons, about 500,000 children in the U. S. have not been able to continue living with their parents. Based on three studies that have published data on the reasons children were placed in foster care (Fanshel & Shinn, 1978; Gruber, 1978; Jenkins & Sauber, 1966), a very rough estimate would be that 19% of the children in foster care came into the system because of mental illness of the mother, 17% because of physical illness of the mother, 13% because of severe neglect or abuse, 10% because of divorce or desertion of the parent, 10% because of abandonment, 8% because of personality or emotional disorders in the child, and 4% because of parental death. The remaining 20% entered foster care for miscellaneous reasons including parental unwillingness to provide care, awaiting adoption, and jailing of parents.

In general, natural parents who have children in foster care, compared with other parents, have less income and education, are more often divorced or separated, are more often dependent on public assistance, and are disproportionately from minority groups. To cite just one example of these characteristics, a recent survey of 300 adoptive children in North Carolina (Governor's Advocacy Council, 1978) found that 90% were from divorced, separated, or unwed mothers; the average parent had completed 8 years of schooling; and the average income was less than $200 per month for mothers (or $400 for fathers).

Among the important types of information needed about foster care is the characteristics of children who enter the system and who stay in the system for various periods of time. As in any case in which we would like to know about changes over time, only longitudinal data will provide accurate information about the effects of foster care. Apparently, there has been only one such longitudinal study (Fanshel & Shinn, 1978), but the information it yielded is of great interest. First, Fanshel and Shinn found no evidence of IQ declines while children were in foster care. Indeed, many children showed increases in IQ over the 5 years they were followed. These generalizations applied to both children in foster families and those in institutions. With regard to the mean level of IQ performance, children in the Fanshel and Shinn study, unlike those in previous foster-care studies (e.g., Gruber, 1978), were of about average intelligence at the time of placement, after 2.5 years, and after 5.0 years. As usual, there were ethnic differences in IQ (the study included blacks, whites, and Puerto Ricans), but no group defined by ethnic and age characteristics ever scored below 91. Indeed, by the end of the study the mean IQs of Puerto Rican and black children were about 100, while that of white children was about 103 (Fanshel & Shinn, 1978, Table 7.12, p. 190). Given the socioeconomic background of these children, it would appear that claims of deficit intellectual development by children in foster care may be somewhat exaggerated.

Nor is there very good evidence that children in foster care have serious emotional problems. Based on parent, teacher, and social worker reports of symptomatic behavior as well as figure drawing tests, children in Fanshel and Shinn's study (1978) showed moderate levels of behavior disorder, comparable in most cases to levels reported in studies of normal children. There were no behavior problems or symptoms of emotional illness on which foster-care children appeared to be obviously maladjusted. Fanshel and Shinn (1978) conclude: "On the level at which we were able to measure the adjustment of the children we could find no . . . negative effect [of foster care]" (p. 479).

Given this brief survey of foster-care effects, one is forced to raise the question: if children are not substantially harmed by the current system, what is wrong with foster-care policy? There are three answers to this question.

First, as is widely recognized, guidelines for removing children from their parents are quite arbitrary and vary from state to state or even county to county within states. It is difficult to imagine a more basic right than that of parenthood, including the right to rear children according to the values and practices favored by parents. Since seemingly arbitrary laws can deprive citizens of so basic a right as that of parenthood, explicit and uniform policy describing the circumstances under which the state can remove children from their families is essential. It should be noted that this aspect of foster-care policy has absolutely nothing to do with effects of foster care on children; it has only to do with parent rights.

This is not to suggest that defining the circumstances under which children can be removed from their parents will be easy. On the contrary, achieving this definition is both the most difficult and the most urgent question in the analysis of foster-care policy. On what grounds is this definition to be achieved? How can we balance children's rights with parents' rights? It is certain that no obvious answers to these questions are available. But by appealing to the extreme case of severe child abuse, for which almost everyone can agree that children should be removed from their parents, we can also be certain that a policy is necessary. Developing such a policy, and fully elucidating the grounds on which it is based, is the single most important question of foster care policy.

A second set of questions that shows the need for improvement in foster-care policy concerns how the state deals with children and parents once children have been removed from their families. What type of professionals, working under what types of conditions, are best suited to work with foster parents, natural parents, foster children, the courts, and other social agencies? Today, these roles are usually filled by a social worker administratively located in a county or city department of social services. Although there is nothing inherently wrong with this system, in practice it has proven to have serious shortcomings. There is rapid turnover among foster-care workers, they usually have tremendous caseloads, and they are often overloaded with paper work. A recent survey in North Carolina, for example, found that many counties reported a mean employment duration of less than 2 years for foster-care workers, that workers in half the counties carried caseloads between 25 and 80 children, and that up to 70% of social worker time was spent on paper work. Further, in some counties, the average foster child had four different social workers during her stay in foster care (Governor's Advocacy Council, 1978).

Another problem with the current foster-care system is that many children spend years in a kind of limbo between natural families and adoption. Foster care should be seen as a temporary arrangement between two permanent living arrangements or between the time a child leaves and returns to his natural family. But in practice foster-care has been anything but temporary. Fanshel and Shinn (1978) reported that nearly half the children in their study had been in foster care more than 3.5 years. The North Carolina study mentioned above (Governor's Advocacy Council, 1978) found that the average foster child had been in two homes in less than 4 years, that 10% had been in five or more homes, and that 3 of 326 children surveyed had been in 10 or more homes.

An even more serious problem with the duration of foster care is that in most states and counties there is no way to know how long a child will be in foster care, no guidelines for what the natural family must do to get their child back, and no limit on how long the department of social services can keep a child in the shifting limbo that is foster care. To counteract these problems, recently there has been a movement to use something called "permanency planning." A 1973 Children's Bureau project—the Oregon Project—demonstrated that periodic examinations of children, plans for permanent placement, reduced caseloads for foster-care workers, and better record-keeping resulted in more permanent placements for foster children (Cox, 1980).

A final question about foster care that needs analysis is the circumstances under which parental rights can be permanently terminated and the child made available for adoption. It seems clear that society needs one set of guidelines for removing children from their family on a short-term basis and another for permanently terminating parent rights. Although both sets of guidelines will be very difficult to devise and are of grave import for parents and children, the second set of guidelines will be the most difficult as it directly and permanently violates the most fundamental of parent rights. As Caldwell (1980) has argued, an important objective of policy is to do everything possible to avoid this final confrontation of parents' and children's rights by helping families resolve the difficulties which prevent them from providing a safe rearing environment for their children. Indeed, one of the original justifications for foster-care placement was to provide an appropriate environment for children while their parent or parents worked toward resolution of family problems. Although the logic of this approach seems reasonable, in fact the foster-care system usually provides little direct help for families. This is not surprising in view of the data presented above showing that foster-care workers have large caseloads and spend most of their time on paper work. In any case, one might wonder whether permanent termination of parental rights is very appropriate until the state has made a serious effort to help the family by providing financial assistance, counseling, job training, day care, and any of various other services designed to help families stay together or reunite.

A final word about the analysis of foster-care policy is in order. Much of the rhetoric about foster care—like that about infant screening programs and mental health programs—holds that the most important and most neglected aspect of foster care is prevention. It is now quite popular to argue that preventive services are more efficient than services delivered after the condition is manifest because, as the old saying has it, "a stitch in time saves nine." However, the analyst must recognize that the issue of prevention can be persuasive only if: (1) families at risk for having the condition can be identified with a high degree of accuracy; (2) effective means of treatment are available; and (3) the treatment is relatively inexpensive. In other words, the case for prevention must rest on data showing that preventive efforts are cost effective. Unless such data can be accumulated, analysts may be better off to recommend that scarce resources be invested in helping families that are in imminent danger of losing, or have already lost, their children. Taking 50 stitches to save 9 is neither good economics nor good policy.

CONCLUDING COMMENT

Our intent in this volume has been to define and illustrate social policy analysis. We have not made grand claims for the past or possible future success of this emerging discipline. Rather, we have attempted to demonstrate, both by explaining methods and showing specific applications, that a rational approach to social policy may hold some hope for improving social programs and for spending public funds wisely. The social problems discussed in this concluding chapter represent a broad cross-section of the types of social policies that could be improved by judicious and creative application of the procedures described in previous chapters.

None of this should be construed as a denial or denigration of the less cerebral activities that have always played a major role in democratic decision making. A rather modest but realistic objective of social policy analysis is to create a discipline that can play an important though limited role in crafting our nation's social policies. We hope the volumes in this series will amount to a small but certain step in this direction.

References

Adamson, F., & Dobelstein, A. *Supporting children and establishing paternity: Title IV D of the Social Security Act* (Bush Institute for Child and Family Policy). Unpublished manuscript, University of North Carolina at Chapel Hill, March 1981.

Alan Guttmacher Institute. *Eleven million teenagers: What can be done about the epidemic of adolescent pregnancies in the United States?* New York: Author, 1976.

Berger, P. L., & Newhaus, R. J. *To empower people: The role of mediating structures in public policy*. Washington, D.C.: American Enterprise Institute, 1977.

Burnett, C. Personal communication, November 1, 1980.

Caldwell, B. M. Balancing children's rights and parents' rights. In R. Haskins & J. J. Gallagher (Eds.), *Care and education of young children in America: Policy, politics, and social science*. Norwood, N.J.: Ablex, 1980.

Coelen, C., Glantz, F., & Calore, D. *Day care centers in the U.S.: A national profile 1976–1977*. Cambridge, Mass.: Abt Books, 1979.

Cox, M. *An analysis of alternatives for dependent and neglected children*. (Bush Institute for Child and Family Policy). Unpublished manuscript, Univ. of North Carolina, 1980.

Cutright, P. Timing of the first birth: Does it matter? *Journal of Marriage and the Family*, 1973, *35*, 585–595.

Fanshel, D. & Shinn, E. *Children in foster care: A longitudinal investigation*. New York: Columbia Univ. Press, 1978.

Friedman, M. *Capitalism and freedom.* Chicago: Univ. of Chicago Press, 1962.
Furstenberg, F. *Unplanned parenthood: The social consequences of teenage childbearing.* New York: Free Press, 1976.
Garfinkel, I. *Child support and welfare reform.* Unpublished manuscript, University of Wisconsin, 1980.
Gil, D. G. *Unravelling social policy: Theory, analysis, and political action towards social equality* (2nd ed.). Cambridge, Mass.: Schenkman, 1976.
Glendon, M. A. The American family in the 200th year of the Republic. *Family Law Quarterly,* 1976, *10,* 335–355.
Glick, P. C., & Norton, A. J. Marrying, divorcing, and living together in the U.S. today (*Population Bulletin,* 1977, *32,* No. 5). Washington, D.C.: Population Reference Bureau, 1977.
Governor's Advocacy Council on Children and Youth. *Why can't I have a home: A report on foster care and adoption in North Carolina.* Raleigh, N.C.: Author, 1978.
Gruber, A. *Children in foster care.* Boston: Human Sciences Press, 1978.
Gutman, H. G. *The black family in slavery and freedom, 1925–1975.* New York: Pantheon Books, 1976.
Haskins, R. Day care and public policy. *Urban and social change review.* 1979, *12,* 3–10.
Herzog, E., & Sudia, C. E. Children in fatherless families. In B. M. Caldwell & H. N. Ricciuti (Eds.), *Review of Child Development Research* (Vol. 3). Chicago: Univ. of Chicago Press, 1973.
Hetherington, E. M. Divorce: A child's perspective. *American Psychologist,* 1979, *34,* 851–858.
Hetherington, E. M., Cox, M., & Cox, R. The aftermath of divorce. In J. H. Stevens & M. Matthews (Eds.), *Mother-child, father-child relations.* Washington, D.C.: National Association for the Education of Young Children, 1978.
Hill, C. R. Private demand for child care: Implications for public policy. *Evaluation Quarterly,* 1978, *2,* 523–546.
Hirschman, A. O. *Exit, voice and loyalty.* Cambridge, Mass.: Harvard Univ. Press, 1970.
Jenkins, S., & Sauber, M. *Paths to placement.* New York: Community Council of Greater New York, 1966.
Keeley, M. A., Robins, P. K., Spiegelman, R. G., & West, R. W. *The estimation of labor supply models using experimental data: Evidence from the Seattle and Denver Income Maintenance Experiments* (Center for the Study of Welfare Policy, Research Memorandum 29). Menlo Park, Calif.: Stanford Research Institute, 1976.
Keniston, K. *All our children.* New York: Harcourt Brace Jovanovich, 1977.
McCarthy, J., & Menken, J. Marriage, remarriage, marital disruption and age at first birth. *Family Planning Perspectives,* 1979, *11,* 21–30.
Moore, K. A., Hofferth, S. L., Caldwell, S. B., & Waite, L. J. *Teenage motherhood: Social and economic consequences.* Washington, D.C.: Urban Institute, 1979.
Moynihan, D. *The politics of a guaranteed income.* New York: Vintage Books, 1973.
National Center for Health Statistics. *Montly vital statistics report: Final statistics, 1978* (*29,* Supplement No. 1). Rockville, Md.: Author, 1980.
National Research Council. *Toward a national policy for children and families.* Washington, D.C.: National Academy of Sciences, 1976.

Nelson, R. R. *The moon and the ghetto.* New York: Norton, 1977.
Nelson, R. R., & Krashinsky, M. Public control and economic organization of day care for young children. *Public Policy,* 1974, *22,* 53–75.
Office of Management and Budget. *Special analyses budget of the United States Government: Fiscal year 1980.* Washington, D.C.: U.S. Govt. Printing Office, undated.
Ogbu, J. *Minority education and caste: The American system in cross-cultural perspective.* New York: Academic Press, 1978.
Oohms, T., & Maciocha, T. *Teenage pregnancy and family impact: New perspectives on policy* (Family Impact Seminar). Washington, D.C.: Institute for Educational Leadership, George Washington Univ., June 1979.
Pechman, J. A., & Timpane, P. M. (Eds.). *Work incentives and income guarantees: The New Jersey negative income tax experiment.* Washington, D.C.: Brookings, 1975.
Plotnick, R. D., & Skidmore, F. *Progress against poverty: A review of the 1964–1974 decade.* New York: Academic Press, 1975.
Rawls, J. *A theory of justice.* Cambridge, Mass.: Harvard Univ. Press, 1971.
Rivlin, A. *Child care and preschool: Options for Federal support* (Congressional Budget Office Publication). Washington, D.C.: U.S. Govt. Printing Office, 1978.
Steinfels, M. O. *Ethical and legal issues in teenage pregnancies* (Family Impact Seminar). Washington, D.C.: Institute for Educational Leadership, George Washington Univ., 1979.
Stokey, F., & Zeckhauser, R. *A primer for policy analysis.* New York: Norton, 1978.
Thurow, L. C. *The zero-sum society: Distribution and the possibilities for economic change.* New York: Basic Books, 1980.
Titmuss, R. M. *Social policy: An introduction.* New York: Pantheon, 1974.
U.S. Bureau of the Census. *Statistical abstracts of the U.S.* (100th ed.). Washington, D.C.: U.S. Govt. Printing Office, 1979.
U.S. Bureau of the Census. Characteristics of the population below the poverty level: 1978 (*Current Population Reports,* Series P-60, No. 124). Washington, D.C.: U.S. Govt. Printing Office, 1980.
Waite, L. J., & Moore, K. A. *The impact of an early first birth on young women's educational attainment.* Paper presented at the annual meetings of the Population Association of America, St. Louis, April 1977.
Wildavsky, A. *Speaking truth to power: The art and craft of policy analysis.* Boston: Little, Brown, 1979.
Wiles, P. *Distribution of income: East and West.* New York: Elsevier, 1974.

Footnotes

[1] I do not mean to imply that all analysts must always use all "universal" critera. Rather, universal criteria are ones that occur with sufficient frequency that analysts would be well advised to at least consider whether these criteria are appropriate for the policy problem at hand.

[2] Charles Burnett, a graduate student in the Bush Institute at UNC, has been instrumental in helping me reach some understanding both of divorce and the types of policies that might be advanced to mitigate its effects.

[3] I wish to acknowledge my debt to Martha Cox, a professional fellow in UNC's Bush Institute, whose work has been most influential in shaping the approach to foster-care policy taken in this section.

Author Index

SUBJECT INDEX

buffalo shit, and when you tried to stand, you slipped and fell again." Jay chuckled.

"Yeah, but then he spun around and landed on his stomach with his face in the shit," Willy said. Jay and Willy laughed uncontrollably at their friend's expense.

Roscoe turned his head to look at the two, and in a sarcastic tone, he said, "Ha, ha, very funny!"

"That's why we're laughing," Jay managed to say between laughs.

"All that's bullshit!" Roscoe protested as he threw his hands into the air.

"I think it was bullshit actually." Willy cried aloud with laughter as Jay grabbed at his stomach.

Roscoe couldn't stand it, and he joined in on the laughter. Willy put his arm around his short friend, pulled him close, and rubbed his head. "I think he had more hair then too."

"I think we all did," Roscoe said, pointing at Willy's thinning hairline.

"Probably. Now, where is this guy at?" Willy asked after he released his friend.

"He said they'd be here at eleven. Let's give him a few more minutes, and if he doesn't show, we'll go in and grab the bag and go."

"Okay," Willy replied and walked toward his rare car. The 1965 Shelby had been Willy's dream car ever since he was a kid, and fifty-six years later, he finally owned one. When he got to the car, he leaned into the window, grabbed the water bottle off the passenger seat, and took a long drink. Today was the day he and his two friends had been waiting five long years for. After this meeting, Willy had plans to pick up his daughter from work and take her back to her place to pack her stuff, and the two of them would drive out of Las Vegas once and for all. He smiled at the thought of the two of them sitting on the beach in Pensacola, Florida, watching the navy's famous

Blue Angels flying overhead on the Fourth of July. "Just a few more minutes," Willy whispered and dropped the water bottle back in through the window. He looked off into the flat desert landscape, where he saw something shiny reflect off the desert floor.

The sniper had been in the desert since the previous evening. He had been watching the three men stand around in front of the old camper trailer since they arrived in two separate cars. Now, he was reporting what he saw back to his employer.

The sniper lifted his eye away from the rifle scope. "I have them in sight at your one o'clock."

Willy opened the glove box, took out an old pair of binoculars, and peered in the direction of the reflection he had seen. After a moment of searching the landscape, he found the shooter lying behind what appeared to be a long-range rifle. He also saw someone behind a mound of dirt. Willy turned away from them both. He dropped the binoculars in the seat and walked back to the rear of his car. "Come check out this car of mine!" Willy yelled at his two friends as he opened the trunk.

Roscoe and Jay started toward their friend. "What do you want us to see now? You showed the car to us last night at dinner. And during the entire five years we spent in prison, you showed us pictures of it every day."

"I know, but there's something back here you got to see," Willy suggested with a look on his face that the other two recognized and knew well.

Jay and Roscoe knew something was up and that Willy had something to share. They moved close to him and took up a position on his left and right.

"What's up?" Jay asked as he looked at the arsenal laid out in the trunk.

Willy ran his hand over the rear bumper and pointed to the tailpipe. "The front of my car is our twelve o'clock. We got a man with a high-powered rifle on the ground three hundred

Jack did as his boss told him to do. He had hated protecting the "three grandpas" as they became known while they were in prison. Jack and the others had to make sure nothing happened to them if they wanted to get paid. Right now, they were about to. Willy and Jack walked inside the old trailer alone, leaving the others outside.

"Kind of hot today, isn't it?" Roscoe yelled to Hal and Rob, who appeared uncomfortable standing in the sun in their cotton pants and polo shirts.

"Fuck you, Roscoe!" Rob yelled back.

Roscoe looked at Jay and smiled. Roscoe had the knack of pissing people off and getting them off balance. Off balance was right where he wanted both the men to be.

"C'mon now, Robby, don't be like that. I thought we were friends. Don't you remember how I saved you from getting beat to hell by Big Rick in the prison yard?"

"You didn't help me with shit!"

"You're right. I actually paid Big Rick to kick the shit out of you."

Hal could see Rob was getting irritated by Roscoe. "Shut the fuck up!" he yelled back to Roscoe.

Inside the camper, Jack took about three steps in and stopped. He looked around at the broken furniture, animal tracks, and dirt. "I can't believe somewhere in here, hidden among all of this shit, is five million dollars."

"Well, there is," Willy stated.

"Where?" Jack held his arms out to his side, palms up, and twisted his upper body back and forth while looking around the shabby camper.

Willy smiled and started down the small hallway. "In the bathroom shower."

Jack pulled his gun out from behind his back and pointed it at Willy. "Stop!"

Willy turned around and saw the gun in Jack's hand. He

slowly raised his hands into the air. "This is how you guys do business?" Willy asked in a loud tone.

"Keep your voice down. We have guys in the desert ready to take your two friends out if I give the order. Now slowly go into the bathroom and get the money."

Willy walked into the tiny bathroom while Jack kept his gun on him. Willy bent down and unlatched a secret lever, releasing the shower pan from the floor. He lifted the pan and used an old plunger to prop the pan against the back wall. In the hidden compartment were two bags covered in dust.

"You need help getting that out? I mean, you being old and feeble and all, they may be too heavy. After all, it should all weigh just over two hundred pounds. The casino you guys robbed over five years ago got everything back, except for ten million dollars in one-hundred-dollar bills."

Willy glared at the younger man. "I think I can manage it, and it was only five million that they didn't get back. The casino inflated the number to ten million so they could collect more from the insurance company."

"So you say."

"Yeah, I say, because that's what they did."

Jack shook his head and grinned. "Hold on, why don't you go ahead and slowly take out that nine millimeter from your waist that I saw hidden under your shirt. Lay it on the counter by the sink," Jack ordered while motioning toward the filthy sink with his gun.

Willy did as he was told. He started to reach into the hidden compartment for the bags but saw the most venomous rattlesnake in all of Nevada. With its olive-green color and its diamond-shaped blotches along its back, the Mojave green slithered into the corner of the hidden compartment, away from the money bags. Willy was surprised by the three-foot serpent, but he didn't jump or step back. Instead, he got an idea.

"What are you waiting for? Pull it out and give it to me," Jack ordered.

"What's taking so long in there?" Hal yelled from outside.

Jack looked out the dust-covered side window of the camper. "We'll be out in a second."

Willy saw his opportunity, and he took it. The elderly man grabbed the deadly snake behind its head, pulled it out, and tossed it at Jack. The snake landed right on the man's gun arm. Jack was startled, to say the least, and he desperately tried to move away from the snake. Suddenly, the snake struck forward and caught Jack in the cheek. He dropped his gun and grabbed the snake with both hands, but it was no use. The venom was already coursing through the man's body. Jack tried to scream, but nothing came out.

Willy grabbed his gun off the counter, then picked Jack's gun up from the floor and slid it into the small of his back. He then returned to the bathroom and lifted the bags out of the compartment. Willy heard the others talking outside. As he carefully stepped over Jack's convulsing body, he made his way to the door and stood there, out of sight. Willy didn't know what to do next. His plan ended after he'd grabbed the rattlesnake and tossed it onto Jack.

"C'mon, what's taking so long?" Hal yelled.

Willy stood there for a moment more. "To hell with it!" The Vietnam veteran dropped the money bags on the floor, pulled Jack's gun from his waist, and rushed out of the trailer firing the two pistols at Hal and Rob.

Jay and Roscoe quickly grabbed their weapons and did exactly as the three men had planned.

The sniper in the distance looked through his scope for a target. Roscoe covered Willy as Jay dropped to the ground behind the Shelby with the M249 in front of him. He sprayed the mound of dirt in the distance, and the two men hiding behind it ducked for cover.

The battle lasted for more than ten minutes. Nearby, hikers telephoned the police and watched the gunfight from a distance. When the police finally arrived, they found three bodies and a few blood trails that led to tire impressions in the sand. The tire impressions came from three different vehicles. They also found numerous empty casings lying on the ground from different types of guns.

After a month-long investigation, there were no leads. Then some teenagers riding their motorcycles along an old dirt road came across a burned-out Suburban parked next to a dry creek bed. Inside the charred Suburban were the remains of three unidentifiable bodies and what was left of an AR-15, an M249, and three pistols. Next to the Suburban were some emptied out suitcases and personal papers belonging to three elderly men who had recently been released from prison.

Chapter 1
Shelby

The diner just outside of Las Vegas was busy with people either driving into or leaving Sin City. Shelby, a beautiful woman with long blonde hair, hustled from one table to the next, delivering food and taking orders. It was four o'clock in the afternoon, and she was exhausted from working three doubles over the past three days.

Her boss, Frank, walked around the diner, ordering his employees around. Frank was in his forties, overweight, and a pervert. Shelby and the other waitresses had found him spying on them in the bathroom on more than one occasion. If Frank wasn't making comments about the girls' figures, he was putting himself in a position to rub his body against theirs or cop a feel when they walked by him carrying a heavy tray full of food for a table.

Shelby had been waitressing at the diner for six months, while her boyfriend, Carter, worked on his golf game. Carter had gone to college on a golf scholarship. For the past five years, he had been trying to make it onto the pro tour. Being the supporting girlfriend she was, Shelby worked two jobs at a time, hoping one day Carter would soon be taking care of her with the millions he was earning as a professional golfer. She was thirty-five years old, had never married or had kids, and had fallen in love more times than she could count.

"You need to pick it up, and you need to smile more!" Frank ordered when Shelby walked up to the counter to check for her customer's food.

She stared at the man for a moment and smiled sarcastically. "I'll make sure I do exactly that, Mr. Frankie!" Shelby replied in her Southern accent. The accent and her sarcasm were attributed to her short time spent in the South as a child.

"Look, redneck, you better shape up, or I'll send you out on your cute ass," Frank threatened.

Shelby glared at the man and then stood on her tiptoes at the pickup counter to examine the cook's food for her table. She was five foot four, and having problems reaching things or seeing things at a height taller than her was something she commonly referred to as a "short girl problem." Frank, who never seemed to miss an opportunity, walked behind and squeezed her right butt cheek.

Shelby turned around and faced the nasty man. "Don't ever grab my ass again or—"

"Or what? Nothing, that's what. Your country ass needs this job just like the other girls," Frank declared.

Shelby bit her lip. She did need the job, no matter how little she thought of it or Frank. She'd rather have worked in one of the casinos, but a felony conviction on her record prevented that from ever happening. It was either the diner waitressing tables or at the strip club dancing on them, both of which Shelby had some experience doing. "Just don't do it again, Frank," Shelby stated in a more pleasant tone.

Frank smiled, then turned and walked out to the dining area where a thin, balding man in a dark suit stood, waiting for the establishment's manager. "Would you like a seat?" Frank asked politely.

"No, well, yes. Um, I'm actually here to see a Shelby Finn," the man explained.

Frank stared at the man. "Are you a cop or something?"

The man shook his head. "Oh no, I'm an attorney, you see, and I have something for Ms. Finn. Is she around?"

"Yeah, she's here. That's one of her tables over there. You can have a seat, and she'll be right out, but don't keep her long. It's our rush hour right now. I need her helping out with our paying customers," Frank explained and walked back to the kitchen.

Shelby was still looking over the food she had carefully placed on a tray. She was just about to take it out to a large group when the local news came on the TV set Frank had sitting on the counter, out of view of the customers.

"The bodies found in a burned-out Suburban recently have been identified as Roscoe Thomas Westland, Jay Trent Johnson, and William Michael Finn. The sheriff's office has confirmed the three men had extensive criminal records and had recently been released from prison," the news anchor reported.

When Shelby heard the name William Michael Finn, she nearly knocked her tray over as she rushed around the counter to see the TV screen.

"Foul play is suspected," the anchor said right before Frank walked up.

"William Michael Finn, is he some relative of yours?" Frank asked. He knew Finn was Shelby's last name.

A tear formed in the waitress's eye, but she quickly wiped it away when she heard Frank's comment. "No, not that I know of," Shelby softly answered, but it was a lie. She knew William Michael Finn all too well.

"Well, it sounds like he's a crook, so it wouldn't surprise me if you were related. By the way, you got someone in your section who wants to talk to you."

Shelby looked at her boss with a clueless expression. "Who?" she asked.

"I don't know. Just get that tray out to its table, go see the guy, and get back to work. We're shorthanded since your friend Karen called in sick again."

"I think she's having trouble with her mom. You could cut her some slack."

Frank looked at Shelby with a disgusted look on his face. "Why would I give two shits about her? Just get your ass back to work!"

"Okay," Shelby replied. She lifted the heavy tray onto her tiny shoulder and carried it out to the table. When she was finished, she rushed to the man sitting in her section.

"You need to see me?" Shelby suspiciously asked of the stranger.

The man looked the woman over for a moment. "Interesting, you look nothing like your father."

"My father, what do you have to do with him? If you know—or knew him, I should say, then you're probably just as bad as he was, and I don't have time for you," Shelby stated flatly and started to walk away.

"Wait, I'm Tanner Scott, and I'm an attorney representing your father's estate."

"Estate? What estate, and how are you here right now? I heard them report that they just identified his body along with his two cronies. My Uncle Roscoe and Jay!"

"Actually, they identified his body a few days ago, and it's just now being reported in the media. They reached out to me because I had represented your father and his two associates in various legal matters previously," Tanner explained.

"So you're a defense lawyer. You represent people at the bottom of the barrel. Now, what could my father ever leave me? He never had anything of value to begin with. Well, except for my mother, and she died fifteen years ago waiting for him to get out of prison, again."

He gestured toward the booth's seat with his left hand. "Your father had some assets that are now yours, and if you'd sit down for a few minutes, I can have you sign some documents and hand those assets over to you." He offered a friendly smile.

Shelby stood there for a moment, looking at the tall man in his dark suit. "Very well, what do I need to sign?" she asked and sat down. If the truth were told, she really didn't care about what her father had left her. In her mind, it was probably nothing more than a few trinkets from her childhood.

"Well, first off, he has a letter for you in this envelope. Second, here's a deed for the property, and third, here's a bank statement with the money he left you in the amount of four hundred fifty thousand dollars."

Shelby's eyes widened. "What?"

"Yes, for the past ten years, your father, William, Willy, Finn had invested some of his money into different real estate ventures that paid out while he was in prison."

"Oh my word! What is the deed for?"

"Your father purchased a beach house on Pensacola Beach. Here's a picture of it," Tanner said and then handed Shelby a photo of the beach house.

Shelby looked at the photo and smiled. She remembered when the photo was taken.

"It's near—"

"I know where it is," Shelby said, gazing at the old blue beach house her parents had rented for the first ten years of her life. There, she, along with her mother and father, stood posing for the photo.

"There are only two more things I need to pass on to you. One is parked right there," Tanner stated as he pointed at the 1965 Shelby sitting in the parking lot.

Shelby looked at the namesake sitting there with its

Wimbledon white paint job and blue racing stripes. "I guess he finally got it."

"Looks like it. Lastly, this is five thousand dollars in cash in this other envelope. Now, if you can sign here and write in your bank account number here, I can have the money wired to your account by tomorrow," Tanner explained, pointing at two lines on the paperwork he had brought with him. He slid the envelope with money in it toward her.

Shelby signed the document as instructed, and when she was done, Tanner gathered his belongings, thanked Shelby for her time, and walked out of the diner. Shelby didn't know what to do. She was still sitting there looking at the keys to the car in one hand and the deed in the other when Frank walked up and stood next to the table.

"Are you going back to work anytime soon?" Frank asked.

"Oh, yeah," Shelby answered. She stood and picked up the things off the table.

"Good, now get that sweet ass back to the kitchen. You got another order that's up," Frank said and looked at Shelby's backside. He smiled, and with his right hand, he slapped her butt cheek hard.

That was all it took. Shelby quickly came to the realization she no longer needed the job or Frank's constant harassment. She looked at the metal napkin dispenser sitting on the table, picked it up, and spun around, hitting Frank across the bridge of his nose. Frank dropped to the floor as his blood ran down his face onto his white shirt.

"I'll—"

"Don't even think about calling the cops. I'll sue your ass for sexual harassment, and I'll get the other girls on board with me. That man was my lawyer. You'll be flat broke and out of work faster than you could spit if you come after me." Shelby turned and walked out of the diner to the applause of the other waitresses.

When she got outside, she stood in front of the Mustang. She didn't get in it right away. She just admired it for a moment. She took out her cell phone and was about to call Carter but decided to surprise him with everything when he got home. Besides, now the two of them had enough money for her to stop working for a little while.

The powerful V8 purred as Shelby drove it down the interstate toward her apartment. She started to imagine what it would be like traveling with Carter to more golf tournaments as he tried to make the pro tour. With Shelby working and Carter playing golf or practicing at the range, the two barely had time together.

"That's all about to change," Shelby called as she pressed the gas pedal to the floor and allowed the car to run wide open.

When Shelby got to the apartment complex, she had to park in the guest parking space because Carter's car was sitting in their assigned spot. Shelby walked to Carter's car and looked at it for a second. *I guess he stayed home today*, Shelby thought and then headed upstairs to the apartment to share the day's good news.

Upon opening the front door, Shelby was surprised to find that Carter was not in the living room or kitchen. As she started down the hall, she heard Carter's voice coming from the bedroom. The door was partially open. She slowly peeked inside and saw Carter and another woman having sex on the bed.

"Yeah, baby!" Carter yelled, unaware Shelby was standing right behind him.

"Fuck me!" the woman shouted, in a voice Shelby recognized immediately.

Shelby slowly walked to the side of the bed without saying a word. When Carter saw her, he froze. He couldn't say anything. He just stared at the women he had betrayed.

"Don't stop, Carter! I'm almost there!" Karen yelled.

"What's wrong? Why'd you stop?" Karen turned around and found her best friend staring at her.

"It's not—"

"Carter, don't say it's not what it looks like. Because from where I'm standing, it looks a whole lot like you're fucking my best friend!" Shelby shouted. She then walked to the closet and took out her suitcase.

Karen covered herself with the sheets from the bed while Carter followed Shelby around the apartment, trying to get her to stop packing and talk to him.

"Shelby, please. I love you. Karen and I were just fucking. That's all it is. We wanted to tell you."

Shelby stopped and looked at the man she had worked countless doubles for, the man she had fed, clothed, and sponsored in many golf tournaments. She didn't know what to say or do, then it came to her. She saw it sitting there, and she knew what she had to do.

Carter saw the smile on Shelby's face, and he took it to mean something it wasn't. "Baby, now see, I knew you couldn't leave me. Why don't you come back into the bedroom where the three of us can discuss this?"

Shelby kept smiling at Carter as she walked to the eight-hundred-dollar driver she had just bought him. It was sitting there in his golf bag, right where she could grab it. When she pulled the expensive driver from the bag, Carter knew her smile was not one of understanding.

Shelby removed the cover from the driver's head and made her way to Carter's trophies, gripping the club tightly. "I bought this because I thought you were something special."

Carter held his hands in the air. "Shelby, calm the fuck down!"

Karen, who was still sitting on the bed, afraid to move, heard Carter's command. "Fuck," she mumbled and held the pillow over her head. She knew telling a woman to calm down was not the right thing to say in a moment like this.

Shelby reached back with the driver and brought it forward, into the trophies. The impact sent the man's memorabilia crashing against the opposite wall.

Karen pulled the pillow down from her face to her stomach and listened to the two of them once more.

"Calm down?" Shelby yelled.

Carter stepped back from the scorned woman with his eyes and veins bulging. "You're one fucking crazy bitch!"

"Oh shit, Carter," Karen mumbled and covered her head with the pillow again.

Shelby laughed aloud. "Crazy? I'll show you crazy!" she yelled. She swung the club at everything breakable and didn't stop until the driver's head snapped off. When she was done, she walked back into the bedroom, took out more of her clothes out of the closet, and stood next to the bed.

Karen thought Shelby had walked out and that she was alone. She pulled the pillow off her head but found Shelby still standing there, looking directly at her.

"I don't—"

Before Karen could finish, Shelby punched her former best friend in the face. She then walked into the living room, where Carter had begun picking up his shattered memories.

"I hope you're happy," the upset and still-naked man said. He got up and angrily walked toward Shelby.

Shelby dropped her suitcase on the floor, and when Carter was within striking distance, she stepped forward and drove her knee right into his groin. Carter fell to the floor, where he rolled around in agony. Shelby picked her suitcase back up, walked out to the Mustang, and sped out of the complex without a second thought.

Shelby didn't know where she was going, but nothing was keeping her in Las Vegas anymore. She was a free, independent woman with nothing but her future in front of her. She gripped the steering wheel tightly, took a deep breath, and looked at the picture of the old beach house that she had wedged into the sun visor.

"It's time to take care of myself and to do for me." She pressed the pedal down and headed down the highway with the sun setting behind her.

Tanner Scott waited out of sight in the parking lot of Shelby's apartment. He was surprised to see her go in and come back out so fast with her suitcase in tow. It didn't matter if she left now or later to him and the people he worked for. They just needed her in Pensacola, where they could keep an eye on her. There was too much money on the line for things to get messed up now. Tanner reached into the passenger seat and picked up his cell phone. He dialed the number on the sticky note and waited.

"It's me," Tanner said into the phone when the other man answered. "Yeah, looks like she's leaving for Pensacola now."

Chapter 2
Beach Bound

Warden Henry Baker sat in his leather executive chair inside his office at the Nevada State Prison. He was waiting impatiently for an important phone call when his secretary knocked on his door.

"Come in."

"Warden Baker, there's a man from the FBI out here to see you," Shelia announced.

Henry felt his heart race. "Um, show him in," he nervously said. He then stood too fast and was reminded of his injury. He winced in pain and then took his cell phone off his desk and placed it into his pocket right before the FBI agent walked in.

"Good afternoon, Warden Baker," Brian greeted as he walked into the office. Brian was a tall man, wearing a black polo and black slacks. The man had an air of confidence when he moved, and others noticed, including Warden Baker.

Warden Baker shook his visitor's hand. "Afternoon, Agent. What brings the FBI all the way out here?"

Brian looked at the chair in front of the warden's desk and the nameplate on the desk that read: Henry "Hal" Baker. "I have a fascinating case I'm working on, and I thought maybe you could help me with a few things. May I sit down?"

"Certainly," the warden said and gestured to the chair. He slowly eased himself in his own seat, careful of his injury.

Brian watched the warden slowly sit and couldn't help but notice the man appeared to be in pain. "Are you all right, Warden?"

"Yes, I pulled my groin playing basketball in our gym about a month ago, and it hasn't gotten better yet."

"I've heard groin injuries can take a long time to heal," Brian replied. He looked at the warden and wanted to laugh. Somehow, he couldn't imagine the short and slightly overweight warden playing basketball, or even running around on a court. Besides, Brian knew how the warden really injured himself.

"Well, I'm hoping for the best. Now, what can I do for you?"

"I imagine you've already heard about the three men who were former inmates of yours, who were found inside a torched Suburban."

The warden thought about it for a moment before saying anything. "Yes. We sent their medical records to the coroner's office as quickly as we could. You know, it came as no surprise, really. I mean, we have a lot of inmates who leave here and end up getting into trouble again. Some of them come right back here within a year or two after being released."

"Yes, I'm aware of the high recidivism rate among inmates. Some people just can't be reformed."

"No, no, they can't. Now, what would you like to know?"

"What can you tell me about Roscoe Westland, Jay Johnson, and William Finn?"

"Well, they were sentenced to eight years for robbing a casino. They did five years, they were released on parole, and then they were found in that Suburban. What else can I tell you?" Warden Baker asked, hoping he had said enough to satisfy the FBI agent.

Brian thought it was odd the warden didn't have anything else to say about his former inmates. "How was their time here? Were they a problem? Did they have friends? Associates? Anything you could tell me may help in finding out just how they came to be in that Suburban." Brian was fishing for any information; he needed to know what the warden knew about the three former inmates.

"Well, Roscoe and Jay were cellmates. Willy had a few different cellmates, but none I could say were ever close to the man. The three hung out together most of the time at dinner or in the yard. They weren't a problem, as far as I can remember."

Brian wrote everything down in his notebook. "Were they assigned to any work details, or did they hold a job in the kitchen, machine shop, or anything?" The agent looked up from his notebook. He couldn't think of much to ask about, but he knew he had to ask more questions, even if he already knew the answers, because that was what a real FBI agent would do.

"Roscoe worked in the machine shop. Jay was assigned to the kitchen, the infirmary, and the laundry. Willy worked in our community outreach program, where he helped to train animals to work with people with disabilities."

"At least they kept busy—"

"I don't really know much about the men. I can have Shelia, my secretary, get the guards who worked their cellblock scheduled over the next few days so that you can interview them if you'd like."

Brian wasn't sure how to approach the next topic, so he just put it out there. "There's only one guard I'd like to speak to, but I can't."

"Who would that be?" Warden Baker asked, even though he already knew who the guard was.

"Jack Waller. He was killed about a month ago in the desert, along with two other men who have yet to be identified."

The warden pretended to be shocked by the news. "We've been wondering what happened to Jack. He was scheduled for work but hadn't shown up for about… well, for almost a month now. Two weeks ago, we contacted the Bureau of Prisons, and the last I heard was that they were working with the local police and… I thought you guys too. Can you tell me what happened to him?"

Brian was caught off guard by the question. He should have known that Jack being killed would require involvement of the feds. "Yeah, we're looking into it. That's why I asked about it. Anyway, it looks like he got bit by a rattlesnake. In the face, of all places."

"Where—how, I mean… What or how did that happen?"

The warden was overselling his ignorance of the ordeal, and Brian knew it, even if the warden did not. "It looks like he was part of a shooting in the desert that took place near an old camper, along with two other men."

"Wow! He really wasn't that great of an employee either. I guess for some people who find themselves around criminals all day, they can't help but fall into the same lifestyle."

"So he wasn't a good guard?"

"No, as a matter of fact, I have his personal file here on my desk. Our HR department asked that I review it before we fired him for cause when and if he finally showed back up for work. I guess that won't be necessary now," Baker said and handed the folder to the man he still believed was an FBI agent.

"May I keep it?" Brian asked as he looked through the folder.

"I'll have Sheila make you a copy on your way out. I really need to get back to work, unless you have something else you need help with."

Brian stood. "I understand. You're a busy man. Thank you for your time."

"No problem. Sheila, can you make the agent a copy of CO Jack Waller's personnel file?"

Sheila walked in, took the file, and escorted the agent out of the office.

Warden Baker waited for the agent to leave before taking his cell phone out of his pocket. He scanned his call history and found Rob's number.

"Yeah."

"Look, the FBI was just here, asking questions about those three fuck-ups and Jack," Hal said into the receiver.

Rob listened to his boss and heard the nervousness in his voice. "Do they know anything?"

"Not yet, but it won't take them long to put it all together. Where's the girl?" Hal asked.

"I watched her at the diner, and you'll never guess who showed up to visit."

"Who?"

"The Tan Man came by and dropped off her old man's car."

Henry thought about what he had just been told. "Do you have Jimmy tailing her?"

"Yeah."

"Good, if he gets the chance, have him take the car."

"You know Jimmy. He'll want to take more than the car."

"Make sure he knows we need her alive. We just want the car for now."

"Anything else?" Rob asked, already knowing what Hal wanted him to do.

"Yeah, why don't you talk to Tan Man and find out what he knows."

"All right. I'm sitting outside his place now. By the way, Hal, how's the leg?"

Hal reached down and rubbed his thigh, around the area where the bullet went through. "It hurts like hell, but it'll be worth it if we get our hands on the money," Hal answered and ended the call.

Tanner Scott had returned to his small house off Eastern Avenue after transferring the money. He was tired, and his body ached. The meeting with the woman had taken a lot out of him. Now, all he wanted to do was go to his room, turn on the window AC unit, and rest for the evening. He thought about making some dinner, but his stomach had other plans. The cancer medication was taking its toll on the man's body, mind, and overall well-being. He had been warned about overexerting himself, but the meeting with the woman had needed to take place.

After filling an ice bag, Tanner shut the door to his room, turned the AC on high, lay down, and placed the ice bag on his armpit. One of Tanner's lymph nodes had been damaged from the radiation treatments, and it was swelling. The swelling, the pain, and the Nevada heat that accompanied it were unbearable at times. Next to his bed on the nightstand were numerous medication bottles and a half-empty glass of water from the previous evening. He grabbed two oxycodone pills and washed them down with the lukewarm water. Tanner had just about fallen into a deep sleep when his bedroom door burst open.

"Good evening, Tan Man," Rob said as he entered the room.

Tanner lifted his head and immediately recognized the man standing there. "Robby, how the hell are you, you dirty shit bag?" Tanner asked in a groggy voice.

Rob didn't say anything. He stepped to the bed and delivered a hard fist to the feeble man's lower jaw. The blow sent Tanner back on his pillow. Rob pulled the sick man up by his shirt and got ready to hit him again. "Who'd you meet with today and why?"

"Your old lady. She needed some lovin'. Apparently, you've

been coming up a bit short in that area," Tanner answered and laughed aloud.

Rob, being the violent man he was, hit Tanner over and over again. When Tanner finally passed out, his tormentor grabbed the glass he found on the nightstand and threw the water on his victim's face to wake him up.

As Rob waited for Tanner to come to his senses, he read the labels of the different medication bottles sitting next to the bed. "Are you dying or something?" Rob asked without a hint of remorse in his voice.

"Yeah, and I got nothing to say to you."

"No? Well, we'll see about that," Rob said threateningly and grabbed Tanner once more.

Tanner laughed again, and Rob paused. "What's so funny?"

"You're nothing. Guards like you and Jack are nothing but weak men who take advantage of people who have no way of defending themselves. You know, that's why Roscoe paid to have you beat down in the yard. By the way, I chipped in too."

Rob became angrier, and he started back at Tanner. He gripped his shirt tighter and was about to hit him again. Suddenly, Tanner gasped for air and grabbed at his chest. Rob released his grip, allowing the man to fall back onto the bed. He stood there as the cancer patient clenched his chest and then took his last breath.

Rob looked down at the dead man. "Fuck."

Brian walked out of the prison, climbed into his sporty coupe, and tossed the stolen FBI badge and forged credentials into the passenger seat. He then started the expensive car, drove out of the prison's sally port, and sped away. When he reached the highway, he took out his cell phone and called the number on the sticky note. The phone rang twice before his call was answered.

"It's me. I just left the prison... Yeah, Warden Henry 'Hal' Baker' is nervous... He's trying to cover his tracks; he created a fake personnel file for Jack... I know where the car is. It and the woman are about an hour outside of Las Vegas," Brian said, looking at the tracking app on his cell phone. "That's not what we agreed to... Yeah, I'll do it for that much... Okay, I'll keep you informed." Brian ended the call and looked at the tracking app once more. "See you soon, sweetheart."

Hal was sitting on the bed in the shady hotel room, watching the evening news as he waited for Rob to call him. The Stay and Play was on the outskirts of Henderson and far enough away from Las Vegas that he wouldn't be recognized. He felt stressed from his meeting with the FBI agent and decided he needed some female companionship. His first call was to April, a prostitute who was also a former inmate at the women's prison. When Hal had met April, he was a deputy warden at the women's prison, and she had been assigned to housekeeping. April's job brought the beautiful young woman into his office regularly, where they spent a lot of time together. For April, their relationship in prison afforded her certain benefits that other inmates didn't have. Since her release over a year ago, she had returned to her old profession but kept in contact with Hal. He had threatened to expose her to her parole officer if she didn't perform certain favors for him and his men.

April was standing at the foot of the bed, putting her clothes back on. "Are you going to tell me what happened to your leg?

"I wasn't planning on it."

"Fine, don't then. I need some money."

Hal looked up at the woman and chuckled. "Then you better get back out there and start selling."

"Asshole!" April yelled and stormed out of the room.

Hal was still watching the news when his cell phone rang. He looked at the number and answered it.

"What did you find out from Tan Man, and why did you wait so long to call me back?" he asked in an angry tone.

Rob paused before answering. He was drunk and knew Hal would be pissed off when he found out. "Tan Man is dead."

Hal sat up on the bed. "You're drunk. I can hear it in your voice. How did it happen?"

Rob took another drink before answering. "He was sick with cancer. I didn't know. I think he had a heart attack."

"Did he tell you anything?"

"No, but I looked around his place and found some documents. I don't think he forged them."

Hal stepped off the bed and limped around to the end of it. "Really, you don't think they were forged? He was a forger! It's why he was in prison! You idiot!"

"Wait, I checked some of them out. One document was a copy of a deed for a beach house in Pensacola, Florida. I checked it out. It belonged to Willy."

"What else is there?"

"He left her four hundred and fifty grand and the car," Rob said.

"Is there anything else?"

"Yeah, I went back to the diner where she worked. I spoke to her boss, who she did a number on, and I paid him a few bucks to tell me anything he knew about the man who came by to see her."

"Did he tell you anything important?"

"Not really, all he saw was that the man gave her an envelope and some keys and had her sign a document. I think it's part of the ones I found at Tanner's place," Rob explained.

"What was in the envelope?"

"He didn't know, and Tanner never mentioned it. What do you want me to do?"

Hal didn't respond right away. He thought about it all for a moment. "Get down to the beach house. I'll have Charlie meet you there, and the two of you can work something out. Maybe Charlie can get close to her and find out what's in the envelope."

"Anything else?"

"Yes, make sure Jimmy doesn't kill the woman when he goes for the car. I mean it! You better make sure he understands. Don't you guys mess this up," Hal threatened before abruptly ending the call.

Shelby drove the Mustang for nine hours straight. She stopped for gas, dinner, and gas two more times before pulling into a truck stop gas station in Albuquerque at about one thirty in the morning. She used the bathroom inside, grabbed a hotdog and soda, and returned to the Mustang she had parked between two semitrucks. Shelby was tired, and her mind had been spinning ever since she left Las Vegas. Her thoughts ran the gamut from turning the vintage car around to staying on the road and continuing to the old beach house in Pensacola.

If she went back to Las Vegas, it would be the same old thing. Carter would be coming around, trying to make up for his infidelity. Shelby being Shelby would probably forgive him because their relationship was something she was familiar with. Familiarity was Shelby's crutch in life, and she knew it. Another crutch in her life were men in general, who seemed to always be there and always seemed to use her for their benefit.

Wait. I'm not going to be used anymore. I'm taking care of myself. I don't need Las Vegas, I don't need Carter, and I don't need men telling me what to do, Shelby thought, right before she fell asleep in the driver's seat to the sound of the two idling diesel engines.

Jimmy had been following the Mustang since she left Las Vegas, and he was eager to meet the woman driving it. He was told he couldn't kill her, but he figured he could at least have some fun. Jimmy had been patient and was waiting for the right time. He thought about going after her in the car, but with her being parked so close to the two semis, he felt it was too much of a risk, especially if she fought back or screamed for help. In the end, he decided to wait quietly in the darkness of his car until she made a mistake. Then he would take her. He was experienced in this type of behavior. He knew it would be a matter of time before she made herself available. Now that she was parked and looked to be settling in for a break, he needed to find something that would help him in securing and concealing the car.

Chapter 3
Truck Stops

Shelby awoke shivering at about four o'clock in the morning. During her short nap, the New Mexico temperature had dropped significantly. She reached into the back seat for her suitcase, found one of Carter's white UNLV hoodies, and slipped it over her head. The semi-truck parked on her left had pulled out sometime during the early morning hours. A yellow rental moving truck had taken its place. She was still sleepy, but she also wanted to get moving again. She reached down and started the car.

I better use the bathroom first, Shelby thought and turned the car off again. About one hundred yards away from her was the truck stop convenience store and the bathrooms. An uneasy feeling came over her. She looked around at the dimly lit parking lot before unlocking the car and getting out.

Shelby stood next to the Mustang as a cool westerly wind blew across the parking lot. She shivered again and turned toward the convenience store. When she reached the rear corner of the moving truck, she noticed two ramps laid out behind the box truck. She stopped, peeked around the corner, and found that the cargo door was open. "What in the—"

"Come here, bitch!" Jimmy yelled. He reached down from the carbo bed of the truck and grabbed the woman by her long blonde hair.

Shelby was surprised and unprepared. With both hands, she desperately grabbed at the unknown man's hand and muscular forearm and tried to pull away, but his grip was too strong.

Shelby started to scream, but Jimmy was ready for the ambush and knew she would scream. He had a lead-filled leather sap in his right hand, and he used it. The impact of the weapon on Shelby's temple knocked her out. Her tiny body went limp. He dropped the sap on the bed of the truck and then lifted her inside. He looked around the dark parking lot, and when he was confident no one had seen anything, he pulled the door closed.

Brian left Las Vegas, and when he stopped in Flagstaff for gas, he found, to his dismay, he had a leaking radiator hose. After waiting for a new one to be delivered to the repair shop and then another hour to repair it, he was three hours behind the woman. While he waited, he constantly checked the tracking app on his phone to see if she had stopped somewhere for the night. When Brian finally got back on the road, he was tired and in need of rest, but he knew he had to keep up with the woman and the car.

When Brian was a couple of hours outside of Albuquerque, he saw the woman had stopped somewhere along the interstate. Brian believed she was either stopping for gas or getting a room. He hoped it was the latter, as he was ready to find a nice hotel to get some sleep. As he drove along the lonely road, Brian thought about his future and his past. The past was something he wished to forget but could not. It was his past and the bad decisions he had made that had taken some of his youth. Now, he was desperate to make up for lost time, but he needed money for that, and the girl and the car would do just that if things went as planned.

When Brian entered the city limits of Albuquerque, his tracking app indicated he was very close to the Mustang. He took the next exit and pulled into the parking lot of a truck stop. The red light on the app grew larger and larger, indicating the car was close, but when he surveyed the large parking lot, he didn't see the car anywhere. Brian changed the view on the app, making it bigger. As he drove through the parking lot, he stopped a few hundred feet away from where the car should have been located. Still, he didn't find anything except for one large semitruck and one yellow moving van. Brian parked his car and walked between the two trucks, where he searched the ground for the tracking locator that had been attached to the Mustang. He couldn't find it. However, he did hear music coming from inside the moving truck parked next to him. His app also indicated that the Mustang was sitting in the same spot as the truck.

The sound of jazz music was the first thing Shelby heard when she came around. She tried to sit up but found her arms had been handcuffed to the wall above her head. A gag had been tightly tied around her head and covered her mouth. She had also been blindfolded. Shelby was groggy, but she still tried to peek out from under the cloth covering her eyes.

Earlier in the evening, when Jimmy had left the woman where she was sleeping in the parking lot, he drove around the area until he found a moving truck rental company near the truck stop. He hotwired one of the cargo trucks, drove it over to the truck stop, and waited until the woman made herself available.

"You're finally awake, good," Jimmy said. He was sitting on the hood of the Mustang, smoking a cigarette. After securing the woman, he used a come-along that he had attached to the back wall to pull the car into the cargo area.

Shelby desperately pulled at her restraints to no avail. She soon realized she was no longer wearing her hoodie, and the tank top she'd worn under it had also been removed. "What are you doing?" Shelby asked with fear in her voice.

"I'm stealing your car, and well, now you and I—"

Suddenly and unexpectedly, the cargo door opened slightly.

Jimmy rushed around the car and looked at the door but didn't see anyone. "What the fuck?"

Shelby used her right shoulder to pull the gag away from her mouth and screamed.

Jimmy panicked. He ran to the back of the truck, pulled the cargo door closed, and latched it. He rushed back to his victim and was about to hit her with the leather weapon once more when someone grabbed him from behind. Shelby heard two voices and what sounded like a scuffle taking place just a few feet in front of her. Once more, she used her right shoulder and partially pulled the blindfold off her eyes. Shelby's vision was blurred. She couldn't make out either of the men, but she could tell the fight was intense. Suddenly, she saw the glare of what she thought was the blade of a knife shining in the light of the cargo truck.

Shelby pulled and tried to free herself when she heard one of the men scream in pain. She then heard her kidnapper's voice. "Now, I'm going to put it in you deep. Then I'm going to do the same to her."

"C'mon then," the other man replied confidently.

"No, no..." Shelby heard more scuffling, someone falling to the bed of the truck, and silence. She desperately tried to see what was going on, but she couldn't remove the blindfold any farther down her eyes. She sat there quietly. Then she heard the footsteps of someone moving toward her. "No, please," Shelby begged.

Without warning, someone pulled the blindfold and the gag back in place. "No, let me go, please," Shelby cried, and to her surprise, she felt her hands being unshackled. Someone lifted her up and propped her against the wall. She whimpered and passed out.

Hal was sitting in his office at the prison, looking over Rob's information concerning the property in Pensacola. The warden couldn't help but think back to when he had first spoken to Willy about the robbery in the old man's cell sometime back. Hal had worked it out for the three men to be released on parole early, as long as they agreed to pay him half the money they had been able to hide before being arrested for the casino heist. After the meeting with Willy, Hal and his crew decided to take all the three men's money and kill them after.

The day at the camper, Hal and his men never thought the three old men were capable of anything like what had gone down. The warden reached down and rubbed his leg injury, and as he did, he recalled the moment Willy came running out of the camper, firing at him and Rob. One round had found Hal's upper thigh and went straight through it. When the shooting was over, Hal had nothing but a hole in his leg, a few dead men, and some of the casino's money. After reading over Rob's information, Hal pulled up Willy's record. He was about to read through it once more for anything that could help him locate the rest of the money when there was a knock on his door. He looked up and saw Sheila opening the door.

"Mr. Baker, there are men from the FBI here to speak with you," Sheila announced.

Hal looked at her with a surprised expression. "Show them in."

The warden stood and watched as two men wearing suits walked into his office.

"Hello, Warden Baker, I'm Agent Thomas, and this is Agent Rizzo."

Warden Baker reached over his desk and shook both the men's hands. "What can I do for you fellows?"

"Warden Baker, we're here to speak to you about one of your employees, and two unidentified men," Agent Thomas answered and handed the warden a picture of a very dead Jack Waller and two other photos of the two men he had hired out of Texas.

Hal pretended to be surprised. "Yeah, what can I help you with?" He asked after taking his time to look at each photo individually.

"Do you recognize the men?" Agent Thomas asked.

Hal handed the photo of Jack to Agent Thomas. "Yes, this one is Jack Waller, but I don't recognize the other two men," Hal answered and then handed the other two photos to Agent Rizzo.

"Can you tell us where Jack Waller worked in the prison? We'll also need the names of the inmates with whom he had direct contact with during his employment here," Agent Thomas said.

"Not a problem. By the way, do you know an agent named Brian Forbes?"

The two FBI agents looked at each other and shook their heads. "I don't know anyone by that name," Agent Thomas replied.

"I don't either," Agent Rizzo answered.

"Why? Is he a friend of yours?" Agent Thomas asked.

Hal answered with a lie, now knowing he had been played. "No, I just met him in one of the casinos about a year ago, and he told me he was trying to get reassigned out here." *Who's Agent Brian Forbes?* Hal thought to himself and then sat at his desk to answer the agents' other questions.

The coolness of early morning had turned to sweltering heat from the sun shining through the Mustang's windshield. When Shelby awoke, she was sweating, and her head ached. She reached up and felt the cut in her hairline and then she recalled the horrific events that had caused it. She frantically looked around, but only found that the moving truck was gone, along with her kidnapper.

Shelby feverishly reached down to lock the door, but it was already locked. She took a deep breath, started the car, turned the air conditioner on high, and rested her head back. Finally, when she felt safe, Shelby tilted the rearview mirror to examine her head, expecting the worst. Instead, she found her head wound had been cleaned, along with her face. There were no signs that she had been kidnapped and assaulted. Her wrists were red and slightly bruised, but there was no blood anywhere on her. Her tank top had been put back on her, and the only thing missing was her hoodie. Her cell phone was in the passenger seat. She looked at the time. "Ten o'clock," she mumbled. She closed her eyes and tried to recall the events that had taken place inside the moving truck.

She remembered getting out of the car, walking toward the back of the moving truck, and everything going dark. She rubbed her head, trying to remember, but she was startled by someone knocking on the driver's side window. Shelby quickly opened her eyes and found a man standing there. She blinked over and over but saw nothing but the cigarette-smoking man.

Shelby screamed. She placed the car in drive and sped out of the parking lot.

Danny, the young truck stop attendant, watched as the frightened woman sped out of the parking lot. He was left standing there holding a cold bottle of water. He had brought the cool beverage to her after a concerned truck driver reported that a woman was sleeping inside a hot car in their parking lot. Danny shrugged it off and started back to the convenience store to clean the bathrooms. As he strolled back toward the building, he stopped and drank some of the water.

"That's good," Danny said after the cool water quenched his thirst. He then turned his attention to a group of truck drivers who had gathered at the corner of the store to look at something. He walked over and stood next to them. Off somewhere in the New Mexico desert, a large cloud of black smoke drifted to the sky. He believed it was about two miles away.

"What's on fire?" Danny asked.

One of the drivers was holding a pair of binoculars. "Looks like some type of box truck."

Danny watched the smoke fill the air until the fire department arrived. He then headed back to the bathroom to clean it. He opened the men's bathroom door and was nearly knocked down by a tall man wearing a hoodie covering his face and carrying a black bag.

"Sorry, sir," Danny stated.

The man didn't say anything back. He just walked past Danny with his head down.

Danny shrugged it off and continued into the bathroom. He started by picking up the trash on the floor and moved to the shower stalls. When he opened the last shower stall, he stepped back in shock as to the amount of blood he saw on the walls and floor.

"I'm not cleaning this!" he declared and angrily walked out of the bathroom to tell the manager.

Brian made it back to his coupe and started back down

the road, chasing after the woman in the Mustang. He had been tired before he arrived in Albuquerque, but after the incident in the box truck, he was exhausted and badly injured. He took out his cell phone and called the number from the sticky note once again.

"It's me… I had a situation… Yeah, I took care of it… I'm going to need a cutman when I stop somewhere… I don't know where. It'll be up to her… I'll call you back when I stop for the night… No, she got roughed up a bit, but she'll be okay… I got it," Brian said into the phone and ended the call.

The sign ahead informed Shelby she was about to enter the town of Amarillo. She had not stopped since leaving the truck stop except to fill up once. She still couldn't recall most of the events that had occurred inside the truck. The only thing she knew was that she was checking into a hotel this evening. Sleeping in the car was no longer an option.

"No more truck stops for me. I'm staying in a hotel tonight," Shelby whispered. When she stopped for gas, she checked her bank account and found the money left to her had been deposited and credited to her account. "I'm staying somewhere nice." She pulled into the parking lot of the Emerson Suites. The hotel was exquisite and expensive, but Shelby wanted to stay where security officers patrolled the hotel's halls and had a secured parking garage.

Brian let out a sigh of relief when he saw the Mustang turn into the Emerson Suites parking lot. He drove past the parking lot, and when he saw another hotel on the same side of the road, he turned into it and parked. Brian watched and waited until he saw her come back out of the hotel. When she drove the car in the parking garage, he drove back to the Emerson Suites and went inside and got a room as well.

Brian took a warm shower, where he examined the six-inch cut along his ribs. For the most part, the bleeding had stopped, but the wound was deep. His opponent had been a skilled knife fighter, but in the end, Brian was better. The only thing really bothering Brian was that he should have been carrying a gun and had it with him before climbing into the back of the box truck. After his shower, he walked into the suite and was about to sit on the bed when the phone rang.

"Hello."

"This is Kim at the front desk. You have a visitor, a Mr. Smith, here to see you."

"Yes, please send him up." Brian stated and then hung the phone up.

A few minutes later Brian heard someone knocking on the door. He picked up his pistol, walked over to the door, and looked out the peephole.

Standing on the other side of the door was a man wearing a suit and carrying a brown bag.

"Yeah?" Brian spoke at the door while keeping an eye on the visitor.

"Someone called for my services," the man answered and then looked down the hall in both directions.

Brian opened the door and allowed the man to enter. He then quickly shut it and latched the lock behind him. He looked at the man cautiously while holding the .45 in his hand. "Mr. Smith, I guess you're the cutman?"

"I'm a doctor, if that's what you mean."

"It is," Brian answered and showed the doctor the cut on his ribs.

The doctor bent down and examined the wound. "You should go to the hospital."

Brian shook his head in disbelief. "C'mon, man, you know I can't. That's why you're here."

"I know, but I'm still going to give you my professional opinion before I work on you," the doctor replied and pointed at the bed.

Chapter 4
Extra Towels

Shelby's suite was on the top floor and had a view of the city. Kim, the receptionist at the front desk, had suggested the room. Shelby thought the hotel was nice for a city like Amarillo, but it was nothing like the hotels on the strip in Las Vegas. However, it was perfect for a woman who was passing through who needed to feel safe and secure. When Shelby got to her room, she immediately latched the door and pulled on it, ensuring it was closed. The previous day's events still had her shaken, and she wasn't taking any chances of someone coming in on her during the night. Now, all she wanted to do was climb into the large tub the front desk girl had told her about when she described the room to her downstairs.

Shelby unpacked her lightly packed suitcase, and upon doing so, she realized she didn't have much to wear. In the turmoil of leaving Carter and rushing out of the apartment, she had neglected to pack underwear, shorts, shoes, or toiletries. All that was in the suitcase were two pairs of jeans and three T-shirts. Instead of stepping into a nice warm bath, she took a quick shower, changed clothes, grabbed her purse and room key, and made her way back to the hotel lobby. When the elevator doors opened, Shelby stepped out and walked to the reception desk, where Kim talked with another hotel employee.

"How's the room?" Kim asked when she saw the hotel guest walk up to the counter. Kim was an attractive woman who had just turned thirty. She was also recently divorced, and she was about to leave the hotel for the day.

Shelby looked around the lobby and then back at Kim. "The room is great. I just have a small problem."

"Oh, what's that?" Kim asked, concerned there was a problem with the suite.

"Well, I left my place in Las Vegas in a hurry, and all I packed were some jeans and T-shirts. I need to buy clothes. Can you suggest a good place to do that?"

Kim smiled; she recognized the look on Shelby's face. Kim believed that the woman was running away from someplace, someone, or something. "Wolflin Village is about two miles from here. There are a lot of shops and small boutiques there."

"I guess that's where I'll go then." Shelby felt and heard her stomach groan. "Are there any good places to eat in Wolflin Village?"

"Yes, lots. If you need a good drink, there are good places to go for that too," Kim remarked in a soft voice so the other employee wouldn't hear her.

"That's good. I think I could use a good drink." Shelby was about to walk away when she had a thought. "Kim, I don't want to make this awkward, but would you like to grab some dinner? My treat."

Kim looked at Shelby. "Well…"

"Never mind, I shouldn't have asked. I mean, you don't know me, and um, I appreciate the advice about Wolflin Village—"

"I was going to say yes. I would love to go to dinner," Kim said and walked out from behind the counter. "I just didn't want my relief to hear me."

"Then I guess it's a date. I mean, it's a deal or a… Shit, let's just go eat!" Shelby blurted.

Kim laughed. "I know what you mean. We're good, girl!"

Brian was sitting on the bed, biting his lip as the doctor stitched the wound closed. Meeting doctors in hotel rooms wasn't a new experience for Brian, but it was getting old. He knew the lifestyle he had been living only had two types of endings for most people in this business: prison or death. Neither was an appealing option for the man. For Brian, this job needed to be his last, and if everything went as planned, it would be. In a few months, he hoped he would be somewhere running his own construction company. The time had come for the felon to finally make an honest living.

"You need to be careful moving around, or you'll probably tear your stitches out," the doctor ordered.

"I'll do my best."

The medical professional moved his head from side to side, taking note of the various scars on his patient's body. "I don't know if I believe that. After looking you over, I can't imagine you ever take it easy in anything you do."

Brian looked at the man and smiled. "It's all part of the job, Doc."

"Sounds like a dangerous profession. Have you ever thought about getting into a different line of work? Maybe something legal?" the doctor asked in a pompous tone.

Brian didn't respond at first. He thought about what the man said for a few seconds. "Yeah, I have. Have you?" Brian asked in turn. He was irritated by the man he felt was judging him. A type of man who probably had everything handed to him in life. A man who was in a hotel room getting paid to treat another man who couldn't walk into a hospital for treatment.

The doctor was surprised by the man's question. "I just thought you should maybe think about doing something other than what you do now."

"Doc, do you think you know me?" Brian asked rhetorically as he stood. "You know something, you think the two of us are two very different men, don't you?"

The doctor listened as he packed his medical supplies back into his bag. "I think we are two very different men."

"How are we different?" Brian asked.

"I'm a medical professional, and you are, well, an um…"

"A criminal or felon?" Brian asked. "Was that where you were going?

"Well, yes, actually," the doctor answered with his pompous tone once more.

Brian smiled and made his way to the door. "Doc, I think you need to take a good long look and then ask yourself a few questions before you start judging other people and pointing fingers."

The doctor followed his patient to the door. "What kind of questions do you think I should be asking myself?"

"I'd start with, how do I, a man with a degree in medicine, end up patching up criminals in hotel rooms? How is it that the criminal underworld knows my phone number? How did I fuck my life up so bad, I need to practice this kind of medicine for money? You see, Doctor, we're the same. Don't go splitting hairs about what we do for money. The people who pay you for being here are also paying me for being here. They're the same, and we're the same," Brian explained. He unlocked and opened the door. "Good night, Doctor."

The doctor looked at Brian but didn't say anything. After all, he knew his patient was right, even though he couldn't bring himself to admit it or to acknowledge it. He was, in fact, a criminal too. In the end, there was no difference between the two men.

Brian locked the door and swallowed one of the oxycodone pills the doctor had left. He set his .45 on the dresser and checked the tracking app on his phone. It appeared the woman and the car were in for the night, so he turned the lights off and went to sleep.

Shelby and Kim first stopped at a Mexican restaurant inside Wolflin Village, where they had a bite to eat before heading into the mall. The two new friends then walked from one store to the next, shopping for Shelby's new wardrobe. It was the first time in her life Shelby didn't have to look for the sale racks in the store or check the price tag before she picked something up. After they finished, the women got into Kim's car, and the two started back toward the hotel.

When they got to a traffic light, Kim looked over and saw The Thirsty Bar and Grill on the corner. "How about that drink?" Kim asked and pointed at the bar.

Shelby looked at the bar and then at Kim. "Do they have a good margarita?"

"Yeah, they do," Kim answered, turning into the parking lot.

They were seated at a corner table where they had a clear view of the entire bar. The place was decorated in an old Western theme, with cowhides, horns, and ropes along walls painted in a distressed wooden pattern. The two ordered mango margaritas and a bowl of fries to share.

"How does a Vegas girl find herself in Amarillo of all places, with a fairly new cut in her hairline?" Kim asked as she pointed at the wound on Shelby's head.

Shelby bit her lip. "Well…"

Kim apologized with sincerity in her voice. "Look, I'm sorry. If you're not comfortable talking about it, I won't be offended, and I won't pry."

"No, it's just a long story. I would really like to talk to someone about it, if you want to hear about it."

Kim tilted her head to the side and grinned. "Well, I do. I guess we'll have to have a few margaritas tonight. By the way, the fries here are bottomless!"

Hal left work and was almost home. He was tired and nervous. The FBI agents had taken up most of his day, and they had asked too many questions. The warden was getting concerned that everything was falling apart. It was only a matter of time before he was associated with the three inmates, his dead guard, Jack and of course the two hired guns out of Texas, who were associates of another inmate in his prison. Then there was the hole in his leg that he couldn't explain. Finally, there was Rob and Tan Man. Hal was getting paranoid, and he allowed his mind to run wild with thoughts.

"I can't oversee everything from here. I don't think I can even stay here. What if they got DNA off the ground where I got shot? Would there still be blood on the ground? Maybe the FBI already knows I'm involved. What if they're just waiting to arrest me?" Hal asked himself as he turned into his driveway.

By the time Shelby and Kim were on their second margarita, the two knew a lot about each other. Shelby had explained how she came to be in Amarillo, how she got the cut on her head, and where she was going. Kim told her new friend about her divorce, her job, and what she was planning on doing next. Eventually, they talked about the men who had come into and out of their lives. That particular topic brought about their first shot of the evening.

"So, are men totally out of the question? I mean for a little while anyway?" Kim asked and took a drink of water.

Shelby laughed. "Are they ever totally out of the question?"

"No, I don't guess they are."

"Shit, I'd just like to find a good one," Shelby said.

"I saw one today. I mean, I don't know if he's a good one, but damn! He was fine."

"Where? Did I miss him when we were in the mall?"

"No. He wasn't at the mall. He checked in right after you."

"Really?"

"Yeah, he came in needing a room. Well, everyone who comes in needs a room. Sorry, I'm a little drunk right now. Let me focus a minute." Kim closed her eyes for a second, while Shelby waited patiently for her to start her story again. "So he walked up to the desk, and in a very sexy voice, he asked if we had a room available."

"Because that's what people need when they come into a hotel. They need a room, right?" Shelby asked and laughed.

Kim giggled and then closed her eyes again and held up one finger. "Do you want to hear about Billy… Wait, Bobby. No, maybe it was Brody… Well, shit! I can't remember his name now. Anyway, he had black hair, olive skin, beautiful blue eyes… He was yummy."

"Was he tall?" Shelby asked and bit into a fry.

"Yes, he was. Like I said, he was yummy."

Shelby thought about it for a minute. "Nope."

"What do you mean?"

"Too perfect. Something's wrong with him. How did his body look?"

"Well, he wore a T-shirt, and I could see he was tight."

Shelby shook her head from side to side as if to say no.

"What now?"

"He's got to be gay," Shelby stated.

Kim thought about it for a minute. "Maybe, he did have a

weird-looking man in a suit carrying a bag come by to see him a short time after checking in."

"See. I knew it. Gay!" Shelby declared and slapped the table with her hand.

Kim sat there a minute, drunkenly staring at the new margarita sitting in front of her. Shelby saw disappointment in her eyes.

"What's wrong?" Shelby asked.

Kim picked up her margarita and took a long drink from it. "Well, I don't care. When I think about him later, he's going to be straight."

Shelby laughed again but managed to speak. "You mean fantasize? When you fantasize about him later?"

"Whatever. When he calls the front desk in the morning needing some towels, I'll have to run them up to him," Kim explained.

Shelby laughed even more. "Is that the fantasy?" she asked between breaths. "He needs towels?"

"It's the one that seems most likely to happen," Kim answered.

The women stayed at The Thirsty Bar and Grill until after midnight. They took a rideshare back to the hotel. Kim walked Shelby to her room, where they said good night and then agreed to have lunch before Shelby left Amarillo. Kim checked into an empty room across the hall from Shelby and spent the night.

Shelby once again secured the door after tossing her bags on a chair. Her mind was spinning, along with everything else in the room. She stumbled to the bed, kicked her shoes off, and allowed her jeans to fall to the floor. She unclasped her bra and pulled it out through her sleeve. Finally, she pulled the sheets back and made herself comfortable under the covers, where she immediately fell asleep.

"No, no!" Shelby shouted and sat up in the bed. She was sweating, and her heart was racing. She desperately glanced around the room, and after she realized where she was, she dropped back onto her pillow. She checked the clock on the dresser. It was ten-thirty in the morning, and the sun was shining brightly outside. "What the hell was that dream about?" Shelby asked aloud, then her room phone rang. She looked at the phone, surprised it was ringing. She rolled onto her side, lifted the receiver, and listened for a moment.

"Hey, are you there?" Kim asked.

"Yeah, I'm here," Shelby answered in a sleepy voice.

"You still want to grab lunch in the hotel restaurant before you take off?"

"Yeah, but first, can you meet me in the hallway?" Shelby requested.

"I'm not dressed," Kim said.

"Neither am I. It'll only be for a second. I need to give you something," Shelby explained.

"Okay, I'll go there now," Kim said and hung up the phone.

Shelby jumped out of bed and ran to her bags. She shuffled through one until she found what she was looking for. She then ran to the door and cracked it open. Across the hall, she saw Kim standing behind her door.

"What is it?" Kim whispered as she looked to her left and right.

Shelby stepped out into the hallway, half-dressed, and handed Kim a summer dress she had bought when they were out shopping. Shelby then rushed back to her room before the door closed.

"What's this? Kim asked.

"It's the dress you saw yesterday. You said you liked it."

"I do, but you didn't need to buy this for me."

"I know, but you didn't need to take me out yesterday and listen to my sob story."

Kim tilted her head and smiled. "Thank you."

"You're welcome."

"I'll be ready at twelve if you want to walk down together," Kim said.

"Okay, but are there any really hot front desk guys working right now?"

Kim laughed. "No. He's ugly, so don't bother calling the front desk for more towels."

The two laughed for a few more minutes before shutting their doors to get ready. Shelby took out the clothes from her shopping bags and spread them out on the bed. "What am I going to wear?" she asked herself, then she heard her cell phone chirping. She walked to the dresser where the phone was plugged in and read the text Kim had sent.

Thanks for the dress again. By the way, the front desk receptionist may be hideous, but the detachable shower head in your bathroom has a lot of pressure. Enjoy!

The text made Shelby smile. She immediately sent back a smiley face and a water emoji.

Chapter 5
Dreams and Memories

Shelby and Kim took the elevator down to the lobby and were seated near the front of the hotel's restaurant. The two made small talk about Kim's job at the hotel and Shelby's trip while waiting for their lunch. When their food arrived, they both dug in as if they had not eaten for days. Halfway through their meal, they looked up and saw each other with a mouthful of food, and they realized they had not said anything since the food arrived.

Shelby wiped her mouth. "Oh my gosh, I'm so hungry. I know we had a taco last night and some fries, but man, I didn't know I was so hungry."

"I didn't either, but it's twelve-thirty right now. We had that taco at what, six o'clock last night? The fries were somewhat filling, but it's been like eighteen hours since the last real meal and maybe twelve since we ate a fry. We're due for a meal," Kim said as she took another bite of her chicken sandwich.

"I like how you explained that. I'm going with it," Shelby stated and took a bite of her hamburger.

"How did you sleep?" Kim asked.

Shelby lifted her head and twisted her lips for a second as

she thought about her answer. "I guess it was good, but at some time, I had some weird dreams or flashes of images."

Kim had a quizzical look on her face. "So was it a dream or flashes of images?"

"I don't know if it was a dream. It's like I had experienced what I saw."

"Were they memories?"

"Maybe."

"What were they flashes of? I mean, can you describe them?" Kim asked.

"I'll try," Shelby answered and then closed her eyes. "I see myself in a bathroom mirror, and there's someone beside me, kind of like carrying me. Then I'm in a shower, I think. I can see someone wiping my face, and he keeps telling me I'm going to be all right."

Kim was drawn into the mystery. "Do you think it's the guy who kidnapped you?"

"No, but I saw him too. He's not in the bathroom; he's in the truck sitting on the hood of the Mustang smoking his cigarette, and I'm still handcuffed to the wall," Shelby said and rubbed her still-bruised wrist.

Kim looked at Shelby's hands. "I still think you need to call the police."

"No, I just want to forget about it, get to Pensacola, and start my life over. I want to forget everything that happened at the truck stop." Shelby took a deep breath. "Now, what about you? You're single now. You can go anywhere and do anything you want. From last night's conversation, if I recall correctly, you mentioned moving out of Amarillo and going back to school for nursing."

"Yeah. I have the money from the divorce, but I don't know where I want to be or where I want to go to school."

Shelby understood. She didn't know what she wanted in life either. "Well, if you make it down to Pensacola, I could use some help renovating an old beach house this summer."

"Are you keeping it or fixing it up to sell it?"

"I don't know yet. I'm going to play it by ear."

"How far are you driving today?"

"Tyler, Texas," Shelby answered and took the last bite of her hamburger.

Brian awoke a little before eleven o'clock. He showered, dressed, checked out of the hotel, and ate breakfast at the restaurant across the street. While he waited for the woman and the Mustang to leave, he looked through his phone at the various news media websites in and around the city of Albuquerque. After a few minutes of searching, he found what he was looking for.

One news outlet had reported the moving truck fire on the outskirts of the city near a popular truck stop. The only thing missing from the article was anything about the body of James Thomas Hanson. Brian had left the man's body inside the truck before he set it on fire. Brian had found the man's name on his Nevada driver's license in his wallet. He didn't know who he was or why he was after the woman and the car. However, he did assume Mr. Hanson was employed by or worked with Warden Henry "Hal" Baker.

It's only a matter of time before they locate Mr. Hanson's body, but there's not much left of him or anything in the truck to tie him to me, Brian thought. Brian didn't like killing the man, but he had no other choice. It was either Brian or Hanson. It was similar to the situation that had got Brian incarcerated the first time, for six years.

It didn't take long before Brian saw the Mustang pulling out of the parking garage with the woman behind the wheel. When she turned out of the hotel parking lot onto the main road, she looked different. He didn't know what was different, but there was something. Brian waited five more minutes before he pulled onto the main road and then onto the interstate heading east, just like the woman in the Mustang. He pondered if she would stop once more for the night or drive on through to Pensacola. Brian looked up at the cloudy skies overhead and decided she'd stop somewhere for the night. She didn't seem like the type who would drive in the rain.

Hal made his way through security and to his terminal gate. He spent the entire night in bed tossing and turning, thinking that at any moment, the FBI would burst through his door. At five o'clock in the morning, Hal couldn't take it anymore. He sat in front of his computer and bought a plane ticket. He spent the rest of the morning, before leaving for the airport, packing his things and preparing his medical leave paperwork. He then sent it to his supervisor, the deputy director of Nevada's state prison. Hal knew the deputy director would be surprised by the sudden leave of absence, but Hal didn't care. He wasn't planning on coming back to Nevada any time soon.

When Hal stepped on the plane, he felt as if a burden had been lifted. He found his seat and placed his carry-on in the bin above it. He then sat next to a large man who had already claimed the armrest to his left and right.

Rob landed in Pensacola at ten o'clock and immediately called Charlie, who he learned was already set up and ready to go when Willy's daughter arrived. Rob tried to convince Charlotte 'Charlie' Stevens that they should stay together to keep an eye on the woman, but she had other plans and thought it was best that they weren't seen together. Rob relented and rented an expensive luxury car at the airport.

He drove to Pensacola Beach to look for the old beach house Willy had left his daughter. After driving across a long bridge, he entered Gulf Breeze, where he stopped for an iced coffee. He took his drink to go, and before long, he found himself on another bridge that brought him to the island community of Pensacola Beach. The tourists were out in full force enjoying the warmth of the sun, tanning their bodies as they jogged, walked, bicycled, or skateboarded along a paved trail next to the road.

Rob followed the rental car's GPS until he found the beach house at 1417 Maldonado Drive. He slowed to get a better look and wondered why anyone would want to buy a rundown place like the one he was looking at. He pulled along the curb and got out of the car, then a woman in a tiny leopard-print bathing suit walking her dog approached him. The woman was a tall and thin brunette, whose dog seemed to be angry with her. The tiny chihuahua barked and bit at its collar while the woman forcefully dragged it along.

"Are you looking for a specific house?" she asked in an unpleasant tone.

"Well… I was looking for a place to rent. I just got here," Rob answered as he glared at the woman.

"Yeah, I thought so. You're not really dressed for the beach. You should call Clear Sky Realty Vacation Rentals. I'm sure they can help you find a place to stay," the woman said. She walked away with a suspicious glare directed at him.

Rob stood there and watched the woman walk away before getting back into the rental car. "Fucking bitch!" Rob said and then decided it was probably better to look like a vacationer than to stand out in khakis and a black polo.

On the other side of the road, in front of a two-story beach house that happened to be directly across the street from the

1417 address, was a rental sign. "Clear Sky Realty Vacation Rentals. I got it," he said.

The drive to Tyler, Texas, took Shelby about seven hours. She found a well-lit hotel, parked under one of the lights, and went inside to book a room. The hotel receptionist was nothing like Kim, so soon Shelby was missing her new friend. When she got to her room, she latched the door, unpacked her suitcase, and took a quick shower.

She peered out her window at the Mustang. The car appeared to be okay, and so did she, but she had an uneasy feeling that she was being watched. She blew it off and made her way to the bed. She took her phone out and started browsing through her social media accounts. She laughed when she came across a picture Carter had posted. He was sitting in their apartment living room in the middle of his shattered trophies. He had captioned the photo with the words *"bitch destroyed my stuff."* It looked as though he was seeking sympathy from his friends, but instead, everyone was posting comments about how he'd probably deserved it. Some people said it was about time Shelby had left him and that she was way out of his league. Shelby laughed as she read through the various comments.

At ten o'clock, she plugged her cell phone in, turned the lamp off, and lay there in the darkness, unable to sleep. She closed her eyes and tried to recall the night at the truck stop. She had so many unanswered questions.

Who was the man in the box truck who kidnapped me? Who was the other man who saved me? Was he the one who cleaned me up in the bathroom, or did I clean myself up? How did I get in my car? Why did he just leave me there? Where was the box truck when I awoke?

Brian rented a room in the same hotel as the woman. Once he locked the door, he sat on the edge of the bed and browsed the news media outlets in Albuquerque once again, and it was much easier to locate the moving truck fire. It seemed everyone, including the national news, had picked up on the story, but why wouldn't they? There was a body inside it.

Brian read the clever headlines and took the time to see if any information would indicate to him that the police had a lead to go on. Luckily for him, there were none as of yet. He then took a shower, where he allowed the cool water to run over the wound on his side. It had started feeling warm to the touch, and he believed he needed to clean it anyway. After getting out of the shower, he carefully dried the wound off, rebandaged it, and took another oxy before climbing into bed.

Hal was met at the airport by Rob, who was angry that he had to drive back into town to pick up his boss. He also didn't like the fact that Hal had come to Pensacola because he didn't think Rob and Charlie could take care of things on their own.

"Why are you here?" Rob asked as he drove back toward the beach.

Hal looked out the window, and after a moment, he looked back at Rob. "It's not that I don't think I can trust you. I just needed to get out of Las Vegas. I think the FBI is closing in on us," Hal explained.

"What are you going to do or say when you get back?"

"I'm not going back. This is it for me. Once I get my part of the money, I'm out of here, and you and Charlie should do the same."

"Have you heard from Jimmy?" Rob asked.

Hal looked at him with a concerned expression. "When I had my layover in Atlanta, I got a call from the Albuquerque Police Department," Hal said.

"And?" Rob asked, encouraging his boss to continue.

"And, they had a truck fire of some sort, and they found a body inside it. When they were going through the charred remains, they found a wallet. Inside the wallet, they found Jimmy's old department of corrections inmate identification card from when he was on parole," Hal explained.

Rob couldn't say anything. He just looked out the windshield and then back at Hal a few times.

"What? It's all closing in," Hal said. "I went ahead and rented a condo some distance from you. I'll get a car tomorrow. Here's the address we're heading to."

"What's the plan?" Rob asked.

"I don't know. I guess we wait for Willy's daughter to show up, and then we'll have Charlie get close to her. If we're needed, we'll be here. At the end of this, we'll either have a few million and we'll be wanted by the FBI, or we'll be flat broke and will still most likely be wanted by the FBI."

"So this is it?"

"This is it. I'm here to play rough if we need to."

Shelby got up early and made her way to the parking lot. She filled the car up, grabbed a breakfast sandwich from a drive-thru, and headed east toward Pensacola. While she drove, she asked herself the same questions she had gone to sleep asking. There was one more question she had added to her list.

Why would someone save me, clean me up, and just leave me like that?"

Brian saw the woman heading out of the hotel at the same time he was. He was able to stay out of sight until she had gotten into her car. He then got behind her on the interstate but stayed far behind her. When they passed through Shreveport, Brian received a phone call.

"Yeah... Good... I can do it... Yes, I can do it for that much... Is it close to her? That's a little too close, don't you think? I know... I'll stay close." Brian ended the call and placed his phone in the center console. He gasped a little when he sat back in the seat. His side was sorer this morning and driving in a car for so many hours didn't help.

The drive from Tyler took nine hours, and at around five o'clock, Shelby was cruising down Via De Luna Drive. She rolled the window down and took in the ocean air. She felt butterflies in her stomach. The closer she got to the old beach house, the more childhood memories were brought on. She saw the old restaurants and recalled a memory of each and every one. Shelby smiled when she passed the swim park on the sound side of the island. It was where she and her mother had spent many days splashing in the shallow water.

Eventually, Shelby's phone indicated she needed to turn right onto Avenida 23. After turning down the familiar road, she gazed at the beautiful beach houses built on tall piers. Most of them were less than twenty years old, and many were being used as beach rentals. When she got to Maldonado Drive, she turned right again, and before she knew it, she was pulling up to and parking in front of the old blue beach house at 1417 Maldonado Drive.

She stood next to the car and stared at the weathered structure that had been built sometime in the fifties. The beach house wasn't the oldest on the street, but it was close. At one time, all the homes on the street had been built during that era. Still, one hurricane after another took them out one by one until there were a handful left, including the old blue one that Shelby now called her own.

Chapter 6
Old Blue

After standing in front of the beach house, taking a before photo and a selfie, Shelby moved some trash from the driveway. The home needed a lot of work on the outside. She then got back into the car and parked in the driveway of her new home. It may not have looked like much, but it was hers. Shelby had never been a homeowner, and as she sat in the car, she felt a wave of emotions come over her. She took a breath and wiped her eyes; the old house had some fond memories.

She imagined an eight-year-old Shelby walking next to her mother as they returned from the convenience store on a sunny afternoon. Her mother carried a few groceries while Shelby drank a fruity slushy drink that ran down her chin and onto her bathing suit. The blue sticky beverage was all over the child, who didn't seem to mind. Shelby remembered the white shorts with a red one-piece bathing suit under them. Her flip-flops were red as well and had a seashell print.

Shelby recalled what her mother had looked like that day. She thought her mother was the most beautiful woman she had ever seen. Whitney, her mother, or Whit as her friends had called her, walked next to the young Shelby, wearing a red bathing suit top, white shorts, and white flip-flops. Her long blonde hair blew wild as winds from the Gulf swept past them.

"Let's go, Shelby," Whit said after stopping and looking back at her slow-moving eight-year-old, who was more concerned with her slushy drink than getting home.

The young Shelby ran to catch up. "I coming, Mommy."

Shelby held on to the memory for as long as she could, when suddenly there was a knock on her passenger window. She jumped and looked to her right where an elderly woman stood. Shelby got out and walked around the car, approaching the visitor.

"Hello," Shelby said as she put her hand out in a friendly manner to greet one of her new neighbors.

The elderly woman didn't reciprocate the gesture. She just pointed at the driveway. "I'm Evelyn and I live in this neighborhood. You can't park here. Beach access is farther down the main road," the elderly woman said and walked back to her place, occasionally glancing back at the young woman.

Shelby was taken aback at first. Still, Shelby smiled after realizing her new neighbor wasn't aware that she was the new owner. "No, you don't understand. I own this house," Shelby said proudly. She used her thumb to point back over her shoulder toward her new house.

"What! I thought it was going to be torn down. You keep it down over here. My husband is sick, and he needs his rest," the elderly woman ordered. She then turned around and walked away, smiling.

Shelby was surprised by the woman's comment. "No, it's not getting torn down. I'm going to fix it up. Come back in a few weeks and see it… Bye… Evelyn." Shelby watched the woman walk back across the street to her newly built beach house. Shelby turned around and looked at her own beach house. "Maybe a few months," she whispered and headed toward the front door with the keys in hand.

Rob's beach rental was immaculately decorated in a beach house theme. The living room had a coffee table made to look like a surfboard. The dining room table was made of distressed wood, and the walls around it were covered in pirate décor. The outside was painted a light green, with a white deck on the front and another on the back. The back of the beach house had a pool and a grand view of the Gulf of Mexico. The front of the home had a view of the other beach houses and the sound side of the Gulf in the distance. The best part of the view to the front was that directly across the street was the home of the woman he had been sent to keep an eye on, which was precisely what he was doing at the moment.

The living room was nicely furnished, the air conditioner was on, and Rob sat there comfortably watching Willy's daughter talk with an elderly woman. When he saw Shelby at the beach house, he thought she looked different than she did at the diner in Las Vegas. She was wearing a flattering white summer dress that whipped around when the wind blew. He turned his attention to the white Mustang she drove, and he thought about just knocking her out and taking the car. He had mentioned that plan to Hal in Las Vegas, but Hal wasn't sure the money was in the car, and he wanted the envelope too. The warden wanted to take things slow and gather as much information as possible before they made a move on the car or the girl. Rob wasn't a slow-moving type of guy; he was more into doing something now and then figuring out what to do next if things didn't work out the first time.

"I wonder what Charlie's up to," Rob said to himself after he watched Shelby walk into the beach house.

Brian made it to Pensacola Beach, but instead of following the woman to the beach house, he drove to a grocery store to pick up some supplies. He had already been texted the address of his beach rental, the combination, and the deposit confirmation for the additional funds that had been sent. When he got out of the car, he abruptly stopped as a surge of pain hit him. He flinched his body to the left, favoring the injured side of his torso.

"Fuck," he said and sat back down in his car to collect himself. After he caught his breath, he slowly eased himself out of the car, shut the door, and made his way inside.

As he grabbed a grocery cart, he noticed the other shoppers wearing their tank tops, board shorts, and flip-flops. Brian quickly concluded he appeared out of place in his jeans, boots, and T-shirt. *I'll need some new clothes to fit in*, he thought as he pushed the cart down the first aisle.

Hal found the condo to be quite comfortable. He had spent the day settling in, finding a rental car, and making a contingency plan. Now, the warden was sitting at the dining room table, logging into his laptop. He tossed back a shot of whisky and logged into the Nevada inmate database. He wanted to search for prior inmates who had left the state of Nevada and were living in or around the city of Pensacola. After about ten minutes, he found a few prospects and wrote down their names, offenses, and last known addresses.

By six o'clock, Hal had become restless. After growing tired of watching the sailboats from his balcony, he decided it was time for a bit of excitement. When he checked into the condo the day before, Hal saw a banner behind the check-in desk that advertised the monthly "Condo Conclave" in the Shipwreck Tavern next to the lobby. He wondered what type of people attended an event like that. When he stepped off the elevator, he made his way to the check-in desk once more.

"Conclave. Who came up with that?" Hal asked right before he turned and walked inside the Shipwreck Tavern to join the other condominium guests and residents.

Old Blue, the name given to the old beach house by the new owner, was almost as bad on the inside as it was on the outside. It had a small living room that greeted visitors when they walked in the front door, and behind that was a small kitchen. As Shelby moved through the house, she detected a familiar odor that hinted at something from her past. Shelby couldn't recall the scent or associate it with anything right away. However, it gave her a feeling of safety. When she walked down the hallway, more memories came rushing back. She imagined herself running down the hallway into the kitchen where her mother was preparing breakfast.

She stopped when she got to her old bedroom and looked around at the chipping pink walls. There was trash lying about, and the tile floor was cracking in places. After walking through the entire house, she took a seat in the living room on the worn sofa that sat against the wall.

In the master bedroom, she had found clean bedding, and in the bathroom was clean linen. The kitchen had a set of dishes that were all pieces of other sets. Not one glass, cup, or plate matched another. The appliances, although working, were also a hodgepodge of different brands and colors. The refrigerator made Shelby laugh because it was new, but it was pink and designed to look vintage. At the same time, the other appliances were brown and actually vintage.

After making a list of the things she needed, Shelby drove to the grocery store she had passed in Gulf Breeze. She hurried down each aisle, grabbing what she needed as well as things she didn't know she needed. It didn't take long before she was checking out and loading her purchases into her car.

She crossed the bridge back onto Pensacola Beach and detected the aroma of something delicious in the air. It reminded her she had not eaten anything since lunch, which had been nothing more than a chocolate chip cookie from a gas station at a convenience store. She looked to her left and saw a few restaurants sitting on the sound side of the island. Images of fried shrimp and grits came to mind, both of which influenced her into turning into the parking lot of one of the restaurants.

Captain John's Seafood on the Beach looked to be a popular place to eat. Shelby had to drive around twice before she found a parking space near the front. After Albuquerque, she wasn't taking chances on anyone trying to steal the Mustang. She walked inside and found the place packed with people who, like herself, were craving seafood. To say the place was busy was an understatement.

"One or two for dinner?" the hostess asked.

Shelby was slightly embarrassed that she was eating alone. Why she was embarrassed, she didn't know, but she was. "Well, I…"

The older hostess noticed the guest's apprehensiveness and interjected. "I have a seat at the bar. Follow me," she told the guest and didn't wait for her to say no.

Shelby followed the hostess who sat her at the end of the bar, away from other people. Shelby scooted herself onto the barstool while the hostess placed the menu in front of her. "The bartender's name is Stacie. She'll take care of you. She'll even run people off if you want her to," the hostess said with a smile.

Shelby gave a friendly smile back. "Thank you."

"Nothing to it. Let me know if you need anything else," the hostess said, giving the bartender a nod, and walked away.

Shelby was browsing the menu when the red-headed bartender came to her. "I'm Stacie. What would you like to drink?"

"Anything diet."

"Got it. Let me know if you have any questions about the menu," Stacie stated and walked away to get the diet soda.

Shelby was still looking over the menu when a man walked in and started to sit on the barstool next to her. "How are you doing?" the man asked.

Before Shelby could say anything, Stacie returned with the drink and put it in front of her. "She's doing just fine without you, Billy. I got your seat down here with Carl and Sam. C'mon down here and visit with them."

Billy looked at the bartender. "I want to sit right here!" Billy, who appeared to have already been drinking, proclaimed.

Stacie leaned on the bar, getting really close to her regular customer. "Billy, baby, you can go sit with your friends down there at the other end of the bar, or you can go sit at the bar at Oysters across the street. Now, if you sit with Carl and Sam, I'll buy your first drink. What would you like to do?"

Billy looked at Shelby and then back at Stacie. "Can I come back over here later?"

"No," Stacie answered quickly.

"But you'll buy the first drink if I go down there with Carl and Sam?"

"Yes."

Billy took one last look at Shelby. He smiled at her and then walked away to sit with Carl and Sam.

Shelby looked at Stacie and then covered her face with the menu so no one could see her laughing. Stacie laughed too but quickly walked away to get Billy his first drink.

Shelby was waiting for Stacie to return to take her order when she looked around the bar and noticed an attractive man sitting alone at one of the small tables in the bar. He was tall, had dark hair, and appeared to be very fit. He wore white-and-blue board shorts and a blue T-shirt.

Stacie caught Shelby looking at the good-looking man who was sitting alone. "Have you decided on what you want? Besides him I mean?"

Shelby turned back toward Stacie, unaware she had been staring at the man until that moment. "Oh my God! Did I make it look that obvious?" Shelby asked as her face turned a little red.

"No—well, me and some of the other single women who are in here checking out good-looking men may have noticed, but he didn't. He's a man. They never notice."

"You're right about that."

Stacie picked up the menu. "What's it going to be?"

"Shrimp and grits," Shelby answered.

"Good choice. It'll be about ten minutes," Stacie said and rushed off.

Shelby couldn't help herself. She turned around to look at the man once more, and when she did, he caught her. The two locked eyes for a moment. Shelby, now embarrassed, quickly turned back around.

While waiting for her food, Shelby drank her soda and resisted every urge to turn around to see if the man was looking at her. *I just got out of a relationship*, she thought as Stacie walked over carrying her dinner.

Stacie placed the shrimp and grits in front of her guest. She reached under the counter for silverware and put it on the counter with a napkin. "Did you see Mr. Eye Candy leave?"

Shelby spun her head around and looked for the man who had caught her staring at him. After not seeing him, she looked back at Stacie. "No, how long ago did he leave?"

"I think right after I took your order. He didn't even wait for his food."

"What?"

"Yeah, he ordered the same thing you did and then *poof* he was gone. I didn't even know it until I brought the plate out from the kitchen."

Shelby listened with a stunned look on her face. "He didn't say anything?"

"Nope. Just gone. Well, he did pay for the food, and he left a nice tip. Oh, and he had a beer. He did drink that before he left," Stacie said and walked away.

Shelby shrugged it off and took her first bite of grits. When she finished her meal, she drank one more diet soda and had a taste of the banana pudding Stacie dropped off.

"Where you visiting from?" Stacie asked. She set Shelby's receipt on the counter and used a clean spoon to scoop herself out a bite of the dessert.

Shelby looked at the bartender and smiled. "I'm not visiting. I'm going to be here for a little while."

"No shit! You live on the beach?" the bartender asked and took another bite.

"I own a house on the beach," Shelby said, not knowing how to really say it for the first time.

Stacie stood and looked at Shelby with a suspicious grin. "Are you a rich girl? You don't look or act like one of those, you know…"

"I do know, and no, I'm not. It's a really old place that needs a lot of work. My father left it to me after he passed away recently."

"Oh, I'm so sorry. I didn't—"

Shelby put her hands up in front of her. "No, we weren't that close. I hadn't seen him in years before I found out he died."

"All right, I didn't want to say anything out of line, you know."

"No, I understand. So what kind of person do I look like?"

Stacie liked a challenge. She finished off the dessert, stood back, and looked Shelby over. "You look like one of us."

"Us?" Shelby asked, hoping it would persuade Stacie to explain further.

"Yeah. Us. People like me who work in places like this. Catering to others, hoping we get a decent tip."

Shelby was intrigued. "How'd you know?"

"Well, you treated me well. Something tells me that you've spent some time behind this counter or out there running from one table to another. Tell me I'm wrong."

Shelby shook her from side to side. "Nope, you're spot on. Two days ago, I was running trays out to tables in Las Vegas."

"No kidding."

"No, no kidding."

Chapter 7
I'm Shelby

Rob watched the house across the street for Willy's daughter to return, and at around midnight, he saw a small light moving around inside the old blue beach house. He turned the lights off in his place and then got down low to peer out from the bottom of the window.

"Who is that?" he asked himself.

The light and the person carrying it moved from room to room.

"Somebody's looking for something," Rob whispered and then it hit him. "Fucking Charlie!"

Shelby had spent the better part of the evening at the bar talking to Stacie and some of the other staff. She had been there for so long, Stacie had her bring in her perishable groceries so they could put them in the refrigerator for her until she left. It wasn't until after twelve when Shelby walked out of the restaurant with her groceries in tow, and the phone number of a new friend as well—a friend who planned on coming by the beach house in the next day or two.

As Shelby drove back to Old Blue, she thought about the friendly people she had met thus far on her trip. She wondered what Kim was doing. She decided she would take a picture of the Gulf tomorrow and send it to her. *Maybe Kim will come visit one day,* Shelby thought as she turned onto Maldonado Drive.

Rob was still watching the person he believed was Charlie from his window when he heard and then saw the old Mustang coming down the street. He grabbed his cell phone and tried to call Charlie. "C'mon, answer the phone," he said while Charlie's phone rang until it went to voicemail. He tossed the phone in a nearby chair and thought about what he could do.

Shelby turned into her driveway, shut the car off, and unloaded some of her groceries. She put the key into the lock only to discover that it was already unlocked. "I'm sure I locked it when I left," she said to herself as she twisted the doorknob and walked inside. The house was dark, and nothing happened when she reached for the light switch and flipped it upward.

"Damn it!" Shelby mumbled. She set the groceries down, reached into her purse, and felt around until she found her cell phone. Once the phone was in her hand, she pressed the flashlight icon, and right when the tiny bulb illuminated, she saw a masked intruder standing in front of her. She gasped as the intruder knocked her phone from her hand and grabbed her by the arm.

Shelby tried to pull away and was about to succeed when she was hit from behind. Suddenly, two people were attacking her. Shelby screamed and swung her hands and arms madly. Flashbacks of the box truck kept running through her mind. "No, stop it!" she cried.

One of the intruders released her arm, and the other intruder let her go as well.

Shelby scrambled back against the wall on her hands and knees. To her surprise, someone grabbed her, pushed her into the hallway, and stood in front of her. She couldn't see much, but of what she could make out, three silhouettes were fighting in the darkness. She heard people breathing hard and the sound of people being hit.

The third person, who appeared to be a man, the one who had pushed Shelby into the hallway, seemed to take blow after blow from the other two intruders. Still, he never wavered, no matter how many times he was hit. He kept fighting back, keeping her safe from the other two.

"What's going on over there?" the elderly woman from across the street yelled. "I've called the cops, and they're on their way." She then hurried back into the safety of her own home.

Two of the silhouettes ran out of the house. The third walked to Shelby and stood over her.

"Please don't hurt me," she begged.

"I'm not. Are you okay?" the man asked. "Here, take my hand."

Shelby felt for the man's hand, and when she found it, she held it tightly. The man lifted her off the floor.

"Who are you?" Shelby asked in a trembling voice, releasing the stranger's hand. She slowly walked to where her phone was lying on the floor and picked it up.

"I'm Brian," the man said as Shelby shined the light on his face.

Shelby moved closer for a better look as she kept the light on him. "You're the guy from the restaurant."

"Yeah, I guess I am," Brian said, using his right hand to block the light from his eyes.

"Who… I mean… What?" Shelby struggled to speak as she walked into the kitchen and turned on another light.

Brian had to come up with something fast. This wasn't

part of the plan. "I'm staying next door, and when I got home, I heard you screaming. I ran over here and found, well, all of this. Who were those people?" he asked, attempting to redirect the line of questioning.

Shelby cautiously walked back toward the handsome stranger. "Why'd you leave the restaurant in such a hurry earlier?"

The redirect didn't work. "I haven't been feeling well since I got here, and I thought I was going to get sick. I paid for my food and walked out to the beach. The next thing I know is I'm lying on the sand, and it's after midnight," Brian said as the sound of police sirens got louder and louder.

Shelby looked at Brian and placed her hand on his forehead. He was burning with fever. "Come over here and sit down," Shelby ordered, just as her rescuer passed out and fell to the floor.

When Rob got back to his place, he kept the lights off and sat on the floor, spying on the events unfolding next door. First, there were two police cars, then a third. Next came an ambulance, which carried off the man who had come in and attacked Charlie and him. He tightened his jaw and gritted his teeth when he thought about how Charlie may have ruined everything for them. He waited for the police and the ambulance to leave before he crawled into the back bedroom, where he shut the door and took out his cell phone.

He texted Charlie and then waited. *What the fuck was that about?*

I didn't need any help!

Rob read the text and gritted his teeth. *The fuck you didn't! I saved your ass.*

Whatever! Who was the guy?

I don't know. I'll see if Hal has an idea. Rob answered.

Don't interfere with me again!

Fuck you! Rob typed and then dropped the phone between his legs.

Shelby went to the hospital to be treated for some minor injuries, along with the man she knew only as Brian. One of the responding deputies followed her to the hospital and got her statement. She answered as many of the deputy's questions that she could, which wasn't many. After all, she didn't know who the other two intruders were. She never got a good look at them, nor did she know what they were after or where they had run off to. The only thing she was sure about was that Brian had come over and saved her from unknown harm. She also knew he was a mystery man whom she wanted to learn more about, and it was why she stayed at the hospital after being treated for minor scrapes and bruises.

"I'm Doctor Williams. Are you Mr. Brian Suther's next of kin?" the treating physician asked.

Shelby thought about the question for about half of a second. "Yes, he's my fiancé. Is he going to be okay?"

The doctor looked at her with a suspicious glare, and Shelby knew he was questioning what she had just said.

"I mean, I'm just so worried. We were at dinner earlier, and he said he didn't feel good, so we went out to the beach, and he passed out. I ran into the restaurant to get some help, but when I got back, he was awake. I wanted to bring him in then, but he refused—stubborn ass. Anyway, when we got back to our beach house, we were attacked. You can ask the deputy; I think he's still here." Shelby halfheartedly started to stand as if she were about to go locate the deputy.

"No, that won't be necessary," the doctor said, interjecting. Your fiancé has an infection."

"An infection?" Shelby blurted as her mind thought about specific infections.

The doctor looked at her with raised eyebrows. "Yes, like I was saying, he has an infection. Can you tell me how he got that deep cut on his left side?"

Shelby looked at Brian, who still appeared to be unconscious, and back at the doctor, not knowing what to say. "How did he get the cut on his side?" She repeated the question hoping to buy some time.

"Yes, how did it happen?"

Shelby opened her mouth but felt Brian's hand on her arm.

"Where am I?" Brian asked.

"You're in the emergency room at Baptist Hospital. You and your fiancée were brought in after you were attacked. She was just about to tell me how you got that cut on your side, that appears to be infected."

"I fell off the roof at one of my job sites. I'm a custom home builder, and right before we left for vacation, I slipped and slid over a piece of roofing flange that had a sharp edge. It cut me pretty bad. My doctor back home stitched it up," Brian said, lifting his left arm to examine the wound himself.

"Well, the stitches tore loose from whatever you two got into this evening, but the cut was infected before then. I've given you some antibiotics that should take care of it. I would like to admit you for the night for observation."

"Is it really necessary?" Brian asked.

"Well, I wouldn't have suggested it if it weren't, would I?"

Brian chuckled and looked at Shelby. "If my fiancée promises to take care of me and to watch over me, would that be good enough?"

The doctor looked at his patient and rolled his eyes. "I don't care if you stay the night or not. If you want her to watch you, then that's up to you. You will be leaving here against medical advice. I'll send you home with more antibiotics, guidelines to follow, and what to look out for regarding infections. We've covered the wound for now, but the wound itself needs to stay open for a little bit longer. In a few days, come back, and we'll close it up. Keep it clean and apply a new dressing every day."

"Okay, then that's what we'll do," Shelby answered, seeing the doctor was getting impatient with his patient.

"It'll be a few minutes. Sit tight, and someone will come back and sign you out," the good doctor stated and walked out of the room.

Brian looked at Shelby. "Fiancé?"

"I'm sorry, I didn't know what else to say. I wanted to make sure you were okay, and he wasn't going to tell me unless I was your next of kin."

"All right, I understand, but whose place are we staying at tonight?"

"Oh no, I'm staying at my place, and you're staying at yours. I'll come over and help you if you need anything. I'll give you my number, and you can call me," Shelby replied, clarifying immediately. "Oh, and you need to call this man tomorrow." Shelby handed Brian a business card.

"Who's this?"

"It's the deputy who took my report. He needs your statement."

"What about you?"

"I already gave him my statement. You were asleep."

Brian looked at Shelby while she looked out the door toward the hall. He thought she was beautiful. "What's your name?"

Shelby looked back at the half-dressed, good-looking man lying in the hospital bed who just happened to be the same man who had protected her. "I guess we haven't been formally introduced, have we?"

"No, we haven't. I mean, I told you who I was, but you never told me who you were."

"Well, you did pass out."

"Yeah, I guess I did."

"I'm Shelby."

Shelby and Brian took a rideshare back to the beach house and got there at about five o'clock in the morning. After they walked through her place to make sure it was safe and to get the lights back on, Brian walked back to his. When Brian walked inside, he found his cell phone right where he had left it before running over to Shelby's place earlier. He picked it up and saw he had numerous missed calls from one number. He called the number back and waited for him to answer.

"It's me… Yeah, things got bad last night. Someone made a move on her… Yeah, she's fine, and so am I. Thanks for asking… No, I don't know who it was… It was dark… I don't know… Well, I was over here, and I saw someone moving around inside her place with a flashlight as she was coming back from dinner… I went over there and found two people attacking her, so I stopped them… I don't know. They took off… Yeah, fine. I got to get some sleep," Brian said and ended the call.

He checked the locks on his doors and windows before he headed to his bedroom. When he got to his bed, he took a seat on the edge and looked at his .45 sitting on the nightstand. "That's twice now I needed you, and you weren't there for me," he said and picked the gun up. He figured the infection and the fever had clouded his thoughts, which caused him to run out of the house without the weapon. "That had to be it, right? Or was it something or someone else distracting me?"

Shelby walked into the bathroom and turned on the

shower, but nothing happened. She turned both knobs, but no water spewed from the showerhead or the faucet. She tried the hot and cold knobs on the sink, and to her delighted surprise, water rushed out. She took her clothes off, wet a washcloth, and bathed herself over a towel. "This will have to do for tonight," she mumbled.

After Shelby's birdbath, as she called it, she put on clean clothes and rechecked the front door and windows, making sure they were locked. She grabbed an empty glass bottle she had found in the yard and carefully balanced it on the front door's knob. If it were opened, the bottle would fall to the tile floor and make a loud shattering noise. It was a trick her father had taught her when she was a teenager.

When Shelby fell asleep, she was haunted by faint and broken memories from the night at the truck stop in Albuquerque. This time, she had different memories or visions.

Once again, she was in the back of the box truck. She found herself being carried by someone wearing a red-and-white hoodie that covered their head and darkened their face. Shelby felt calm and safe as the man carried her through the parking lot toward the convenience store, where the glow of the fluorescent lights blinded her. She closed her eyes and heard him whisper, "You'll be all right." She heard the bathroom door open and opened her eyes. The lights inside were just as bright. Unexpectedly and to her delight, she saw the man tilting his head down to look at her. Shelby got excited; she could almost see his face.

A chiming noise came from somewhere outside her memory, and just like that, he was gone. Shelby was lying in her bed right next to her phone, which was ringing on the dresser.

Shelby rolled over and looked at her phone. It was noon and Brian was calling. "Hello," she said in a tired but cheerful voice.

"I need some help," Brian stated.

Shelby quickly sat up. "Are you okay?"

"Yes, but can you come over here, please?" Brian asked in a quiet voice.

"I'll be right there."

Shelby dressed quickly, put her hair into a ponytail, and took one last look in the mirror. She grabbed her cell phone, unlocked the front door, and hurried to the beach house next door.

Rob was dressed and getting ready to leave to meet with Hal when he saw the woman rush to the beach house next door. "What's this about?" he asked aloud.

Chapter 8
Lance and Brenda

The beach house is picture-perfect. Brenda typed it just like that and texted it with a picture to her daughter back in Ohio. Brenda and her husband, Lance, were in their sixties and had come to Pensacola for the summer to look for a new house to retire in. Lance had found the summer rental online and spoken to the owner. The owner informed Lance the rental unit was available and that it was being sold at the end of the summer. When Lance showed Brenda pictures of the beach house, she immediately fell in love with it. She especially loved how it was designed and built with an Italian villa theme. It was a light-brown stucco with a dark-brown clay-tile roof. The beach house had a large deck in the back with a saltwater swimming pool.

The couple had spent the first two weeks looking at other homes on Pensacola Beach, in case there was something available they liked better. Still, in the end, they decided on the one they were renting, the one Brenda had already fallen in love with. They told the owner they had decided to purchase the beach house. The owner generously agreed to allow them to stay in their future home rent-free until they closed on it during the first week of August. The couple was ecstatic about their future home, and Brenda told everyone she met on the island about it, including a stranger named Charlie.

Charlie said she was also in Pensacola looking for some property. When Lance and Brenda met Charlie, the three immediately hit it off. The couple invited their new friend back to their place for dinner. Charlie seemed excited for the soon-to-be retirees. They generously gave their visitor a tour of what was to be their new home.

The home tour ended in the garage, where the couple's brand-new luxury car was parked. They had purchased it the previous day. Charlie convinced them to get inside the car for a photo Brenda could send to their daughter.

Now, a few days later Charlie's back was sore from the burglary and the fight. When she returned from the old blue beach house, Charlie needed something to ease her lower back pain. After looking around the bathroom for some pills, she walked downstairs to the kitchen and noticed a foul odor.

Charlie looked at the door leading to the garage. It was time to check on Lance and Brenda, who were still in the garage, sitting in their car with a bullet in their heads. She opened the door and found the source of the foul odor. Lance and Brenda had gotten quite ripe. Charlie quickly shut the door and decided something needed to be done with the couple before other people in the neighborhood started smelling their decomposing bodies.

Shelby rushed into Brian's place expecting to find the man in a bad way, but instead, she found him sitting on a leather sofa with a roguish grin and watching golf of all things. Shelby stared at the man with a sullen expression.

"I thought you needed help," she said as she walked into the room.

Brian stood and took a good look at the beautiful woman who rushed over to help him. "I do. I need help eating that pizza over there. I ordered it, and when it arrived, I took one look and knew I couldn't eat it all myself," Brian said as he pointed into the dining room.

Shelby didn't respond. She walked into the dining room and looked at the pizza box and the two bottles of beer sitting in an ice bucket next to it. "Does this place have ranch dressing?" Shelby asked and sat down.

"It does. I'll be right back," Brian stated as he rushed into the kitchen.

Hal sat patiently at the picnic table, waiting for Rob. Hal had thought about what he needed to do when he got back from the Condo Conclave the previous night. After more careful deliberation, he decided to steal the car. His decision didn't come easy, but after Charlie told him nothing had been found in the beach house, there were only so many options left. If the money wasn't in the Mustang, then Willy's daughter had to know where it was. Hal figured he was down to either getting the car, the letter Tan Man delivered, or the girl. One of the three had to lead the warden to his retirement.

Rob found Hawkins Recreational Park off Munson Highway in the town of Milton. He didn't know why Hal wanted to meet this far away from Pensacola Beach, but it didn't matter. Hal was the boss, so he called the shots. When Rob pulled into the parking lot, he found Hal sitting near the river at one of the picnic tables.

"Why are we meeting out here?" Rob asked.

Hal looked at the people around them. "You carrying?"

"Yeah, why?" Rob answered as he pulled his shirt up, revealing the handle of his 9 mm.

"Good. We're meeting José Hernandez and his brother, Mateo."

Rob raised an eyebrow as he looked at his boss suspiciously. "You think we need them?"

"Maybe; Charlie called and told me there was nothing in the beach house. So either the cash is in the car or there's information in the envelope Tan Man delivered that will lead us to it."

"If there isn't?"

"Then we always have the girl."

Rob looked down at the table. "Yeah, but now she has help."

"How good is he?"

"He took on Charlie and me. He didn't seem to mind being outnumbered in a fight," Rob reluctantly said.

Hal thought about it for a moment. "Do you think he's a pro?"

"Possibly," Rob answered as two men walked over and stood next to them. Rob recognized the two men, so he moved around the table and stood behind Hal, ready to pull his gun if needed.

José and Mateo Hernandez didn't know what to expect when they got the call to meet with their former prison warden. Since they were both still on parole, they figured they had best make the meeting.

"Warden," José said and looked up at Rob.

"Fellas, how's life on the outside treating you? Contributing to the betterment of society, I hope," Hal said sarcastically.

"What's up? Why you in Florida? We ain't violating parole. We got permission to be here," José replied, while Mateo continued to keep his eyes on Rob. Mateo recognized the prison guard.

"No, you're not in violation."

"Then why you fucking with us?" Mateo asked.

Hal stood and walked closer to the two men. "I'm not. I'm here to offer the two of you a job. If I remember correctly, you guys are for hire. Correct?"

The two brothers looked at each other with a curious expression. "You want to hire us?" José asked.

"Yes."

"It's a trap. We agree to do something and then you revoke our parole."

Hal shook his head. "No, you don't do what I need, and I'll revoke it. So you have two choices here. Either you do what I need done and make some money, or you walk away and I make some phone calls to send you back," Hal stated and then dropped ten thousand dollars on the picnic table.

Shelby and Brian moved into the living room after they finished eating. They sat close to each other on the sofa. Shelby enjoyed the man's company, and it didn't hurt that he was easy on the eyes.

Brian also enjoyed looking at and talking to the woman he had saved twice.

Shelby pulled her legs under her and twisted her body to face him. "So, tell me about Brian Suthers."

"Suthers? I don't remember telling you my last name."

Shelby gave a cheeky grin. "The doctor said it before you came around last night. I also read it on your discharge papers too."

"Oh, I see."

"What do you expect? You came in when I needed help and probably saved my life. I wanted to know who you were. Now, I would like to find out more about you," Shelby explained and took a sip of her beer.

"Well, I'm Brian Suthers. I grew up in North Carolina. My

parents still live there. I joined the US Army after high school and spent some time overseas."

"What'd you do in the army?"

Brian didn't know how he should answer the question. He hesitated.

"That bad?" Shelby asked when she saw the blank look on the man's face.

"No, it's just not what some people want to hear about."

Shelby understood. She had once asked her father what he did in Vietnam, and he'd had the same look. "We don't have to talk about it. So what did you do after getting out of the army?"

Brian looked at her once again with a blank expression. Before Shelby could say anything, he blurted, "I spent six years in prison."

Shelby was in shock, and her face showed it. "Interesting."

"If you want to leave now, I understand," Brian said and moved to stand.

Shelby reached over and grabbed his arm. "No, stay here and tell me about it." There was something about Brian that drew her to him. She wanted to know everything about him.

Brian took a deep breath. "When I got back from my last deployment, I was in a different place mentally. I went out one night to a bar and drank heavily. This guy came over, and he saw my haircut. He assumed correctly that I was in the military. He wanted to buy me another drink. His name was Walt, and he was really drunk, and he had two friends with him," Brian said and then took a moment.

Shelby saw it was hard for him to share his story. "Go on. It's all right."

"Well, I was young, and I wasn't in the mood for company, but Walt wouldn't stop. I told him I wanted to be alone. Walt put his hand on my shoulder and spun me around when I tried to ignore him. I stood up and pushed him away. He came toward me again, and I wasn't having it. I grabbed a heavy beer mug and hit Walt in the head with it."

"Did you kill him?" Shelby asked.

"No, but what I didn't know was that Walt had a brain injury from a car crash he got into a few years prior to that night. The blow from the mug caused him to have a seizure that paralyzed his right side."

"You were charged."

"Yeah, first-degree assault causing bodily injury. The army discharged me, and I did six years in prison for it."

Shelby set her beer on the coffee table. "My father was in and out of prison my entire life. He was always after the big score that never seemed to pan out. When I was really young, I used my crayons and drew him a picture of us in front of the beach house. My mother sent it to him in prison, but he never wrote back or ever said anything about it."

"What about your mother?"

"Oh, always the faithful bride. She waited for him to get out of prison each and every time he was sent away. She died of pancreatic cancer when I was fifteen. I pretty much stopped going to school and took care of her."

Brian took the last drink of his beer and set his bottle next to hers. "Where was your father?"

Shelby shifted her eyes upward. "Prison, of course. She died on a Friday, and he was released the following Monday."

"Did he walk away after that?"

"No, he tried to be a father. He got a job selling tires, and he kept it the entire time I was in school."

"I thought you stopped going to school."

"I did, but after my mother died, I went back. I did everything I could to stay out of the house and away from him."

Brian gave her a questioning look. "I don't understand. Was he an abusive man?"

"No. Not at all."

"Did he drink?"

"Yeah, but he wasn't an alcoholic or anything like that," Shelby answered. The questions made her start to think. "Enough about me. Tell me more about you."

"Like what?"

"How did you adapt to prison life? Or is that too personal?"

"No, I can talk about it. It was bad at first. I didn't consider myself one of them. I saw everyone around me as a murderer or rapist. Now, don't get me wrong, I've killed people in war who were trying to kill me, so I'm not a saint, but I never killed an innocent person."

"How did you get by?"

"It was hard. If I wasn't in a fight, then I was in solitary because I had been in a fight. That went on for like six months. Then one day, I get out of solitary, and when I get to my cell block, there's this old guy in my cell."

Shelby lowered her head. "Was he a hardened criminal?"

"Criminal, yes. Career criminal actually, but not hardened by any means."

"Well, what happened?"

Brian shrugged his shoulders. "Nothing really. He wasn't a murderer or a rapist. I tried to act hard at first, but he blew it off."

Shelby raised her head. "You tried to be hard."

Brian laughed. "Yeah, I walked in and said I'm taking this or that. He didn't argue about it. I was rude to him for like two weeks straight. Then I started to notice a pattern."

"A pattern?"

"Yeah, every time I did something to this guy, I got a shitty work assignment the next day. Eventually, I learned that his old man was running the show."

"Really!"

"Yeah, he had guards on the take. He never did anything he didn't want to do. This guy got special meals, rec time, and gifts."

Shelby had a look of curiosity on her face. "Gifts."

Brian nodded. "Yeah, he got gifts from people. We had a small TV, a toaster oven, and once every month, he got us ice cream."

"Ice cream."

"Oh yes, it was vanilla ice cream that had chocolate chips and caramel mixed into it."

"You got to eat it too."

Brian leaned forward onto his knees. "Well, yeah. You see, I caught on really quick to this guy running things, so I stopped being an asshole to him. Then one day in the rec yard, this other inmate starts in on him about something and tries to stab him. For some reason, I stepped in and stopped the inmate, and from then on, I was his guy."

Shelby squinted her eyes. "His guy?"

"Yeah, I made sure nothing happened to him."

"Kind of like with me the other night, a bodyguard of sorts."

Brian shrugged his shoulders. "Yeah, I guess."

Shelby looked out the window at the Gulf of Mexico in the distance. She then looked back at her bodyguard. "I haven't walked on the beach since I've been here. You feel up to it?"

"Yeah."

The drive to the Florida-Alabama line took Charlie about an hour. An hour with two decaying bodies in the trunk was more than she had bargained for. More than once, the killer had to stop and take a break, out of the car from the stench. A dirt road off Mobile Hwy took the killer into the woods near Styx River.

Charlie drove the luxury car about three miles down the dirt road until she reached a clearing near the river's edge. Charlie parked the car and casually looked around. She wasted no time pulling Lance and Brenda out of the trunk and dragging them to the riverbank. The last thing Charlie saw of the couple was their bodies sinking deeper into the water as the current carried them away.

Charlie opened the doors and the car's trunk to let it air out before heading back to the beach. The killer then lit a cigarette and smoked it while reading the text message Hal had sent.

Meet us at Rob's beach rental at nine o'clock. We're taking the car tonight.

"Finally," Charlie mumbled. She tossed her still-lit cigarette to the ground and got ready to leave but heard someone walking out of the brush behind her. She quickly turned around and found two men dressed in camouflage.

"You lost?" one of the men asked as he approached her. Beau and his brother had been shooting birds when they came across the woman who was alone and looked helpless.

Charlie knew the type of men they were. She knew she needed to leave, and soon. "No. Just passing through. I'm leaving now," she said as she walked around the car, closing the doors and trunk.

"Whew. You smell that, Wilbur?" Beau asked.

"Oh yeah, brother, something's dead in that car, or there was something dead in there," Wilbur said and leaned on the driver's door preventing the contract killer from getting inside.

Charlie looked inside the luxury car at her purse, which had her gun inside it. She then looked at the shotgun Wilbur held. She knew she needed to make a move if she were to have the upper hand. *Two more bodies in the river*, she thought and grabbed Wilbur's gun. He wasn't ready for the move, or the one that followed. The shotgun blast sent Wilbur over the hood.

Beau lifted his own shotgun when he saw the woman turning around to face him.

Charlie quickly pulled the slide action back on the gun to chamber another round, but it was empty.

Beau stepped forward with his shotgun, raised it to his shoulder, and pointed it at the woman's head. "Bitch!"

The shot echoed through the woods and down the river.

Brian and Shelby walked down the beach, running into the water with the tide going out and then hurrying back when a large wave approached. They laughed and played like children on vacation. At some point during their frolicking, Shelby grabbed Brian's arm, which eventually led to them holding hands. As the sun dipped closer and closer to the Gulf, the two stood closer to each other.

Shelby shivered. "It's getting cooler."

Brian put his arm around her. "Come closer," he whispered.

Shelby put her arm around Brian's waist and moved into him. He looked down, into her green eyes. She was mesmerizing. Brian moved her long blonde hair out from her face. He pulled her closer and kissed her softly.

Chapter 9
Date Night

Brian walked Shelby back to the old blue house a little before six o'clock. Shelby told Brian about the problem she was having with her shower, and he agreed to look at it. When they walked inside, Brian stood in the living room and looked around for what all needed repair or improvements. His face said everything. He walked around the room, looking at the walls closely. He picked up a glass bottle from the windowsill and twisted it back and forth in his hand.

Shelby did not remember putting the bottle there. She didn't even remember removing it from the doorknob when she had rushed out earlier. *Odd*, she thought.

"It needs some work," Brian said as he placed the bottle back.

"It's bad, isn't it?" Shelby dismissed the bottle as a lapse in memory from rushing out to make sure Brian was all right.

"It's not too bad. It just needs some TLC. The walls are concrete and can be painted. The floor is covered in carpet and tile, both of which can be replaced. The ceiling leaked at one time, and I'm guessing it can use some new TPO."

"TPO?" Shelby asked.

"Yeah, it's a type of thermoplastic that goes on flat roofs."

"Oh."

Brian laughed. "Where's the bathroom?"

"Down the hall on the left," Shelby said and pointed.

Brian walked down the hall with Shelby right behind him. He spent a few minutes looking at the faucet and the knobs. He then sat on the toilet and looked at the sink. He turned the knobs, and both the hot and cold water came on. "Hmm."

"Hmm, what?" Shelby asked.

"I don't know."

Shelby raised an eyebrow. "I thought you built custom homes."

"I do. This isn't a custom home, and I don't do the plumbing myself. I hire most of the work out to other trade professionals. I run the project, sending bids out and making sure things get done on time," Brian explained.

"So you have no idea what's wrong with it?"

"Actually, I do. Somewhere, the water line going to the shower has been capped."

Shelby looked at the man with a blank expression. "Why would it be capped?"

"I don't know. I can look at it tomorrow, maybe follow the line from outside back into the house and see what's going on."

Shelby's shoulders dropped. "Tomorrow?"

"Yeah, why?"

"I really wanted to take a shower."

"I got a shower."

Hal and Rob were sitting in the Red Fish Restaurant's bar section, eating an early dinner. While they enjoyed raw oysters and boiled shrimp, Hal thought over a few things that had been bothering him. He thought maybe he needed more help, other than two convicts he wasn't familiar with.

"Rob, the sniper you hired in the desert to cover us when we met with Willy at the camper, is he available?"

"You mean the guy Jack hired. I don't know, but I can call him again. After he took care of the old guys by the creek bed, he kind of disappeared," Rob answered with a mouthful of bread.

Hal narrowed his eyes and pursed his lips. "You never met him?"

"No. Jack knew him and hired him. I got his number out of Jack's phone after he died."

"How'd Jack know him?"

"He was an inmate."

"Do you know his name?"

"No. Jack called him Smooth."

"Smooth?"

"Yep."

Evelyn looked out the window at the young woman who had moved into the old blue beach house across the street. She watched as Shelby made her way to the house next door, carrying her suitcase. Evelyn had met Shelby when she first arrived, and Evelyn hadn't been very nice to her, but it wasn't the time or place to make introductions. She really didn't need to talk to her about anything. She just wanted to see Shelby up close.

"What are you looking at?" Evelyn's "husband" asked.

"I'm just watching her."

"What's she doing now?"

Evelyn didn't answer. She just watched her and smiled.

"What's she doing?" He asked again.

Evelyn walked away from the window. "She's going over to his place, carrying her suitcase."

"What!" the man yelled as he stood and hurried to the window. "What does she think she's doing?"

"I don't know, but she's gorgeous, and I think he's taken notice."

Brian walked Shelby upstairs, grabbed her fresh towels, and showed her where the bathroom was. He stood at the door, waiting in an uncomfortable silence. Shelby placed her makeup bag on the countertop and reached for the door.

"You want to eat somewhere nice?" Brian suggested, finally breaking the silence.

"That would be nice. Do you want to maybe make us dinner reservations?" Shelby asked.

Brian realized he was just staring at her. He was embarrassed. "Yeah, I'll go downstairs and call around. You go ahead, do whatever you need, and use whatever you need."

"Okay," Shelby said and then slowly shut the door.

"Um, I'm going downstairs," Brian said once more and walked away.

Shelby turned on the water, undressed, and stepped into the shower. It was invigorating. She let the warm water run down her face as she closed her eyes and thought about Brian. She thought he was good looking, strong, and confident. She also thought things between them may be moving too fast, but maybe fast was what she needed.

Brian rushed downstairs and called a bunch of nice restaurants but didn't have any luck getting a reservation on such short notice. He sat on the couch and looked up restaurants that weren't on the island. He was about to call one more when he got a phone call. He looked at the number.

"Yeah... Why are you yelling... I'm keeping her close... I know that's not part of the deal... Me coming out here wasn't part of the deal, but that changed too!" Brian yelled into the phone and abruptly ended the call. He paced back and forth in the living room, thinking about what he should do. He headed upstairs.

Shelby got out of the shower and dried off. The humidity had caused the mirror to fog up. She removed the towel and wiped the mirror off, but the moisture in the room was too much. She opened the side window and then walked to the door.

Brian was about to knock on the bathroom door when it suddenly opened. He couldn't move. He couldn't blink. All he could do was stare at the beautiful, naked woman in front of him.

Shelby was just as surprised, and she froze for a second. She quickly shut the door.

"I'm sorry," Brian called.

Shelby fell back against the door. "It's okay. Did you need something?"

"There's nothing available on the island. I thought about calling somewhere else off the island. What do you think?"

Shelby thought about it for a second and then it hit her. "Give me a second. I have an idea." Shelby grabbed her phone off the toilet and texted Stacie.

I need food and I have a guest. Can you get us in? Please, please, with banana pudding on top.

A few seconds went by before Stacie texted back.

Yeah, he better be good looking!

Shelby snickered with excitement. "I got us in somewhere," she said through the door.

"Where?"

"I'll tell you when I come out."

"Okay, I'll go back downstairs. Come down when you're ready."

Hal and Rob were still sitting at Red Fish Restaurant. Rob continued to fill up on shrimp while Hal sat there thinking. Some things didn't add up, like the sniper, the old men in the burned-out Suburban, Agent Brian Forbes, and Willy's daughter.

"This sniper guy, do you know why Jack chose him?"

"Yeah, he said he was an Army Ranger. He did some tours in Afghanistan as a sniper or something."

Hal leaned forward, wrinkling his nose. "How do you know he killed Willy and the others?"

"He called me and told me after it was done. The coroner compared the medical records to the bodies that were in the Suburban, and they checked out. It was the three old guys."

"I guess. How did you pay him for the hit?"

"I dropped it where he asked. I mean, he did cover our asses at the camper. If it weren't for him, we wouldn't have gotten the one money bag. We got what was owed, and it's because of him."

"Yeah, it was, wasn't it? We got what was owed," Hal said and sat back in his chair. "Are you done?"

"Yeah, why? We still have time before we meet the others. You want to go somewhere else?"

"I want to go back to my condo before we head over to get the car."

Brian and Shelby took his car to Captain John's Seafood on the Beach. The parking lot was almost full, but Brian found a spot in the back. He ran around to the other side of his car to open the door for Shelby. When Shelby got out, she put her hand behind Brian's head and kissed him passionately.

Brian smiled when she finally pulled away. "I hope they can't get us in."

Shelby laughed. "We'll get in. I got connections."

"You got connections?"

"Yeah, I got people."

"Okay, we'll see."

The two walked in, and the men in the restaurant each turned to look at the gorgeous woman wearing a silky red shirt with white shorts. Shelby also wore the white high heels that Kim had picked out for her in Amarillo. She felt pretty, and Brian was making sure she did too. When he saw the other men looking at her, he got a little jealous. He placed his hand around her waist and pulled her close to him.

Stacie saw Shelby walk in and smiled at her. She then saw the man she was with, and her smile grew. She gave her a thumbs-up and rushed over to greet her and her date. "I have a table right over here for the two of you."

The couple followed the bartender to a table and sat down. Stacie stood by for a second, waiting for them to get comfortable.

"Here's our menu. Our special tonight is red snapper over rice pilaf. Can I start you two off with something to drink?" Stacie said as she handed both a menu.

"A white wine would be nice," Brian answered.

"Great. Do you need time to look at the menu?" Stacie asked.

"I think I'll have the shrimp and grits," Shelby said and looked across the table at her date.

"I'll have…"

"The shrimp and grits as well," Stacie stated before Brian could finish.

"How'd you know what I wanted?"

"Because you ordered it the other night. I kept it in the refrigerator. I'll warm it up and bring it right out to you," Stacie joked and hurried away.

Brian looked back at Shelby, who was laughing. "I guess she's one of your people, huh?"

"Yeah, she is."

"You don't think she really has my dinner from the other night, do you?"

"I don't know but probably not." Shelby answered and then started laughing again.

Brian shook his head and laughed along with her. "We're swapping plates when the food arrives!"

"Oh, no!"

When Hal got back to his place, he took out his laptop. He had a suspicion, and he needed to check it out. Rob took a seat and kept quiet as his boss waited for his computer to turn on.

"What are we doing here? What are you looking for?" Rob asked.

Hal logged into the prison database again. "I want to check on something."

"What?"

"Give me a minute. Now, what was that sniper's nickname?"

Rob scowled and pursed his lips. "Smooth. Why?"

Hal didn't answer. He typed the name Smooth into the alias box on the screen and pressed the enter key.

Rob leaned forward and propped himself on his elbows on the table. "Are you going to talk to me?"

Hal didn't answer. He kept his eyes on the screen until Smooth's picture appeared. "You gotta be kidding me."

"What?" Rob asked.

"It's Agent Brian Forbes," Hal said and turned the computer so Rob could see it.

"That's the guy next door. He's the one who stopped Charlie and me last night," Rob said and hit his fist on the table.

"We got a problem, but it could be all for the best. I need to call José and Mateo."

Shelby and Brian laughed throughout dinner, and they laughed some more over dessert. This time, Shelby shared the banana pudding with her dinner date. It was nearly eight o'clock when they ordered another bottle of wine. Shelby enjoyed spending the evening with Brian, and she liked how he made sure that she was the center of attention.

"The old beach house is needing so much work. I hope I can manage it. When you go back home after your vacation is over, may I call you for some advice?" Shelby asked.

Brian smiled; he knew what she was beating around the bush about. "My schedule is wide open right now. I'm thinking about staying here a little longer. Maybe I could help you out for a bit."

Shelby put her head down so he wouldn't see her grinning with glee. After she collected herself, she looked back up at him. "Do I look that helpless?"

"No, I think you'll be all right no matter if I help you or not."

Shelby was listening to Brian when suddenly her head felt heavy, and her eyes blinked rapidly. She dropped her spoon on the plate and grasped the table. Then Shelby was back in the box truck. Images of the kidnapper and the man who had saved her came rushing at her.

"Shelby, are you okay?" Brian jumped from his chair and caught her before she fell to the floor.

Stacie rushed over and stood on the other side of her. "What happened?"

"I don't know. She was fine one minute and then she turned pale and almost toppled over," Brian said as he held her in his arms.

Shelby heard the two of them talking. She was no longer in Albuquerque; she was back in the restaurant. "I'm okay. I don't know what happened. I just kind of lost myself for a minute."

"Maybe we should call an ambulance," Stacie said.

"No, I'm okay. It's probably just the wine."

"Are you sure? You've been through a lot lately," Brian said.

"I'm sure. Can you take me home?"

Brian looked up at Stacie and shrugged his shoulders. "Yeah, absolutely."

Brian paid for their food and left the restaurant after Stacie made him give her his phone number. The concerned bartender also took a picture of him. It made him laugh, but he understood why she was so careful. He was a stranger, after all.

When they got back to the beach house, he helped her onto the couch and sat next to her.

"How do you feel?" he asked.

Shelby looked up at him. "Better now."

"What happened back there?"

Shelby looked away.

Brian gently placed his hand on her chin and turned her face back toward his. "Tell me, please."

Shelby looked into his eyes and felt the need to tell him everything. Over the next thirty minutes, Shelby detailed the events that had brought her to Pensacola Beach. Brian listened without interrupting her, even though he already knew most of what she was telling him.

"So now, since the attack in Albuquerque, I've had these glimpses or flashbacks. I keep seeing this guy carrying me away. I'm sure he's the one I saw in the box truck fighting the guy who grabbed me. Sometimes I feel that if I close my eyes, I'll see him standing there. And—"

"And, you probably have a concussion. I think we should take you back to the hospital tomorrow and have them do a scan or something," Brian suggested, before she had any more memories come back.

Shelby tossed her hands into the air. "I don't know; maybe I should."

Brian looked into her eyes once again. He ran his hand down her neck and placed his other hand on the nape of her neck. He slowly pulled her close and kissed her gently.

Shelby pulled away and looked deeply into his eyes. "Slowly, okay," she whispered.

"Whatever you want," Brian whispered back. He then stood and picked her up.

She placed her arms around his neck and kissed him once more. He carried her up the stairs to the bedroom and laid her on the bed. He kissed her again and then removed his shirt and dropped it to the floor, revealing his muscular body.

Shelby slowly unbuttoned her top and slid out of it. She locked eyes with him as she unfastened her bra and laid it at the end of the bed. Brian admired her beautiful body for a moment before easing himself onto the bed. Shelby unbuttoned her shorts and slid them off. She wrapped her arms around his torso.

"Ouch!" Brian said when she bumped his wound with her arm.

Shelby quickly pulled back. "I'm sorry. We can stop."

Brian laughed. "Really, stop now? No, it's okay. I'll fight through the pain."

Shelby laughed too.

Hal had everything in place for when the couple returned. He stood at the window of Rob's beach house, keeping an eye outside. He looked at his watch. It was only a matter of time before he would have all the money. Soon, he would be on his way to someplace where no one knew who he was, but first, he needed to take care of some unfinished business.

"It'll all be over soon," Hal said as he looked at the Mustang sitting in the driveway across the street.

Chapter 10
Visions

Brian and Shelby lay in bed, wrapped in each other's arms. The night had been fantastic. Shelby had her reservations about getting involved with another man so soon after her breakup with Carter. Still, lying next to Brian, she couldn't imagine it being any other way. She could hear Brian steadily breathing and knew he was asleep. She slowly rolled away from him and crawled off the bed.

Shelby picked his shirt up and slid it over her head. She tiptoed across the bedroom to the bathroom. Once inside, she eased the door closed and turned on the light. Shelby stood in front of the mirror and looked at herself. "Shelby, Shelby, Shelby, what are you doing?" she asked herself. She turned the faucet on, splashed her face with cool water, and looked for a towel to dry off.

"Damn!" she whispered when she found the towel rack empty. Shelby opened the cabinet doors but couldn't locate something to dry her face. She then looked at the corner and saw a pile of towels. *How many towels can one man use?* she thought as she shook the water off her hands. When she was about to turn off the bathroom light, she saw something in the laundry pile that caught her eye.

Brian was awakened by a noise. He looked around the room but didn't see Shelby. He quickly scooted off the bed, opened the nightstand drawer, and pulled out his .45. Brian stayed low and surveyed his surroundings, and he saw the light glowing from underneath the bathroom door. He took a breath, believing the noise he'd heard was Shelby going to the bathroom. He slowly stood and didn't move for a second.

Then he heard something or someone downstairs. Brian slid his pants on, looked at the bathroom door, and decided to go downstairs to see what or who was there.

Shelby slowly walked over, stood over the pile of dirty clothes, and stared at what looked like a white hoodie. She bent down and pulled the garment out of the pile. The letters UNLV were clearly visible on the front, along with bloodstains that covered a large portion of the hoodie. Shelby dropped to her knees, and without warning, she was back in the box truck.

She felt the man's hands on her. She then saw him standing there, smoking a cigarette. Shelby tried to recall more, but there was nothing except the sounds of the two men scuffling and then it stopped. A moment later Shelby felt someone carrying her.

Shelby opened her eyes, and she was back in the bathroom. "No, no, I need to know," Shelby cried. She took a deep breath, held the hoodie close to her, and closed her eyes.

Brian walked down the stairs with his .45 at the ready. He stayed in the shadows to conceal his approach. When he reached the landing at the bottom, he heard someone moving around in the kitchen. He paused for a moment and surveyed the darkness around him. He then slowly moved toward the kitchen.

Shelby tried to take herself back to Albuquerque, but she couldn't stop crying. "Stop it! Concentrate," she told herself, and again she closed her eyes and imagined being carried by the man in the hoodie. She already knew who it was, but she needed to see it. She needed to see him.

Once more, she was back there, in his arms. Again, she heard him say, "You'll be all right," and he started to look down at her.

Brian walked into the kitchen, slowly opened the swinging door, and found nothing but a bright flash of light.

Shelby kept her eyes fixated on the man carrying her. As the two entered the light of the convenience store, she finally saw him.

She opened her eyes just as the sound of a gunshot rang out. "Brian!" She shouted and ran out of the bathroom, down the stairs, and into the kitchen.

"Nice of you to join us," Hal said as he walked around the large granite counter.

Shelby looked at Brian, who was lying on the floor as his blood pooled around him. She dropped to her knees and put her hand on his back. "Who are you?" she yelled as she looked around the kitchen at the people standing there.

"Grab her!" Hal yelled to José and Mateo.

The two brothers grabbed her by the arms and lifted her.

"What do you want with me?"

Rob stepped forward and gripped Shelby by her face. "We want to know what your father left you in that envelope, and we want the car."

"It's all next door," Shelby admitted.

"Then let's go get it," Hal said.

The two brothers escorted Shelby out the door and into the yard, with Hal and Rob following close behind them.

When they were between the two houses, Rob stopped and grabbed Hal by the arm. "Wait. Where's Charlie?"

Hal looked around and didn't see Charlie anywhere. Charlie had not called or answered Hal's text earlier, but the warden thought his contract killer would have still shown up, knowing what was at stake.

"Stop!" Hal ordered José and Mateo.

Both men stopped and looked back at their employer. "What's wrong?" José asked.

Hal suspiciously looked around. "Something's not right." He looked to his right and saw someone moving out from behind the old blue beach house. He squinted his eyes to try to see who it was.

"I gave you a lot of money, but it wasn't enough, was it? You had to have it all, didn't you? Greed, it's a compelling thing."

"Yes, it is, Willy," Hal said.

"What?" Rob asked and stepped forward for a better look. "You were right. He's alive."

"Yeah, he set it all up. He had his old cellmate Smooth run interference for him. Jay worked in the infirmary and changed their medical records. Then he arranged to have Jack hire Smooth to cover us in the desert, but he wasn't covering us, was he, Willy?"

"No, Brian Suthers or 'Smooth' as we call him was covering us, and he did a good job of it too. By the way, Hal, how's the leg?"

Hal chuckled sarcastically. "Funny."

"Dad, is that really you?" Shelby asked.

Hal stepped closer to her and placed his gun at her head. "C'mon on out, where we can see you better—nice and slow, like with your hands in the air."

Willy did as he was ordered and kept his eye on the man holding a gun to his daughter's head. He glanced to his left and saw the one thing he needed. He started walking toward Hal.

"That's far enough," Hal ordered.

Willy didn't listen. He kept walking forward.

"Stop!" Hal ordered.

Willy didn't hesitate.

"Stop!" Hal yelled once more and aimed his gun at the elderly man.

"Now!" Willy yelled and then dropped to the sand just as a bullet whizzed by.

Mateo didn't know what hit him. The .308 round entered his skull right between the eyes. He dropped to his knees and fell forward into the island beach sand. Hal ran to his right and found cover behind one of the piers supporting the beach house.

A wounded Brian looked over the scope of his rifle at Shelby. "Run to me!" he yelled.

José ran for cover and yelled something in Spanish. Then two of his associates came running out of the shadows, firing wildly in Shelby's and Willy's directions. Willy rolled to his left and looked up at Shelby, who was frozen with fear. Bullets hit the ground around her.

"Smooth, cover me," Willy ordered as he got up and ran to his daughter.

Brian got to his knees and fired at the two men who'd appeared out of the shadows. He caught the one on his right with a bullet to his chest. The other man found cover behind a small sand dune.

Rob was still in shock, hiding in the street behind a car. He didn't know what to do, but when he saw Willy running for his daughter, he carefully aimed his pistol at him.

"Robby, how are things?"

Rob turned around and found Roscoe standing there, holding a 9 mm on him.

"Don't even think about it!"

Rob didn't listen. He raised his gun and quickly fired his weapon. Roscoe was faster, and he placed two bullets into the man's chest. The round Rob fired ricocheted off the road and caught Roscoe in the shoulder, which sent him running behind another car for cover.

José dropped down and hid behind one of the support piers under Rob's rented beach house across the street. He saw his brother go down, and it drove him to get to the man who had killed him. He peered through the darkness and saw the man Hal had shot in the kitchen of the beach house taking cover on the deck. He looked hurt, but he wasn't dead, but he soon would be if José could get to him.

When Willy got to Shelby, he grabbed her by the arms and pulled her toward Brian's beach house. At the stairs, she started to struggle.

"I thought you were dead!" she yelled and pulled away from his grasp.

"Not now, sweetheart," Willy ordered and grabbed at her again.

Shelby pulled away once more, just as a bullet found Willy's right leg, fired from Hal's gun. The elderly man dropped to the ground while Shelby screamed and knelt over him.

"How's that feel, Willy? Just returning the favor!" Hal called as he slowly moved from one pier support to the next, getting closer to his intended target.

Brian heard Shelby screaming. He got up to run. Bullets whizzed by him, then one found its way into his arm. Brian fell back on the deck with a gunshot wound to his arm to go with the one he already had in his chest. He knew the direction the bullet came from, but he couldn't stand without getting hit again. "Shit," he mumbled.

"Cover me!" José ordered his other man as he walked down the side of the beach house to the back deck. The other man stood and directed the barrel of his pistol at the back deck as José made his approach.

José got ready to surprise the man who had killed his brother.

"Now, Smooth!" Jay yelled as he opened fire with his Thompson submachine gun on José's cover man, killing him before he knew what happened.

José spun around toward the shooting.

Brian heard Jay's command, and with everything, he sat up and found José standing there at the edge of the deck. He aimed his gun at José's head. "Psst."

José quickly turned his gun back toward the man on the deck. Brian pulled the trigger, and José fell backward onto the sand.

Shelby was treating Willy's leg when Hal walked up behind them. He placed the gun barrel against Shelby's head. "Don't move."

Shelby froze in place and gazed at her father. "Please stop!"

"As long as I get the money, you'll live," Hal said with a smile.

"What's going on over there?" the elderly woman from across the street yelled from her porch.

Hal looked up, and that was all it took. He never heard the shot, but he did feel the bullet from Brian's .308 as it ripped through his heart. The warden dropped his gun and fell to the ground. Police sirens wailed in the distance. Brian dropped the rifle and collapsed.

Suddenly, a black SUV pulled up with Jay and Roscoe inside. "We gotta get out of here!" Jay yelled as he ran around the front of the vehicle to help Willy get inside.

"Get Smooth and place the bags of cocaine in his place," Willy ordered after Jay eased him into the back seat.

Jay took off toward the beach house to help the younger man.

Shelby stood next to her father. She was in shock.

Willy reached out and took her by the hand. "Everything will be okay."

"What's going on? What do I do now?" Shelby asked.

"Nothing. You know nothing. Now, go over to Evelyn's place. You were over there when this gang war happened."

"I don't understand," Shelby stated as she watched Brian being placed into the back seat, next to her father. He was still conscious, but he looked terrible. Shelby ran to the other side and grabbed his hand.

Brian opened his eyes and looked at her. "I'll see you soon," he said in a soft whisper.

Jay pulled Shelby away from the vehicle and passed her off to Evelyn. The two women stood there and watched as the SUV sped away.

"Come on, honey," Evelyn said as she put her arm around Shelby and pulled her toward her beach house.

It had been six months since that night, and Shelby had not heard from her father or Brian since. She and Evelyn had talked to the police when they arrived. As far as the police were concerned, the two women had been out all evening and had not seen anything until they saw all the emergency vehicles on their street. Evelyn did most of the talking while Shelby agreed with what the elderly woman told them. Willy had made all the arrangements, and he was selling the entire incident as a drug deal gone bad.

Shelby learned that Evelyn was Jay's younger sister and, to Shelby's surprise, her father's girlfriend. Apparently, Willy and the others had planned on leaving the United States after they faked their deaths in Las Vegas, but Warden Baker had other plans for them.

It started out as a simple plan to get Shelby safely out of Las Vegas after the camper ordeal, but it had turned into a huge fiasco.

Evelyn told Shelby how her father had snuck into the old beach house and checked on her as she slept one night. Willy had come back to Evelyn's place that night beaming with pride when he found the bottle sitting on the doorknob. He had boasted to Evelyn that his daughter was using a trick he had taught her. Willy had made a promise to himself that he would show Shelby how to beat the bottle on the doorknob if she'd ever let him.

Shelby sat in Evelyn's beach house, watching the evening news. The two had had a late evening of dinner and drinks with Shelby's friends, Stacie and Kim. Kim had come in from Amarillo for a visit. Shelby and Evelyn had plans of spending the next day at the beach with them both. As the two women were making plans, the local news came on. Suddenly, they stopped what they were doing to listen to the reporter on the television. An image of Brian's rented beach house filled the screen. Shelby picked up the remote and turned the volume up.

"The Escambia County Sheriff's Office has concluded its investigation into the shooting that took place at the beach house right behind me six months ago," the news reporter stated.

Shelby and Evelyn watched and moved closer to the screen when Warden Henry Baker's image appeared next.

"It has been determined that Nevada State Prison Warden Henry Baker had come to Pensacola Beach to sell cocaine to a local drug gang when the shooting occurred. Since the shooting, the police have connected inmates and local gang members to some of the Nevada Prison System employees. The sheriff's office is working closely with the Nevada Department of Corrections to determine who is involved and who may still be involved. An anonymous source identified Warden Henry Baker as the ringleader of this multi-state drug ring. The warden was one of the people killed here, along with one of his prison guards. In the end, we may never know exactly what occurred here on Maldonado Drive. I'm Heather Shields, Channel Six News, live at Pensacola Beach."

Evelyn turned and looked at Shelby. "We should get ready to leave after this weekend."

Shelby looked at Evelyn. "You think so?"

Evelyn smiled at the young woman. "Yes, I do. I think we need a vacation."

Shelby beamed. "Where?"

Epilogue
Vacation

The sun was already setting by the time Shelby and Evelyn made it to Costa Rica. The car that met them at the airport was driven by a very nice man. He offered the ladies cold water bottles that he had chilling inside the plastic cooler next to him, in the passenger seat. Shelby was not accustomed to traveling to such exotic places. When she learned of their vacation destination, she downloaded a Spanish-speaking app and began learning the language.

Shelby had two concerns, and her thoughts shifted from one to the other during the flight from Miami to Costa Rica. First, she wondered if she and Brian would be able to start where they had left off. Second, she didn't know how her relationship with her father would be. She still had mixed emotions about her feelings for him. Over the past six months, with Evelyn, she had developed more of an understanding about her father. It included his life and who he was as a man, friend, and husband to her mother.

Now, it was up to Shelby to decide what kind of father he was. As the driver took them closer to their destination, Shelby pulled the envelope that had been given to her months ago in

Las Vegas from her purse. She looked to Evelyn, who scooted closer and placed her arm around the young woman. Shelby opened the envelope for the first time and took out an old, wrinkled sheet of paper. She carefully opened it up, and a single tear dropped from the corner of her eye as she looked at the crayon drawing of her family in front of the beach house. After a moment, she smiled and decided that she was willing to try to work things out if he was.

When the car pulled up to the house on the beach, Shelby saw Willy, Roscoe, and Jay standing there in the driveway, waiting for them. Behind the three men on the porch was a taller man. He was wearing a white cotton long-sleeve, button-down shirt, blue board shorts, and white deck shoes. Shelby recognized Brian right away. He was smiling, which to her was a good sign. As the car came to a stop, Brian rushed over and opened the door for her. Shelby jumped out and threw her arms around his neck. He kissed her deeply and passionately.

Willy and the others just watched the young couple. "How are you going to deal with that?" Jay asked, at which he and Roscoe laughed aloud.

Willy looked at Jay with a grin on his face. "I guess the same way you have to deal with this," Willy replied as he walked toward Evelyn, took her into his arms, and kissed her.

"That's not right!" Roscoe declared and laughed even louder.

Shelby looked at the two men. "What's so funny?" she asked.

Willy smiled at his two friends and then turned toward his daughter. He held his arms out. Shelby looked at him for a second and stepped into his arms.

"Hi, Daddy."

About the Author

Michael grew up in Pensacola, Florida, where he spent the summer months as a youth at the beach, tubing down the river or splashing around in a pool near his grandmother's home. After graduating from high school, he joined the US Army and served in the Military Police Corps. After nearly seven and a half years, Michael left the military. He took a position at the Colorado Springs Police Department, where he served the community for ten years. An injury on duty forced him into early retirement from policing. Currently, Michael is the Department Chair of the Criminal Justice Department at a local community college. Michael earned a Bachelor of Science in Sociology with an emphasis in Criminology from Colorado State University and a Master of Criminal Justice from the University of Colorado.

Michael started his writing career as a ghostwriter for a publisher of textbooks. Eventually, he co-authored a textbook. Michael has always had the desire to write fiction. Through the encouragement of his family and friends, Michael started writing mystery fiction and hasn't stopped. Michael's wife, Stefanie, still catches him daydreaming as he drives down the highway thinking about different stories. The facial expressions that he makes reveal to her that somewhere in his mind, he's reviewing a chapter, scene, or dialogue between characters for a new book.